VARIATIONS ON A
TEACHING/LEARNING WORKSHOP

SCHOLARS PRESS
Studies in the Humanities

Variations on a Teaching/Learning Workshop

Pedagogy and Faculty Development in Religious Studies

by

Linda L. Barnes

Scholars Press
Atlanta, Georgia

Variations on a Teaching/Learning Workshop
Pedagogy and Faculty Development in Religious Studies

by

Linda L. Barnes

Publication of this volume has been made possible in part by a grant from the National Endowment for the Humanities. The opinions, findings, and conclusions or recommendations expressed in this publication are those of the author and do not necessarily reflect the views of the National Endowment for the Humanities. Funding for this publication also has been provided by Lilly Endowment Inc.

Library of Congress Cataloging in Publication Data

Barnes, Linda L.
    Variations on a teaching/learning workshop : pedagogy and faculty
    development in religious studies / by Linda L. Barnes.
        p.   cm. — (Scholars Press studies in the humanities ; 23)
      ISBN 0-7885-0530-0 (pbk. : alk. paper)
      1. Religion—Study and teaching. I. Title. II. Series: Scholars
    Press studies in the humanities series ; no. 23.
    BL41.B29   1998
    200'.71'1—dc21   99-19774
                                        CIP

Printed in the United States of America
on acid-free paper

To my father, By Barnes,
for his dedication to the art of teaching,
and
to my mother, Florence Maddix,
for her gifts of voice and presence.

Contents

Foreword

The future of the academic study of religion in North America depends primarily on the quality of teaching and learning in colleges, universities, and theological schools. Moreover, a new awareness is developing both within and outside the academy that educational institutions of all kinds must focus on the primary work of faculty and students in the classroom. But the importance of good teaching and learning is more personal that. The quality of the lives of teachers and students is enhanced when they experience the liveliness of learning and the excitement of discovery—the pure pleasure of good teaching and learning. That is particularly true in the study of religion, which directs our attention to the ways in which peoples throughout history and around the world have shaped their personal and group identities and sustained their fundamental commitments through their religious beliefs and practices. As part of a major focus on teaching, the American Academy of Religion inaugurated a series of workshops on teaching and learning in religion that gather scholars who are already fine teachers to reflect on good teaching and to explore for all of us what makes for effective teaching and learning.

Workshops on teaching have intrinsic value for the staff and participants, who regularly report that such workshops are transformative. It is important that, in addition, a broader audience be able to share and learn from the experience of the workshops. What elements create success in workshops and other initiatives about teaching? Are there significant issues that must be addressed? What are the most creative ways to help teachers reach their potentials? Linda Barnes is a skilled ethnographer who, as a participant/observer of the entire process, helps answer these and other important questions. She brings to the task her graduate training in both anthropology and religious studies. She is also a recipient of the Certificate of Distinction in Teaching from the Derek Bok Center for Teaching and Learning at Harvard University. Her book presents the first thick description of the workshops on teaching and learning, thereby providing a valuable resource for everyone committed to excellence in teaching in religion.

This lively description of the teaching workshop experience focuses on what works and what doesn't. Although as a thick description of the experience itself the book is not topically arranged, it does deal with crucial issues of teaching and learning in religion and other disciplines as well—diverse learning styles, faculty identity in the classroom, syllabus development, assessment, advocacy, gender, leading discussions, information technology, and career development. These and other significant topics can be accessed through the index. The cumulative effect of Barnes' description is to provide a sharp and colorful snapshot of the teaching of religion in colleges and universities at the turn of the century. It is also a hopeful picture because the participants display commitment, wisdom, skill, humor and excellence in their reflection on teaching and learning. We can all learn from that.

Raymond Brady Williams
Chair, American Academy of Religion Lilly Teaching Workshop Committee
LaFollette Distinguished Professor in the Humanities
Wabash College

Acknowledgments

I thank Sharon Parks for proposing my name to the American Academy of Religion when the national workshop committee was looking for a participant observer, and Raymond Williams and Barbara DeConcini for choosing me to play that role. The commitment of all three individuals to pedagogy and faculty development in religious studies has been an ongoing inspiration. I have found it an inexpressably rich and valuable experience to spend these years discussing matters of teaching and the field of religious studies in the different regions of the AAR, and I thank all of them in particular for giving me the opportunity to do so.

I thank Warren Frisina and Tim Bryson who have been worthy administrators in this process, and Steve Herrick for his always thoughtful and gracious management of logistics and details.

I owe a great debt of gratitude to the Lilly Endowment, whose understanding the importance of religious studies as a discipline and whose vision of what is possible in pedagogy and faculty development in this field have translated into the generous support they have extended to the workshops. The National Endowment for the Humanities has also provided important support. All of us who have been part of these workshops want them to know how much this has mattered to us.

Thanks, too, to the staff and participants of the original Wabash workshop. Your engagement led us all to explore further what made the workshop model so effective.

My greatest thanks go to the sixteen members of the different staffs and to the sixty participants. This book is a story of what we did together. Although I cannot name any of you, as we know, the bond of the workshops remains.

And finally, my ongoing love and gratitude to Devon, my friend and heart's companion, who has listened to these stories, and many more about teaching, students, and pedagogy.

I

How It All Came About

This is the story of how a series of workshops was designed with the objective of focusing on the identity of religion scholars as teachers. To the amazement of those initially involved, the experience not only succeeded in consolidating the self-understanding of the participants *as* teachers and in refining their pedagogical skills; it was also described by staff and participants alike as profoundly transformative. Each subsequent series resulted in the same outcome.

Following the first series, I was brought in as an ethnographer to document the next four, and to try to discern some of the factors that had led to such results. To my own surprise, what began as a series of reports gradually took shape as a study not only of the workshop process, but of the current state of affairs in teaching in the study of religion. Inasmuch as the various groups discussed pedagogical strategies and techniques, they also talked about the challenges and dilemmas they confront in teaching in this particular field and in their own disciplinary areas. Some of what was said was specific to teaching in the study of religion; much of it also crossed over disciplinary lines into broader questions of what it means to be a teacher in today's academic environment.

But how did it all begin?

For some time, Raymond Williams had been thinking about designing a program in which young faculty in the study of religion could come together and talk about the part of their professional lives most routinely undervalued in their profession—namely, teaching. Williams, who teaches at Wabash College, was convinced that if one sought out some of—as he puts it—"the brightest and the best?" and conveyed to them that who they are and what they do is special, over time it could have a transformative effect in the academy. He was supported in this by Barbara DeConcini, the executive director of the American Academy of Religion (AAR), the learned society of religion scholars and faculty in North America, as well as by others at the national level of the organization. After all, it was argued, college and university teaching is what many of us spend a significant part of our lives doing, with the hope of influencing how our students go out into the world thinking about religion. It should, therefore, be more highly valued not only in principle, but in practice. The question was, how to do so?

Williams's original idea had been to hold a week-long workshop on teaching in the study of religion, an idea he took to Craig Dykstra at the Lilly Endowment in Indiana. Dykstra listened to his idea, and then, as Williams tells it, said, "Why only for a week? Why don't you plan something that will extend throughout the academic year?"

Startled, but excited by the thought, Williams said, "All right!" That was the beginning of the workshops.

Williams, with three other faculty well established as teachers in the study of religion, and with support from Lilly, chose fifteen pre-tenure faculty as participants, most of them from the Midwest and some from other regions. They came together for a week during the summer of 1991, met again for two weekends (one in the fall and one in the spring) and then convened for a final week-long meeting at the beginning of the summer of 1992. The focus was on teaching; each participant was expected to work on a teaching-related project over the course of the workshop, culminating in a presentation during the final week.

By December, the staff at Lilly had received a formal report from Williams and in-process evaluations from the participants in the Wabash group. The latter were well aware that they were part of something new and understood that their engagement would provide data to support continuing the workshops. Their accounts and Williams's report made it clear that the experience had proved successful beyond anyone's expectations. Delighted, the Lilly staff met with Williams to talk about supporting further workshops.

Through a series of discussions, it was agreed that the AAR would submit a proposal for four additional workshops, two of which Lilly would fund in full; for the other two, the foundation would provide half the funding, with the understanding that the AAR would raise the rest of the money through other sources. In response, the AAR went on to formalize the reasoning underlying the larger workshop project:

> The need to cultivate a greater understanding of religion has never been clearer. The influence religion continues to have on just about every area of contemporary life makes it vital that we examine religion in all its forms and from many different perspectives. As a learned society dedicated to promoting the academic study of religion, the AAR recognizes that effective teaching is the most important factor in cultivating a greater understanding of religion among college and university students. For this reason, the AAR is deeply committed to exploring ways to cultivate superior teaching in courses on religion. In this, we share with other learned societies a growing awareness of a need which has been largely ignored by graduate institutions. Put simply, to become good teachers, young faculty must have successful teaching experiences early on in their careers.[1]

One of the problems, as the proposal also pointed out, was that few people entering college or university teaching in any of the academic disciplines had ever received much training related to teaching. Rarely did they later teach in a setting where they could reflect on their experiences in the classroom or receive support in their efforts to develop creative courses, or to refine their skills. The AAR and Lilly saw the workshops as one countermeasure to this lacuna in the academic study of religion.

The objective was to hold the four additional workshops by the summer of 1996. This would bring the AAR halfway toward its more immediate goal of holding one round of workshops in all ten regions.

---

[1]   Grant Proposal to the Lilly Endowment Inc., p. 1.

Beginning in 1992, the organization would start publishing "Spotlight on Teaching" as a section of its larger publication, *Religious Studies News*. In this way, teaching-related materials would reach its membership on a regular basis, thereby providing ongoing evidence of its own commitment to this priority. The longer-range goal was to institutionalize the workshops in all the regions, as an ongoing service to the profession. Williams, DeConcini, and others were convinced that the workshop initiative would have far-reaching influences. They made the case to Lilly that, colleges and universities would be unlikely to provide total funding,[2] and that the foundation's help was essential.

Although enthusiastic, the Lilly staff also wanted to move carefully, even slowly. Was it primarily a coincidence that this series had been so successful, or was there something to be learned from it that might prove transferable both within the AAR and potentially to other academic disciplines as well? Would it be possible to identify some of the elements and dynamics that had made things work so well? Such reflections were directly tied in to a larger question raised by Dykstra: Was the Wabash experience replicable and, if it was, to what degree and how? For that matter, what most characterized that experience? Participants and staff alike had talked about the workshop as something "life-changing?" What did that mean, and how had it happened? What, too, did it mean to talk about something "transferable," and how to avoid creating what might prove to be little more than a reductionistic template?

In the hope of figuring out some of these things, it seemed necessary to have an ongoing process of observation at the future workshops. The Lilly staff wanted to see a pattern suggesting consistent outcomes before making a longer-term commitment, and especially before expanding the model into other arenas. They wanted to keep the project going, but not to get too far ahead of the evaluation process. For that reason, it was decided that the next workshops would, like the first one, have the same focus on pre-tenure faculty and teaching, and would select for excellence. This

---

[2] Workshop directors, they hoped, would also enlist the support of their host institutions, from whom they would request as many "in kind" contributions as possible.

was not to be a remedial program, but one that would take teachers who had already proven their abilities. The teaching workshop at Wabash would remain the core model. A team of four staff members would lead the workshop, having been chosen according to criteria defined by the committee. Likewise, their proposal would have passed through a process of selection and refinement.

One of the issues that arose during these discussions was the question of whether proposals based on the use of outside specialists, experts, or consultants fit the paradigm. It was decided they did not. The point, as the members of the committee reflected, was to build communities of tenured and untenured teacher-scholars who would work with each other to develop their understanding of teaching. It was feared that reliance on outside experts might weaken the dynamic that had proved so powerful in the initial series of workshops. It would also modify the original design of the Wabash workshop, thereby complicating the experiment.

In addition to the kinds of people involved, there would be several other constants:[3]

- Each workshop would have fifteen active participants. Strong preference would be given to applicants in the early stages of their careers, particularly those who had taught fewer than seven years.... Preference would also be given to applicants from within a single region, in the expectation that this would contribute to a sense of collegiality, and because fifteen faculty could be expected to constitute a critical mass likely to be able to exercise significant influence at the regional level. Each region could decide to reserve, as well, up to three places out of the fifteen for advanced graduate students.
- Applicants would have to propose a project that would be the focus of their work during the sessions. The project itself could be related to active teaching and learning; course development; goals, evaluation, and grading in courses; multicultural initiatives; curriculum materials; departmental structures; student development, as well as other issues. Although diversity of projects would be strongly encouraged, all would have to deal with aspects of teaching religion.
- Each workshop would begin by meeting for one week in the summer. There would be two weekend meetings during the academic year, and a second week of meetings following the academic year. By framing the academic year this way, participants would be able to refine the plan for their teaching project during the first week. During the two weekend meetings, they would have the opportunity to discuss how their

---

[3]   From the AAR Grant Proposal to the Lilly Endowment Inc.

their project, and evaluating their overall experience. In addition, the Lilly Endowment generally required that a Researcher/Observer be present to record information that would allow for effective assessment. The same would hold true for these workshops.

It had been suggested to the committee that they choose someone for this last role who would not make the staff and participants uncomfortable, who could work well with the staff and not be perceived as a threat, who had good personal qualities, who would recognize the limits of participation and yet not be totally silent, and who would be a good listener and interviewer. They were advised to select an educator who could bring to bear a variety of conceptual lenses (such as different appraches to developmental psychology and educational theory), who had a theoretical base in which to ground his or her observations—without being wedded to any particular theory—and who understood undergraduate education as well as the graduate institutions and processes. The workshop directors would be informed that this person would observe all four workshops, meeting with the staff members during the workshops themselves, interviewing the participants, and reviewing all related documents, reports, and evaluations.

The phrase used repeatedly to describe the desired outcome was "thick description," a term originating with anthropologist Clifford Geertz, and referring to the interpretation of an event from multiple perspectives. The eventual thick description that would emerge would attempt to identify what makes the workshops effective, and what should be changed and improved. Eventually, this would take the form of a monograph that would be helpful to anyone developing teaching workshops or reflecting on the nature of teaching and how it can be improved. This is where I came into the picture.   During the summer of 1992, I became the Parti-cipant/Observer/Ethnographer for the teaching workshops.

Over the course of the four workshop series, certain aspects of this role remained constant; others underwent a process of ongoing redefinition. In part, this happened as each group of staff quizzed me about why I was there, particularly because I had initially been presented as the "evaluator" from Lilly. I quickly learned that it was more fruitful to describe myself as an ethnographer—although that, too, had its complications. Likewise, I discovered that I was sometimes a puzzle to the participants. Insofar as I sat in on staff meetings, I fell into the category of "staff." On the other hand, insofar as I joined in on all the group sessions and activities, hung out with participants, and spoke when I had things to say, I was one of the group. Then again, as I was the only one to spend a good deal of her time scribbling copious notes in a curiously crabbed shorthand sprinkled with Chinese characters, I was neither.

Some of this was consistent with being an ethnographer, who is engaged as fully as possible in what is happening while, at the same time, sustaining a bystander's stance. This means not letting stray remarks slip past—including the jokes and the arguments—without recording them, even while laughing or gauging the tenor of the conflict. At the same time, I occupied none of the roles that those present had adopted for the duration of the liminal time out from their academic lives. That made me all the more liminal.

Moreover, the teaching workshops were different from other cases of ethnographic observation for several reasons. Ordinarily one goes into a different group, another tribe. The engagement between the ethnographer and this other group may lead to thinking of oneself as a hybrid version of what one used to be, because through the experience one absorbs aspects of different ways of seeing and being. At a certain point, though—however many intermittent visits there may subsequently be—one returns to one's own setting. Here, however, that was not so simple. At the time I began my work as the project ethnographer I was completing my doctoral work. I was, therefore, undergoing initiation into the tribe myself. Eventually, when I finished, I too began teaching, thereby going further into the very definition of tribal identity. This meant that I was studying colleagues, few if any of whom were accustomed to being the object of an ethnographer's inquiry.

Part of the whole dynamic, of course, involved the process of establishing relationships and even friendships with the people about whom I would be writing. Self-disclosure, in that context, becomes a delicate matter. Although it is, in part, the stuff of which relationships are made and therefore constitutes a crucial piece of the experience underlying an ethnographic account, questions of confidentiality loom large. In general this is true; in this context it was so for additional reasons. The vulnerability of pre-tenure faculty is high these days, particularly as tenure is undergoing erosion through failures to re-hire following retirements, accompanied by attempts to introduce contract hiring or, worse, poorly compensated adjunct positions. Therefore no identifying details could be included. This aspect was further complicated by the number of people involved in the actual workshops that were part of the study— seventy-six, all together. It was, practically speaking, not possible to describe all four workshops, in all of their similarities and differences, and create seventy-six pseudonymic personae whom a reader could reasonably be expected to keep straight over the course of the book.

Ultimately, I decided to retain what had been said and done, but to eliminate all the usual markers of identity where the participants were concerned. In certain respects, extremely significant information is therefore missing. The consequence, stylistically, is that individuals—including myself—become "one person," "another person," "someone," "someone else." This is far from ideal, but knowing that this study would be read by the participants' colleagues and possibly tenuring committees, issues of confidentiality outweighed what would otherwise have been ethnographic priority. The larger "character" was the workshop and its variations; the real problem, one of exploring how far its basic design could be stretched. Where did it fray, without tearing? How could the fabric be made stronger?

The exceptions to absolute anonymity were the staff members, for whom I used pseudonyms. This in part reflected their being in more secure positions professionally; it also served to differentiate them at least by role. At the same time, although some of them were willing to be openly identified, others were not. The use of pseudonyms and disguised identities therefore seemed prudent.[4]

Self-disclosure on the part of my consultants did, however, have an effect on my role in the workshops. As such interchanges

---

[4]   The manuscript was also reviewed by a director from each of the staffs, as well as by others in the national committee, specifically with issues of confidentiality in mind.

took place, I also became the sometimes confidante to both members of the staffs and to some of the participants. In systems theory, this is known as playing the role of the bystander, about which I shall comment later in the study. Playing this role sometimes served to diffuse tensions or to propose new ways of conceptualizing a given situation. This was all the more the case as my own experience of these workshops grew.

Gradually, as the only person to have attended all but the Wabash series, I also became the historian—the carrier of a collective memory, the transmitter of earlier experiences—and even at times the consultant. The challenge, then, was to remain non-prescriptive, respecting the centrality of each group's freedom to define its own workshop, while providing comparative data for those making the choices. One colleague refers to this as "mucking with the data." I think this is inevitable. Therefore, I am responsible for *how* I do so, keeping in mind the larger objectives at stake.

Other methodological questions emerged over the four years I was gathering my field data. During the first two series of workshops, I carefully documented the different activities in which people engaged, and a fair amount of what they said both during and after these sessions. This was a natural focus insofar as these first two groups focused on classroom techniques and methods, albeit with different emphases. In the second two series, however, the sessions involved fewer of such activities and consisted instead of more extended discussions between people sitting around large circles of conference tables. The stuff of the sessions *was* the discussion and a given group's responses to it.

This shift informed my account of these different workshops. The first two blend descriptions of the various strategies modeled, with edited versions of the related discussions. The latter two, however, consist primarily of dialogue, with few descriptions of activities. I point to this stylistic difference as an attempt to reflect some significant differences between the workshops themselves.

Over time, my own understanding of the function of this book has expanded to encompass four objectives. First, insofar as the study discusses both practical and theoretical issues directly related to teaching religious studies, these first four chapters are also intended to serve as a resource for other faculty. An ethnography is not the usual vehicle for conveying material related to pedagogy, but in this case I hope it will prove accessible and engaging. The index at the end provides a guide to these topics in particular, for those to whom discussions of teaching strategies may be the most interesting. As such, it is intended to provide a guide to major topics in teaching religious studies.

Second, it is an attempt to convey something of the *experience* created by these variations on a common structure.[5] As will emerge through the following narratives, the four approaches to reenacting this structure proved to be remarkably diverse. The first four chapters therefore describe, session by session, what took place in the four workshops, stepping back regularly to discuss both the things that did not work so well, along with those that did. The objective here, on one level is to illustrate some of the different possibilities tested in practice, and to provide future planners with ideas and related commentary. On another, it is to demonstrate the resilience of the underlying structure. Each series was seen by both staff and participants as a real success. Thus, the answer to the initial question as to whether the Wabash experience was, in some way, transferable, is yes. What becomes all the more interesting is that this was so, even with the great differences between the specific groups, an issue to which the sixth chapter returns.

Third, returning to the question of what did, in fact, contribute to making the various workshops a success, the fifth chapter will discuss conclusions from the evaluations and interviews with staff and participants, and will suggest what seems to be essential. This section is also aimed at future planners of workshop series whether in the study of religion or in other disciplinary areas. It should be held in creative tension with the multiple variations explored in the

---

[5] Because I was not present at the Wabash series, this study does not include a discussion of the events of the workshop that was to become the prototype for those that followed. Where the participants of this series do appear, however, is in the two final chapters, which discuss factors contributing to the success of the workshops, and the implications for faculty development. There, the Wabash participants are present in their comments about their experience. Yet although their story is not told in its details, had it never happened, none of the others would have occurred.

earlier chapters, on the one hand, and the individual initiative, intuition, and creativity of the planners themselves on the other. Although not intended to be read as a template, it is the direct response to the question of what permits the transferability of the core experience of the teaching workshops.

Finally, the book also suggests, if not the state of religious studies as a field, at least a take on where some of its members currently find themselves in relation to the discipline. It therefore constitutes an ethnographic record of reflections on teaching in the 1990s, and on related issues at stake in faculty development. The conclusion, in particular, addresses the implications of the teaching workshops with regard to faculty development. Here, the statements of those who have experienced the workshops speak most directly and eloquently not only to this issue, but to the more general experience of living in the academic world. These voices make the strongest case of all that not only has the original workshop experience proved transferable within a particular field; they suggest as well that there is good reason to expect it would prove effective in the context of other academic disciplines. Above all, they are certain it should continue to be extended to faculty in religious studies .

II

The Tools of Teaching:
The New England/Maritimes Workshop

The August Week

The Planning

"For many years AAR/New England has experienced a programmatic paradox. While we have made consistently strong contributions to AAR on the national level, our regional programs have remained among the weakest. Most observers assign this pattern to the fact that the large number of major research universities, seminaries, and colleges in New England orients our colleagues to engage in responsibilities at the Academy's annual meeting and national programs rather than to participate in regional activities."[1]

It was part of the region's plan to focus on teaching and increase its initiatives toward younger colleagues. The regional conference each year had increasingly developed the reputation as a forum for graduate student papers, and the regional board hoped that, without discouraging the involvement of graduate students, they might also strengthen this branch of the AAR by encouraging

---

[1]   Proposal, New England/Maritimes Region, AAR, p. 1.

untenured faculty to take a more active role. The AAR/Lilly Teaching
Workshop Program was seen a potentially important way to do this.

By the time they learned about the possibility of funding for
teaching workshops, the two members of the New England/ Maritimes regional board of the AAR who decided to follow through on
the idea didn't have much time to write their proposal. The only
paradigm to go by was the prototype workshop series held at
Wabash College during 1991-92. They decided to follow the Wabash
model in its presentation, organization, and procedures, and to rely
on a strong staff with expertise in teaching/learning issues and
workshop formats, and a broad conceptual approach. Various of
them had worked together before, some of them having taught at
the same institutions at one time or another. They began, therefore,
with some sense of each other's working strengths and styles.

Natalie, the director, was a historian of American religions
and of women's history in particular, as was Michael. Matthew was
known for his work on the Methodist tradition, and Charlotte was a
sociologist of Chinese traditions, with considerable background in
teaching and learning theory. Between the four of them, they
represented schools around New England: Natalie and Charlotte
taught at large urban universities, Matthew at a divinity school, and
Michael at a private women's college. This blend, they thought,
would prove useful insofar as they could speak knowledgeably about
the demands of these different environments. Their initial plan also
allowed for one day at Charlotte's school with specialists in
computer-related technologies.

Reading the evaluations from the Wabash workshop, they
concluded that, while the participants there had experienced the
discussions of philosophies of teaching as rewarding and transforming, they would also have like more of a focus on the nuts and
bolts of teaching—the tools. The latter, they decided, would
therefore orient their own goals.

"We have the following goals for our Workshop," they wrote:

> ... (1) to discuss the study of religion in the context of the liberal
> arts; (2) to focus the attention of the brightest young

scholar/teachers in the field on teaching and to develop their confidence and self-esteem as teachers; (3) to develop fundamental skills for teaching, including leading discussions and preparing lectures; (4) to develop teaching resources; (5) to review and revise course syllabi; (6) to provide opportunities for discussions of career development and (7) to provide training and experience in the use of hyper-text in conjunction with innovative audio-visual technologies such as CD-ROM, Laser Disc, and Compact Disc in the classroom."[2]

Following the Wabash format, they would give preference to those who had taught fewer than seven years, with new appointments having to be nominated by the chairs of their departments. Graduate schools could each nominate one student for one of three spaces.

Although not one of the geographically larger regions, the New England/Maritimes nevertheless included major seminaries from virtually all the principle American religious traditions, and an educational world dominated by private, often religiously based universities and colleges far more than by public institutions. At least in the perception of the staff, the region also included one of the most diverse student populations in the nation.

One of the regional challenges targeted by the staff was the growing diversity among and within schools in the region. A corollary to this was the growing tendency for students to identify themselves in terms of their religious tradition and ethnicity. How, in this context, to present highly charged sources and issues? They would, they decided, frame their goals around three central themes: "Who are our students? How do they learn about religion? and How can we best teach them?"[3]

They would also stay with the original time frame, with a week-long session being scheduled late in the summer of 1993, a weekend that fall, and another in the spring of 1994, and a final week during June, shortly after the end of the academic year. The idea was to focus on building community and an open discourse during the longer sessions; the weekends would be dedicated to reports on the

---

[2]   Ibid., p. 5.
[3]   Ibid., p. 3.

participants' projects and "enrichment programs on career development and special issues requested by participants."[4] Broadly speaking, the staff would draw on their own strengths in teaching and would give related presentations during the mornings, to be followed by plenary discussions. The afternoons would provide time for reading and for the participants to have conferences with staff members; evenings would be dedicated to further presentations and discussions. As in Wabash, applicants would propose a year-long teaching project which they would develop over the course of the workshop and test out during the academic year. The projects themselves would play a central part in the workshop experience, and project presentations and reports would take place at regular intervals. In short, the New England proposal did, indeed, walk pretty directly along the guidelines set down by the Wabash program, the primary difference being the decision to focus on the nuts and bolts of teaching.

To recruit people to the program, Natalie put an announcement in *Religious Studies News* and sent out a notice to the members of the AAR in the region, along with notices to be posted in the different departments. Departmental chairs were also asked to nominate qualified graduate students. These notices were, in their own right, a significant screening mechanism. They told potential applicants that they could expect to discuss religion in the context of the liberal arts, enhance their confidence and self-esteem as teachers, work on various teaching-related skills, learn about computer-assisted technologies, and discuss the development of their careers. Although the notices said nothing explicit to the effect that the workshop was not intended to be remedial, they did say that "it will be designed to . . . focus the attention of the brightest young scholar teachers in the field on teaching." The idea was to take those who were already good and help them become even better.

A person who did not already care about becoming an outstanding teacher would not have bothered to apply. A second factor was the uncertainty of the job market. Many applicants in this

---

4   Ibid., p. 5.

and the other workshops would later say that they had applied in the hope that being accepted by an AAR-sponsored program based on the quality of their teaching would help them either in getting a job or in their tenure review. Even with that, the recruitment of participants took some work. Natalie discovered that the announcement in *Religious Studies News* did little to bring in applicants. It was the personal letters that made the difference.

When it came time to select the participants, she met with Matthew to review the sheaf of applications. Charlotte, who was not directly involved in the study of religion, did not come. Michael, who was, had not returned Natalie's calls inviting him to the meeting. She had not altogether expected he would; he was known for being hard to reach. Fortunately, Natalie was quick to perceive the more ridiculous dimensions of any challenge, and it didn't take her long to come up with a few in this one. Her ability to do so would get a fair amount of exercise during the following year, which the group would come to appreciate not only because it was done without malice, but because she enjoyed herself even more when she could direct the same humor toward herself.

Both Natalie and Matthew had studied and ranked the proposals in advance. Now, the issues that arose in making their choices included some effort to get distribution by different kinds of schools, but most of it was based on the proposals themselves. Several people were rejected because their proposals seemed incomplete, others for not yet having their degrees. Letters of recommendation were also not weighed equally.

"You can tell whether or not a letter really says something," they agreed. "If we focus on excellence, it's not going to be hard to get diversity; it will just happen."

Did the person qualify in terms of the number of years he or she had been teaching? In a few cases, the choice fell back toward strong graduate students who had submitted more impressive proposals than other candidates who were already faculty. When pressed to specify their operating criteria, both staff said they were looking at each proposal as a whole—at how well organized it seemed and how much connection there was between someone's teaching, publications, and proposal. But ultimately it was the project that was the most important element. Was it coherent and was it something one could imagine actually being taught?

All in all, it took about half an hour to decide. The outcome was eleven women and four men. Two participants were of African descent—one from the United States, one from Trinidad. One person was from India. The four members of the staff and the rest of the participants were Caucasian. One person was Jewish, one a Muslim; the rest were Christians from various denominations, including Seventh-Day Adventist. Their teaching settings ranged from community colleges to larger universities both public and private, with a number of smaller private colleges in between.

Somewhere before the end of the meeting they reached Michael at home and he entered the room by speaker phone for the final clearing of the agreements they had reached. The patterns of a systemic style were already being set in motion.

Day One: Sunday, August 1

It was terribly hot. The dormitory rooms at Michael's college looked out on idyllic stretches of trees, grass, and water—and it was still terribly hot. No one had anticipated record-breaking heat during this one week when the Faculty Club, where all the future sessions would be quartered, was unavailable. Now there was nothing to be done about it.

A carefully arranged fruit basket sat on the desk of every room, however, welcoming each arrival. It was a gesture that had been recommended by Raymond Williams, the organizers of the original workshop at Wabash, and was intended to encode the message to staff and participants alike that what they were doing was important. As Williams put it, "It doesn't matter whether it's a fruit basket or something else, but you need to make these folks feel that they are valued." So, Natalie had labored to put these baskets together for everyone.

The first full meeting of the staff took place on the library steps, where they met to review the plans that Natalie had compiled from their various suggestions. They already knew each other in a number of ways: Natalie had worked with Charlotte and Michael; Michael had worked with Matthew; Matthew had known Natalie through the AAR. On the steps they found they could all laugh together.

The opening reception was to be at Carver House, a restored old mansion that belonged to Natalie's university. Large trays of hors d'oeuvres had been laid out on tables set around a winding staircase—the kind intended to stage elegant descents in evening wear—and the new arrivals wandered from one large parlor to another, beginning to make each other's acquaintance. Dinner was equally elegant, served at two large tables by uniformed waiters, and moving through various courses.

It was a vegetarian meal. Particularly because of the religious complexities of the situation, Natalie had decided to keep dietary matters simple. So, for every meal served to the group as a whole, she had ordered the vegetable option. Finding herself in charge of negotiating arrangements at a school where she had no formal connections, it also simplified the process for her by a little. It was not her fault that the caterer's idea of vegetarian consisted of three or four choices, each of which was repeated with minor variations in every conceivable sequence, over the course of the workshop.

It was clear that women constituted the majority. Had Natalie and Matthew been asked to explain the imbalance, they would have said that who they chose reflected excellence, regardless of other variables. In this case, it had resulted in greater numbers of women. Throughout the reception, dinner and, later, the discussion, the four male participants—who found themselves in what, for most of them, was the unfamiliar situation of being in the distinct minority— had clustered together. This was not a particularly deliberate move, but a noticeable one nevertheless. By the next morning, it was no longer the case; nor would it happen again. Only the indirect effects of the numbers would later be quietly expressed in the evaluations of the program through one participant's brief but plaintive request— "More men."[5]

---

[5]   In contrast, in some other groups, the numbers favored the men.

and needed little prompting. But as an opening strategy designed to serve as an introduction to each person, it didn't work.

The staff was quick to recognize this and move on. It was the first illustration of needing to be light on their feet and capable of turning anything and everything into the occasion for teaching. In this case, as they saw that their plan had fallen flat, they moved on to the next item, sets of feedback forms. The point of these was to encourage the participants to inform the staff of any difficulties or frustrations they were experiencing with regard to the workshop. The staff hoped in this way to establish a collaborative model that would attune them to the undercurrents of opinion and allow them to make adjustments to the program along the way.

The schedule as it had been laid out was full, with all but two of the afternoons already booked. Although the original hope had been to keep most of the afternoons free, the staff also saw using them as the only way to include various requests that had come in from various participants. They were thus heading into a week of intensive activity.

Day Two: Monday, August 2

For the rest of the week, the meals were in one of the school's cafeterias. This insured that people would have a place to continue their discussions and get to know each other more informally. It had become apparent at Wabash—and would prove to be the case in this workshop as well—that the meals functioned as a crucial time for people to engage in the weaving together of a community. It was during this down-time that significant work was being done.

Building a group takes the form of any number of informal challenges which fill in the cracks and provide the support for the more formally defined ones. For example, when the group reconvened in a large, carpeted room in the library that morning, they discovered there to be two styles of chairs, half of them obviously more comfortable than the others. Joking about ranks and privileges, they agreed that everyone would, during the course of any given day, switch their seats after the recesses. Everyone mattered enough to have a turn at a good chair during the day.

Matthew led off with a case study, an approach to teaching that he himself both favored and was good at. He was eager to demonstrate its applicability to a broad range of classroom settings and course materials, in accord with the staff's decision to model their various skills and use these as the basis for discussions about different classroom strategies. The case itself involved a young professor teaching in a denominational school, who found that one of his courses had the unanticipated consequence of leading several of his students to come to him with stories of personal catastrophe which had led them to doubt the sincerity or depth of their own faith. The professor, in turn, was confronted with questions about his own identity as a teacher and a scholar. The case also raised questions about the potentially oppressive role a religious teaching can play.

The group stepped into the discussion, mulling its way through the various dimensions of the dilemma, assessing possible stances and responses. It was a situation in which they could each imagine themselves, which lent it greater immediacy. Working out the ideas and exploring questions of responsibility and identity in teaching also began to give the group a shape. Matthew pointed out that to use a case involves being clear about what one wants to accomplish with it. One then has to think about how to lead off the discussion, defining its different segments, connecting each of these, and including everyone in the process. One can also ask questions:

Open-ended: What are your reactions to . . . ?
Diagnostic: What is your analysis of . . . ?
Information-seeking: What was . . . ?
Challenge: Why do you believe that . . . ?
Action: What needs to be done to . . . ?
Priority: What is the first step to . . . ?
Prediction: If your conclusions are right, what might occur . . . ?
Hypothetical: What would have happened if . . . ?
Extension: What are some implications of your conclusions about these different aspects of the case . . . ?
Generalization: Based on your study of . . . what are the major forces which . . . ?

One must also consider the elements of what makes a good case.[6] There has to be a dilemma without an obvious solution.

"The case works better when it's drawn from real life—made-up ones don't work as well—and when it includes delicious detail, irony, nuance, and dialogue to bring it alive." Then there are the teaching notes, the meta-commentary on the case that allows the professor to lead students more deeply into the complexity of the case dynamics and appraise the situation it presents.

Things got slightly more delicate when Charlotte moved the group into a discussion of what they had just experienced—delicate because they were, at the same time, being asked to comment on the work of someone on the staff whom most of them had just met the day before. Charlotte, however, succeeded in keeping the focus on the paradigm of modeling and debriefing, the point of which was to get the group to reflect on the experience of different strategies and to explore how they might adapt them in their own teaching.

This was a model that showcased the expertise of the staff and transmitted valuable teaching tools that they had refined over the years. At the same time, on occasion, it also conveyed the unintended message that the staff were the experts and the participants the learners, leaving some of the latter questioning the authenticity of the idea that this was a gathering of colleagues and even peers in learning. Some felt as though they being treated like graduate students again, and were confused about what seemed to them a contradictory set of messages. At the same time, they also recognized that, in certain respects, they were, indeed, learning from more experienced teachers, and very much appreciated the opportunity to do so. None of it was black or white, and such ambiguities made the dynamics in the group more complex.

During the afternoons, everyone dispersed, some to the campus library to work on their teaching projects, others to swims or walks where they continued discussions about the working sessions,

---

6   From handout, New England/Maritimes workshop. Taken from C. Roland Christensen, David A. Garvin and Ann Sweet, *Education for Judgment: The Artistry of Discussion Leadership* (Harvard Business School Press, Boston, 1991), pp. 159-60.

the staff, and their own lives. This "down-time" was to prove one of the important variables in the workshop experience, insofar as it allowed for different layers of integration to occur and for relationships to take shape.

For the staff, who had decided to make themselves available for one-on-one meetings with participants, the afternoons were, by and large, working sessions. As all the staff took seriously the idea of mentoring younger faculty, they spent hours listening to, and counseling the various participants in matters concerning the latter's teaching and careers. It was in this regard that the staff had decided to have Charlotte give a presentation that evening on developing a teaching portfolio. Many of us had never heard of the term, but Charlotte in this—as in all that she presented—was prepared with overheads and handouts methodically outlining and detailing not only what it meant, but how one did it.

At the heart of the portfolio is the issue of evaluation. As all faculty know, teaching involves multiple layers of review whether by one's students, colleagues, departmental head, dean, or senior administration. These different assessments of one's work constellate into one portrait of the teaching and researching self— and sometimes a portrait over which a person has relatively little control. The point of the portfolio is to assemble a self-portrait through the compilation of statements about one's own teaching philosophy, the teaching goals underlying the design of one's courses, responses to evaluation forms that one has designed, letters from students and colleagues responding to one's teaching, and any other materials that round out the picture of what one has been doing in the classroom.

Although the overt function of the portfolio is to make the case for the strengths of one's teaching, it has a less obvious function as well. To formulate the teaching philosophy and goals underlying a course pushes one to think through precisely what those might be. Moreover, it allows one to track just how well one is meeting those objectives throughout the actual course of teaching. Thus, it has the potential to serve as a tool for thinking about what one is doing and why. Indeed, knowing how to design such a tool seemed sufficiently important to the staff that they decided to have participants begin a portfolio in relation to the final report on their projects. In this way, the staff reasoned, the experience of doing one would take on the significance of actuality and not remain an abstract.

Day Three: Tuesday, August 3

One of the workshop institutions, it is said, is the Rebellion. The Rebellion may or may not actually take place, but it is always anticipated, usually sometime during the first week, and if nothing looking like it happens, the particular staff are then left wondering whether they will meet up with it further down the road in some other disguise. The tradition of the Rebellion began with the Wabash workshop. Around midweek, the participants rose up to challenge the layout of the week, introduce some of their own ideas about how they thought things should go and, as it was later recognized, to make the workshop their own. In the light of various theories of group dynamics, this was seen as not such a bad thing.

Thus, the staff of this new workshop had been instructed to be on the watch for evidence that a group is coming into its own. This grows out of the ideal that, over the course of the workshop, the participants will increasingly define the content of what is happening. In general, the staff is expected to do most of the planning for the first week, and has the choice over how much response to invite from the participants in advance. Having gone through that week, however, the participants are generally invited to suggest their own ideas for the remaining sessions.

Usually a long wish-list emerges, and it then becomes the task of the staff to figure out how to cluster and combine these different ideas into manageable working sessions. Since the review and request process takes place at the end of each meeting period, the list can also become perilously long, at which point the synthetic abilities of the staff leap into the play, as they are pressed by this necessity to discern meta-themes with which to organize the future sessions. Thus, by the final week, the staff essentially become the facilitators of the participants' requests, remaining free, at the same time, to give the particularities of shape and form to how these requests are executed. When done well, both parties feel fulfilled.

But it has come to be assumed that for this full transfer to be effected, it may take the Rebellion. Having been so advised, the New England staff was therefore ready and waiting, which is not the same thing as to say that they were trying to bring one about. The Rebellion, it was said, just happens as a part of group process.

Or does it? As we shall see over the course of this book, there were cases when it didn't—which raises a question as to what brings it about. Are there factors that make it more likely and others that minimize that likelihood? Is the Rebellion, in itself, necessary for the health of a group insofar as it also runs everyone through the gauntlet of conflict, forcing them to test some of their own limits as a group and to discover that they can, indeed, survive disagreement? Does it form a particular kind of bond necessary to the formation of a certain quality of community? Or, were it to prove neither inevitable nor necessary, what kinds of more deeply-seated discords may it serve to express? What risks does it reflect and even intensify?

In the New England/Maritimes group, the staff—again borrowing from the Wabash experience—had decided that it would be a valuable exercise for the participants to have the occasion to observe themselves in action and to receive constructive critiques from their colleagues. Each person would present some aspect of his or her teaching project that Thursday, and would be videotaped in the course of doing so. These videos would then be presented the following day for group viewing and discussion. This plan was mentioned on Sunday evening and announced again on Monday.

The muttering behind the scenes grew to low rumbling and, by Tuesday morning at breakfast was gaining in volume. At least several of the participants felt caught off guard in being asked to prepare a presentation on short notice and to be filmed doing so.

"They didn't give us any warning."

"They can't expect us to pull something together without any resources on hand."

"We had nothing to say about the decision."

The gist of the complaint had to do with feeling—as they had when asked to describe an embarrassing teaching moment—that they were once again at some risk of embarrassing themselves. They were arguing not against the value of learning to assess their own teaching style or of seeing those of others; it was the suddenness of the exercise coupled with the feeling that in this artificial setting among their peers, the videos would "not be a real picture of me." The resistance to the possibility of being seen performing badly was also a measure of some of the vulnerability that accompanies the pre-tenure role.

The staff had felt that, despite the artificiality of the setting, the videos would still capture important things about people's style. They had not anticipated that the exercise would arouse this degree of resistance. When the participants attempted, on Monday, to express some of their opposition, the staff's initial response was a mixture of reassurance and humor, suggesting that the participants could get over their anxiety. The staff showed no sign of altering the plan. By Tuesday, the resistance had grown. I became of aware of being perceived as a potential go-between when several of the participants brought the matter up over breakfast and asked my advice. I suggested that at very least they should take advantage of the suggestion form or, better, that they should raise their concerns directly with the staff.

I faced a dilemma at that point, and one that would inform how I would go on to define what it meant to play the role of ethnographer, participant, and observer in the context of these workshops. I had already influenced the situation to some degree by counseling the participants to talk with the staff. Should I then simply let everything play itself out, knowing that the staff could get blindsided by an attack, or should I bring the situation to their attention so they could think about how to respond? Was my obligation simply to track the natural course of the workshop or to speak in some way intended to facilitate a more fruitful discussion? Which was the priority—a disengaged record of events, or an engaged account in which I, as a participant, recognized that the very presence of any observer modifies an event, and took responsibility for determining the ways in which mine would do so?

The work of systems theorist David Kantor suggests that, in any group, there are four roles—or "psychopolitical actions"— which the members of the group take turns playing: the mover, the follower, the opposer, and the bystander.[7] Movers propose ideas and actions. They initiate. Followers agree, playing a supportive role to what has been proposed. Opposers challenge the idea, either openly or behind the scenes. And bystanders step back to observe and sometimes to comment on whatever is going on, without siding with any of the other parties.

In general, people occupy each of these functions at different moments in the dynamics of a system. The person who, in one context, initiates an idea and promotes its execution may, in a different context within the same group, play the part of the follower, the opposer, or the bystander. Kantor argues that for a group to work effectively, all four functions must be present, although problems can arise when any one of the players gets stuck in a particular role. A group can also become disabled when opposition is not allowed or when there is no bystander to reflect back to it what is going on. In this sense, the ethnographer is a bystander, with the option to remain in the role of the observer who says little about what she sees. Once the bystander intervenes, however, the dynamics of any system change.

During the staff meeting after breakfast, I brought the staff up to date, and suggested that they might want to consider a more fluid approach to the planning. They were relieved to have located when and where the Rebellion would take place, and joked about how it had finally arrived. When the group all came together, Natalie presented a revised schedule—but one that still included the video sessions—and invited questions and comments.

These were quick in coming. The group wanted to keep the staff presentations, but they also wanted to come up with more ways

---

[7] David Kantor and William Lehr, *Inside the Family* (New York: Harper & Row, 1976).

to draw on each other as resources. To this end, they wanted to discuss each person's project as a group. They wanted to make the whole thing more collaborative, and to learn from each other. Yes, they might like some smaller discussion groups about specific topics, but they remained resolute in their opposition to including video sessions that week. They proposed, instead, that they each arrange to be filmed on their own turf and that these videos serve later in the program in the way that had originally been proposed. It was agreed that the group viewing of these tapes would be postponed until the final week.

The staff, pleased that the participants were, in fact, taking on the task of making their own case for the kind of workshop they wanted, readily agreed to these different ideas. From the perspective of the participants, it had now been proved possible to challenge decisions made by the staff and to influence the direction of the workshop as a whole. It was not the last time it would happen, and there would not always be such quick resolution—this had taken perhaps half an hour—but the fact of a conflict addressed and resolved was now a piece of their collective experience. This was important to the constituting of the group.

With that settled, they moved on to the morning session. Matthew took the first half to encourage the participants to think about how they might use a case study in connection with their own teaching, even if it meant writing the cases themselves. Going around the circle, some found this easier to envision than others. Generally, those who were teaching contemporary topics could readily imagine materials from their fields that might translate well into case material. One might, for example, find a promising life situation, gather the data through interviews and observation. Others who were teaching Biblical studies found the task more difficult to conceive, to which Matthew responded with a number of historical events that might lend themselves to formulation as cases.

For those who had never encountered case studies before, some of the difficulty stemmed from a lack of familiarity with the method itself. Not everyone was convinced that it was sufficiently versatile to be useful in their own courses, and some found it hard to combine the two tasks of presenting their projects and thinking through how to imagine potentially related case studies at the same time. Even so, the discussion raised new prospects. There were also some participants who felt that more sessions had been given over to case studies than they needed. The three sessions could, for have example, been condensed to one, accompanied by handouts on how to write a case. Still, the group generally agreed, they had found it useful to become better informed about this approach.

It then came Michael's turn, as he put it, "To show his stuff." In this case, that meant the leading of discussion. Again, the idea would be for the group to participate in his approach and then step back to reflect on the experience.

The night before, Michael had passed out materials on Mother Ann Lee and the Shakers. Some of these were primary sources, some secondary. During the working session, he supplemented these with a brief lecture fleshing out the historical context, ethical issues, and some of the more problematic dimensions of the text. Therefore, everyone entered the time reserved for the discussion already having heard a mini-lecture and having read the sources.

Michael's objective in a class was first to get students working off the primary sources. In so doing, he then wanted them to discover that they, too, could function as interpreters of American religious traditions and texts in their own right. To bring this about, he had three students sign up for each class session—in this case, three workshop participants—to prepare a short paper summarizing what they took to be the major issues in the sources and responding both appreciatively and critically. They were also expected to give reasons explaining their responses. Michael collected these papers at the beginning of a class, and put the three sets of ideas side by side on the board, summarizing their contents in ways intended to provoke a response.

"The last lick then goes to the paper writers," he said. "I ask them to check what I've put up there and see if it gets at their ideas. Do they have any changes they want me to make?

"If they don't, then what's on the board becomes the foundation for the class discussion. I assume that open discourse and free inquiry are valuable. If a student comes too much under attack, I will come to her defense, but I will also push each one of them to sharpen her points and develop them. I also question any comment the class seems to have accepted uncritically."

The virtue of putting the statements on the board—and one which arises spontaneously—is that rarely do all three agree. Thus, the professor does not set the agenda; instead, it grows out of students' responses to the materials. Moreover, it requires that students be intellectually responsible to their peers. During the last part of the class, the professor begins to pull things together—to bring to the surface that which still remains embedded.

Following the exercise, Michael explained how he understood what he was about, in this approach.

"I define my role," he said, "as intellectual provocateur, defender of those students who cannot yet defend themselves, amplifier and clarifier of the commentators' positions, summarizer and critic of the class discussion, supplier of additional questions and perspectives to make the class's encounter with the text as comprehensive as possible, and modeler for free inquiry. Of course, not everybody likes this approach. I guess I just say, 'I'm going to roll like this, and you'll learn to keep up.'"

Charlotte then stepped in to define other dimensions of Michael's classroom persona.

"He took some time to start things while he was putting the summaries up on the board," she said. "This gives people the chance to transition their way into the class. The summaries also empowered the group as primary sources themselves, and by laying out the arguments and checking them with the authors, he made sure that nobody would feel misrepresented.

"His use of rapid speech and of movement set a certain mood, but he stayed up front at that point. His movement especially conveyed enthusiasm, engagement. Only after the students started talking did he move into their space. He kept his eyes focused on the person who was speaking, which is an indirect way of instructing the other students to look at that person, too.

"He encouraged people to talk by saying regularly saying 'um-hmm,' which isn't necessarily the same thing as agreeing with them, and he asked a lot of open-ended questions, which let people know they could say whatever they wanted. When cross-talk started, he got out of the way. But he also beckoned a lot with his hands—that welcomed people to speak, too. And when the discussion is going on, he's liberal with praise and makes it clear he really means it. But he also works to get an argument going."

Someone made a joke about a testosterone-based discussion style that favored argumentation.

"Actually, I think about it sort of like theater," Michael interrupted. "It's like working the room. It's important to think about *how* we say things. You can actually tape yourself and listen to how you're using your voice. Think of it as theater or as a pulpit. You're writing, producing, costuming, and starring in a production."

Charlotte nodded. A couple of people chuckled at the idea of costuming—Michael's notion of classroom dress had, so far, consisted of denim or khaki shorts, light-blue, short-sleeved sport shirts, and frayed sneakers with slipping ankle sox. Not precisely anyone's idea of the spiffy ensemble. The point was not lost on Michael, who grinned.

"Well," he said, "at least it gives the message that things are comfortable in my classroom."

Charlotte laughed. "The other thing," she said, "is that nobody else's style will work exactly for you." She looked pointedly at Michael's sox. "Anything you observe in someone else will have to be adapted to your own personality."

What the group was learning through the structure of these presentations by the staff was a process of modeling and reflection. First they engaged as participants in an exercise; then they stepped back, turned things around, and looked at them as observers both of the method being demonstrated and of their own engagement within it. It was useful to see the staff analyze each other's work in the debriefings. Through this process of meta-analysis, the participants were learning tools with which to observe their own styles in a classroom. Unwittingly, they also were absorbing the skills with which they would eventually assess the videos of their own teaching.

"A few other things," said Charlotte. "When you do a lecture, make a folder for background material to go along with it. Put in summaries or outlines of different books. Read something new each time you give the lecture, and change the syllabus, a bit at a time. If you can, re-do about a quarter to a third of your lectures each time you give the course. And be sure to put in more details in your outline than you'll need, because even if you think you know them this year, you may not remember them next year." Like much of Charlotte's advice, these were practical, down-to-earth, usable suggestions. She wasn't a fancy dancer, but she had a keen sense of what worked and could tell you why it did.

That evening, she rounded out the discussion of the materials that might go into a teaching portfolio with a presentation on how to prepare and assess student evaluations. There were the evaluations designed for "consumer use" by other students trying to decide whether or not to take a course. Then there were those used in personnel decision-making—the ones that at least have to ask how effective a teacher is and how much the student has learned. Finally, there were the evaluations intended to help someone improve his or her teaching. Those were the ones that need a longer form with greater detail. She walked the group through each one, using overheads to summarize her points, and everyone came away with a fat sheaf of useful stuff.

Day Four: Wednesday, August 4

"Is what you're teaching the same thing as what people are learning?" Charlotte looked over her glasses at everyone. "How do you assess the effect you really have on your students, and how do you know that you're really getting through?"

A good working assumption, she went on to observe, is that if we improve our teaching, we will also improve the learning that happens in the classroom. To do that, you have to establish clear goals and objectives—clear, that is, not only to yourself but also to your students. Pushing yourself to define these kinds of goals actually helps you to focus on designing specific tasks to bring them about, to discern the places where things don't work, and to understand where and why you haven't yet met some of these goals. It can become a motivating process in its own right. You can spend as much or as little time on it as you like, but once you start to do it, it becomes a process of understanding that deepens your appreciation of all the variables at work in the classroom.

To help students understand their own part in mastering these goals, they need feedback early and often, before they get to a midterm exam, and some of it should be ungraded. Everyone is idiosyncratic, and early feedback is a way to let them know what is important to you as the professor before they actually get a grade. You might, she concluded, consider in-class writing and asking them to talk about what they still don't understand.

With the morning half over, the group paused for a break. It has, up to this point, been an invisible fact that every morning session in this and all the other workshops was divided in two by a break. Actually, the breaks also fall under the broader heading of "Food at the Workshops," in this case representing not just a chance to stand up and stretch, or maybe grab a fast cup of coffee. The Break meant abundant baskets or platters full of fresh fruit and baked goods. Even though everyone had had the occasion a few hours earlier to eat a solid breakfast, the Break presupposed that each person still possessed and inordinately speedy metabolism that could be counted on to burn it all up in a wink. Few there did, of course, but it was fun to pretend, even if most people's waistbands did snuggle in on them a bit more each day.

The food at the workshops was one of the variables that contributed to the overall feeling of being well cared for. It was, for the most part, beautifully prepared and probably more than anyone was in the habit of eating in the course of an ordinary week—not to mention having a waiter at dinner and maybe at lunch every day.

The environment created by the meals in turn generated a setting for good talk. There was the leisure to pick up and follow through on things we hadn't finished up during an earlier session, to tell stories about how life was going well—or not so well. Like stories of a department chair who had told someone that just because she was a woman he wasn't going to hold her hand (not that she had ever asked him to). Older priests on the faculty in another school—most of them without doctorates—who resented a younger woman colleague for her accomplishments; it was quietly suggested that she keep these to herself. The trouble-talk and other kinds of thinking out loud that lay down the lines of connection between folks. Put more simply, people got to know each other. And the Break was part of all that. So, even though it shall not be mentioned again, imagine its occurring somewhere midway through the description of any given morning; remember that somewhere in between references to the end of "that morning" and the beginning of "that afternoon," or just before any discussion of "that evening," the people of each group are there in those pauses, gathered in the fellowship of food and talk.

During the second half of that particular morning, the group split up for the first time into different discussion sessions led by the staff and organized by topic. Each participant would have the time to attend two of these, with each session lasting forty-five minutes. The choices would fall between "Syllabus Techniques," "Discussion Methods," and "Assigning and Grading Student Materials (such as exams, papers, etc.)."

In his session on grading, Michael suggested blinding out the names of the students, in order to focus on the work itself. It is important to be clear about which aspects are being graded, he said—the quality of the critical reading, for example, or of the writing. One can always encourage students to turn in drafts ahead of time, and then meet with them to talk about their writing. Papers or exams can be divided into batches and the batches compared, to see if there is a need to adjust the grades. However one goes about doing this, it is most important to be able to say why one is giving a particular grade. There must be comments interpreting and explaining it. One can write these on the computer, so that they can also be used later in assessing the student's work for a final grade, a letter of recommendation, or the summary of one's argument, in case the student should challenge the grade.

Matthew, who focused on the leading of a discussion, first raised the issue of choosing which kind of process one wished to promote—to have everyone talking and interacting, to cover certain material, or some mix of the two? Or, for that matter, was it a case of teaching the students how to *do* certain things? Should you choose a mix, the number of points you hope to cover must be modest; otherwise, it becomes a quasi-lecture-discussion. If the point is to discuss a set of readings, then you can set up questions with which the students can structure their reading. They can also be asked to write response papers, giving four points and a personal reaction, or selecting their favorite quote, summarizing the main point, and again offering some response to it. They should turn in a certain number of these, and are a good way to keep people up with the reading, attendance, and participation. It matters that you write something on these response papers, so that the students know you read them. If it's a large class, the students can divide into smaller groups, each one addressing a different assigned question and, about half-way through the class, reporting back to the larger group.

Many students don't know how to preview a book—how to look at the title, reading line, table of contents, and index (to see which headings have the most entries), and then how to read the introduction, beginnings and endings of chapters and paragraphs, and the conclusion, in order to start out with a sense of what the book is doing and where to focus in it. Sometimes one has to teach them how to do this. What does the layout say about the book and its intentions? What terms does one not understand?[8]

One should also be careful in assigning readings. The greatest tendency—particularly with newer faculty—is to assign too much, or to fail to take into account the degree of difficulty of the reading.

---

[8] Mark also suggested assigning Mortimer J. Adler and Charles van Doren, *How to Read a Book* (New York: Simon and Schuster, 1972).

"With primary sources," he said, "you excerpt. And try to encourage your students to go to the library orientation."

To sum up at the end of a class, have students write a one-minute paper about the most important issue from the discussion—either that, or about whatever it is they still don't understand. Different options would be for the professor, or the group, or a pre-selected note taker to sum up where the discussion has gone. One way or the other, these strategies function to pull together whatever has taken place.

On that note, the session came to a close.

The afternoon and evening had been left open for informal meetings and conversations, and so it was during this time that an unexpected affinity group agreed to gather, to address a particular challenge faced by some of the women in the workshop. It came about like this: over dinner one evening, one woman said to another, "So, when you start teaching, are you going to cut your hair?"

The response was brief and forceful. "Hell, no."

"What are you going to do?" the first woman said. "I've figured I'll have to cut mine, because it doesn't look professional to wear it down."

"I'll put it up," said the other. "But I'm not about to cut it."

"I don't know how to put mine up."

"We'll fix that."

Word spread. By the next afternoon, enough of the women with longer hair had heard about it that they had decided to hold a hair workshop. By dinnertime, every woman with hair long enough to pin up, twist, or braid had a new hairdo. Some were on their second, going for more than one look, on the principle that it's good to keep your options open. The tone stayed light, but it still grew out of the root feelings that your hair shouldn't be held against you, and you shouldn't have to cut it if you didn't want to.

Day Five: Thursday, August 5

The day had been set aside for project presentations. People had turned in paragraph-long summaries of their projects, and these in turn had been circulated among everyone else. The issue now was how to organize the morning and afternoon so that each person could verbally present what he or she was doing, and receive feedback and help from the group.

As often happens when people go around in a circle to describe their work or talk about something important to them, the participants going first tended to speak at greater length. Consequently, the available pool of time remaining continued to dwindle, to the point where those who came last had less to work with. By then, they were feeling slightly frustrated and, because it's more tiring when the time isn't structured, everyone in general tended to feel somewhat scattered and distracted. The swing factor in such cases lies in there being a timekeeper.

There was another dynamic at work. Even though the session was not being videotaped, people had still been asked to make a presentation about their projects. At the same time, it had originally been suggested that this would be an occasion for them also to demonstrate their teaching style. Some therefore stood to give a ten-minute lecture, as though actually speaking to a class. Others, who had understood the task to be the giving of an overview fleshing out the paragraph summaries, made a presentation about their plans for the larger project. Still others sat to explain what they were doing. As some of the participants noted later, the freedom they had been given to structure things as they wished also left them uncertain about how to shape the presentations, not being altogether certain what the objective of the task was.

What the group was intended to offer in response to the presentations had been left open-ended. Thus, although the staff made suggestions, the participants said less, not being quite sure how far they were being invited to go in critiquing the other proposals. Nevertheless, a series of handy tips came out of the discussions, and many of the participants later felt they had learned a great deal from the experience as a whole.

One of the topics that surfaced repeatedly during the discussion was the preparation of syllabi. Here, Charlotte had a number of useful suggestions. She pointed to the wisdom of spelling out precisely what you expect from students: "Prepared participation, for example, is required." This precludes students' contesting a lower grade based on lack of attendance. For that matter, all the expectations must be in writing—the length of the papers, the stylistic requirements, and so on—because the syllabus functions as a contract with the student.

Structurally, the reading selections one makes must be pointed, and the broader topics of the syllabus should flow into, and build upon, one another. The content should be designed in ways that allow for comparisons between the materials during a given week, as well as between those from one week to the next. This also means doing all one can to lay a good foundation at the beginning, so that a basic point of reference is established.

In choosing readings, it is important to remember that one can be inventive. For example, if the objective of a course is to explore how a tradition is transmitted, one can be creative in the choice of materials. Have the students read primers, catechisms, children's stories, and even (as in the case of India) comic-book versions of classical stories along the lines of similar versions of literary classics in the United States. The point is to show how a person absorbs a particular tradition. Newspaper stories and other media can also be useful to show how the popular imagination is being shaped about a given topic. Jonathan Z. Smith was invoked for his advocacy of assigning fewer readings (the "less is more" principle), using no formal textbook, and conceptualizing the intro course as an introduction to college writing, speaking, and argumentation.

In discussions, the professor faces multiple challenges, not the least of which is having enough of an idea about the direction he or she would like things to take, so that everyone doesn't wander too far off into the woods. Then, as Natalie pointed out, there is also "the sow's ear into a silk purse" phenomenon—the off-the-wall point that one has to work to bring back around to what one is actually trying to do. If setting up an advocacy for a particular position, one has to make the case to substantiate it or, better yet, set it up as various cases that could be made, and train students in how to assess the evidence for each one. Things should be defined as problems to be explored.

"In a discussion," said Charlotte, "*you* are the structure." The ideal is to grow flexible enough so that everything can be turned into part of the learning.

This brought up a different question about the role of faculty, particularly in the study of religion: What to do when a student comes with a personal problem or even crisis, and assumes that, because you teach about religion, you are also there to serve something of a pastoral function. The staff told stories about different instances of their own experiences of this. It was agreed that for a number of reasons, students often expect that an individual teaching in the broad field of religion will be more responsive to such dilemmas.

Paradoxically, even when a professor is a religiously committed person deeply rooted within a particular tradition, he or she still may not feel willing to respond as the student hopes. The most commonly given reason—and it held true in this workshop as well—is the sense of lacking either pastoral or counseling skills and training. Better, the thinking goes, to refer the student to the counseling services or to a student hot-line. Many faculty feel ill-prepared to do more than that, and also question allowing what they understand to be an essentially academic role to be expanded into a quasi-pastoral or therapeutic one as well. Indeed, some faculty resent being asked to cross over into areas they feel do not fit their own understanding of their job description. How to draw the line?

The confusion traces back to some of the ambiguities surrounding the separation of the study of religion from the academic preparation for ministry, the rabbinate, or other more formally defined religious roles. In students' minds, the distinction is not always so clear-cut. They often assume that a person who has dedicated his or her life to the study of life-forming traditions will probably be open to discussions concerning the forming of a life. The one, they discover, does not necessarily follow from the other.

"I don't feel I have the training to handle these situations," said Natalie. "So I say to them, 'No one should have to go through this alone.' Then I refer them to the student counseling services." Others agreed.

It is a complicated question. Sometimes what students are trying to figure out is where their education fits into the larger life they are struggling to envision. A question about whether to pursue doctoral work may, in fact, really be a question about whether or not it is really all right to go off instead and work on being a writer. On other occasions, as a frequently cited example attests, the loss of an earlier version of faith, due to the encounter with new traditions and challenging ideas, rather naturally leads a student back to talk with the person perceived as having contributed to the crisis in the first place. Does one walk away from these questions, or pass them on to somebody else?

There is no easy resolution to these questions. Ultimately, it may necessarily remain a matter of personal decision based on how one understands one's role. Nevertheless, the issue would appear to confront faculty in the study of religion more frequently than in other disciplines, often leaving them at a loss over how to respond.

Day Six, Friday, August 6

Even though the videotaping of people's teaching styles had been postponed, the staff recognized that a number of the participants remained nervous about the whole thing. To allay their fears, Matthew had volunteered to serve as exhibit number one. This morning, he would show not just one, but two videos—the first, of himself delivering a lecture, the second, of himself being coached by an aide in his school's teaching center in how to watch and critique his work in the original video. He grew a bit vague when asked to describe the first film, saying he thought he'd learned a lot from the critique. The rest of the staff admired his willingness to offer himself up.

In fact, he'd gone them one further. He figured that if he presented a video of himself doing a fairly bad job, the participants would be left secretly confident that at least anything they brought in would be better. So, he had selected an excerpt in which he appeared as a talking head reading off his notes from behind a podium. Pointing out that few of us are aware of the personae we project in our classrooms, he then reviewed excerpts from the filmed critique—

including his initial reactions to those characteristics of his lecturing style of which he had been oblivious.

He warned that almost everyone spends the first moments of watching such a tape certain that they look terrible beyond repair It is therefore better to view the tape with a colleague, who can check one's fears to this effect. He also suggested that for one's own purposes it is a good thing to work through the whole tape, in order to explore issues of pacing and of the larger classroom dynamic.[9] But when, as in this workshop, the point is to solicit constructive critique from others, it is generally more useful to view a short excerpt of no more than ten minutes.

The exercise had the desired effect. It diminished much of the participants' anxiety about being filmed and viewed, and reinforced the staff's argument that this could be a valuable exercise. Matthew, who had to leave the workshop at that point to attend a weekend program somewhere else, made his exit to enthusiastic applause.

The morning moved over to Charlotte, who was to talk about the nature and effects of different learning styles.

"Take a moment and write your name," she said. Everyone wrote their names.

"Now switch your pen to your other hand, and write your name again." Everyone did that, too, although in most cases much more awkwardly.

"Do you see how uncomfortable some students may feel when asked to learn through an approach that is unfamiliar or relatively more difficult for them?" She had made her point.

When listening to a lecture, she observed, students usually retain about seventy percent of the content from the first ten minutes. If nothing happens to shift the rhythm of the class—that is, if the professor simply keeps on lecturing without any pauses—after that, it drops to some twenty percent. Worse still, most people's attention and interest fade out almost entirely at about twenty

---

9   In this regard, it is a good idea to request that whoever is doing the filming include shots of students in the class. For further suggestions on viewing videotapes of one's teaching, see selected materials in Appendix.

minutes. After four months, students often know only about eight percent more of the material than students who never took the course at all.

"The tuning out is going to happen to some degree, no matter what you do," said Charlotte. "The question is, how to minimize and even forestall it. Probably the most important thing is to help your students be aware of their own preferred learning style, and to know your own. Are you only replicating your own preferred style in the lecturing and teaching you do? If you are, what you are doing may be effective for the people who share your preference; it may not work so well for some of your other students.

"You might try handing out a questionnaire to find out how the people in your class like to learn—through lectures, visuals, short or long papers, discussions—with an interest to figuring out how to integrate these different approaches into your syllabus. Ask them what their most rewarding learning experience in a class has been. You can even use the exercise of writing with different hands to illustrate the difference in styles and the importance of understanding one's own.

"For people who learn better visually, be sure to provide charts, or other things that can function as maps of what you're doing. Use the board, use handouts. Slides, films, field trips—all of these stay with people. You can use music at the beginning of a class to help students come into the class. In my classes on Chinese sociology, I usually have a video clip from Chinese television running as students come into the classroom. It gives them an interlude to make the transition into the class content.

"During a lecture you have to illustrate things, or shift the activity in order to sustain your students' attention. At the twenty minute point, for example, pause to ask a question. It shifts the direction, so that students can regroup their attention."

So far, the workshop had not gone into the issue of how to lecture effectively. This was one of Natalie's strengths, and she would be leading a session on it that afternoon. When the staff had laid out their plan for the week, Natalie had originally been scheduled to demonstrate and discuss her lecturing style on Wednesday morning. When the plan changed, following the Rebellion, her session got postponed to Friday afternoon. This meant that for much of the week, while the other members of the staff were presenting the various things they were good at doing, Natalie had little occasion to show her own classroom approaches. She had led several of the small group discussions on Wednesday, and had met privately with many of the participants during the open afternoons, but it wasn't the same.

Her own engagement and enthusiasm made it difficult for her not to enter the different discussions at full tilt—especially, as she later said—when she didn't quite have anything to do until the end of the week. Without meaning to, she interrupted others frequently, and talked more then she had intended. In this she was not alone. Michael tended to interrupt right back, and carry on at high speed himself. Some of these interruptions occasionally ignited the impatience of the other staff (Matthew, at one point, turning to say, "Shut up, Michael!") and of the participants. At the same time, where Natalie and Michael had both shown themselves to be open to and excited about the ideas raised by everybody else, there was also considerable humor (Michael's more energetic insertions leading to a few jokes about the advisability of Ritalin) and much forgiveness. Furthermore, in their own daily meetings, the staff engaged in critiquing their own work. Natalie and Michael were aware of needing to hold back; in practice, it just wasn't always that easy. Still, the ongoing ability to step back and assess their own work was one of the strengths of this staff.

That afternoon, Natalie distributed a few brief materials on the Nuremberg Code, to lead into the broader issue of the moral and ethical choices related to research ethics. As she noted, an ordinary class would have read more than this in preparation for the lecture. It was when she began to speak that the group saw the transformation of her conversational exuberance into a strong and compelling lecture style. It became easy to see why she had won teaching awards. After about ten minutes, she stopped, but already the group was sold. Clearly this was the person to ask about all the difficulties they themselves had run into while lecturing.

"What do you do when students correct what you've said? It's so embarrassing."

"You thank them for the correction."

"What if someone disputes a point you've made?

"I co-opt the point. Like, I'll say, 'You know, you're right, and even *more* than that (using the point they've made) . . . !' Then I go on to give my own, stronger example of what they've just said. Sometimes it will happen because a student is more advanced. Then it's a good idea to address the question briefly at their level, after which you pick it up in a more general level for the other students."

"What about when two people get into a disagreement in the class, and they won't stop?"

"I try to remind them of the main point and get them back on track. If they won't do that, I send them out for coffee together."

What about when someone is doing something distracting, like knitting, and saying that it helps them concentrate?"

"I say that *I* need to concentrate more."

"What do you do when they don't do the reading?"

"I tell them that the angrier I get about this, the harder the exam will be. Of course, you also have to *use* the readings in the class, and you have to figure out the baseline at which they are prepared. One approach, if they're not doing the reading, is to assign less, until they *are* doing it. Then you show them how to use it to get them engaged. Find the lowest common denominator and build on it.

"I also try to summarize the key points from the last class at the beginning of the next one, and then begin building on them. It's a good idea, too, to mix telling stories, summarizing, analyzing, and asking questions, to shift genres. Get students to discuss things in small groups, too. It all helps you to keep their attention."

The connection between attention and how one styles oneself in the classroom is an increasingly complicated one. Some students lack the ability to follow a sustained, slowly unfolding piece of reasoning without going off the track somewhere around the middle. How much of that to attribute to a natural drop-off occurring at the twenty-minute point and how much to a lack of discipline is hard to separate out. As the group noted, newer forms of media have contributed to the dilemma by structuring students' attention to favor the short, the colorful, and the arresting.

The staff, aware of these challenges, had decided to pull in a few other approaches designed to engage other styles of learning. One of these, a simulation game called "Star Power," had been scheduled for the evening. The game, which relies on the structured trading of chips, each of which represents a certain cash value, is all about group dynamics and, not all that subtly, social inequities and class conflict. It is intended to replicate some of the broader dynamics of a capitalist economy, particularly the ethos that everyone stands a fair chance at making it to the top. The larger group is divided in four, and each of these assigned a sector of the room—one of which is given the most luxurious of whatever chairs are available, the next the slightly less so, the third nothing but wooden ones, and the fourth, the floor.

Based on the value of the chips one receives in a small envelope, a person moves into one or another of these sectors. Through trading segments, during which one's net worth increases or diminishes, one relocates. What complicates the matter is that the game leaders are also tinkering with the contents of the envelopes at regular intervals. Those who receive envelopes containing the lower values are invariably at a disadvantage, and have virtually no chance of reaching the domain of the comfortable chairs.

In some sub-groups, people form alliances, pooling their chips or in other ways trying to promote the welfare of their particular members. In others, they will try to advance one person in the hope that he or she will then be better situated to reach down and help those from the original sub-group. What few seem to recognize is the other option of simply refusing to play. More often, they settle for griping about being set in competition with each other. More often, they settle for griping about being set in competition with each other.

Yet, as educator Sharon Parks used to tell groups at the end of a session, "The problem with being part of the rat race is that there's only one part it lets you play—that of a rat." The very fact of not seeing the various ways to step out of the process itself then become part of the discussion.

Even as a game, Star Power raises strong feelings. When a prize is awarded at the end—often something like a cake or a pie—groups sometimes refuse to accept it. Either that, or they insist on dividing it equally between everyone, as one way of offsetting their distress at engaging in unmitigated competition with each other.

This group hated the whole thing. For some, it was because they didn't like the premise of the game in the first place. For others, it was because they didn't like anything resembling skits or charades, and they resented being asked to play this particular role. But another, more significant reason, was that no one had been quite certain as to why they were being asked to play the game, other than for the sake of having a different experience. It had not been clear where it fit in to what they were being asked to learn, or how they might think more explicitly about using it in their own teaching. Moreover, up to this point the group had worked collaboratively together. To be set in competition, even in an the antagonisitic framework of a game, proved unexpectedly distressing.

The strength of the group by this time, however, along with the genuine regard they had come to feel for one another, allowed them to say these things straight out. Through this discussion, the importance of establishing a context for a classroom activity, and for explaining to students the logic underlying any given assignment, became all the clearer. In the end, it served to demonstrate that, with some attention, virtually any experience can be adapted into an occasion for teaching and learning.

Day Seven: Saturday, August 7

The group spent the last morning evaluating their work together and planning for the coming weekend in November. It had been pretty well decided that the one full day of that session would be dedicated to computer-based resources, so most of the discussion focused on how people had experienced the week and what they hoped would still be forthcoming. By this time, everyone seemed to speak candidly, suggesting a certain level of trust and confidence. There were sure to be things that people elected not to say, but by and large they tuned in and contributed to the wish list for their future sessions.[10] Then, knowing that they would come back together in three months, everyone gathered up their bundles, computers, fans, and other luggage, closed the doors on their dormitory rooms without regret, and headed home toward the start of a new season of teaching.

The November Weekend

Day One: Friday, November 12

"So," said Michael, tapping on a glass to get everyone's attention as the servers in the faculty-club dining room began bringing out the dessert. "We sent you some instructions to think about the question 'What two or three elements from the August workshop have I incorporated into my teaching?' Would anyone be willing to speak to that ?"

It took a moment for people to gather their thoughts. Many of them had come to the before-dinner reception directly from teaching or from meetings, and had been busily catching up with each other then and through the meal. Although they hadn't yet had much time to look around, it was clear that the faculty club was a cut above the college cafeteria and the dorms. (For one thing, the furniture wasn't bolted down in the rooms.) As one person murmured upon entering the dining room, "Well, Toto, we're not in Kansas anymore." Raymond Williams had also come. Indeed, it would become customary for him or another representative of the central workshop committee to make a visit at some point during a series, to extend the good wishes of the national AAR and the funders.

---

[10] Discussion of the assessments will be presented in Chapter VI as part of the broader question of what made the workshops work effectively.

"I've learned to come out from behind the podium and interact more directly with my students."

Others commented on how their approaches to their syllabi had changed. Goals were clearer, assignments better formulated. It seemed easier to experiment with the designing process, moving things around until the flow seemed smoother. One person had even experimented with involving students in the planning:

"I promise my students a final syllabus after two weeks, when I've seen the level of the group. I have to order books, but I can lengthen or shorten what I give them. So this is a process in which they get involved."

Some of the discussion techniques had proved useful.

"When someone asks a question, I now invite others to respond, to convey to the students that they are all primary sources."

"I brought in copies of an article, we read it for ten minutes, and then we discussed it right there."

"I hand out study guide questions, but I give different questions to different groups. When we come back together and they report to each other, it's livelier."

"I put the main points on the board at the beginning of class now. It helps my students see where we're going and where we've been, and for the people who learn by seeing things laid out, it seems to work better."

There were those who were experimenting with different writing assignments—asking students to turn in response papers on their reading, or having them write for a minute at the end of a class on "the muddiest point" and turning that in for the professor to think about how to wipe away some of the mud for the next class session. One person now allowed students to submit either a rough or final draft by a preliminary due date; she then retained the option of deciding whether or not to hand it back to be reworked. If she did hand it back, she included suggestions for the re-write.

Not everyone had had uniformly good experiences, as one person reported:

"This has been one of the worst classes I've ever taught. I asked them to generate discussion guidelines—they split into two camps and refused to come to an agreement. So, I tried doing a fishbowl exercise with one group listening to the other's point of view, but they only jumped all over each other. I used the suggestion of asking them to write about what had been meaningful to them so far, and they didn't have much to say. A few things worked a little better—I had them do a case study with role playing, they liked some of the slides I showed, and I did have myself video-taped. But it hasn't exactly been an easy semester. At least I can come here and talk with all of you about it."

The effects for many had been more intangible—having a better grasp on how not to allow a discussion to run away, being able to focus more on the students and what they are absorbing, feeling generally less nervous, and breaking through to feel more confident. But above all, it was the sense that now there was a community into which one could bring these accomplishments and observations, express one's doubts, and ask one's questions. If it brings about nothing else, Raymond Williams observed, the first weekend meeting serves to consolidate the perception of staff and participants that they do, indeed, constitute a group.

Day Two: Saturday, November 13

The staff had originally hoped to include a field trip during this weekend session, but gave up the idea when they realized they were trying to do too much in too short a time. Instead, they decided to postpone the excursion for the final week (even though they began to have the uneasy feeling that the list of things to carry out in June was quietly but steadily multiplying to potentially unmanageable lengths) and to focus this session instead on working with computer-related teaching materials.

Broadly speaking, this can be a particularly daunting topic for the academic who didn't grow up using a computer, particularly when colleagues more fluent in computerese speak rapidly about FTPs, URLs, HUBs, LANs, WANs, Gophers, and RAM. Worse yet, those who have mastered the language usually have a hard time remembering which things they once found especially difficult to learn (it's something built into the language itself that makes you forget that part), so they're often not very good at explaining to anybody else how to speak it. "Telnetting in" sounds like something you have to wear special gear to do; so does "surfing." And the idea of setting up a home page into which to move your syllabi doesn't feel the least bit homey when you can't figure out the rudimentary mechanics of entering the Web, much less of viewing how at home every body else appears to be at *their* Web address. The idea behind the day's activities was therefore to demonstrate some of what could be done in the classroom with a few of these technologies, and to introduce a number of the rudimentary terms from the Internet.

The group piled into a large van from Natalie's university. With Natalie straining to see over the steering wheel and complaining about the difficulties of reaching the gas pedal, and various cracks about "Camp Lilly" and singing AAR campfire songs floating forward from the back seats, the van with its happy campers lumbered out onto the highway and made its way into town.

Using a presentation program—in this case, "Powerpoint"— Natalie and Charlotte had put together an illustrated lecture on eighteenth- and nineteenth-century mourning traditions in the United States. It was all loaded on Natalie's computer, hooked up to a projection mechanism in the classroom, and set so that whether she wanted to show outlines, charts, photographs, or drawings, she could push a button on the computer and advance from one image to the next as though she were simply showing a set of slides.

Shots of funerary jewelry and casket jewel-boxes, followed by scenes of empty stone cradles and armchairs flashed up on the screen one after another, as Natalie talked about mourning societies, nineteenth-century patents for embalming that allowed the deceased to be preserved like jewels themselves, and the transformation of cemeteries into neighborhoods with signs marking the lanes and paths, and housing corresponding to the heavenly home. By the time she got to the scenes from the Forest Lawn cemetery, where music is piped in for the dead, she had amply illustrated why it was no longer clear whether this really even *was* death we were now talking about.

Then stepping out of her role as professor in the classroom, Natalie went on to explain how this particular presentation fit into a larger course she teaches, "The Meanings of Death," in which she also shows films and slides, and takes students on field trips to graveyards, meeting houses, and museums. The point of the trips, as she would illustrate during the final week, is to look at different sites and objects as both text and experience.

As the presentation came to a close, Charlotte—herself a media specialist and the workshop's guide through the various computer facilities—explained some of the features of the presentation program the group had just seen in action. They would not be learning how to work it; the point here was to demonstrate how it could be brought into actual classroom use. She had, for example, had some of Natalie's slides digitalized and put on a CD-ROM, so that they could be shown off the computer.

That afternoon, the group went to the university's Media Resources Center, where members of the center staff spent an hour talking with them further about the different kinds of things one could do with CD-ROMs and with videos. The participants were then given a choice between remaining in the Media Center to continue this discussion, attending demonstrations in the Multimedia Development Lab, or learning about accessing the Internet and, with Matthew at the helm, navigating some of its resources for doing research.

Day Three: Sunday, November 13
In thinking back over their experience the day before, it was the hands-on aspect that had been useful. It had also been good to be exposed to the available resources. As one person wrote:

"We were given a picture of what was possible. Now we can investigate what our institutions can provide and be prepared to influence some of the decisions on acquisitions. It was supplemented by the discussions of the *value* of the technology and ways to modify it for our classrooms."

There were those who doubted they would use much computer-assisted technology in their own classrooms, primarily because their schools were too small and lacked the necessary resources. But they did hope to begin doing more with playing music at the beginning of classes, or with showing slides or videos; they nursed hopes of eventually being able to explore some of these other, more elaborate possibilities. Some felt their subject matter didn't lend itself to images in the first place. While they found the technology interesting, it seemed more immediately applicable to their own research than to their teaching. Others envisioned developing presentations on video or CD-ROM, although they acknowledged they would still have to learn how to do this and were not sure how they would find the time or the support.

One person planned to start using computer-generated handouts and overheads; another, to set up a computer bulletin board for one of her classes. A third was figuring out the logistics of a computer journaling process through which students would first write responses to their reading and then comment on each other's observations. A dialogue would thus begin before they ever came to class. Others thought they might have their students use e-mail in some way for writing projects.

Overall, the workshop had left them feeling somewhat more capable of finding ways to integrate these methods into their own work. The idea as a whole seemed less formidable, although the actual mechanics remained in many ways a mystery. The major obstacles were time, the lack of institutional support or encouragement and, for some, the cost.

There were also unexamined philosophical issues concerning the implications of adopting these technologies. The working premise had been that to do was beneficial. Was this necessarily and entirely the case?

"The technologies themselves are interesting," wrote one person, "but they are tools, not an end in themselves. I feel strongly that more of a pedagogical and/or philosophical framework should have bracketed our sessions—i.e., what can one do that is new or different with this technology that was not possible before, by way of creating more meaningful learning experiences for students? Why and how is technology a more effective way of teaching?"

Does a computer presentation with Powerpoint project with the same clarity as slides? Does the use of prepared outlines instead of using the blackboard prevent a more spontaneous written tracking of a discussion and, even if it does, is this disadvantage offset by the possibility of providing students with a clear presentational format? Just as the day's presentation had opened new possibilities, it had also illustrated that the trade-offs involved remain open questions.

The March Weekend

The Planning

Little in any of the participants' academic experience had prepared them to stand before groups of different sizes and kinds, and many felt that their delivery could use some work. They intuited that, in addition to learning the techniques for leading discussions or the technologies for illustrating their lectures or the tools for engaging students in the readings, it all worked better when something came together in the person at the head of the class— which posed the question, how to *act* before a class? Is it better to speak formally, in a voice distinct from daily speech, or informally, in a voice both authentic and distinct? Voice was the issue at hand.

It had been proposed that someone with a background in theater come to work with the group that weekend. Enough people had responded to the idea with enthusiasm that the plan had been put in place. Her name was Frances West. Trained as a Shakespearean actress in England, she had, more recently, spent some years studying with two master teachers in the United States, Kristen Linkletter and Tina Packer, and was now teaching others their methods for refining the use of voice in performance.

Thus, there was little else to plan, except for a few logistics. There would be the Friday evening gathering for people to reconnect with each other, Frances would lead the morning session the next day, and the participants would have the afternoon to work on their projects, meet with staff, or gather in small, informal affinity groups should they choose to do so. Sunday morning, they would evaluate the weekend's work.

Day One: Friday, March 8

The group came together, only to find that not everyone would be present for all the events. Michael, it happened, would be unable to join them because of another engagement. Several people had religious services to attend—a choice the staff had felt they should support, even though they worried about the effects of absences on the group as a whole and the coherence of the shared experience. A few others would miss parts of the weekend because of family events or conference presentations. Each announcement was presented as a *fait accompli*. Then, during the reception, Matthew quietly announced that he had been appointed to the presidency of a school—an appointment that would, as part of his entry into it, require him to go to a series of meetings. These would coincide with the final week of the workshop. In the midst of packing and other preparations, at most he might be able to come for the first day or so. Beyond that, he would not be there. This troubled him, but he could see no way around it.

By this time, Natalie had gradually assumed more and more of the responsibility for the planning and logistics of the workshop sessions, but this also increasingly left her as the lone figure of authority without much power of enforcement. Although it had been stipulated from the beginning of the first session that each person was expected to be present for the entire workshop, beyond executing the policy to dock people's stipends, there was little else she could do to penalize absence. The interplay of these and other variables resulted in a working culture in which people made behind-the-scenes choices on their own about when to be present and when to go do something else. Thus, Matthew's announcement was not so incongruous as it might have been in another group. What remained to be seen was how much absence the group could tolerate.

In the meantime, the group used the evening to catch up. Three had gotten tenure-track jobs; three had completed their doctoral work; two had obtained fellowships. Two had undergone difficult spring quarters, but were able to talk about their experiences in the supporting circle of the group. They had come together once again.

Day Two: Saturday, March 9

Frances West started out the morning with a series of movement exercises designed to loosen the body and, by extension, the voice. She moved from there to sounds, having the group slide from soft to loud, then highs to lows and back, explaining that rarely do people know the full range of the instrument they have at their command. She then turned to a technique known as "dropping in."

Over the years, each word in our repertoire accumulates layers of meaning and emotional association as we encounter it in multiple contexts. Whether we are aware of it or not, any given word thus becomes the repository for an idiosyncratic bundle of associations, each one with its own emotional tone. "Dropping in" sifts out these different meanings and, in the process, refines a person's awareness of the subtle emotional shifts that accompany each one. Ultimately, he or she develops the control—and freedom—to express these differences, literally broadening and deepening the range of the voice given to things.

"Dropping in" is done with a partner. You sit down, the partner standing behind your chair, working text in hand, feeding you the words one by one.

"Red," says the partner, for example, if that is the first word.

"Red," you say, thinking of some red thing and its associations, dwelling for a moment with that memory of red.

"Red," says the partner again.

"Red," you say, this time calling to mind some other red meaning. It goes on like that until red has been plumbed. Then you continue with the next word. Word by word, the team works its way through the text—with actors, most often a script—the performer weaving new threads of meaning into it through this attention to every word. In the process, different possibilities for voicing things emerge. This would, of course, be difficult to do with a lecture, and the method would require modifying—pausing, in one's preparation, for example, to reflect on the words being used.

Frances had also asked everyone to bring a brief excerpt from a piece of writing that mattered to them. She called on each person to read, making them stop and begin again, until they reached the point where their voice sounded sure and true. For most, this took multiple stops and starts. But she wanted each person to locate an experiential frame of reference from which to gauge whether or not they were "on voice." Most of us, she said, rarely are. By knowing what it feels like, she concluded, one can work toward returning to the experience in performance or, in this case, in the classroom.

That afternoon, three participants were scheduled to meet one-on-one with the three staff, in order to pre-view the videos of themselves in the classroom which they had sent in advance. Charlotte had insisted on the pre-viewing, pointing out that it allowed the staff person to review the problematic dimensions of the tape privately in a focused session with the individual, and then to speak more affirmingly in the public gathering with everyone else. In the meantime, everyone else headed off to sit in on a number of small focus groups, to go on walks, take naps, or work on their projects.

In one of the focus groups, they continued the discussion of voice. For some of the participants, the morning's session had been liberatory. It had given them a number of exact tools with which to listen to themselves, and to discern when they were speaking in a voice that was truly their own. There was, they recognized, much power in this.

"I am always aware," one person said later, "that the more relaxed I am during a class, the more comfortable, energetic, and animated I am—not to mention that I enjoy the time much more. She gave us some practical ways to prepare and trigger relaxation."

Another would write, "She helped me to be aware of how important it is to view speaking and presenting as a skill which requires practice, along with physical as well as psychic presence. There is a performance aspect of teaching, and the workshop began to address these issues."

Some felt the exercises would help them be more aware of their delivery:

"I hope to remember to think about and experience the images that arise in my lecturing and to express the richness of those images through my voice. I also hope to remember the warm-up exercises for relaxing my body. I'm going to try slowing down when I lecture, taking deeper breaths in order to give more power to the words and the images themselves."

But for others, it had been a more disquieting experience.

"I found her work thrilling," said one person. "I want to continue to work on finding my voice and speaking more powerfully. But it feels dangerous, too, in this academic world where I live as an untenured faculty woman."

"Frances West's work," wrote another, "was deeply meaningful both in the techniques she tried to teach us and in the larger philosophical questions her presentation raised. The latter remain unresolved in many of our minds, however, and she is, through no fault of her own, unaware of the possible repercussions of finding and expressing our 'authentic' voice as untenured faculty. To suggest that this is a choice without peril is ingenuous."

The question of voice remained an ambiguous one. Does the authenticity have to do simply with the character of one's vocal expression? (After all, an actor can render a chillingly authentic portrait of a villain.) Or does it refer to telling the truth of one's convictions, even in an institutional environment which may not be friendly to these? Can one fully separate the two? As one learns to discern a style of vocalizing that is true, will it become increasingly difficult to speak out of anything other than one's real convictions? What are the possible political consequences if one gets it wrong? The group had no answers to these questions.

That evening, they watched excerpts from classes in which three of the participants had arranged to be filmed. Before starting, though, each person described to the group their experience of having met with members of the staff during the afternoon to discuss what was going on in the tapes:

"Matthew was very helpful in helping me articulate what I was trying to do in the course in general and in this class in particular," the first person said. "He talked with me about how to best achieve that. While we were viewing the video, he pointed out what I did well and asked me questions to help me discover what I could have done better. From a very short clip, I learned three important things and got very motivated to try them out and videotape myself again."

"The most helpful aspect," said the second, "was having Natalie watch an entire session of my class on video and affirm my teaching techniques. I realized that just about my only feedback on my teaching is from students, since we don't sit in on each other's classes at all at my school. Her suggestions about how I could change the tempo in the middle of the class and on how to end a class were very helpful, too."

"It was very helpful," said the third person. "It raised questions such as:

"How do I begin a class?

"How do I raise questions?

"How do I summarize?

"How do I affirm students?

"How do I transition discussion questions?

"How do I express myself with gestures, voice, and stance?"

Before presenting their excerpts, each of the three led off with a brief description of their class and of what they had been trying to do in that particular session. It helped to have that brief explanation of the setting and the particular class, along with the summary of the dilemmas the presenter had faced. As some people noted, it also gave them a window into each others' teaching worlds. Once the group had seen the excerpts, the staff modeled the process of critiquing, allowing everyone to see the fundamentally constructive intentions behind the whole process. Between Matthew's presentation during the first week, and now this evening's, the ground had been laid for the rest of the participants to go forth and be videoed for their presentations during the final week.

Day Three: Sunday, March 10

During the review of the weekend and the planning for the final session in June, several differences emerged in how the participants defined what they were still looking forward to. Although many of them continued to be interested in addressing nuts-and-bolts issues such as the integration of field trips into their courses and the preparation of effective lectures, those who were more experienced were beginning to raise additional questions concerning faith in the classroom, dealing with difficult texts and issues, and the tensions between scholarship and research in their institutions. The staff realized that they would have to find a way to balance these various concerns.

Natalie had worried that the news of Matthew's departure might cast a pall over the weekend. Over the weekend, he seemed less connected to the group, although he was perceived as being actively involved in the video sessions. As Natalie later remarked, "To use the language of small-group dynamics, *he* had terminated with the group, but his leaving was still new to everyone else." Others were concerned about the long-term effects.

"I think we can rise above it, but I do think we should openly acknowledge that it is disappointing. I can't help feeling a bit abandoned by the absent faculty members—that somehow the workshop is more important to me than to them, etc. In other words, I don't think we should say nothing and pretend it's all right."

The participants agreed that to take upon themselves some of the leadership for the final week, to offset the loss of a staff member. As one person put it, "Someone on the staff could just as easily have been ill for a segment of the workshop. We can help by pooling our own experience and teaching each other. This could be really exciting." Together they decided that three of them would give presentations on the use of non-textual materials during the final week. That, and open discussion, they felt, would help them address whatever problems they might have with this unexpected departure. The transition, it seemed, was in the works.

The June Week

The Planning

No staff meetings got set up this time to organize the final week. The planning, in this case, amounted to a telephone conversation between Natalie and Charlotte, with Natalie gamely doing what she could to work out the logistics. There would be the video-viewing and related preview sessions with the three staff who would be present, along with sessions that would address the various requests she had gathered from the participants during their last meeting.

The week would be short by one day. Between religious services and the coinciding dates of the commencement exercises of people's different schools, it now made more sense to hold the first session on Sunday. On the other end, the College Club inn would be available only through Friday. There would, therefore, be six days instead of seven. Natalie compensated for this by moving the reception to earlier on Sunday afternoon and by setting up working sessions both before and after dinner. The workshop would continue through Friday afternoon. The total meeting time was thus essentially what it would have been had the group met for the full seven days, minus one session. It was a creative solution, and nothing could be done about it, but there was still the sense of not having a full week and of things being crammed in.

The schedule went out in May, along with two short readings on difficult issues in the teaching of religious studies. The participants were also invited to contribute materials pertinent to several of the focus groups, sending these to Natalie in advance for copies to be made. Projects were initially to be due by the last day of the June session, but this was subsequently revised, and tied in to receiving the stipend for the final week.

Day One: Sunday, June 12

Aside from the folks who had commencement exercises the previous day, most of the others had wrapped up their teaching for the year a few weeks earlier. If the exercises were the closing of the spring, the workshop felt like the front door into summer.

To maximize the number of working sessions, the custom of following the opening reception with something of a check-in had been dropped. Although the members of this group knew each other well enough by now that they could manage to go straight into a discussion, the more subtle underlying effect was one of having skipped the step of bringing the group back together again through the usual checking-in with how things had been going during the previous months. It didn't start things on the wrong foot, but it did make them stumble slightly.

During the first week of the workshop, the group had touched on the practical dimensions of the current tension between teaching and research in the life of the academic. Teaching, many of them had been given to understand in their institutions, was not really valued as one builds a career. One person had even been told that large enrollments could potentially be detrimental, insofar as those evaluating her work might infer that the popularity of her courses might derive not from her teaching skills, but from their being too easy. Even when the institution claims to value teaching, one is still expected to have completed two books in order to pass tenure review. Teaching, it is said, is good for the initial hire in some places, but not for getting tenure.

For this session, the group had read Stephen Boyer's *Scholarship Reconsidered*—a study of ways in which one might integrate teaching and scholarship more effectively.[11] Matthew led the discussion, which proved desultory at best. The hope had been that Boyers's recommendations might inspire people to explore new possibilities. However, many in the group found the actual realities they faced too daunting for the book to serve as a good opener. So, Matthew circled around to a different issue.

---

[11] Ernest L. Boyer, *Scholarship Reconsidered: Priorities of the Professoriate* (Princeton, N.J.: The Carnagie Foundation for the Advancement of Teaching, 1990).

"Our socialization as teachers," he said, "usually focuses on the question 'What does it take to be a success?' We forget to ask, 'What is it to *enjoy* what I'm doing?' or 'Where would I need to be in order to do what I enjoy, regardless of the prestige?' Test your internal temperature."

After dinner, the group turned its attention to issues particular to the teaching of religious studies in primarily liberal arts environments. Matthew, who was leading the session with Michael, threw out a question, which the rest of the staff—perhaps in a well-intentioned effort to prevent another discussion from flagging—promptly proceeded to answer. Nor did the participants challenge their doing so. The unintended effect was to re-assign the participants to the role of passive observers. Matthew, who recognized what was going on, attempted to divert the course back to the participants, even saying at one point, "Michael, before you hijack the discussion . . . " The ploy didn't entirely work, but eventually the participants began to find their voices.

The teaching of religious studies, it was argued, operates along two axes: 1) the relationship between the teacher and the student, in which questions of faith and identity—as, for example, in the case of tensions between "believers" and "unbelievers"—are likely to arise, and 2) the relationship between oneself and one's institution, insofar as one may be part of a field which is not necessarily integrated into the institutional vision of one's school.

People began to related stories from their own experience. The anecdotes were sharp and even confessional. They included what—had this been the original opening night—might well have fallen under the heading of "Most Embarrassing Teaching Moments." This time, however, there was no hesitation. The audience now consisted of known factors. It had all been a matter of timing. Almost everyone had some tale to tell about students wanting to know "what the professor really believes." There were no clear-cut ground rules for deciding how much to reveal of one's own stance. There were those, for example, who made it a point to keep this information to themselves, arguing that their job was to present other traditions so faithfully that their students might rightly get confused about their actual affiliation. Others simply told.

This was distinct from the issue of students who assumed that having been raised in a tradition is the same thing as being a full authority about it, and who either dismiss the content of a course because it diverges from their own understanding, or find it rocking their faith in deeply distressing ways.

"If it's a history course," said Natalie, "you can present things in light of historical method and differentiate by saying, "You have to understand the history and show you understand it before you can judge it. What you're really doing is helping them to become better-educated believers, along with learning when and how to bring in their own experience."

"I use the following set of ground rules," Michael added. "I tell them that sensitive material requires everyone to be respectful. You are only allowed to ask questions about someone else's tradition if you are willing to ask the same questions about your own. You will engage in collaborative discussions based on the assumption that everyone is an expert.

"I try to make it clear that part of my function is to train students not only at the level of content, but also on a methodological plane based on reason. That means they have to learn to discuss different positions on the basis of clearly articulated values and judgments. For the sake of equity, all the positions must meet the criterion of argued demonstration." The discussion continued in this vein, picking its way through the thorny challenges of teaching in this area.

Natalie had consulted with an expert in small-group dynamics, seeking advice on how to address Matthew's departure with the group. She and Matthew had agreed that he would participate in the afternoon and evening sessions on Sunday, at the end of which he would talk with the group and have time to take his leave. It was approaching eight-thirty, the time for Matthew and the group to say their good-byes before he departed at nine to head on to his new position. The hour arrived. Matthew suddenly leaned over to

Natalie and whispered that he had to leave. As the discussion went on, he stood, waved to the group, and walked out of the room.

Not having heard what he had said, everyone continued to talk for the next few moments, expecting that he would soon reappear. Gradually, however, it became apparent that he was gone. What could anyone say? They concluded their discussion, collected their things, and returned to the campus for the night.

Day Two: Monday, June 13

The study of religion, from one perspective, addresses the allegiances that people may hold more tightly to their hearts than they do most other things in their lives. From another perspective, it is about the study of how those same allegiances have defined the convictions of the members of a particular group, those of non-adherents and, less neutrally, of enemies. It is also about how these others have been treated in the name of conviction. All of which is to say that, sooner or later, a class is likely to run into what is often referred to as "the difficult text," a matter which cannot be separated from the question, "Difficult for whom?"

To date, many of the requests from the participants had focused on the practical aspects of teaching—how to prepare and deliver good lectures, how to write syllabi, how to lead discussions, how to grade, how to organize pedagogically significant field trips. The staff had been more interested in issues such as race, gender, and religious differences in the classroom. Monday's materials represented an attempt to bring all of these things together through the readings that had been chosen and the trip the group would take that afternoon.

Natalie had sent out "Satan," a chapter from *The Autobiography of Malcolm X*,[12] in which Malcolm Little converts to Islam and becomes Malcolm X. The chapter walks through the various events that lead to the conversion, including the explanation by the Honorable Elijah Mohammed about cosmology and the

---

[12] Malcolm X, *The Autobiography of Malcolm X*, (New York: Ballantine Books, 1965).

creation of the races as understood within the Nation of Islam. In this account, white people are referred to as devils.

Natalie began with a brief lecture, but quickly moved into modeling how one might lead a discussion on this particular text. As she did so, she pointed to different teaching issues raised by the text, not the least of which is the question of truth. Those students who find themselves in the face of a creation story different from what they know, are prone to assume that their own is on some level true, whereas the other is a myth—particularly if they are part of the group portrayed as a race of wicked deceivers. It can be harder for them to recognize the mythic dimensions within their own convictions, making it important in the study of religion to teach how mythic discourse operates. One might, for example, contrast this particular creation story, and the role it assigns one race, with the Biblical story in which Ham, son of Noah, is condemned to servitude—a text often pressed into service by those who sought to legitimize the enslavement of Africans and their descendents.

The Autobiography of Malcolm X, until the more recent rise of the Rev. Louis Farrakhan, is often used to illustrate a position of racial separatism from an African-American perspective. Neither race nor racism are topics that students in a classroom find easy to discuss. The challenge with this and other texts that focus on unresolved injuries and injustices perpetrated by one group toward another is that of sorting out the range of issues involved, and presenting them in a way that students can, in fact, talk about them. This might include introducing the analytical skills with which to figure out the issues at stake—and for whom they represent different kinds of difficulty.

There may also be issues that some students fail to recognize altogether. In the process of a discussion, the text can then become difficult in a different sense, confronting the teacher with the question of how far to press things. Some aspects of a text may be taken as such a given, that none of the students thinks to question it, even though it may in fact represent an unjust set of circumstances. The risk is to find oneself suddenly ranged against one's students.

A different problem can arise when one has a conservative students in the group, whose views may become the target of other students' attacks.

"I keep a few examples of even more conservative positions than theirs in mind," said Natalie. "That way, if somebody jumps on their ideas, I can bring in these other examples—which are really just more extreme versions of the same ideas. It protects the conservative students as individuals, and allows everyone else to address the issue at the level of ideas and not personalities." An analogous move, when the attack comes from conservative students and is directed at more liberal views, is to formulate a rebuttal from within a conservative framework. (One may need to consult with colleagues, to have such responses ready in advance.)

The discussion then moved to a case study involving a teaching fellow who, in the midst of leading a discussion on Confucius, had one of the women in her section blow up about the Confucian tradition in general and the practice of foot binding in particular. What to do when some aspect of the materials one is teaching provokes a passionate, embittered reaction? How to keep the students from attacking one another while, at the same time, making room for their differences to find expression?

The group adjourned for lunch along a nearby river. It was a warm day, and everyone fanned out to catch either full sun or shade, eat their submarine sandwiches, engage in a bit of a gossip, drowse to the rushing of the nearby waterfall, and watch the ducks mob the bread crumbs thrown down to the river's edge. Then, after a while, they picked themselves and everything else up, and wandered over to the cemetery across the street, where Natalie had brought them to see some of the stones which, in our own day, have become more theologically problematic—stones about the curse of Cain, or about how, after death, a good slave "by the blood that Jesus shed" had been "changed from black to white."

From there, they went to see murals painted by a local artist in the town post office and library, which depicted Native Americans being led off in chains to slavery, while being blessed and consoled by the minister who had converted them to Christianity. Both settings prompted further discussion of how sites in one's own area can be used to introduce religious history, along with the ways in which relationships between different groups are represented over time in one's own material environment. As it happened, the post office had never had a tour group go through it before, and a number of the patrons joined the group long enough to head over to the library to look at and talk about the second mural.

At the end of the long afternoon, Natalie led the group to an ice cream parlor. By this time, the behind-the-scenes murmurings were about her consistency with the group, her steadfastness. She had, through the outing, brought the group together again and again. Which is why, over dinner out in an Italian restaurant that evening, the same murmurings turned into anger over how Matthew had executed his departure. The more generous conceded that maybe he had found it just too hard to stay long enough to talk with them all about his leaving. Either way, he had been highly valued, and they would have liked to say good-bye and tell him so.

Day Three: Tuesday, June 14

The power of a field trip, the group agreed, lies in the actual experience of being there, as they had found at the post office the day before. It would have been hard to miss the impetus to inquiry that emerged while they had been viewing the murals, and they wondered whether some of that spirit got deadened under the pressures they all felt in their routines. Thinking about how they might apply the day's experience, they acknowledged that seldom would their classes have the opportunity to discuss a reading in the morning and then go out on a trip in the afternoon, and the debriefing would very likely happen not the next day but the next week—or, in the bus on the way home. Nevertheless, yesterday's trip had given them ideas about how to integrate an excursion into a class plan—for example, as one historian of American Judaism said, "like going to see churches that used to be synagogues."

"You can send them out on their own with a list of questions," said Natalie. "It's not as effective as going with them, but if you have them write the answers or write a reaction paper, they're more likely to go and then think about what they saw. But there's no point in sending them out on a trip unless the content is well integrated with the rest of what you're doing in the class. A lot of times, students will ask questions they might not ask in the classroom. I also sometimes invite class visitors. Like, I'll have pastors in the area come in for a section on understanding the Bible, and they pretend they're the different gospel writers who have come to dispute the different stances represented in the gospels."

"My school tends not to encourage bringing in outside speakers," said someone else, "but you can have colleagues come in."

The logistics get more complicated once the numbers go much beyond twenty or twenty-five. Out of a class of forty, if a trip is optional, maybe some ten or fifteen at most will come.

"But," said Natalie, "since it's optional, there's no need to nag. You can tell them to get themselves somewhere. Also, if it's not required or if you're not providing the transportation, then you're not liable. What gets a little trickier is the issue of mixing your role of professor with being tour guide, sheep dog, etc. It brings up the issue of your own authority, like the question of the distance or closeness you establish with students, and of boundaries. I'd suggest always dressing a little better than the group you're taking. If you need to, have the guide at the place give the tour. Do the kind of field trip *you* can do."

The rest of the morning had been planned as a response to the continuing interest in some of the basics of classroom teaching— grading papers, writing and grading exams, and developmental issues. The three topics would be offered simultaneously, with two sessions of each one. The participants could therefore choose to focus on two out of the three.

For the group working on grading papers, the staff had handed out samples of undergraduate student papers in advance. The participants were to grade these before coming into the small group, where they would then compare their own approaches to grading and commenting on student work.

To prepare for the second group on the writing and grading of exams, everyone had been asked to bring copies of the exams they had developed for their teaching projects. As they reviewed these, they asked themselves what their objectives were with a given exam and what corresponding criteria they should use to insure that the exam actually worked toward those ends. If, for example, one objective were to have students demonstrate basic mastery of the material, then questions allowing them to show their familiarity with the course content would figure large, and could include everything from multiple choices, to straight answers, comparisons, and/or identifications. It might also include multiple styles of questions, to take into account the different learning styles and levels of ability in the class.

Then there are the issues involved in determining how to grade student responses.

"I don't take off as much for bad spelling or problems with grammar when it's an exam or in-class writing," said Michael. "Set up criteria for yourself about what an 'A' answer is. Have as clear a sense as you can of what a 'B' means. Does a 'C' mean they have to show basic familiarity, a 'B' that they do some integrative analysis, and an 'A' that they formulate some original observation? None of these schemas is neutral; they each imply a hierarchy of values in terms of what we are trying to get students to learn."

The practical trade-off, the group agreed, involves the time it then takes to grade everything, particularly if one has no assistance. Identification questions, for example, can be time-consuming. Whatever the decision, a good exam question should contain implicit suggestions as to how to go about developing an answer.

Then, as the third group discussed, there is the question of where the students are developmentally.

"At one end of the spectrum," said Charlotte, "you have the students who say they have 'no idea'; at the other end are the ones who have too definite an idea of how the world works. You can end up with these kinds of differences in one class, along with cultural differences, not to mention a few graduate students. The challenge is how to design your materials so that you reach everybody.

"One of the functions of your course may be to train students in a range of skills, like how to formulate and defend a hypothesis, or how to read and analyze a piece of writing. I sometimes hand out a newspaper article at the beginning of class and then take some time to have them identify the issues. Maybe they have to compare the article with something else. Maybe I give them study-guide questions to go with their reading. With each of these approaches, I try to help them become more aware of the assumptions on which they base their own arguments—which can be especially important in teaching religion."

After lunch the reviewing of the video-taped classes began. Each participant had been assigned to work for one hour that afternoon or the next with a member of the staff, insuring that everyone would be given one-on-one critiques of their classroom work. Although neither Natalie nor Michael had done this before, Charlotte had provided them with instructions.[13]

The process was grueling for the staff. The combination of the shortened week and the all-afternoon video-viewing sessions put them on deck for virtually the entire day. It also made it more difficult for them to find time to meet as a staff except for half an hour hastily inserted after lunch. This was, on occasion, frustrating for the other participants to whom they could not be as available. At the same time, the reasons for the crunch were clear. The participants recognized the pressures under which the staff were laboring—which included being short-handed—and in their later evaluations of the program were unanimous in their praise for the staff's dedication, flexibility, enthusiasm, and especially their humor.

Later that afternoon Natalie struggled to unload a cooler full of ice from the back of her car.

"I went out to get more ice," she said, punctuating the important points with her characteristically enthusiastic emphasis. "I pulled ahead of some guy into a parking space at the market and

---

[13] See Appendix.

he gave me a dirty look as I was coming out with all these bags of ice. So, *I* said, 'Oh, I'm transporting these *donor* organs, and I had to get all this *ice* to keep them *cold*!' And I pointed to the cooler, and he didn't know what to say!" Doubling over with laughter then and later, when she repeated the story to the others, her greatest amusement lay in the joke on herself.

While the staff were working on the video clips, the other participants had the option to attend several informal focus groups. This part of the plan fell through the cracks, as it had never been made entirely clear where they were to meet. Nobody was much bothered by this, however. Instead, they went off to work on their projects or to socialize with each other.

That evening and the next, they gathered to watch a ten-minute segment from each person's video, followed by comments and observations from the rest of the group. The clips had been chosen either to illustrate a particular strength or present a specific problem. Most of the tapes were strong, but few of the participants found it easy to be generous when viewing their own work. Again, knowing this, the staff had operated on the principle of pressing their critiques somewhat more strongly during the private one-on-one sessions and being generally more affirming in the large-group meetings. The rest of the group followed suit.

"After the first session in March," Natalie was to write, "several individuals who had not had their tapes viewed commented that the time was too short and that people were too affirming and should be more critical. After this first session in June, however, these same people modified their views rather dramatically."

Despite their initial resistance to the whole exercise, by the time it was done the participants had become convinced of its general usefulness. The very fact that several of them had chosen to show excerpts in which they had not done well testified to the trust that had grown up within the group since the previous summer. The only modification to the viewing process suggested by several of them would have been to split up in the evenings and have smaller groups view and critique each excerpt. Six people a night, they thought, had been a lot.

Day Four: Wednesday, June 15

The participants had, for some time, hinted that they would like to learn more from each other. Once it became apparent that something would have to be done so that the full load of the final week would not sit hard on the heads of the staff, the group suggested that several among them might be tapped to teach something of their own strategies. Three agreed to do so.

The first gave a presentation drawn from her course on "Women, Religion, and the Early Church." Using chronologically arranged slides of artistic depictions of Mary and Joseph, she pointed to how these spoke about the face of God. She moved through early Christian depictions, to images such as Veronica's veil and different windows done in stained glass.

"You don't know what this image is, but what do you *see*? Where does your sense of identity go—to which figure? Why? What does this paradigm for holiness inspire? Mary, here, is imitating Christ—but the image also gives the message to imitate Mary. *Look* for the messages given independent of the text.

"See, here," she continued, "how Joseph is becoming more central—and here, even Madonna-like. Why is he so important to the women saints? And what are the paradigms for the family?" With the changing of the slides, excerpts of music followed one after the other—plain chant, Hildegaard of Bingen, the Stabat Mater from 1735:

"The musicians are part of a community of memory, too," she said. "They participate in the ongoing reworking of these memories through their music. Hymns are another kind of theology. I use them together, and try to teach my students to read and understand both of them. I also try to get them to see the difference between these things in context, and the contemporary popularity of things like Chant, in the world-music movement, where it is presented only as sound, or the fashion of wearing pectoral crosses these days without any religious understanding of them. It's like the old ethnical scriptures, where things were ripped out of their own settings and meanings. It's this new cultural context in which symbols are robbed and dislocated. I want them to understand that."

So, as one of their assignments for her course, students collect related images from current magazines—a number of which she includes in the presentation. Their work then also becomes material for the course and for their discussions together.

The second presenter introduced the Image Bank, a collection of 5,500 teaching slides compiled by Richard M. Carp and Jana Carp, and donated by religion faculty from a wide range of disciplines.[14] This allowed the group to begin to think about different ways of integrating slides into a lecture or presentation. The collection is designed to facilitate this process: One of its strengths is its cross-referencing of the slides by tradition, theme, and geographic area. Furthermore, most of the faculty who donated slides also contributed accompanying explanatory text, making it possible for someone else to speak about the particulars of any given slide in some detail when using it in the classroom.

"Most museums," she added, "will allow you to take slides without a flash, if you ask their permission. It works best if you use 1000 ASA film and a tripod to still the camera."

The third presenter turned the discussion to her experiments in developing a computer journaling process for her students. Using a Mac-based computer network, she had set up a folder for the class on the central system. Within that folder, each of the thirty-five students had a personal folder assigned to him or her. Every person had a password to get into the class folder as a whole, and any of these folders could be accessed by any of the students in the class. In this way, each student could make a weekly entry and respond to the weekly entries of others. Each of them was also to maintain an original of whatever they had written.

The computer journal would count for about 20-25% of the grade. Assignments had to be on time, and connected to the reading. If an assignment met those two criteria, it received one hundred points. The students had to make their own entries by 9 a.m. on Monday, and write their responses to other people's journals by 9

---

[14] Copies of slides from the Image Bank can be ordered through the Center for the Study of World Religions at Harvard University.

a.m. on Thursday. For any part of this not turned in on time, they lost 5 points. At the end of the semester, they had to submit hard copy of five of their best journal entries, with reflections on these as a whole. They also were required to be respectful of those to whom they were responding.

How did they know whose work to comment on? They began with the person below them on the file list. The next week, they went to the following person, and so on. They could read everyone's comments on their own work by looking up the entries in the other folders. The professor checked on Monday mornings to see that the entries had been made. The exercise as a whole had an immediately positive effect on the responses to her lectures and in discussions.

The other assignments in the class included 1) a research paper with footnotes, bibliography, etc., 2) a multimedia presentation done as a group, and 3) a take-home exam which they were usually on top of because they had been doing the reading and writing in their journals all along.

She didn't go in to the files to respond to their journals; it was the students who responded to each other. The process was continuous and, she found, improved over the semester. Over time, she found she had to modify one aspect of the exercise: Because the students could go into each other's folders, on two occasions in order to camouflage that they themselves had not done the work, one or possibly several students had gone into the others' folders and discarded everything they had written. A backup system had prevented the ultimate loss of everything, but the sabotage had weakened the morale of the group and eventually led the professor to stop the requirement that the students respond to each other's writing. This notwithstanding, she continued to find it a great enhancement to the course.

In their final evaluations, one of the experiences to which many of the participants would point was this one, of having been taught by their peers. Ten out of the fifteen noted that this had been one of the most helpful sessions of the week (in contrast to seven who said the same of the video viewings). On one level, this response simply reflected their appreciation of the content and methods they had learned. On another, however, it expressed a certain satisfaction over having the occasion to assert their own mastery. If only briefly, they had taken possession of the larger workshop and leveled the field in ways that the group had hitherto not fully succeeded in doing, and would not do again.[15]

Day Five: Thursday, June 16

The question of how to prepare and deliver a good lecture is a besetting one, especially early in one's career as a professor. For that reason, it kept bobbing to the surface each time the staff cast out their nets for ideas from the participants about what they wanted in the upcoming sessions. Because the precise blend of engaging content and performance so elusive, no amount of presentation on the matter quite seemed to capture a satisfying answer.

The staff decided to combine two tasks in one: an exercise in designing a lecture and one in small-group work. The larger group would be divided in three, each with the assignment to prepare—as a team—a lecture on Clifford Geertz's classic essay, "Religion as a Cultural System."[16] It was up to them to figure out who their imagined audience would be, the course in which the lecture would occur, and the form in which it would be presented.

"The staff," as Natalie would later note, "had a two-fold goal. First, small-group learning is emphasized throughout the pedagogical literature; many of our group routinely use it in their classes. This exercise would give them a chance to *experience* small-group work while fulfilling a second of our goals, namely, seeing different presentations of the same material."

The idea was to foster team teaching in a multidisciplinary way, with people bringing their different disciplinary backgrounds to the task. The groups were each given several hours to prepare a twenty-minute presentation. Each of them went off in search of a

---

[15] The discussion of the day ends with this session, as the afternoon and evening sessions continued the video-viewings discussed above.

[16] Clifford Geertz, "Religion as a Cultural System," in *The Interpretation of Cultures* (New York: Basic Books, 1977), pp. 87-125.

working area—a task complicated somewhat by having to share the conference space with what proved to be a large law-enforcement group, all of whom seemed to pour into the common areas for loud and frequent coffee and doughnut breaks.

What confounded the teams at first was a confusion over what it meant for a group to prepare a lecture—a performance most of them conceptualized as a one-person show. Eventually, each of them settled on a different solution to the problem. The first group, for example, decided to play the parts of experts called in to represent different specialties. They would sit on a panel before a senior seminar, and discuss amongst themselves the strengths and weaknesses of Geertz's contributions to the field. Even this arrangement had been arrived at only after much disagreement among the participants in the group, who found themselves almost unable to complete their task.

The second group—who had worked well together but disagreed nonetheless over how to present the material—proceeded in a similar vein by opting for a lecture-discussion format directed to an upper-level religious studies class. They differed from the first group, however, in opening their discussion after a while to the "students" for questions and comments.

The third group arrived at an almost immediate agreement over how they would make their presentation: one person would represent them. The course would be an introductory-level one in religious studies. They would begin their presentation by calling on the "students" to elicit and then critique the issues defined by Geertz.

The staff thought the group had done well and that the exercise had effectively illustrated how the same material could be presented in a number of ways. It had also got at some of the pitfalls in small-group work. That the participants did not share their feelings became apparent that afternoon when the group sat down to discuss its future involvement in the regional AAR. In and around the planning, the conversation returned to the morning's experience.

The Geertz essay, as some of them noted, is difficult to teach in its own right. That much the assignment had succeeded in modeling. But a group process is also difficult and, they felt, it had not been made sufficiently clear what this aspect of the task had been intended to achieve. This was further complicated by being asked to design a lecture as a group—something none of them had ever undertaken as a collective venture. They had felt frustrated in the midst of what, from their perspective, had been colliding goals.

"We were trying to do too many things at once," one person later wrote. "They gave us too much autonomy and too little time. I would have liked there to be more structure to the group process, as opposed to being dumped in the water."

"I do want to learn more about preparing a lecture," wrote another, "but the group process part of it made it difficult to translate any of what we did into anything resembling a lecture."

"What got modeled was how teaching collaboratively can be awful in the planning and weird in the execution."

"I think a small-group process was a great idea, and afterwards I could see the benefit of the experience of group dynamics. It helps me to empathize with my students and the task of collaborative exercises. On the other hand, I would have been less frustrated and more enthusiastic if I had been alerted to this reading earlier in the week. A shorter article, I think, would have worked to reduce my frustration. I wouldn't have minded developing a lecture and presenting it, given more notice."

"We should discuss at the beginning of the whole workshop what it is to be on display both as teachers and as participants in the workshop—especially being on display to our peers."

Herein lie some of the core issues, a number of which represented replays of earlier challenges from the group. The first of these was timing. Just as there had been protest during the first week against the idea of coming up with a project presentation in two days, the complaint was now against being given only a few hours to undertake a complicated task, the directives for which, they felt, had not been made sufficiently clear. This tied into the second issue: that of the short preparation time creating the experience of being "on display"—also a variable in the group's objection to telling embarrassing stories about themselves on the opening evening.

In and of itself, performing in front of each other was not the issue, as had been illustrated by the success of the previous day's program and of the video-viewing sessions the two previous evenings. Rather, it had to do with the perception of being put at the risk—involuntarily—of performing badly in the eyes of one's peers and superiors. It was one thing to choose a problematic excerpt from a video in the interest of asking advice on how to improve what one had done; it was another to find oneself in the midst of carrying out a task poorly when the circumstances seemed not to have been arranged in a way that might allow one to do one's best.

At stake, underneath it all, lay an expectation the workshop had created—that one would not be put on the spot. Precisely because the participants experienced the staff as fundamentally trustworthy and the workshop as good, they rebelled when some piece of the experience seemed, to them, not to hold up under that assumption. Indeed, their affection and respect for the staff was abundantly clear when the group gathered for their final evening together and the participants took the lid off their own conclusions to the workshop. In a move that simultaneously reincorporated the absent Matthew Henries and ritually roasted him for his defection, they presented the following case study:

> A liberal arts school which puts high value on *teaching*, Research College seemed to assistant professor Henry Matthews the ideal place to begin his career of discovery, integration, application, and disintegration. The new course he was about to start teaching was entitled "Religion and Everything" and had an excellent reputation. Since most of the student body felt that they already knew something about at least one element of the course title, it attracted a wide range of students including basketball forwards, chemically enhanced and grooving mystics, environmental ideologues, and sensitive new age guys. Because Research College had a reputation of pioneering innovative teaching techniques, this course was *team taught*. Professor Matthews's colleagues for the semester were self-selected to balance Matthews's own substantial strengths in the field of "Religion and Everything."
>
> Responsible for the section subheaded "Death, What a Bummer," Professor Natalie Notta Problem, a brassy redhead, brought to the course her expertise in dynamic lecturing and

unfazed chutzpah in the face of sensitive subjects. She was invaluable for her field trips, as she possessed a lifelike Class B chauffeur's license. A powerful female professor, she attracted many women students to her office for counseling, where she was often overheard to say, "No one should have to go through this alone." Most effective, according to her course evaluations, was her section (optional) on "Planning Your Own Funeral."

To supplement the team was Professor Michael Hyperkinetic Orsini, recently appointed part-time President and Provost of the College. Bringing a background in multi-culturalism, ministerial studies, grant-writing, and Euro-fashion (socks in particular), Professor Orsini contributed to all areas of the section subheaded "Religion." Without formal training, he acted as a consultant for students who chose final projects in such topics as "The Dress for Success Movement: A Critical Reappraisal," "I Don't Like to Argue: An Irenic Vision of a New Heaven and a New Earth," and "Silence: The Last Word."

Fortunate to have the resources of a media think-tank and learning center, Professors Matthews, Notta, and Orsini benefited from the close advising of Dr. Charlotte D. Romen, also known as Dr. C. D. Rom. Dr. Rom's deep concerns were divided between helping the professors answer the twin questions: "Are the students learning anything?" and "How do I get tenure?" She encouraged all the faculty to begin assembling a teaching portfolio which would reflect more fully their work as teachers, including course syllabi, assignments, evaluations, fan mail, pressed-and-dried flowers, thank you notes, and a phone log of all-night phone calls from students.

On a recent visit to the class "Religion and Everything," Charlotte had advised the faculty individually. To Henry Matthews she had suggested breathing and grunting exercises to firm and strengthen his penetrating lecture style. To Natalie Notta she had pointed out that covering the ethics of organ donation, the early childhood of Malcolm X and the hermeneutical assumptions of Women Aglow in a single class might prove difficult for those students whose learning style leaned toward the linear. Dr. C. D. Rom had affirmed Prof. Orsini's style of inquiry, assumptions, justification, and debate and asked whether he had noticed, in the video of his class, the huddled form of the woman weeping in the corner.

Sipping coffee at the back of the room was consultant Linda Barnes and Noble, the representative from the endowment which was bankrolling the slides and exhibits for "Religion and Everything." Linda was mistaken by the more mystically inclined students in the course as an "angel or ministering spirit sent forth to serve for the sake of those who are to obtain salvation." Taking extensive notes during all classes, Linda's anthropology training had provided her with skills to write "thick description." In this she had focused on the widening waistlines of the faculty and students in the course. Outside of class, she provided *pro bono* a remedial tutorial in hairstyles for the follically challenged.

It was a warm June morning when circumstances forced Henry Matthews to reconsider his identity as an aspiring professor teaching "Religion and Everything." He had assembled a riveting set of overhead transparencies designed to illustrate how ontology recapitulates phylogeny in the early Methodist movement. Henry was clearing his throat to begin, and looking out over the sea of eager faces, as he instructed his teaching fellow to turn out the lights.

As he began with the first diagram, to his horror he discovered that the images were upside down. He experienced a rush of different reactions. He looked pleadingly at Natalie, Charlotte, Michael, and Linda.

What should Henry do?

The group had found a way to preserve its integrity, translating its disappointment into humor. There was none of it that Matthew couldn't have heard, but Matthew wasn't there. Ribbing him was what it took to get the last of the gall out of their systems. As for the other staff, no one could have laughed harder at the portraits of themselves. The evening ended with the awarding of certificates to the participants, and the giving of gifts to the staff.

Day Six: Friday, June 17

A persisting issue for many of the participants was the general lack of mentoring they had experienced in these early years of their teaching. For those who had gotten no training in teaching during their graduate years, the absence of senior colleagues to whom they could turn for help as they learned to teach only added to the loneliness that many in the group described themselves as feeling within their departments and their schools. Few had found guides to lead them through the purgatory of tenure review, much less through their departments' or schools' internecine conflicts.

For this final session, Charlotte had suggested a case study that focused on the dilemma raised by a possibly racist grading pattern by a pre-tenure professor, and her discussions about it with her department chair. The case study about "Edwina" led the group further into the discussion not only of multi-culturalism, but also of the interaction between pre-tenure and tenured faculty, and particularly of their own situations.

"The issue here is how to find the right person to help you when you get yourself into a jam," said one person. "I'm not sure I can find someone in my department I can trust. What happens if you get burned? If I were to need to seek help, I would feel more comfortable turning to this group. The general situation I face is one in which there is very little mentoring; instead, there's a lot of suspicion. I would like to see more attention given to developing support structures for people in our position, that would help us negotiate these difficulties."

"I got into teaching," said someone else, "because one person was very generous with their teaching strategies, and I want to replicate that. The same spirit of the staff and participants here has been completely different from the posturing you run into in so many academic gatherings. It has let us talk about the ways we feel insecure in our own teaching."

"I'm struck by your isolation," said Natalie. "We have to look at this in what we tell future workshop groups—how alone you feel, the importance of bonding among people who really need colleagues and peers, and what allows that bonding to happen. But I'm really shocked by this level of isolation." Sometimes, the group concluded, there are no sympathetic colleagues. This had made the workshop all the more a lifeline back to others who cared, as they did, about issues related to teaching.

The discussion continued through lunch, and ended with an evaluation of the workshop that week and as a whole, following which the group disbanded, each person heading out into the summer. During the week that followed, each would send in a teaching portfolio related to his or her workshop project, and containing syllabi, class handouts, examination questions, and student evaluations. Over the course of the workshop, each person had discussed these projects with different members of the staff, working along the way to clarify the objectives of their course, render the internal design more coherent, make the instructions for each assignment more explicit, and figure out better ways to reflect their students' engagement in the course. In the process, they had also learned about the actual mechanics of assembling a portfolio.

For many of them, it wasn't easy to end the workshop. For all the ups and downs, they had held in there together, remaining engaged and invested in the workshop.

"I attribute a lot of that to the participants," said one person, "and to the designers of the program, who radiated fun and vigorousness. They made the whole experience a pleasure."

III

Non-Textual Materials and Gender:
The Eastern International Workshop

The August Week

The Planning

When the team from the Eastern International region had initially submitted their proposal to the national committee of the AAR, there had been been some initial concern that it departed from what seemed to be emerging as a workshop practice—a focus on general teaching philosophy or on the nuts and bolts of effective pedagogy developed at Wabash. This group, instead, had proposed to address particular themes—in this case gender and the use of non-textual materials. Would the workshop structure still hold up with such a focus, and what would happen to pedagogy? The national committee decided to let the team go ahead, to see what came of it.

The members of this staff represented a number of fields and methodological approaches to studying religions. Mark, the director, used anthropological theory and ethnography to explore issues of creativity in ritual, religion and art, with a particular emphasis on material culture. Anne had been trained in the History of Religions, particularly in South Asia, and was skilled in the interpretation and uses of text. Sharon's focus was psychology of religion and women's studies. She was also in the final phase of her tenuring process and was especially sensitive to pressures on untenured faculty. She would be the one to propose that the staff help the participants with mock interviews and writing application letters during some of the unstructured time of the workshops.

One of the staff was not present. Peter, a philosopher and friend of Mark's, was not a member of the AAR, but had been invited to be part of the team because he had actively promoted pedagogy for years, and because he was teaching at a community college. It seemed important to represent this experience in the workshop. Mark, Anne, and Sharon had been involved in earlier workshops run by the NEH.

Individual staff members had met occasionally. Mark and Sharon had formulated the grant proposal together at a regional meeting. Both met informally with Anne and me following one with members of the national committee at the annual meeting of the AAR. There, everyone agreed that the most effective way to run meetings would by telephone, setting Mark the challenge of coming up with times when he and four other overextended people could manage to be available. This was a mighty challenge indeed, but he rose to it with considerable spirit.

More than any other workshop staff before or since, this group invested hours in planning as a team. Between sessions, much of this took place over the telephone with bits of it happening through e-mail; during the workshops, many of the afternoons and some of the evenings turned into a process of intensive reflection on how to design team-led sessions. This dynamic first became apparent in the process of selecting participants for the workshop and in laying out the plan for the first week.

A call for applications had been mailed to the members of the region sketching out the workshop in broad strokes. The goal of this workshop, it said, "is to help good teachers become superior ones." Mark also sent out a letter to the directors of the nine graduate studies programs in the region, as the proposal set aside up to three places for graduate students, who were to be nominated by the directors of their programs.

Mark had sent the staff copies of the applications he had received, each pile accompanied by a two-and-a-half page, single-spaced letter suggesting ways to assess them. This letter cued us all in to Mark's working style—walking us through each detail of his thinking to date about the materials, and spelling out a preliminary set of criteria:

> ...1) candidate's strength as a teacher and interest in teaching (remember that these workshops are not to be considered remedial, but that they are to provide the groundwork for good teachers to become leaders in promoting good teaching in their schools); 2) strength and importance of candidate's pedagogical project; 3) candidate's interest in one or both of our special topics—gender and/or use of non-textual material; 4) general benefit that candidates might gain from workshop; 5) likely contributions that candidates might make to workshop.

Giving clear and specific guidelines was only one part of Mark's teaching and leadership style. The other, as the following excerpt from the same letter illustrates, regularly involved two other crucial dimensions: first, explaining the rationale for any set of instructions and, second, emphasizing in ways that overshadowed both guidelines and rationale, his willingness modify either one.

> I'm listing these things here to help facilitate our conversation; since we wil be discussing this via phone or maybe mail, I think some structure for the conversation might be helpful. <u>IF ANY OF YOU THINK SOMETHING ELSE, OR SOMETHING DIFFERENT, NEEDS TO BE ADDRESSED IN ASSESSING THESE CANDIDATES, PLEASE MAIL YOUR SUGGESTIONS/ THOUGHTS TO ME AND ALL THE OTHER STAFF MEMBERS</u>.

It so happened that, by temperment, the three other members of the staff were also disposed to this general orientation—an orientation which regularly led to lengthy discussions characterized by a great deal of explanation, and give-and-take. As a later report stated:

> All four of us share important pedagogical goals. We are committed to empowering students through developing their academic interests and skills. We are accessible to students and value interactive education. While we greatly value teaching structure and clarity of objectives in the classroom, we also value flexibility, fluidity and serendipity in teaching.

It is important to note that these tenets permeated the workshop beginning with the planning process and the relationships the staff forged with each other. There was, therefore, a congruence that ran throughout both the private and the public presentations of the staff.

The process of selecting participants went on for several hours. Each person on the staff had read the applications and had his or her own considerations and criteria to raise. These included the gender, race, experience, regional affiliation (due to several proposals coming from outside the region), nationality (where there were proposals from both Canada and the United States), academic area, and the actual quality of the proposals. Multiple combinations were imagined, discussed, and tweaked in various directions, as different understandings of balance came to the surface. What was striking at the time about this discussion was its quality of extended negotiation, the different variables under consideration weighing in, in different ways.

Eventually, Mark said, "I think at the end we'll find that we're going to be pretty even-handed. Let's try a different strategy. I'm not sure what to use, but let's go down the list and talk about who seems definite and why. Our goal is to try to create a cadre of exceptional teachers, and to engender the issue of pedagogy as a more important one among younger faculty." As a result, the staff tried to select candidates who showed promise in developing as leaders in the teaching profession.

Finally the participants were chosen. Four, rather than three, graduate students had been selected based on the greater strength of their proposals. The fields represented by the group were diverse. Five of the participants came out of schools in Canada, the rest either taught or were completing graduate work at schools in the United States. Two came from outside the region, because even though preference had been given to in-region applicants, these other candidates were seen as being stronger. In the end, there were eight women, seven men; one of the women was African-American but there were no other minorities either among the participants or on the staff—a demographic fact of which the staff lamented. Several were adjunct faculty, introducing the element of the academic migrant worker. The staff was attuned to the tightness of the academic job market and aware of its impact on untenured and adjunct faculty.

"These are all good people with promising teaching careers who can't find jobs. Maybe we should have paid more attention to the issue of instability in teaching positions," said Sharon.

The talk then turned to planning the schedule, deciding on the packet of readings that was to be sent out,[1] and determining how to integrate films and audio-visual materials. Following the Wabash model, and like the New England Maritimes group, the Eastern International workshop group would meet for a week in August of 1993, a weekend in November, another in the spring of 1994, and a week in June of the same year. The group had decided to focus working sessions in the mornings and to use the evenings for more free-ranging discussions of films. The participants were to be invited to bring materials they had found useful in their own teaching. These would be put in a resource library for the duration of the workshop. In addition, two rooms with videotape players and film projectors would be reserved, so that people could take time in the afternoons

---

1   The participants were asked to buy: John B. Carman and Steven P. Hopkins, eds., *Tracing Common Themes: Comparative Courses in the Study of Religion* (Atlanta: Scholars Press, 1991); Mark Juergensmeyer, ed., *Teaching the Introductory Course in Religious Studies: A Sourcebook* (Atlanta: Scholars Press, 1991); Frank E. Reynolds and Sheryl L. Burkhalter, eds., *Beyond the Classics: Essays in Religious Studies and Liberal Education* (Atlanta: Scholars Press, 1990).

Having reviewed a much thicker stack of additional possibilities, the staff eventually narrowed the list of readings to be completed before arrival in August to the following, which were sent to the participants in a packet: Mary Field Belenky, Blythe McVicker Clinchy, Nancy Rule Goldberger, and Jill Mattuck Tarule, "Toward an Education for Women," in *Women's Ways of Knowing: The Development of Self, Voice, and Mind* (New York: Basic Books, 1986), pp. 191-229; Blythe Clinchy and Claire Zimmerman, "Growing Up Intellectually: Issues for College Women," in *Work in Progress* (Wellesley, MA: Stone Center for Developmental Services and Studies, no. 19, 1985); James W. Fernandez, "Education by Puzzlement," in *Persuasion and Performance: The Play of Tropes in Culture* (Bloomington, Indiana University Press, 1986), pp. 172-87; Roberta M. Hall and Bernice R. Sandler, "The Classroom Climate: A Chilly One for Women?" *Project on the Status and Education of Women* (Washington, D.C.: Association of American Colleges, 1982).

to view different selections either alone or in small groups—a plan which was to prove extremely effective.

The staff also discussed the place of the projects in the group sessions. When would presentations take place and how would they help people relate the workshop back to their projects? It was decided to use the full weekend sessions for the project presentation. A letter addressing practical issues would also ask everybody to send in a one-page summary of what they were doing. These would be circulated to everyone else.

More than most groups, this staff also wrestled with the question of how to incorporate a process of meta-cognizing, such that the group as a whole—and the staff when behind the scenes— would regularly reflect on its own process and come to embody a particular dynamic. This was different from the practicums followed by debriefing sessions that had taken place in the New England/Maritimes workshop. There, a teaching strategy was modeled and the experience then discussed. But the group did not then discuss itself discussing. The Easern International group, in contrast, pursued a process of self-scrutiny in the interest of cultivating an ongoing awareness of what was going on in the group as a model for what might go on in a classroom.

No staff in any of the workshops failed to address the question of why each presentation or discussion was being designed and with what aims in mind. It was, perhaps, the degree to which this group did so that distinguished it—the amount of concentrated attention that each member drew into the discussion. This had a great deal to do with the particular personalities involved. It was a process that might have driven another combination of individuals crazy; this group flourished with it and became increasingly creative in the process. By the time the two initial planning sessions were done, a schedule had emerged. By the end of the final week the following summer, the staff would be spending several hours together each afternoon, working together to design collaboratively a week of team-taught sessions. Of all the workshop staffs, this one was an example of high-end engagement.

The letters that went out were detailed and inviting. From early on, they made it clear that the participants were perceived by the staff as people who had already had early successes in teaching. "The staff," one letter from Mark said, "is therefore figuring out ways for all of us to share our 'expertise' with each other." It went on to introduce one assignment, in which the participants would be asked to consider how they would plan to teach a specific topic over several days in a course, depending on their particular field. Other communications reiterated the emphasis on excellence. Indeed, the very letter of acceptance opened by saying:

> You have been selected to participate in the AAR/Lilly Teaching Workshops. Congratulations! We have a group of superb people with wide-ranging interests. We only regret that we did not have space for so many other excellent candidates.

Mark, through these communications, set the tone in other ways as well. "The rest of the staff and I," he wrote, "are extremely enthusiastic about your participation in the workshop."

These various descriptions led participants to have some sense in advance of how the staff perceived them, in what conditions they would be meeting with each other, what they would be doing, and what the tone of the meeting was to be. "There will be seated meals with all of us together for lunches and dinners," another letter went on to say.

> A lot of effort is being made to provide convivial and informal opportunities for us to share our experiences . . . In broad outline, mornings will be largely devoted to formal sessions; afternoons will be used for individual projects and meetings between staff and participants on particular topics; evenings will be used to present audio-visual material and for informal discussions on the use of that and similar materials in our work in the classroom.

Prior to their arrival, therefore, the participants received a fair amount of coaching with respect to the workshop culture into which they were entering.

The staff gathered a day before the participants arrived in order to go over the plans in greater detail. If any memory stays with me, it is of being met by Mark at the airport. Mark, who had recently returned from an NEH Summer Institute in Honolulu about the use of non-textual material in the classroom, was visibly delighted by his bright blue Hawaiian shirt with its red and yellow flowers—an ensemble completed by what was to become a familiar trademark, a battered old leather hat with its sweat-stained hat band. Needless to say, he was also striding along in worn leather sandals. It was as clear a signal as one could want that this was not a stuffy set.

As each person had been assigned to lead different sessions, the point of this working session was to convey to the others what he or she had laid out, and to invite comments. At this point, the plans were fluid, outlines to be more fully filled in. The group, by now, had begun to define some of its own personality differences in humoral terms, two members being described as "hot," the others as relatively more "cool."

They quickly fell into the habit of making observations about each other's style. The one who appeared laid back was not, upon closer contact, quite so nonchalant as one might first think. A dynamic that went less noticed—but one that would prove to require ongoing attention—was the reticence of one member, who found herself being regularly interrupted and cut off by the more vocal members of the team. After a spate of Unitarian jokes, it also emerged that one member of the staff was a Unitarian. The director's style was to state his own position strongly and then to invite other opinions. What allowed this to work was his own willingness to modify his initial stance.

The group as a whole resolved that they had to present themselves to the participants not just as the planners of the existing schedule, but as the facilitators for whatever other things the participants wanted to do. The actual fact of coming together as staff, of having several informal meals together, began in subtle ways to consolidate the connections begun over the phone. Even though, as in New England, some of the staff had known each other in other contexts, it was these working sessions that established their identity as a team.

Day One: Sunday, August 15

For the first set of meetings, the Campus Inn at Mark's school had been chosen to insure that quarters would be comfortable. The entire group, including the staff, would stay there. Mark, who lived only a couple of blocks away, had decided to do so as well in order to be part of the entire workshop experience. Because the whole session took place on campus, it was logistically simple to walk from the inn over to the classroom building where many of the discussions would take place. People drifted in during the first half of the afternoon, and found the staff waiting in the lounge to greet them.

The suggestions from the AAR had been clear: do all you can to convey to these people that they and what they do are special. The food was good. A fitness center, computer rooms, and library services were provided. While not luxurious, neither were the facilities in any way Spartan. Thus, Mark's correspondences, designed to indicate to the participants how highly valued they were, were reinforced by the material surroundings.

Toward the end of the afternoon, the group gathered for their first meeting. In their planning, the staff used the language of building "thought experiments" when discussing this part of the design. It had been decided that, during the first meeting, the discussion would open with the question of why we teach religious studies. The intention was twofold: to start building group cohesiveness and to get the participants talking with each other about their own experience right from the beginning.

The session took place in the lounge in one of the classroom buildings. The team showed up in T-shirts (some of them funny), shorts (some more rumpled than others), and sneakers or sandals. All the visual cues pointed to an invitation to set down among friends and be at home. This invitation would, of course, require reinforcement through a combination of other signals, but some of these had, in fact, already been given through the letters sent in advance. The message had been that this was to be a meeting of co-learners; so far, this was being backed up by other congruent details.

The group hauled their chairs into a circle. During this first actual meeting of the group, Mark's introduction emphasized the ways in which the participants would be responsible for recommending changes to the program, organizing themselves to see films, setting up their own afternoons, and taking part in the planning of future sessions. If anything, he came close to overemphasizing the point that if something seemed not to be working, the staff wanted to hear about it.

The staff opened the discussion with one of its members describing not her academic position and interests, but talking instead about how and why she had gone into teaching religious studies. This was not the performance piece designed for the formal conference, but the more personal tale of one individual's engagement with matters of profound importance to her. Everyone else followed suit, going one by one around the room, staff mixed in with the others. It was against this background that the participants then described the projects they would be undertaking over the course of the workshop.

What did this approach elicit? For one thing, the many wonderful, peculiar, unpredictable reasons for which people had entered their particular fields. For another, the sense of each other as storytellers. One could already get a feel for the various styles of addressing a group. The exercise posed challenges of preliminary trust. Presumably in a roomful of strangers there were still pieces of all those stories that did not get told. Yet the excercise still succeeded in recruiting the engagement of everyone there—even one participant who had written in her proposal that she tended to eschew anything more confessional on her work.

It took time to go around the room, but by the time everyone was done, the distinctions between staff and participants had dissolved a little bit more, and people had begun to target areas of commonality. The exercise had also allowed everyone to open with a statement about what mattered to them. That, in itself, set an opening tone.

The first film chosen for viewing was a documentary by Robert Gardener, *The Nuer*.[2] The accompanying reading was the article, "The Camera People," about a tribe known as "the Ethnographic Filmmakers." None of the staff had seen the film before (it having been recommended by a colleague), which left everyone to engage in the exercise on level footing. The different staff members spoke up quite

---

[2]   Hilary Harris and George Breidenbach, *The Nuer*, Robert Gardner and Hilary Harris, producers (Cambridge, MA: Film Study Center; Del Mar, CA: McGraw-Hill Films, 1970).

regularly and, sometimes at length. Yet because they had already created a sense that hierarchy was, in every way possible, being erased, the event turned into a circle of stories, a first viewing, a modeling of collaboration.

How does one show a film in which there are the visuals of pain? This film, for example, includes scenes of cattle being cut and killed. How does one teach with a film that presents another group in ways that some students may find alienating? What is the objective in showing something that may be difficult for members of one culture to watch? Could one establishes comparisons with the cattle culture of the Vedas? If so, how does one convey the sense of the sacred that occurs through the relationship to a group's cows?

Perhaps one talks about Chuang Tzu on the locus of the sacred being as much in dung as anywhere else. American slaughterhouses as examples of a way of killing without ritual significance. Mary Douglas's discussion of bodily substances and their relationship with notions of purity and pollution. A film about the *Kumba Mela* in India—the great, periodic gathering of holy people along the Ganges where individuals smear themselves with ash and cow byproducts. A documentary on pain and religious ecstasy. By the end of the evening the participants were volunteering bibliography, exchanging syllabi, and organizing small-group meetings.

Day Two: Monday, August 16

The staff had decided it was important from the beginning to establish group learning and to avoid the model of an "expert" presenting material to "learners." In the interest of encouraging the participants to present their own approaches in relation to a common task, they had been asked to read Diana Eck's *Darśan*[3] before coming, and to talk about how they would teach it in one of their classes. The discussion led to suggestions that the book might serve as a springboard for visiting a local Hindu temple and, from there, going to a Catholic church or perhaps an Muslim mosque. But could it be used in courses about completely unrelated traditions? Could it provide a comparative entrée to aspects, say, of Christian

---

[3]   Diana L. Eck, *Darśan: Seeing the Divine Image in India* (New York: Columbia University Press, 1996.

iconography? If so, it might be used to discuss different representations of saints. One could contrast this with other sacred images as well—that of the rebbe among the Lubovatcher, for example. One would want to teach students the pertinent visual vocabularies so as to reduce the tendency for things to be either romanticized or dismissed as incomprehensible and bizarre. It could also serve as an introduction to Hindu understandings of religious experience and, in this way, raise questions about the differing models of religious truth, not all of which are propositional. What, in other words, are the models for acquiring religious knowledge?

Those more interested in the study of the psychology of religion proposed that it might be used to encourage discussion of non-Western models of religious transformation, and to reflect on how our very models of psychology are shaped by the history of Western traditions. How does the act of seeing play a part in one's psychology, and how is one schooled to see? If there are at least three hundred and thirty million gods in India, how does this inform how one sees the sacred? Moreover, people also learn stories about the gods, which may also be represented in the figure. There are thus whole narratives—even multiple ones—transmitted through iconographic cues.

Part of the question concerns what one feels competent to teach and what that competency actually means. It was argued that it is acceptable to use material concerning topics about which one does not necessarily know a great deal, so long as one acknowledges that this is what one is doing—and maybe not in a lecture. (Would this not, one person wondered, wipe out many of one's lectures early in one's career?) The point being raised, however, was that there may be value in the ability to acknowledge what one does not know and to engage in the project of all digging out the truth together.

One might compare this understanding of viewing with arguments in feminist film theory concerning the nature of the viewer, often positioned as male spectator. Who is positioned as viewer in the case of *darśan*? In contrast, one participant described a case at her school in which a speaker had been brought in who, in the course of his talk, gave *darśan* to those present. What did it mean to see other members of the faculty, students, going up and kneeling?

Likewise, if one takes students to a Hare Krishna temple or to a local Zen Center, what does one do if some of them wish to participate? How does one avoid turning others into zoo specimens and oneself into the tourist?

To convey something of what it feels like to be the zoo specimen, there is always the essay on the Nacirema culture, or David Macaulay's *Motel of the Mysteries*—an attempt, five hundred years into the future, to interpret the contents of a motel in a continent buried under a mountain of junk mail. But how does one deconstruct the tourist stance in ways that make the familiar strange, the strange familiar? Can one turn to Audre Lorde and her writings on grief, or to Adrienne Rich on guilt as something other than an immobilized state? What of Anne Cameron who, in *Daughters of Copper Woman* wrote stories about a Native American women's secret society and, though she had been given permission to do so, was later seen as having stolen something? Does one set Angela Davis's speech against the veil in Egypt in tension with writings by Arab feminists, as in *Opening the Gates*?[4]

For that matter, how does one address those students who are seeking and those who are tired of having their cultures plundered, when both are in the same classroom? What are the politics behind the rejection of one's own cultural background or that of others? We know there are few pure traditions, including our own. The Nuer in the documentary were, after all, wearing shorts. We are all susceptible to being mutually influenced. It may, therefore, not be so much a case of rejecting the role of tourist but of learning, instead, to be a good one. Still, there are also embedded class dimensions to the role of the tourist, usually including having the resources to play the part of a certain kind of spectator.

"I," said one participant, "don't like the zoo metaphor."

"My use of it," said the originator, "comes from students wanting to meet someone who is HIV+ or who has AIDS. It wasn't a particular person they wanted to meet, but someone who fit a

---

4 David MacCaulay, *Motel of the Mysteries* (Boston: Houghton Mifflin, 1979); Anne Cameron, *Daughters of Copper Woman* (Vancouver, British Columbia: Press Gang Publishers, 1981); Margot Badran and Miriam Cooke, *Opening the Gates: A Century of Arab Feminist Writing* (Bloomington: Indiana University Press, 1990).

particular category. What's the difference between something being a zoo experience and a teaching experience? This is an important question for people with non-normative sexualities or who are of non-European descent."

That evening, Mark introduced the group to the resources of the Image Bank, which he had encountered at the NEH workshop he had attended in Hawaii. He had also set up a light table, which allowed everyone to examine them in greater detail. Afterwards, behind the scenes, one person expressed her surprise that gender issues had not been brought more clearly into focus by this point, at the same time worrying that fault lines of disagreement were already emerging along different understandings of gender and notions of the classroom. With respect to the latter, for example, was a classroom a safe space or a place in which guided conflict could occur? Were the two necessarily mutually exclusive? Another person countered that it was already far better than she had imagined it would be. She had not expected this level of expertise among the other participants.

Day Three: Tuesday, August 17

Peter began with a raisin.

After handing a single raisin out to each person, "Imagine," he said, "that you are a beginning student in an intro class." As someone started to interrupt, he halted them. Off to one side, someone else whispered, "And after everyone has had a chance to speak, then you *eat* the raisin."

Amidst much chuckling, Peter went on. "Look carefully at your raisin. Notice its texture—how it feels to your fingers—its size, its shape. Notice its color. Does it have a smell?"

One by one, Peter walked through the various ways in which one might have some sensory awareness of the raisin, inviting everyone as he did so to focus their attention on this particular small object. Only after completing these steps did he direct everyone to close their eyes and eat their raisin, noticing at that point how it tasted. What had been their experience of this exercise? In the meta-cognizing session that followed, Peter discussed how such an exercise can remind us that there are many strategies in teaching and that we tend to neglect most of the senses in both our teaching and our own learning. How, then, does one design a generic experiential exercise aimed at suggesting to students different ways of focusing their attention?

"The difficulty," one person responded, "lies in getting students to focus on an object as *I* define it—like Hinduism. How do I name that focus in a way that *they* can connect with it, and what do I want them to take away?"

Others agreed that one major challenge involves finding ways to keep students focused—to which they proposed strategies such as requiring students to take careful notes and then to turn the notes in, encouraging students to stop the professor when he or she starts to wander, asking them for a one-paragraph summary of something they've read, or having them stand up for a stretching break. A distinct but related dilemma involves recognizing the difficulties students have in focusing outside of class time, and designing tasks to promote greater focus, discipline, and understanding.

"I have my students keep journals," said one person, leading the group to discuss not only what one could require by way of content, but also the ethics involved in student self-disclosure and privacy, as well as the criteria by which one actually evaluates journal writing. Many felt that the function of a journal was to prompt student reflection on some issue experienced as provocative, and that such reflection should not be graded on any basis other than the fact of having written something on time.

In the meta-cognizing that followed, Peter asked for reactions to the raisin exercise. He went on to point to the ways that learning is about having a specialized kind of conversation which is, by its very nature, collaborative.

"In the humanities, we somehow sometimes think of collaboration either as a kind of intellectual cheating or as a lesser creative form. We shy away from doing group projects."

"I always hated group work as a student," said one participant. Others seconded the sentiment.

"We also don't learn very good ways of doing it, most of the time," said someone else.

Everyone agreed it would be useful to incorporate some group tasks into the workshop in order to learn more effective ways of strengthening this aspect of their teaching. They decided also to set up a group journal during the course of the workshop, in which they would each be allowed to read what others had written or included—but only after adding something or writing a response.

"All right." said Peter, "Now I'd like you to work on a short writing assignment. Pick one image or metaphor that describes how you think of yourself as a teacher." After giving everyone time to think about it, he sent them off into small groups to tell each other what they had come up with. When he brought them all back together again, it was reported that this group, as seen through its metaphors, included:

> A facilitator and informer (ear and mouth)
> A catalyst (combiner)
> A midwife
> A tutor/listener/interlocutor
> A seed planter/gardener
> The holder of a looking glass
> A bridge with an alternative path
> A kaleidoscope
> The conductor of an orchestra
> A Taoist model of water over rocks
> One who engenders desire and passion using a carrot, not a stick
> An aide in seeing/ a visual opener,
> A modified gadfly
> A detective and an entertainer/story teller
> A dance instructor
> A juggler's assistant
> A nomad, and...
> The little engine that could

Later, in their meeting that afternoon, the staff thought about how working in a group and having one person report back requires a particular kind of listening. They noticed their own tendency to speak too frequently, and resolved to curb themselves—a resolution which their own enthusiasm would lead them break and remake over and over again during the course of the workshop series. Correspondingly, they reflected on how to engage quieter participants by asking them to lead off some of the exercises, and on the messages that would be given by these choices.

Evenings were, for the most part, down time. Mark knew all the good restaurants in that part of upstate New York, and figured that, to offset being in a town with a main street about one blink of an eye long, he'd take us out to as many of the better ones as the conference budget would allow. This one was just downtown—that is, at the edge of the campus and across the street. Dinner was a pure ruckus. Everybody was talking so much, one would think they'd gone to school with each other for years. After that, going back to sit in hard classroom seats to watch a movie made it a little hard to focus, but the group all managed to digest the experience.

The staff had, in the planning stages, been aware of the effects of different settings. "Rooms," as Mark put it, "are important as theater." This had led to reflection on three possible places for the group's meetings—two of them more formal, one an older hall which offered, at the same time, the most democratic arrangements of seats. The staff voted to hold most of the sessions in the latter, even though some of its chairs were less comfortable. And, truth be told, during the following evenings, the remaining films were shown in a lecture hall where the seats were somewhat easier on the anatomy. The point, as the staff noted in its own discussions, was that setting played a part in a group's experience of an event.

That evening, the group watched *Stopping the Church*, a documentary about protests by Act Up against the Catholic Church's policies on homosexuality. More specifically, it included scenes of protesters speaking about their own self-understanding as Roman Catholics and their anger at church policies, along with scenes of disruptions during the mass. While the film elicited strong sympathy and amusement from one part of the group, it provoked equally strong reactions from another part who felt it engaged in simplistic Catholic-bashing. That both groups felt the freedom to state their positions directly had probably been fed not only by the earlier exercises in building a group but by the conviviality over dinner. The sharing of food throughout this and the other workshops repeatedly served as a powerful bond-builder.

Day Four: Wednesday August 18

How, the staff had wondered in their planning sessions, would they use issues of gender to think about questions of race or multicultural contexts? Gender, in this workshop, focused primarily on the subject as it pertained to women, while the different possible meanings of "maleness" had tended to remain unaddressed questions. Not everyone found this satisfying.

The night before, one of the men in the group who, back home, was part of a men's awareness group, voiced his frustration privately that there didn't seem to him to be much room for the men there to talk about definitions of gender as these affected them. He wondered if he should say something before today's session—an exercise known as "the fishbowl"—geared toward learning to listen to a conversation, hear what was being said, and make comments that might be critical but that also had to be constructive. He decided to wait and see how things went.

One of the staff's objectives was both to model different approaches and be subject to critique. But how could the very process of critique be modeled? Sharon had proposed that a fishbowl exercise be attempted, in order to explore one approach to insider/outsider observation and feedback. The fishbowl required one part of the group to sit in a small circle the center of the classroom, with the other part sitting in a larger circle around them. The first group—which consisted of all the men—was instructed to discuss a question to which there is no "right" answer, but for which there are, instead, multiple possibilities. In this case, it was, "In what ways does gender affect your teaching?" The women were told to listen in on the conversation—a conversation being held among people who in at least one respect appeared similar—after which they themselves would move into the center and have their own discussion, observed by the men. All were asked to notice where unexpected lines of similarity and difference emerged. The objective was to help people learn to listen across lines of difference.

In the debriefing that followed, the group talked about the content and process of what they had experienced—its pedagogical importance and the important themes that had come to the surface or been absent. Why, one man wondered, had the men gone first?

"Because," said Sharon, "people have found that when women go first, they have been very uncomfortable, there's been more silence, and they've remained more theoretical in their discussion, instead of talking about their experience. Because of the cultural definition of what it is to be a human being, the people who are in the dominant category tend not to recognize that they're in a cultural category. So it's useful to have them go first, to make them more aware of it."

The reasoning behind conducting such an exercise in this context was to prompt people to question normative constructions of the masculine and feminine, as well as constructions of what it means to be a professor. Together, the two would include questioning the silent biases which, in faculty settings, may result in faculty-to-faculty harassment, and may influence who is empowered to speak in faculty meetings, who gets recruited to serve on committees, and who gets tenure.

Over lunch, the discussion turned from the experience of observing and being observed to that of being observed as adjunct or untenured faculty in one's own institution, and to how tensions between confidentiality and power arise in a range of ways. For a few members of the group this was all the more delicate and painful an issue because of their own sexual identity. In the course of this and other conversations, an affinity group of women and men— some gay, some straight—emerged around the discussion of Gay and Lesbian issues in teaching the study of religion. This group would continue to meet past the end of the workshop series to pursue their discussions and work together. It was the only case of the workshop's generating an independent group which went on to establish tasks and an identity of its own outside of the workshop.[5]

That night Anne had brought *Small Happiness*, a documentary about women in the mainland Chinese village of Long Bow.[6] The

---

[5] During the course of the workshop itself, other small groups organized as well, such that most of the participants and staff ended up being part of at least one. "Some groups," as Mark observed in one of his reports, "such as the one looking at Indian religions, were more casual and might not even be considered a structured group, whereas the China studies group was more formally established." Many such meetings took place over breakfast.

[6] Carma Hinton and Richard Gordon, directors, *Small Happiness:*

recollections of old women—some with formerly bound feet—mingled with comments from a daughter-in-law, a head of family planning, and other unmarried women. One old woman told a story from years before when, made desperate by famine and having too many children to feed, she had been forced to smother one newborn son. As we listened, one participant, herself quite pregnant at the time, began to cry. How, she wept, after the film's end, had that mother been able to bear bringing an end to the life of her own child? It was a powerful reminder that in any given group, there are elements in what we teach that may move people to strong responses in ways that, as teachers, we cannot anticipate.

During the discussion, it was pointed out that the older women in the film had also had the ability to understand the social and cultural restraints that had been imposed on their generation. There were strong connections between them, and they used humor to disguise a great deal of pain. One participant compared the documentary with *Dadi's Family*,[7] a film about one Indian mother-in-law, whose family was placed under considerable stress by societal change, in ways that proved to be a mixed blessing.

Day Five: Thursday, August 19

On the board as the group entered the classroom that morning was the following list:

1. womenless _____
2. women in _____
3. women as a problem, anomaly, absence in _____
4. women's _____ (women as women—includes region, nationality, race, class, ethnicity and so on, affectional preference, and marital status)
5. men's _____ (includes men as men, in the same senses)
6. gendered _____ (women's and men's)
7. reconstructed/redefined to include all

Women of a Chinese Village (Wayne, N.J.: New Day Films, 1984.
    7   M. Camerini and R. Gill, directors, *Dadi's Family* (Washington, D.C.: Public Broadcasting Service, 1988).

The discussion was again to go further with the focus on gender, this time considering different strategies for integrating gender into and throughout one's courses, beginning with the syllabus.

"How," Sharon said, "do we go from never noticing gender to *noticing* that there are women and men involved in (or absent from) whatever we are teaching?" She turned to the list on the board.

"'Womenless,'" she continued, "is when no women are included. 'Women in...' is when you stick in a few of them. 'Women as anomalies' speaks for itself. 'Women's' refers to various *kinds* of women, just as 'men's' refers to various *kinds* of men. 'Gendered' is thinking about 'men' and 'women' as the only two genders there are, while the last category—'reconstructed'—refers to religious experience organized along a spectrum of genders. These then get further nuanced with dimensions of race, class, ethnicity, and so on. This way of dividing things up allows not only the differences across categories to surface more clearly, but also the similarities."

The group jumped in: When we look at a syllabus, are there more men than women, or no women at all? Are there any related theoretical concerns and do the course goals, content, and pedagogical style emerge from the awareness that there are men and women involved? What are the consequences of adding women into the syllabus—and of doing so in ways that go beyond simply sticking in a few women? Are the categories "man" and "woman" adequate in the discussion of gender and, if so, are people like monks or eunuchs "men" in the same way that others are considered "men?" How does one categorize cross-gendered groups? Is there, instead, a range of masculinities and femininities expressed in a given various religious traditions? If so, what do we see once we cease to insert people from these traditions into our own categories?

The discussion then bridged over to consider that a person's ways of understanding these or any other issues is informed as well by the developmental dimensions of experience. To prepare, the group had read Sharon Parks's *The Critical Years*, a study of young adulthood as conceptualized through the use of various Western theories of human development.[8] The gist of Parks's argument is that

---

[8] Sharon Parks, *The Critical Years: Young Adults and the Search for Meaning, Faith, and Commitment* (San Francisco: HarperSanFrancisco, 1991).

the identity formation of young adults with respect to cognition, affect, moral reasoning, and faith has structurally discernible stages. For a person to move toward the capacity to sustain what Parks describes as committed relativism, he or she requires certain kinds of mentoring. This argument bears directly on what it means to teach, not only in the humanities in general but in the study of religion in particular. It is serves as a powerful reminder that students come to us at different points in their journey toward maturity.

There were apprehensions in the group about any theory with evolutionary overtones, particularly one based on certain understandings of adulthood derived from one cultural framework in particular. The focus on a particular understanding of cognitive development was also troubling. The implied categories of knowledge and rationality were, perhaps, rooted in one culture's vision of the world in ways that might relegate other groups to a lower developmental stage.

At the same time, it was also clear from experience in the classroom that students come to a classwith different capacities to appropriate what is being taught. This awareness pushes us to reexamine what we may otherwise take to be a fairly homogeneous group of individuals. In particular, how does one take into account developmental issues that may influence one student to adopt a firm adherence to a narrower interpretive stance, and another to fall into an unqualified relativism? How does one encourage movement beyond either one of these toward the ability to be open to practices and convictions different from one's own, even as one forms critical judgments and the capacity to take informed stands?

The question becomes all the more complicated when we realize that a range of cultural and religious understandings of what it is to be fully human may challenge our own take on what it is to be a mature adult, and that all of these understandings walk through the door with each of our students. In designing a syllabus, therefore, we are confronted not only by the question of how to integrate issues of gender throughout, and to consider how different groups within a culture experience the related categories in their appropriation of a given tradition; we also face the reality that our students' grasp of what we are teaching them is further informed by where they are in the midst of their own growing up.

Later that afternoon, the staff members took pleasure in how rich the discussion had been. The various thought exercises were, it seemed, working well. They turned their attention to discussing Mark's plans for the next morning. Mark, who makes extensive use of audio-visual materials in his classes, was planning to demonstrate how one could use just a few slides and brief video clips—in this case, a segment from Peter Brooks's *Mahabharata* in which the Pandava brothers are interrogating a pool. This excerpt, in conjunction with an essay by James Fernandez, "Education by Puzzlement,"[9] was intended both to illustrate the use of non-textual teaching materials at the same time as the content involved an exploration of the nature of learning. Mark would then go on, he suggested, to introduce the use of a more performative element through his work with masks.

By this time, it should be noted, each staff member's foibles and penchants had become more familiar territory. Sharon, it was decided, was to be assigned the title "The Soul of All Organization" (or, as she put it, either "the untied soul" or "the untidy soul"). Anne, who was often given the cash to hold when the group went out, became "The Keeper of All Funds." And Mark who, struggling against his own more spontaneous tendencies, had attempted to turn himself into a strict timekeeper for each of the sessions, was dubbed "The Master of Untrue Time."

In the course of the laughter over these designations, Anne returned to an issue that had come up over lunch earlier during the week—namely, the vulnerability of adjunct and untenured faculty in the face of being under observation. We reflected on how the presence of an ethnographer could, potentially, be experienced as an extension of this. Mark mentioned in this connection that the study would eventually be published by Scholar's Press. In a flash, a role perceived as essentially neutral took on more problematic overtones,

---

9 Peter Brook, Jean-Claude Carriere, and Marie-Helene Estienne, (Peter Brook, director), *The Mahabharata* (New York, NY : Parabola Video Library, 1989); James W. Fernandez, "Education by Puzzlement," in *Persuasion and Performance: The Play of Tropes in Culture* (Bloomington, Indiana University Press, 1986), pp. 172-87.

as the staff began to wonder whether or not I posed a threat. Why had I not made it clearer that a book was being written about them? The concern this aroused generated a sense of crisis, and led to a series of heated, behind-the-scenes meetings.

Academics are not accustomed to being the subjects of an ethnography. We are, to be sure, used to our conferences and projects being assessed in the form of a final report, but assume that such accounts disappear into the confidential depths of a foundation's internal files. It is quite a different matter to imagine oneself as the member of a tribe into which an anthropologist has come to record our ritualized behaviors, our words and our actions, and the things we disclose while believing ourselves to be in the privacy of our own village.

The situation resolved when it became clear that the national AAR had, in fact, communicated to Mark that a monograph was to come out of the workshops—a fact which, through unintentional oversight, he had neglected to tell the others on the staff. Immediately, I was off the hook as someone who had not fully disclosed her motives. Nevertheless, the question remained as to how insure that the participants fully understood my role, and reassure them that safeguards were in place to insure confidentiality. This led to subsequent discussions with the members of the group and the establishing of review guidelines once the study was completed, to insure that no one would be put at risk. The caution these measures reflects has to do not only with the general ethics of conducting an ethnographic study, but also with the vulnerability of untenured faculty. This group was more acutely attuned to such issues, again because of their own sensitivity to identity politics.

That night, we gathered to view segments from the series *Art on Film/Film on Art*, along with two sections from *Akira Kurosawa's Dreams*.[10] The former unrolled its way through a Chinese scroll, addressing the nature of the viewer and the act of viewing at the same time as it opened something different from a window on a piece of a Chinese world. In *Dreams*, Japanese tales of fox spirits

---

[10]   Michael Camerini, producer and director, *Art on Film/Film on Art* (New York: Program for Art on Film, 1992); Akira Kurasawa, *Akira Kurasawa's Dreams* (1990).

and cherry trees translated into haunting parables. The point was to illustrate ways in which the values of different religious traditions could be traced through non-documentary films. One might, for example, assign the students to view *Dreams* with the objective of discerning as many elements as possible that seem to emerge out of Japanese religious traditions.

As always, after the film the group drifted back to Mark's suite, one room of which had been turned into a common area. A table along one wall held the group's journal, a notebook set up for everyone to jot down useful bibliographic resources, the various introductory textbooks, books and teaching materials brought by everyone for the temporary resource library, and the computer on which one participant spent the late evening hours intently copying disks-full of information about the Image Bank for everyone who wanted them. There were also some seven hundred slides from the Image Bank itself, allowing participants to view the variety of its contents. The staff would usually disappear for a time into Mark's room for a final debriefing of the day, after which they would rejoin the others. It was both the continuation of the day's discussion and an ongoing party, and nobody wanted to go home.

Day Six: Friday, August 20

"What do you want to convey to your students about religion?" said Mark, giving everyone a moment to note down their thoughts. As he would go on to discuss, insofar as the religious involves experience, audio-visual materials can serve as a powerful, if underutilized, means by which to convey something of the nature of that experience. Instead, however, they are often poorly presented as illustrations adjunct to a verbal text, thereby becoming the occasion for students to take a nap. Ironically, the visual exercise then becomes one of the more disengaging activities in the classroom. How, then, to shift this attitude so that the same materials become a primary text generating discussion in its own right? One way is to present an image with minimal explanation—one that catches an action in the midst—and to do so at the beginning of a topic rather than at the end.

"Look at this one," said Mark. "What do you *see*?"

Three men, wearing white robes, their heads shaved, were descending the stairs off the side of an airplane.

"Hair Club for Men?" said one person helpfully. The laughter took several minutes to die down.

"They look like they're traveling for some religious purpose," said someone else. "Maybe some kind of a pilgrimage."

"They don't have anything else by which you could identify them," said the next person. "It looks like they're deliberately engaging in a different identity."

"They are," said Mark. "Actually, they're pilgrims undertaking the Hajj. If I were using this in the class, and if I were focusing on the nature of ritual, I might have had the class read something by Victor Turner and go to the discussion of Turner after looking at this slide."

He then projected a slide of an emaciated and bloodied Christ wearing a large crown of thorns, seated and facing forward—a statue from an Ecuadorian church.

"What do you imagine would be the theologies that would grow up around this figure?" he said. People suggested images of the suffering servant, the indigenous experiences of suffering, the envisioning of liberation.

"I would use a slide like this to teach students some of the elements of visual analysis," said one person. "What is the composition, the color—look at the hieratic stance of the figure. What effect does it generate, and *how* does it do so? What were the meanings for the people looking at it in a particular setting? I also make students pay attention to the illustrations in their texts."

"I usually don't show more than five or six slides in a class session," said Mark. "It took me a long time to learn that—as Jonathan Z. Smith points out in the quantity of text we assign—less can be more. Students are also usually receptive to slides taken by the instructor. There's the human connection, and you can tell them stories about what they're seeing." The point is not to lead the students into an identification game, but rather to open a process of discussion and discovery.

As he then struggled to get the VCR monitor to project something other than loud gray static, Mark muttered, "This is a test. This is only a test." Despite a few moments during which it seemed that will would win out over the machine, the scene from the *Mahabharata* descended once again into technical opacity. Mark finally threw in the towel and decided to model, instead, what you do when your equipment fails—namely, telling a group what you *had* planned to do, and then winging it from there. ("The participants later told me that they appreciated seeing someone handle a situation that did not go as planned," wrote Mark in a subsequent report.)

Instead of always presenting films or documentaries in their entirety, Mark often uses short clips—sometimes lasting no more than a few minutes—to represent key points related to a discussion topic or to particular dimensions of the course content. By excerpting segments, one can more readily teach students to be critical watchers. One can also have them write about the most important aspects of what they saw. The instructor, in order to do this, must be clear as to why he or she has chosen a given excerpt. That it function as illustration is not, from a pedagogical perspective, enough.

The purpose of this particular segment would have been to illustrate how religion is not simply a set of beliefs, but can also be the poetic process of putting oneself in harmony with the universe. Here, the brothers' act of riddling has everything at stake. As in the excerpt from *Dreams*, the characters must engage with something dangerous, learning to think through alternative logics.

"I try to choose not only good videos," Mark added, "but also good movies. Sometimes I wonder if this is a trap. Are we then assuming that a religion is beautiful, true, and absolute? Can we use videos that are not so good, especially if it contains scenes—as we said the other night—that are hard for students to watch?" A full-ranging discussion ensued.

"I find that to be the case with *An Initiation Kut for a Korean Shaman*,"[11] said Anne. The woman fails the initiation because she wasn't given enough sensory stimulation to put her into a trance. She is chastised so severely that in some settings I would hesitate to use it. But it also shows the seriousness of the process, and that not everyone does make it. It depends a lot on how you contextualize it.

---

[11] L. Kendall and D. S. Lee, producers and directors, *An Initiation "Kut" for a Korean Shaman* (Honolulu: University of Hawaii Press, 1991).

Then there's a larger question, which is how you keep the study of women in various religious traditions from being depressing."

One must also remind students that any representation they see takes place in the artificial setting of the classroom. To learn that a religious symbol is, in fact, multivalent is inseparable from addressing its experiential dimensions. But how to deal with the question of experience itself?

"With some films, I'll burn some incense," said one person.

"I pass out *betel* or candies," said another, "so they can experience the taste."

"But you have to be careful with incense," said Sharon. "If someone is HIV+, there could be pulmonary consequences."

"You know," said someone else, "we don't hesitate to bring a sacred text into a classroom, but anything beyond that makes us hesitate. We should think about why that is."

"I am all for experience," said Sharon. "But I do have to raise a safety issue. In a class on ritual, I once took a group to a Hare Krishna temple. The people who performed the prayer also served food. Some of the people in the class felt that if they ate it, they were in danger of becoming part of that tradition, which they didn't want to do. We have to be really careful about things like that."

"Well," said Mark, "in one of my classes on myth and ritual, on the first day of class, I tell the students to choose from this collection of masks I bring to the class. These are all made by students in the art program, by the way. I say to the students in the class, 'What mask is choosing *you*?' They pick one out or, if they want to, they can also make a mask for themselves. I choose one myself as well, to break down the hierarchy of teacher-student. I tell them they can take the mask home with them. They can hang it on their wall, keep it on their desk—whatever gets them to look at it. We read an article by Peter Brook on the Balinese actor who looks at and studies a mask before ever putting it on.

"Their next exercise is to write a story—through the mask. They've read some primary myths by then—ones that have been directly transcribed, and not cleaned up by anthropologists. Things without clear beginnings or endings, at least not from our perspective of narrative. Still they haven't put on their mask. They come to class, they read their stories—but somebody else wears the mask. Now they have heard everyone's story, none of which lasts more than five minutes. If they've written something longer, they select five-minutes worth.

"Then I ask them, 'Who would your *mask* like to relate to?' They select small groups of three or four people—four works well. Only now can they put on their masks. Without words, using only gestures, sounds—any action they want—they undertake whatever series of movements comes to them. I want them to understand the direct impact of actions which convey meaning without language. Afterwards, they talk about what that was like. As they repeat the exercise, a ritualized sequence begins to emerge. A repeated segment begins to happen, one that gradually becomes a performance piece. Finally, during one evening, each group performs their segment for the rest of the class.

"I also have them read Maya Deren's work on the living gods in Haiti and what she has to say about possession, and also watch her film.[12] When the students debrief about their experience of working with a mask, sometimes they'll say things like, 'I honestly don't remember what went on in this performance session.' What they're doing is more profound than I had originally thought when I first started it. Even though it's not the same thing as what Deren is describing, it gives them a different understanding when they read about the experience of some form of possession. Of course, you have to be very available to them, and give them lots of time to talk about their experience. I would not use masks from another tradition. Nor would I have them do a ritual from another tradition. Again, the masks I use have been made by art students at the school."

Mark's presentation prompted the group to think about what the risks might be in undertaking this kind of an exercise. What, for example, if someone had a bad experience with a mask? It was clear that this approach both fascinated them and, for some, stepped outside the bounds of what they could imagine themselves doing in a classroom as a part of their teaching. The point of the workshop,

---

[12] Maya Deren, *Divine Horsemen: The Living Gods of Haiti* (New York: Mystic Fire Video, 1990); Maya Deren, *Divine Horsemen: The Living Gods of Haiti* (New Paltz, NY: McPherson, 1953).

however, was not to convert anyone to a particular style or strategy. More important was actually seeing how wide a range of approaches lies at our disposal, and having the occasion to talk with those who had charted that stretch of the territory. For some, it was easier, for example, to think about using music.

"I compare different examples from similar genres," said one person, "like Tibetan and Gregorian chanting."

"But what if we don't know much about a particular musical genre?" another person asked. "What things *is* it okay for you not to know about?"

"With texts, I feel I have some skill in working with them," said someone else. "I don't want to reinforce the idea that some materials are analyzable and others are not."

"Well, when I use chants," another person added, "it's as one way to show that text is not just words on a page." The group concluded that any of the media one might choose could be used either as an entrée into a tradition, or as another facet of what students had already been learning about a given culture.

In the staff meeting, Sharon—who by now had also been dubbed "Our Lady of Perpetual Responsibility"—led the team's discussion about how to conduct the evaluation of the week's session. It was finally decided that everyone, including the staff, would spend some time that afternoon filling out a questionnaire. (The questionnaire, which would not be read either by the staff or the ethnographer, would be sent to one of the directors of the workshop program who would summarize the contents for the staff.) Everyone would then take part in a group discussion to assess the events of the week. This would also allow the participants to note topics they would like to see addressed in the upcoming sessions.[13]

That night, an assessment of quite a different sort took place, when the wickeder side of the group's sense of humor came to light. Having invited everyone to gather after dinner in the common room, two ringleaders from the group announced that it had been decided

---

[13] During the afternoon, the group assembled to evaluate the week's work. Because their conversation pertains more directly to the question of what made these workshops effective, the content of this particular discussion appears as part of the material in Chapter VI.

to form a new affinity group to be known as the adherents of "EIST," or "Eastern International Standard Time." Its first honorary member would be Mark, the original Master of Untrue Time. The badge of his office would be a travel alarm clock on a piece of string, which they proceeded to hang around his neck. It was, they noted, set four hours ahead.

In the moments that followed, the group broke into a spontaneous spoof of every key word, metaphor, process and distinctive behavior to have emerged over the course of the week. Through the parody of process and content, it rapidly became apparent that in that short time they had constituted a code fully understandable only to themselves.

The group suddenly grew silent and whispers were heard from the other side of the door. Then one person stood and, in stentorian tones, announced "The Analysis of the Mask!" The door opened, and in processed four of the group holding before their faces masks fashioned from photographs of Mark's bespectacled, grinning face (clearly enlargements from a faculty photo directory) glued to handles made out of plastic knives. As an old blues-singer buddy of mine used to say, "Class act, class props!" By this time things were in full swing, and it didn't take long for someone to get the idea for further mischief.

If there was anything sacrosanct on Mark's campus, it was the statue of an ancient king. The target of protests from various groups, it was nevertheless the one figure standing as an ambiguous symbol for the school. A short time later, a small cluster of participants slipped back into the room chuckling to themselves. It was clear that something was in the works. Dark hints about masks being posted in interesting places, telling grins directed at one another—clearly this required investigation.

A second crew headed out to reconnoiter, intuiting that the unfortunate king might be at the center of the joke. Sure enough, high up on his pedestal, he now sported one copy of Mark's face taped over his own and two taped onto his shield.

There were no footholds down below, so two people stood in, allowing one of the participants experienced in rock-climbing to clamber up to reach the masks, with a fourth person spotting for the campus police (who never made an appearance). Nevertheless, when the group returned, they told the others about having been stopped by the police—to whom, they said, they had explained that they were undoing a prank. But, they added, they had not divulged the names of the perps, who now owed them one.

On the surface, these seem like little more than sophomoric jokes and hijinks and, from one perspective, that is so. But if we are, in fact, not only *homo academicus* but also *homo ludens*, then the capacity to enter into a kind of secular carnival in which ordinary roles get laid aside and adult behavior gets redefined to include the ability to play with one another, then something quite significant took place. For a group of professors to establish sufficient trust in each other that they could risk being ridiculous on the one hand, and simply themselves on the other, is a not-altogether-common experience, particularly at an academic meeting in which, at the same time, intensive and serious work was taking place. The very fact that it happened had everything to do with the capacity of those present to work hard at creating a non-competitive environment with minimal hierarchy. One could argue that if anything of significance was modeled by the workshop as a whole, it was this environment as a working possibility.

Day Seven: Saturday, August 21

For the final exercise, which was to be carried out the following morning, the staff had decided to focus the discussion on the challenges posed by designing an introductory course—that is, the kind of course that one is often asked to teach.

"We've been talking a lot about teaching and how we do it," said Mark, "and we've been doing a lot of things individually. *We* need to do an exercise as a group."

They decided that the larger group would split up, with each of the smaller groups working together to design such a course. They would then reassemble to discuss what they had done. The staff would meet as one of the groups engaging in the exercise. The task involved thinking about how to integrate different elements from the group's discussions into a sample syllabus for an introductory course on the study of religion. Each teams was to come back with a ten-minute presentation summarizing their what they had come up with.

The first group defined its course as having two points of focus: first, the assumption that all forms of human activity and experience may have religious dimensions and, second, that all forms of religion are human, social constructions. They organized the course around a series of topics:

- space and time
- sanctioned forms of violence (sacrifice, crusades, *jihad*, ritual pain)
- altered states (drugs, dervishes, *voudun* possession, various approaches to trance)
- eating or not eating (fasting and feasting of different kinds)
- story/ riddling/ *koan*/ silence
- sexuality
- performance/ non-action
- understandings of knowledge
- the relationship to politics
- one student-selected category
- plus the exploration of the overlaps between the categories

The course would include visits to various settings. The planners did not presume that it would necessarily be taught using texts.

The second team discovered that the major frustration they encountered with their course was the realization of all the things they had left out. They had decided, however, to design a course entitled "Twentieth-Century Religious Experience Through Film and Autobiography (with a special appearance by Elvis)." As texts, they had selected the autobiographies of Dorothy Day, Black Elk, Eli Weisel, and Aghehananda Bharati; one autobiographical novel by Chaim Potok; works by Nawal Sadawi, and a study of gay and lesbian religious experience in South Asia. Some of these books had served as the basis for movies; they planned, in addition, to use the film *Romero*.[14]

---

[14] Dorothy Day, *The Long Loneliness: The Autobiography of Dorothy Day* (New York: Curtis Books, 1952); Black Elk, *Black Elk Speaks; Being the Life Story of a Holy Man of the Oglala Sioux*, as told through John G. Neihardt (Lincoln, University of Nebraska Press, 1961); Elie Wiesel, *Night* (New York: Hill and Wang, 1960); Swami Agehananda Bharati, *The Ochre Robe* (London, George Allen & Unwin, 1961); Chaim Potok, *The Chosen* (New York: Fawcett Crest, 1967); Nawal Sadawi, *Memoirs from the women's*

The class would be set the task of carrying out oral-history interviews with someone either from within their own families or from another religious tradition, and given guidelines on how to do this. This would integrate a focus on student writing. Students would be expected to keep journal in which they would respond to and critique the readings and films. The larger objectives of the course would be to train students in an approach to American history which is rooted in the local and the autobiographical, and to do so in a way that is both personalized and political.

The third team role-played that they were the Religious Studies faculty at U.C. Berkeley, chosen because it represented an urban setting with considerable student and faculty diversity. They had discussed how each of them, as a member of the department, would highlight different areas in their respective courses, coming together to teach a world-religions course. They had also spent their time discussing ways in which students seem to want to be evaluated a lot, whether this be done through midterms, reflection papers, or other forms of examination.

The staff team, accustomed to using its time together to discuss how things were going, quickly got off the track of the assignment and fell instead into the more familiar mode. How, they wondered, had the focus on non-textual material and on difference (using gender as the central example) engendered a certain self-selection on the part of applicants that could have been shaved differently? Later I was to look back at the original call for participants. Although it did propose to explore ways to integrate non-textual material and gender into religious studies courses, most of it focused on more general issues related to the art of teaching. For someone who was looking for programs that offered a forum in which to discuss these two issues, the workshop would have stood out. For someone who was not, neither issue was presented in such a way as to seem the primary focus of the program.

---

prison (London: Women's Press, 1986), and *Woman at point zero* (London; New Jersey: Zed Books, 1983); Rakesh Ratti, ed., *A Lotus of Another Color: An Unfolding of the South Asian Gay and Lesbian Experience* (Boston: Alyson Publications, 1993); John Sacret Young, writer, John Duigan, director, *Romero* (Los Angeles, CA: Vidmark Entertainment, 1997).

To the staff it had been clear from the beginning that these were the orienting themes; the call did not make this nearly as clear. Because of the multiple ways the call could be read, there had been correspondingly divergent expectations among the participants. Several, for example, had focused on the non-textual dimension, assuming that this would be the general orientation of the program, while others had picked up on the gender question in similar ways.

Absorbed in this discussion, the staff forgot to plan an introductory course. Just before the working time ran out, they turned to discussing the challenges inherent in team-teaching.

"I know," said Sharon, "why don't we have a typical departmental argument!"

In the plenary discussion that followed, members of the group felt they could have used more time and more information— particularly with respect to the academic setting for which they were being asked to design these courses. Were they doing so in a state university course with a hundred students, or in a small liberal-arts college seminar? What were the pragmatic issues they had to take into account, like the power dynamics within a department?

To close the week, the staff had invited each person to write a brief epigram. Just before going around the room for each person to read his or hers aloud, one of the participants spoke up:

"I've brought a small token for each of you as a symbol of what I think we've done here this week. Please each take one."

He passed a small brown paper bag around the circle, from which each person drew a wooden acorn.

"No, I'm not suggesting you're all a little nuts. We planted something this week and, even though it may seem small to start, I think something quite large will come of it."

Others began to read their epigrams:

"Oliver Wendall Holmes: 'I do not give a fig for the simplicity on this side of complexity. But I would give my life for the simplicity on the other side of complexity.'"

"Learning takes place in relationships."

"By graduate school I was taught to compete in order to achieve; here, I've learned that there are many models of cooperation and ways of speaking."

"After a week-long Seshin, the Zen master said, 'Let us stand and bow to the Buddha three times. We thank the Buddha because we have had a great enlightenment. If we did not have a great enlightenment, then we have had a small enlightenment. If we did not have a small enlightenment, then at least we didn't get sick. If we got sick, then at least we didn't die. So let's thank the Buddha."

Going around the circle until the last person had read aloud, the week-long session came to a close.

The October Weekend

The Planning

The group was now something of a known entity whose intentions and interests could be factored into the planning of the second session. Through another round of conference calls, the staff pulled together ideas for four sessions for the first of the weekend meetings, to be held in October. Two were to be dedicated to discussions of the teaching projects, the other two organized around questions and issues raised by the participants.

It had been decided that it would be a useful experience to hold the workshops at different schools around the region, so that the participants could develop a clearer sense of some of the different working environments they had been describing to one another. This one would be held at a small college in New York, the teaching base of one of the participants who had also volunteered to manage the logistics. (Another participant would do the same in the second of the weekend workshops, held in an urban center in Canada.) This time, as there were no available on-campus accommodations, the participants were put up in a local Econo-Lodge. Because it was not within walking distance of the workshop site, it was not possible to provide a common room for socializing. It was decided, in the subsequent evaluation, to secure such a room for the next weekend.

One difficulty that staff had not anticipated was the effects of the distances some of the people had to travel. Several, for example, had to drive over six hours. As Mark was to note in a later report:

> Two of these people who believed they had allowed plenty of time arrived after the first formal session, because they had taken a wrong turn and gotten lost; one of these people who is

trying to turn a one-year position into a tenure-track position believed she shouldn't cancel her two-hour Friday morning class, since she thought she could just make it on time. One person whose wife was due to have a baby a few days before the workshop sent us his deep regrets. Another woman, who had left her two-week-old baby to participate, left an half hour early rather than catch a plane leaving six hours later. Somehow none of this became disruptive and everyone seemed to understand the circumstances, again a tribute to the generosity and general caring of this group of people.[15]

Day One: Friday, October 22

An opening reception that afternoon gave everyone the chance to arrive at different times and to regroup informally. Having received prior instructions from Mark—along with a blank index card—each person had also brought jottings on "the most important issue you'd like to share with the group." These they passed to Mark who, at one point during the course of the reception, could be seen off in one corner diligently sorting them into little piles.

Receptions are awkward things in certain regards. They are not private enough for more thoughtful conversations and there is always the likelihood that one will be interrupted just at that point when a good story ought not to get broken off. Still, they allow all the elements of the larger entity known as "a group" to move about each other, gradually reconfiguring into whatever collective identity they had been in the process of forming during their last meeting. The connecting joints are recalled and rejoined.

By late afternoon, enough people had arrived for the more formal discussion to begin. What, everyone was asked, had been the effects—if any—of the first workshop on their teaching that fall?

"I'm listening to what my students are teaching me about pedagogy," said one person, "and about what they are trying to say to each other. The students are experimenting pedagogically. I give them a few suggestions and then let it happen. I'm hearing their questions and listening to their interaction in a different way."

"I've had them do simulation exercises, playing the roles of the different groups in their readings—Sadducees, Pharisees, others. Usually one group is silent because it doesn't know what's going on,

---

[15] Director's report, Eastern International Workshop, p. 3.

so I'm breaking the groups up differently over time to make things more interactive."

"I think I'm starting to understand the difference between teaching material and teaching students. I try to make it clear that when I ask the question it's not a game of 'stump the dummy,' especially if I ask them something they don't know. I'm listening to their reasoning and working from there."

This kind of discussion has obvious and yet subtle effects. More obviously, it asks whether the first workshop, in practice, accomplished anything. More subtly, it picks up threads from the earlier meeting, passes them through the shuttle of the intervening months, and re-weaves earlier shared memories, also held as individual ones, back into the collective fabric.

The themes into which Mark had sorted the index cards were loosely gathered, many of them pointing to the practical ways in which people had implemented elements of the previous summer's discussions. Many of them, too, involved other things people had learned about questioning and listening to students. How, for example, to help students understand the importance of getting at a *good* question, as well as figuring out the appropriate level of question to ask? Some people had a new appreciation of developmental issues expressed in the difference between students who wanted answers as opposed to those who wanted something more open-ended. There, too, how to begin with what they know?

"I put a couple of words on the board," said another person, "words like 'myth' or 'ritual'—and ask them for free thought associations. I say to them, 'There's nothing you can tell me I haven't heard before.'"

"I give out what I call 'A Student Manifesto.' It's something like a bill of rights in the classroom. The point of it is to turn the classroom into a democratic space in a way that pairs rights and responsibilities. I give it to them and have them review it. I tell them to take it home and discuss it with other people. I ask them if they want to use it at all. Then they work on revising it together. By the middle of the term, we evaluate how things are going. This keeps holding their feet to the fire. It's one way of asking them to think seriously about what their role in the classroom is going to be. It creates an agreement—a contract—between them as members of a class, and between them and me."

This kind of discussion makes us all authorities of something, if only of that one technique we happen to be presenting at that particular moment. The authority rides on our experience, sometimes as a simple piggy-back, sometimes as a whole family of acrobats lifting chairs, dishes, and flaming birthday cakes up to the top of a carefully composed human tower. Most of the time, the only people to witness this balancing of skills, strategies, and improvisations are our students. Rarely do we get the occasion to perform before an audience of peers who know what it really takes to get the birthday cake up there without the candles blowing out— or who are eager to learn.

Moreover, it is not just talk about techniques. As is especially clear in the case of the Student Manifesto, a technique is both an expression of an existing teaching philosophy and a way of giving form in practice to that philosophy. The same is equally true of the other methods of questioning and leading discussions. What a process like workshop encourages one to think about more precisely, however, is just what that philosophy *is*, along with the approaches that will enable one to enact it well.

Day Two: Saturday, October 23

The letter that had gone out from Mark to everyone ahead of time reported that six people had signed up for this weekend to do presentations on the progress of their teaching projects. There were four other people who didn't mind whether they presented this weekend or the next, so the staff had arbitrarily divided them between the two sessions.

"Please remember," the letter went on to say, "that no one expects a final report on the projects at this time; these are working sessions where the group can explore issues with you. Thus, they should help all of us think about general issues in teaching as well as help participants with their specific projects. I imagine that an absolute upper limit for presenting the topic and for discussing it will be forty minutes . . ."

Actually, it was scaled down to thirty-nine, and that to be strictly adhered to. Comic as this example may sound, the tightness of time is one of the inescapable features of the weekend workshop sessions. People pull in on Friday (sometimes having taught that morning or even that afternoon), reconnect, have Saturday together, spend Sunday morning evaluating what they did and imagining what they might still like to do, and then pull out, hoping to get home in time to prepare for classes the next day. There is little of the leisure that characterizes the week-long sessions. Still, the weekends matter.

The presentations were diverse, the projects including a course on the historical Jesus; the role of wymyn in shaping religious history ("herstory") from the ancient to the modern period; Hinduism, caste, and class; religious ethics and the environment; religion and human values; and two different presentations on introducing the very notion of religion. The syllabi, as texts, could do no more thana hint at the experiences they were intended to represent and to create. What we were seeing roughed out were only excerpted stage directions. The performers were still in street clothes; they hadn't put their make-up on. To change metaphors, I don't know whether architects take as much pleasure in looking over somebody else's blueprints—whether the building takes form in their minds and they begin to envision not only all the interiors to each room but also the overlooks from each window. I would guess that the space, to someone who knows how to read the plans, quickly assumes the phantom form of the imagination.

If you spend a lot of time thinking about teaching, something like that happens when you read a syllabus. And along with it goes a certain wistfulness, as you realize that this experience for which you hold the plans will, at some point, become a real scenario that others will undertake—one that you will probably never actually enter into yourself. So reading somebody else's syllabus keeps you humble that way, as you imagine, and maybe even regret a little bit, all the learning you never will get around to doing.

Day Three: Sunday, October 24

The group began with selections from *The Art and Craft of Teaching* concerning the first day of class, questioning, and the rhythms of a semester.[16] They talked about the connection between lecturing and asking questions, particularly in the effort to break down reified notions of a text. They then moved on to evaluate what they had done over the weekend, inviting ideas for the future sessions. The staff had made it clear that, although they had generated the first week themselves, all the subsequent sessions would attempt to respond to requests from the participants. The idea was that the staff would gradually move further and further in the direction of facilitating, as the participants made the workshop more and more their own.

They also reminded the group of a suggestion from the previous August that, to illustrate a range of lecturing styles, members of the staff would bring videos of popular colleagues, none of them known personally by anyone else at the workshop. This thought exercise would allow everyone to observe and critique other teaching techniques, and would prepare the participants for the idea of videotaping their classroom work for observation during the final week-long workshop. It was hoped that at least some of them would be willing to do so. The process ended with the awarding of the broken travel alarm clock, still on its string, to the participant-host of the weekend.

The March Weekend

The Planning

Holding the workshops at different locations is complicated mostly for the director, who must either work with the conference services at some other school with which he or she is not likely to have much familiarity, or who must convey all the logistical needs either to one of the participants or to someone else on the staff. Even though holding the workshop series as a moveable feast would seem to save the director a lot of work, there are nevertheless certain tasks which only he or she, as the direct liason with the Lilly

---

[16] Margaret Morganroth Gullette, ed., *The Art and Craft of Teaching* (Cambridge, MA: Harvard-Danforth Center for Teaching and Learning, 1982).

Endowment and the AAR, can carry out. Mark was cheerful about these complications, however, and grateful that other members of the group were willing to play host.

In the telephone planning sessions it had been decided to make the exercise of being videotaped an optional one. Suggestions for things to keep in mind would be forwarded to everyone. Different members of the group had also requested that time be assigned to the discussion of evaluation and the power that underlies it, and it was decided to address this during the final week-long session. Peter wanted to introduce at least one case study both for the virtue of the content and as an illustration of how to use a case. And everybody thought it would be a good idea to do more on the dilemmas of teaching an introductory course, focusing particularly on dealing with large lectures.

Mark was also in the process of setting up a list-serve for everyone in the workshop. Although it never became quite the site of ongoing discussion that had been hoped for—people tended to post, instead, their latest news, an occasional teaching question, and every once in a while, a good book they'd come across—it still reinforced the sense that this group functoned as an extended network.

Day One: Friday, March 4
The workshop was being held in Canada, this time, hosted by two of the participants. The group would stay in a motel not far from the campus of the school where the meetings would take place. "You drive along past the old garment industry area of town," the directions read, "then go right. Expect rough road conditions and people double or triple parked." Pass steeples, construction cranes, hotels, more construction, street lights.

The first session opened into a review of what people had found to have been working over the past few months, particularly their efforts to go beyond just lecturing to larger groups.

"My faculty critiqued what I was doing," said one person. "They told me that having all those discussion groups and using movies meant that my course might be getting soft on content."

"There's this whole thing now about trying to quantify the amount of content you transmit. It's a financial transaction model.

It's thinking about students as customers. But if they're customers, how do you measure what they're getting and, if this is supposed to be the equivalent of a market-driven system, how do they know what they want? We're up against this trend toward 'outcome-based' education, but that's now how learning really works."

Discussions of the Total Quality Management (TQM) model, derived from the business world and applied to education, were to appear and reappear at different points during the workshop, reminding everyone that there are cultural pressures to which their institutions and, therefore they, are increasingly subject. Yet while understanding the need to find good ways to assess what students were really learning, this particular version of the commodification of knowledge was perceived as insidious, reductionistic. Some of the most profound and enduring aspects of learning were simply too elusive to be captured in such measures.

The large lecture course only complicates the matter. When you are standing in front of a situation inclined to promote anonymity, how do you grab that many people—a challenge made even greater when it's a required course? And when all the seats are not only bolted down but set up on risers, then everybody's movement is restricted. On the one hand, you *can* at least see what each person is doing. (They, however, can also see what the others around them are doing—which can present a different kind of problem when the class is taking a test.) To reduce the anonymity, one person collects a three-by-five card from everyone on which they have been asked to give a few basic particulars about themselves, along with some question they hope will get addressed somewhere along the way. Another person gives a short writing assignment in which each student is asked to introduce him- or herself and attach a picture.

How, too, to guarantee that critical thinking is taking place? Is this possible *only* in a small group discussion, especially when the topic involves something controversial? Or are there ways to conceptualize the lecture course as a dialogue on a number of levels—first, through raising multiple perspectives and positions within the lecture itself and, second, by turning sections of it into a conversation with the class?

There is no separating how and what one teaches from the institution where it all takes place. This holds true in at least three ways: first, in relation to the expectations on the part of the school and where the course fits into its larger picture. Second, there is the physical environment—the small room versus the big one, the availability of audio-visual equipment, whether the school is located in the country, a suburb, or the city. Then there are the differences involving the students themselves. One participant, describing her experience that spring, wrote:

> My initial shock was upon encountering the differences between the students I was used to (an urban based university setting), and the students at this rural university setting. Similarities existed in age levels, reading ability, intelligence, etc., but the main difference appears to have been in the level of "worldly" exposure. In short, the majority of the students in my classes have had very little or, in some cases, no exposure at all to other cultures/ideas.
>
> When I attempted to teach the fundamentals of religious concepts, I found that I could not utilize examples from various religious systems, because the students knew absolutely nothing about these systems. And the excerpts from "world scriptures" remained meaningless without the historical and/or cultural context of the writings. What was particularly frustrating was that students who had already taken courses in sociology, anthropology, and psychology had not been exposed to any material that elaborated upon the study of religion within those academic fields.

There are thus multiple intersecting cultures at work: those of the professor, of the school, and of the students. As a whole, they constitute a system. All of them, in the context of the classroom, end up informing what actually goes on.

In the New England/Maritimes workshop, Charlotte had talked about one approach to learning styles, focusing on the sensory domains within which people feel most attuned. There are the listeners, who differ from the lookers. There are also the differences between people who prefer lectures versus people who tolerate them but would opt for a discussion any day.

Peter introduced still another set, the personality types arrived at through the Myers Briggs Type Indicator. Growing out of a Jungian paradigm, the test subscales track whether a person is more inclined toward extraversion or introversion, sensory-based or intuitive knowing, drawing conclusions primarily through thinking or feeling, and assessing his or her experience either through judgment or a more open-ended process of perception.

Each inclination tends to coincide with a preference for a different style of learning. More extraverted persons, for example, might prefer to study with others and like background sounds to help them concentrate. They might favor faculty who encourage discussions in class, and say that they need help in reading and in writing papers. More introverted students, however, might value reading and like to study alone. They might say they need help to speak in public. They might need quiet for studying, and want faculty to give clear lectures. Moreover, each type would differ in how they prefer to approach tasks such as writing.

After everyone had filled out the test questions, most of them not knowing what they were disclosing about themselves as they did so, Peter passed out all the explanatory guide-sheets. Everybody sat in silence, intently studying this additional set of categories with which to think about themselves. One looks not simply at a single variable, of course, but at how elements constellate. One could, for example, be a more intuitively inclined extrovert who bases his or her decisions on subjective, person-centered values and who relates to the outer world primarily by adapting to it and by liking to keep her options open to new experiences and information. If you were such a person, you would probably not do as much preparing in advance but would rely, instead, on your ability to improvise.

To render these differences the more visible, Peter then assigned each such constellation to a different section of the room, directing everyone to go to the one occupied by theirs. If nothing else, it established kinetically where the greatest tempermental affinities were likely to lie within this particular group, and likewise the greatest distances. It was a good reminder that any class is going to be just as variably constituted, which helps to explain why some students complain about the very features of the course that other students love. The challenge involves having enough different approaches going on for each kind of person to feel the course is adapted to at least some of the ways he or she learns best.

Day Two: Saturday, March 5

In the course of discussing their projects that day, the group navigated its way through the implications of the minimally hierarchical, learner-centered approach to which many of them felt a strong allegiance. Loosening things up like this was not without a number of complications.

"My students are sometimes intimidated by the apparent lack of structure."

"But this isn't exactly a question of 'structure' or 'no structure,'" said someone else. "It's about a different *kind* of structure. Like, instead of having the structure of pre-ordained tasks in which they have very little to say about the design, teaching them to make up tasks as they go along."

"I think it's also about finding the right match between the content and the classroom method itself," another person said, "so that the method helps them understand something more about the content. If it were a history-of-Christianity course, for example, it could also be a course *on* historiography."

"I go on the working assumption that the professor is a text," said someone else, "that is, another interpretation of certain material—and that the students are just as busy reading the professor-as-text as they are at anything else. The professor is also a cultural critic. He or she should be a spokesperson for people outside the academy who might otherwise never have a presence within it. The professor is also a writer/reader—a reader of the student's writing, for one thing. And then there's the question of whether you're going to be an insider or an outsider. I don't ever want to be altogether comfortable in the academy. I want to be an insider to the extent of having a certain power; I want to be enough of an outsider to remember to be a catalyst for change."

"I want to teach students how to be critical of *any* text," another person said. "And I don't want them to see *me* as the authority." (The group agreed that there can be a big difference between having authority and being an authority figure.)

"But that process is also confusing for them," said someone else, "because often they've learned that texts are authoritative. I tell my students that I'm regularly going to throw them into confusion, because the only way education happens is by working your way out of confusion. So if they're not confused, I say, they're not getting the class. I promise them that they can count on being at sea. But I also promise them that it *will* all come together in the last week, if they can just stick out the confusion, and that I'll be there along the way."

Folk wisdom has it that to go through any challenging undertaking, it helps to have three kinds of companion: the fellow traveller, the veteran, and the professional. Each provides a different sort of insight and, possibly, wisdom about the given phase in which one finds oneself. It therefore may be that an additional aspect of being a professor—above and beyond being text, cultural critic, writer/reader, or catalyst for change—involves alternating between the different roles of the companion in the journeys of his or her students.

Day Three: Sunday, March 6

Anne explained that the video she was about to show depicted what students were *really* thinking about as they listened to a lecture in large class. Voiceovers rambled on about girlfriends, tests in other classes, whether or not to dye one's hair, boyfriends, and not altogether flattering asides on the professor's style of delivery and dress, giving the lie to the ostensibly intent expressions on the faces of many of the students. There wasn't much that could be done to cover up for the three sleeping in the back. They were intent, all right, but not on the lecture.

The video illustrated that, for students, the ordinary conditions and events of their lives operate as the ground about which they spend a lot of time thinking. The professor who walks out onto that ground to give a lecture is one relatively small figure on the landscape. Particularly in a required course, if the student is not to spend the hour paying more attention to staring at the ground than at that lone figure standing out there on it, the professor has the job not only of conveying information but of convincing the students that, in so doing, he or she is telling them something about their ground that they might actually want to know.

In the sixties and into the seventies even, we used to talk about that as making what we were doing relevant. The focus on relevance became so exaggerated that, in some cases, it turned into a parody of itself. But, like any wisdom that gets watered down into pop psychology, that doesn't mean there wasn't something to it in the first place. In this case, the question is how to delve into the ground itself, to talk about something that is an ordinary part of students' experience, and to enhance the awareness of some aspect of that ground *through* the process of discussing the lecture topic. When something apparently foreign to a person's inner terrain can be made to stand out as unexpectedly belonging there, then the things on the ground that surround it are going to look different. The potential for not only transmitting information but for changing that person's entire mode of awareness has just happened. That could be called learning.

Of course, nobody has a stake in precisely all the same things as everybody else in a classroom, which is what can make this task such a daunting one. Figuring out how to address it is a piece of the learning process for the professor, and involves remembering over and over again that, where the classroom is concerned, we teach not material, but students.

The next video, said Anne, showed one of the most popular teachers at her school. Expecting to be entertained, everybody sat back. No one was prepared for what followed. On the surface, it was easy to see why this teacher was popular on his campus. He was delivering a lecture on the book of *Genesis*, and, to all appearances, it seemed to be an easy birth. Along the way, he made a number of comments about the role of women. Somewhere in the process of talking about the early world of creation, he quoted Kipling, made a reference to *The Jungle Book*, and carried it all off in an in-your-face style that would have done Groucho Marx proud. Suddenly one woman in the group spoke out.

"I can't believe you were all laughing at that guy! He's sexist and he's a racist! He made me sick!"

Everyone had been aware all along that the workshop group represented a range of identity politics that included a committed post-modernist theorist; a fair number of self-identified feminists, adherents of three different Indian-based practices; a number of men genuinely convinced that gender was an important issue but who had never really had occasion or inclination to think about the question in more radical terms; and a historian certain that gender biases were not present in nearly as many of the ways as some of the feminists were arguing—because it had not been the case in any of her experience. Everyone had also been aware—as one participant had noted during the first week—that there were at least inactive fault-lines dividing various members of the group along the differences in the degree to which they even thought about issues of gender and then, along the ways in which they did so.

For those who identified themselves along more radical lines, the speaker in the video had been deeply offensive; to others not focused in the same way on that particular political analysis, his jokes had seemed either funny or innocuous. Some of the greatest differences became apparent not only in the stated opposition of opinions, but also in the sheer inability on the part of one group to understand exactly why the other was getting so worked up. As it seemed increasingly clear to the speaker that some of the group—a few of the men in particular—could acknowledge her point but failed to share her outrage, her anger grew. Understanding, she thought, should translate into equally strong rejection.

"How can you not see that Kipling is a goddamned racist who was part of a colonial empire? How can anyone use his work without pointing that out? *Everything* we use in the classroom has political implications, and we have the responsibility to make those explicit!" She was seconded by several others. It was not lecturing in itself that bothered them, but the use of such a forum to speak in ways which, for them, represented repressive political positions masked by humor.

No one knew exactly what to do to bring things back together again, and the working session would be ending within a few minutes. All the qualities that were likable about each person and that had allowed everyone to relate easily with each other now seemed, at least in some cases, to be getting buried underneath other deeply-held differences. None of the particular variables had changed; they had been there all along. It was the background-foreground relationship between them that had shifted. In the group debriefing, it was briefly noted that, because the session was so close to its end, the person most distressed had not been given much room to elaborate on her point, and that the group had not done altogether well with addressing the conflict.

In some cases, the disagreements never did get resolved. There was no time for it in this session and, by the time the group would reunite three months later, the parties most offended would simply resort to staying out of each other's way. As one of them explained, there was no need to form close relationships with everyone in a group. This, of course, is perfectly true. There is, however, a significant difference between a benign lack of affinity and the heat of anger frozen into polite avoidance.

The staff, during their own debriefing after lunch, thought their way through how each person in the group had responded to the blow-up. Mark was not convinced that the staff should do anything about the tensions. It seemed to him that the participants would have to resolve matters themselves. If anything, he was a bit relieved that the participants had shown they could react to something with intensity.Peter, on the other hand, was quite concerned, as were the others, worrying about how the participants would come out of it. They resolved, through various one-on-one conversations prior to the next meeting, to speak with the parties who had seemed to be the most offended. Yet they were unable to come up with a clear strategy for the group as a whole. Up to that point, they had operated on a consensus-seeking model. They now found themselves at a loss when they saw that, around in certain cases, consensus appeared to some like intolerable capitulation.

They were also aware of additional tensions. Several in the group were undergoing difficult tenure reviews. For others, the tensions were related to the precarious job situations in they found themselves. Five, for example, had been unable to find full-time work—much less tenure-track positions—and were struggling with being adjunct faculty—part, that is, of the growing pool of what an editorial in *The New York Times* would, only several years later, call "academic migrant labor."[17] Since three of the group were graduate

---

[17]   Editorial, *The New York Times*, June 29, 1997, p. 14.

students, that meant that out of fifteen people, only seven had full-time jobs. One or two of the men had made cracks about some of the women whose husbands afforded them enough financial support that teaching-related income was not as great an issue. (*The Times* would also talk about the feminizing of the academy as one consequence of the rising trend toward the hiring of adjunct faculty. There was no discussion of the single woman and how she is to survive.) There had, in other words, already been a fair amount of anxiety drifting around the room

By the following June, the fault line would, to all appearances, be dormant once more and would not break open again. In general, the group would return to its earlier camaraderie. What had changed, however, was that now the possibility of that same fault line's shaking the ground was no longer merely a fantastical doomsday prophecy. It had happened, pointing to the possibility in even the strongest of groups for a conflict to surface and for the group not to know what to do with it.[18]

The June Week

The Planning

It was during this final week that the staff, without its ever being a particularly deliberate decision, shifted gears into a different mode of planning. In their previous work together, they had reviewed the gist of each session together but, ultimately, had been left it up to each person to run the ones he or she had been assigned. What changed during the planning for the final week was, first of all, the decision to have many of the sessions led by dyads. In theory, this choice could have resulted in only a little more work for each of the different pairs. However, the team as a whole also decided to enter fully into the actual thinking through of each session.

It became, in other words, an experiment in teaching as a team, with two of the members at a time being responsible for representing the team's reflections and objectives. Had the people on this particular staff not taken such pleasure and interest in each other's company and had they not developed a fundamentally profound respect for each other, engaging that intensively together

---

[18] For further discussion of the issue of conflict see Chapter VI.

during the course of a week would probably never have worked. Their ability to do so also had a great deal to do with their various interests in collaborative teaching. This was a strategy they wanted to learn more about and here was the laboratory in which to do it.

As a team, they discussed each facet of why they were choosing particular readings and assigning them to specific sessions of the week. In so doing, they generated an ongoing process of brainstorming, in which they tested each person's ideas against the questions, objections, and suggestions of the others. It helped that they each had a sense of humor. Much of the awareness of what they were actually doing came to them only during the course of the week. They hadn't consciously intended to make this their behind-the-scenes style and, as their afternoons were increasingly devoured by their discussions with each other, they wondered whether there might have been a way to do it all in a more contained fashion. It helped that there was only a week. Any longer, and they would have burned out the enthusiasm that was moving them. But when they heard that other planning teams had met for maybe half an hour a day, they were unable to imagine how this could have been possible. From the beginning, none of their own meetings had having lasted less than an hour.

On the Saturday before the final week was to begin, the staff came together on the campus of Sharon's school, a private liberal arts college in rural New York. It was only June, but it was already as hot as a scorched August. The group would be staying in one of the dormitories, and there were no air conditioners, and the breeze wasn't making its way in too well, and we were all a bit breathless. After hashing through the remaining details for the next week, cooling off for a couple of hours in a nearby restaurant seemed the only sensible thing to do, along with a swing by the local Walmart to pick up a few cheap fans. Given that no one had planned on fitting themselves out with fans in the first place, it somehow seemed an unjustifiable extravagance to buy anything other than the economy version, all of which were loudly two-tone and could be counted on to offend the color schemes of anyone's homes. Everyone bought them anyway and was glad of it.

Day One: Sunday, June 19

It was just as hot the next day when all the participants arrived. There were more runs to Walmart. Still, when the group assembled later that afternoon, they went right to work. Each person had been asked to come with brief remarks on the most important question or issue he or she would like to explore during the week—the "critical question," in other words:

> What is the role of the academy in developing an ethical, moral frame within an an institution, in a way that is life-affirming?
>
> How do we help each other develop our own voices, styles, pedagogies, and understand where we are in our own process?
>
> How do I move away from being a technique junkie to exploring ways of life committed to justice as an educator?
>
> How does the classroom become a setting in which to combat intolerance, racism, and injustice?
>
> I feel such a tension between content and method. What *is* it that I'm teaching? What *is* Christianity—people? Theories? That kind of uncertainty blocks how I'm preparing my courses.
>
> How possible is it for us to project an authority that is, at the same time, emancipatory—*and* to teach the content of survey courses in religion *as* who one is?
>
> What do you do when you're burned out? And how do you prevent it?
>
> How do I bring these different methods into courses that don't seem to lend themselves to doing so?
>
> I have the problem of teaching in a religious studies department. I don't do theology, which is difficult when I'm teaching about the New Testament, because I shut off the one voice many of my students want to use—namely, faith. Is there any way for them to use that voice without the course becoming about theology?

There were also points raised about realizing the ways in which the larger frameworks of power—the institutional contexts that press in on whatever it is we are trying to do—are continually changing.

In various ways, questions concerning the various permutations and consequences of power could be said to have operated as one of the touchstones of this group. The discussions of gender had been one way of getting at this issue, the focus on non-textual materials another way of challenging the primacy of texts. In their planning, the staff had felt they had slipped a little in keeping a strong focus on gender and especially on non-textual methods, and had resolved to make the effort to consider both in most, if not all, of the sessions during the week.

Mark, for one, wanted to introduce a more theatrical sort of experience by having everyone enact the parties in a historic dispute. While not precisely theater, an exercise in simulation provided one way to integrate the personal and the cultural. Moreover, he argued, it would introduce methods from the arts, about which academics are sometimes suspicious. There are risks, to be sure, but theater learning involves the taking on of a role to discover what it is like to *be* in a particular stance. The risk lies in getting carried away and forgetting that the other is only acting.

This particular simulation was aimed at the people in the group who had said that all this non-textual stuff was fine, but it didn't work for them in Biblical studies. It would concern the Corinthian community of the early church and the crisis brought there about by debates over various issues concerning the Christian faith—particularly the proper role of "spiritual gifts" during worship and the proper role for women in church services. The workshop group would be divided into smaller sections, each of which would represent one of the parties to the debate—the Paulinists, the Petrine group, the Apollos group, and the group designating itself as "Christ's folks."

The parties would come before a council, Pricilla and Stephanas, played by two members of the group. Each group would be given the writings that would have been informing their own positions, and would have fifteen minutes to read these. They would then be given half an hour, as a group, to discuss how they wanted to enact their respective stances. They would play these roles for forty minutes, during which they were instructed to pay particular attention to gender roles, and then would enter a debriefing time during which they could discuss what they had done and what had happened in the process. The exercise was designed for an introductory course in religious studies and, it was hoped, would raise issues that would be discussed during the rest of the week.

The exercise did not yield much of the desired effect. There were a few too many pre-existing layers of awareness and agenda for the exercise to prove altogether successful with this particular group. Those assigned to defend the Pauline position, for example, processed back into the room wearing the arm-protectors from the sofas on their heads, like so many upholstered cowls, and refused to utter anything other than verbatim citations from their texts.

"We did that," they said afterwards, "because we didn't want to defend Paul; we really wanted to embody the society to come."

Some in the group found that their sections had had to spend a great deal of time talking about the background. Mark pointed out that the students usually are given more time to prepare. The debriefing following the exercise is also important because it allows everyone to return from their roles (although the humor, in this case, had much to do with those instances when people stepped out of role). This is especially important when people have role-played a dispute. In one case, Mark recalled, two students—a man and a woman—had continued an argument well beyond the class hour. At the same time, both later said that it was the first time they had been brought to feel that strongly about historically distant ideas. Nevertheless, this pushes the boundaries of a class, and for the integrity of the group, the class requires some means to integrate such an argument into the whole.

Day Two: Monday, June 20

The question of power and the liberation from its more abusive dimensions has come to occupy a certain amount of territory in the intellectual domain of the academy, as well as to function as a natural correlate in the discussion of matters of gender. What was to occupy the group was how to introduce these issues into their courses.[19] Should the primary objectives of a course, for example, be

---

[19] The readings sent out in advance for this session were: Jennifer Gore, "What We Can Do for You! What *Can* 'We' Do for 'You'?: Struggling over Empowerment in Critical and Feminist Pedagogy," in *Feminisms and Critical Pedagogy*, Carmen Luke and Jennifer Gore, eds. (New York: Routledge, 1992), pp. 54-73; bell hooks, "bell hooks Speaking about Paolo Freire—The Man, His Work," in *Paolo Freire: A Critical Encounter*, Peter McLaren and Peter Leonard, eds. (New York: Routledge, 1993), pp. 146-54; Ira Shor, "Education is Politics: An Agenda for Empowerment," in *Empowering Education: Critical Teaching for Social Change* (Chicago: University of Chicago Press, 1992), pp. 11-16; Kathleen Weiler, "Freire and a Feminist

to root out the dynamics of power embedded in whatever we happen to be teaching? Suppose, for example, that the class is examining the aesthetics of the Renaissance, tracing the different meanings of various artistic works both written and visual. The instructor guides the students through the labyrinth of social forces of the time along with their poisonous intrigues, finally exposing the aesthetic as the code for interlocking forms of oppression.

In the course of this, the students learn the sophistications of what it means to be situated. No one, however, discusses his or her actual response to the aesthetic itself. Indeed, once the mask of ostensibly benign beauty has been wrenched away so that one now sees the cruel faces of the Borgia and the *condotieri*, to be drawn to that product and to speak of it as beautiful may even become somewhat suspect. Having deconstructed everything, is there any room left for appreciation? With what are the students then left?

What does it mean to empower students? As some participants argued, for a theologian like Gustavo Gutierrez, liberation is a way of exposing and opposing the First-World socio-economic paradigm of developmentalism. To teach in the mode of liberation pedagogy is, among other things, to carry out that task, confronting students with the ways in which their earlier educational experience has trained them to be the passive recipients of the commodity called education—a commodity whose content reinforces the value structures of an oppressive paradigm.

"Students," said one person, "come not wanting to be liberated; nor is it what their parents think they are paying for. For that matter, most students don't even know they're captives."

"The approach itself came out of Paolo Freire's own experience and belief that if you can help people look at their world, they will recognize the oppression," said someone else.

"You know, we're talking about 'shaping selves,' but even that is still an authoritarian model," another person said. "Students aren't that passive. They won't allow that. Sometimes they're comfortable with who they are."

Pedagogy of Difference," in *Harvard Educational Review*, vol. 61, no. 4, November 1991, pp. 449-72.

"Part of my solution is to recognize that I am not the only educator in their lives," the first person answered. "If I don't take a stronger position in this direction, then there will be nothing to offset the orientations in some of their other classes. I am no longer concerned about bias or objectivity because, despite the claims of other people to be presenting material in an objective way, no one does it. No one *can* do it. I no longer feel I have to be an objective presenter of material."

Within liberatory pedagogy there are models of transformation and practices of shared power within the classroom. Although the power of the professor rests, ultimately, in having final control over the grade, one person described the process by which her students contract to do certain levels of work, each level corresponding to a particular grade. If they do, in fact, carry out this work, they get the grade. Another emphasis lies on creating what is frequently referred to as 'the safe classroom'.

"But there is no way a classroom can ever be a fully safe space," she added. "So sometimes, I send them off to discuss certain things among themselves."

"There isn't a fully safe space, ever," said another person. "All you can to create a safe *enough* place."

"Wait a minute," someone else interrupted. "You're saying that for students to feel safe they need to go out of the classroom? What's *our* role, then?"

"I give them the structure to go out and discuss their concerns privately, and to bring back as much of it as they want to."

"I'm worried that oppression in the classroom gets perpetuated against the conservative students," said Sharon. "How do you safeguard against that?"

"I keep trying to set up situations where the students witness discussions between dueling authorities," said someone else. "I want them at least to learn to question any position that presents itself as authoritative. Of course, I can't do any of that too overtly; I still don't have tenure."

When, one person wondered, did the attempt to distribute power go too far? In her child's first grade class, one of the little boys had called his teacher—a woman—a foul word. The ethos of the school, however, favored free speech and the creation of a "safe space" for the children, who were encouraged to be independent, know their own opinions, and articulate them freely. Consequently, it was structured as a context in which no one could be silenced.

To this, no one had a clear answer. What seemed clearer was that for women, being given a context in which to discover a more powerful voice can be liberating, and has a great deal to do with learning what it means to be oneself. This did not, however, address the dilemma of what to do when the discovery of voice is valued to the degree that there are no norms for crying halt to anything said. Given the ethos of the elementary school in question, suggested one person, the children might have been guided to arrive at a set of rules for themselves along with corresponding consequences for their violation. But the troubling question remained: to what degree, in the safe context, can a group—particularly a class—regulate its members, especially when this involves trying to influence what or how much they can say?

This led the group to reflect on the influence of one's institutional setting. As one person pointed out, "At my school, the faculty think Paolo Freire is fine in the classroom; they just don't want his stuff showing up in their faculty meetings."

"What happens," said another, "when everything in an institution militates against community—when a Ph.D. is a license to maximizing fame, money, etcetera, so that your real audience isn't even really your students anymore—it's elsewhere. Not only that, but we're having to deal with this business model where we're all somehow entrepreneurs who have to market what we do!"

The staff, in their subsequent discussion of what had taken place during this conversation, remarked that it had not been as successful as they had hoped in addressing the readings they had assigned, although these had, in discernible ways, informed the kinds of questions people had raised. Still, they did feel that some of the issues the group would continue to think about during the week had been established.

In thinking through how to conduct each session most fruitfully, the staff found itself experimenting with a range of small-group strategies worked into its plenary discussions. People were thus to experience themselves and each other in multiple combinations which, in turn, encouraged them to encounter each other in multiple ways. The staff also thought through its own presence both in the working groups and in the unstructured ones formed at meals, as people sat at different tables. They deliberately positioned themselves in each of these groups so as to try to distribute their attention well.

That evening, the topic was "What Is Our Role? Religious Studies and Theology." The group had been asked to think of their secret goal in teaching.[20] What was it they went into the classroom *really* intending to do—even though they may never have said a word about it to anybody else? Counting off, they all separated into three groups, sitting out on the grass just as the sun was beginning to go down. It was still hot, but there were the beginnings of a breeze. Different people disclosed what they thought they were really about, in the classroom. The discussions were serious and whimsical, thoughtful and satirical, provocative and exaggerated.

"I want a student who, at nineteen, is a Southern Baptist minister, to get so turned on by reading the *Bhagavad Gita* that he goes to his church in Chattanooga and says, 'We have to read this!'"

"I'm egotistical. I want people to love this stuff as much as I do, because the material is worthy of love."

"I want to stir their curiosity—to hook it—and to follow them without its being obvious. I want to teach by following, so that they generate something I follow and they end up leading. Whenever you

---

[20] The group had also been asked to read: Sheryl L. Burkhalter, "Four Modes of Discourse: Blurred Genres in the Study of Religion," in *Beyond the Classics: Essays in Religious Studies and Liberal Education*, Frank E. Reynolds and Sheryl L. Burkhalter, eds., (Atlanta: Scholars Press, 1990), pp. 141-62; Carol P. Christ, "Toward a Paradigm Shift in the Academy and in Religious Studies, 1986, mss.; William Darrow, "The 'Introduction to Religion' Course: The Template," in *Teaching the Introductory Course in Religious Studies: A Sourcebook*, Mark Juergensmeyer, ed., (Atlanta: Scholars Press, 1991), pp. 15-26; James H. Foard, "Beyond Ours and Theirs: The Global Character of Religious Studies," in *Beyond the Classics: Essays in Religious Studies and Liberal Education*, Frank E. Reynolds and Sheryl L. Burkhalter, eds., (Atlanta: Scholars Press, 1990), pp. 209-220; Huston Smith, "Another World to Live In: Teaching the Introductory Course," in *Teaching the Introductory Course in Religious Studies: A Sourcebook*, Mark Juergensmeyer, ed., (Atlanta: Scholars Press, 1991), pp. 15-26.

see someone following you, it generates not only a sense of authority, but of responsibility."

"I want to get that one student who will outdo me."

"I want to help these students think that religion and spirituality are a good and beautiful thing, and that people do creative as well as perverse things with them.

"I want to teach them to come up with an analysis of religion and spirituality on their own, especially with the problematic nature of the term 'spirituality' and what it means. I want them to understand how dominance and oppression work—to recognize that religion is, at times, the tool of these things and, at times, a tool for liberation. I want to lead them to become more active."

"I want to provide as many ways as possible to read a text, by running them up against each other, so that they see there's no final reading. And I want them to have them to have some sense of being utterly agog—and to see what happens then."

"I want them to discover that critical thinking is applicable to any body of knowledge in terms of asking what we know and how we know it."

"I want to wean people away from fundamentalism. This has to be a hidden agenda or it becomes counterproductive."

"I want to help students think about these issues in a broadly defined spiritual way—not to sublimate that part of themselves in the academic context."

"I want to produce good liberal Democrats."

The issue was agenda, and it was patently clear that everyone had one. They also recognized that, by and large, there were certain other agenda to which some of them felt a kind of knee-jerk hostility—namely the more conservative ones that came in proselytizing. But there were other flash points, one of which was the claim to objectivity.

"It's 'objectivity' that prevents the Other—the person of color, the woman, the poor person—from having a say. If we attend to issues of power, race, and gender—if those things are part of our agenda, is that to say we've lost our objectivity?"

Only what is perceived as inferior, it was proposed, can be controlled. Different fields exercise that control differently. In religious studies, which defines itself in distinction from theology, one way to exert control is to say, "That's a theological position," or "You're not being objective." Thus, if one represents the voices of what is perceived by one group as Other, one is more likely to hear either or both of these charges from some quarters. In that context, "theological" becomes something of a dirty word. When it is not recognized that all positions are, in some ways, advocacy positions, to accuse someone else of not being objective becomes a way to marginalizing them within the academy. One major distinction between more traditional theology and religious studies lies in where each sees the truth coming from, the one finding it in revelation, the other in the "objective" ideals of the Enlightenment. Religious studies came out of an attempt to separate from theology and has worked to differentiate itself as a field. Yet both represent ideological positions from which one can end up proselytizing.

Within a theology faculty, religious studies sometimes ends up as suspect for the ways in which it is perceived as not being meaningfully theological, whereas as in a liberal arts setting, it is equally suspect as not sufficiently a social science and potentially too much a theology. The latter may not be altogether wrong: there may, indeed, be hidden theologies underlying religious studies that we should get at, especially when it comes to understanding how religious studies was originally the product of certain theologies.

What does hold through religious studies now is a disagreement about what "religion" even is. If one takes an inclusive stand, then one adopts a functional definition and many more things become part of "religious studies." If one has a more exclusive definition, then a great deal gets excluded. The contemporary discussion of the matter hasn't reached any consensus, either. If religion, for example, is a world view, then welcome to the world of liberal education; if it requires that there be something supernatural, then it becomes something else again.

Day Three: Tuesday, June 21

Peter had proposed that the group draw on a number of case studies to explore the issue of conflicts that can erupt in a class.[21] The situation described in the first of these involved a woman who faced student resistance, boredom, and dislike in response to an early American novel, a book that she herself treasured and understood to be part of an important literary canon. The case raised issues of who is in charge in the classroom, what constitutes acceptable modes of classroom interaction, what—in this case—had been at the root of her failure to reach her students, and how one defines "good" and "bad" students. And as Peter quickly to point out, *how* one identifies and defines the "issue" in a situation will be informed by a person's moral philosophy.

As we saw with the New England/Maritimes workshop, the use of case studies can go in a number of directions. A case such as this, which focuses on a teaching dilemma, can become one way for a group of teachers to reflect on a classroom situation similar to something they themselves might confront. One reason such discussions work is that, although cases focus on a situation which may feel quite close to home, as stories without clear-cut conclusions they also preserve a certain distance. Likewise, in classroom work, cases can become a means for drawing students out and for bringing up various difficult issues through the use of the open narrative.[22]

It is interesting to see where a group will go with the idea of difficulty. The New England/Maritimes group had talked about Malcolm X and gone on field trips, looking at how a material world gets built up to illustrate and reinforce one people's way of taking

---

[21] For the session, the group had been asked to read: Nancy Davis, "Teaching About Inequality: Student Resistance, Paralysis, and Rage," in *Teaching Sociology*, vol 20, July 1992, pp. 232-38; Kathleen Weiler, "Gender, Race, and Class in the Feminist Classroom," in *Women Teaching for Change* (South Hadley, MA: Bergin & Garvey Publishers, 1988), pp. 125-45.

A useful resource for the discussion of teaching-related cases is: Louis B. Barnes, C. Roland Christensen, and Abby J. Hansen, *Teaching and the Case Method: Text, Cases, and Readings*, ed. ed. (Boston: Harvard Business School Press, 1994).

[22] One collection in particular was cited as useful in raising issues of race, class and gender: Alice Frazer Evans, Robert A.Evans, and William Bean Kennedy, *Pedagogies for the Non-Poor* (Maryknoll, NY: Orbus Books, 1987).

things for granted. In the Eastern International group, they went into a discussion of critical and feminist pedagogy: teaching, in other words, defining itself as a liberatory project. One states up front that there is no such thing as objective pedagogy; all is advocacy. The difference thus lies in making that advocacy explicit.

In their ideal forms both critical and feminist pedagogy undo the dichotomy between theory and practice in the learning process. The starting point resides in the lives and knowledge of those who are part of the discussion—the student and the professor, who co-create a bottom-up knowledge base. Both pedagogies overlap: some of the critical pedagogies include issues of sexism; many women involved in feminist pedagogy have been engaged by the work of praxis-oriented theoreticians like Paolo Freire and Ira Shor. Both assume, although for somewhat different reasons, the importance of beginning with student experience. Both also recognize education to be a political process, and are more likely to engage students in practices like service learning and participatory research.

Based on the analysis of power relations in this and other cultures, both groups assume that conflict is unavoidable insofar as the cultures we know are predicated on inequalities in the balance of power and distribution of resources. Conflict, therefore, is not to be avoided. Instead, one may use it to help excavate one's own allegiances and better understand their implications, all of which requires the building of enough of a classroom community for this to be possible. Hence the emphasis on the creation of a safe-enough space—the place in which it is possible to examine oneself and one's own self-interests as a variable in a disputed perception of the world. Hence, too, the discussion of and agreement upon preliminary ground rules with which to govern discussion. However much one may believe that authentic democracy is unattainable, one nevertheless continues to struggle to attain it.

"It's not about trying to create a true believer," said one advocate. "The underlying premise is not 'that you shall believe this.' It's more that if you account for how your pedagogy is working, then there is no way to avoid asking how it is working for the women, the people of color, and disadvantaged in the classroom." Likewise, it is taken to be nothing but irresponsible not to look at the global environment, the situation of people in the Third World, the effects of class differences in our own culture, and the implications of gender wherever one looks. And "look" in this case becomes intimately implicated in one's ensuing praxis.

"If your goal is social action, there are many kinds," said one person. "Everyone is part of some social action, whatever they're doing. I want my students' participation in the social world to be more informed, more critical. I want them to be able to listen. We make and maintain our world. Given that, how do we engage in shaping it as co-producers of the world?"

"What is the worst '-ism' for you?" said someone else. "How do you work that into your teaching? What is the relationship of your syllabus and your teaching to that '-ism'? Those are the kinds of questions that these pedagogies ask."

Just as the workshop design had been intended to address the multiple approaches to pedagogy, the staff also wanted to insure that the range of teaching settings be represented. It had therefore been decided that Peter, who had won teaching awards within the world of community colleges and was a strong advocate of this network, would lead an optional session that afternoon on teaching in the community college. The following afternoon, someone else led an optional session on training oneself to see as an artist, as a way of enhancing one's ability to help students learn to *read* the visual.

That evening, the group split off into smaller sections to view videotapes that some of the participants had brought to illustrate their own work in the classroom. The assignment to have a class video-taped had been an optional one; about half the group had done it. The staff decided to make this another small-group task, which would take place over two evenings. One member of the staff would participate in each of these groups, all but one of which would have four participants. This allowed for a more in-depth discussion of each person's work. Whether one had brought a video or not, each person was given one hour in which to present and talk about some pedagogical issue that had arisen for them during the preceding year. It might have been a problem with a particular class, a matter of feeling the need to refine a skill, or a dimension of teaching of which the workshop itself had made them more aware.   The point was to have the hour to focus on one's own teaching style and to get help on specific problems from one's peers.

Following the evening sessions, everyone had taken to gathering in the ground-floor rooms of one of the dormitories, hanging out in smaller coteries in the kitchen or the living room or— in the case of the dedicated—in a sun porch to watch the NBA playoffs. (During the previous fall weekend, it had been the World Series.) A couple of additional runs to Walmart had provided the group with enough juice, junk food, and soda (or, as someone put it, "Snapple, crap, and pop") to guarantee everyone who partook of it a bilious night's sleep. It was something else to get to know professional colleagues behind the scenes as people who also lounge around in bathrobes. Still, the winner was the discovery that one of the quieter participants had turned out to be a fiercely avid devotee not only of the playoffs, but of Cheetos.

Those present were reminded, too, that living closely with a group like that also makes one more aware of all the anxieties preying on people's minds at the same time as they are trying to engage in the tasks of a workshop—a sick child, the anxiety over finding steadier work, being in love, the rage over an injustice against a friend, having to relocate. To know these things about each other indicated the emergence of a certain sense of community, however temporary or partial it might have been.

Day Four: Wednesday, June 22

It is usually easy to remember the courses we didn't like; the great ones tend to be fewer. But what, the group wondered, makes for a powerful course and what for a deadly one? They broke into sections to think back to courses that had stood out one way or the other. What had made the difference?[23]

---

[23] To prepare, they had been asked to read: Laura L. Nash, "The Rhythms of the Semester," in *The Art and Craft of Teaching*, Margaret Morganroth Gullette, ed. (Cambridge, MA: Harvard-Danforth Center for Teaching and Learning, 1982), pp. 70-87; Parker Palmer, "Good Teaching: A Matter of Living the Mystery," in *Change*, January/February 1990, pp. 11-16; and Jane Tompkins, "Pedagogy of the Distressed," in *College English*, vol. 52, no. 6, October 1990, pp. 653-60.

When they came together again, they brought with them memories dug up about earlier teachers of their own. The worst ones, it was generally agreed, gave lectures dryly intoned, buried in their notes, pounding on a one-point agenda. One was quoted as saying, "Just because you've been badly educated doesn't mean I have to be remedial." These were teachers alienated from their material, from their students and, most probably, from themselves. It didn't take much to put many of them on the defensive, and they got back by browbeating, humiliating, and dismissing their students. They generated an acerbic, bitter environment and, in some cases, an angry one as well if it was felt they assigned a great many student reports so as not to have to do much work of their own for a class. No one wanted to *be* them.

But then there were the professors who had taught the powerful class. These were the people who embodied a love for their material. Being around the passionate professor made it easier to fall in love with the stuff oneself. These were the ones who were true to who they were, thereby giving sanction to the pursuit of authenticity and engagement. They somehow knew how to design what they taught in ways that caught up everyone there. This had something to do with their being able to make learning a common enterprise in which they were invested just as much as their students. Sometimes you put your pen down when you were listening to them because you became so engrossed in what they were saying.

These were teachers who managed to create communities of scholars within their schools, and they didn't hesitate to refer students to one another. They seemed to trust their students. Sometimes they assigned a lot of work but their enthusiasm made you feel it was worth doing. In some cases, they made it clear that they held strong opinions. At the same time, they stayed open to other perspectives and argued with them fairly. In fact, your arguments—especially if you disagreed with them—usually got better in the process. They weren't afraid to be funny, and often they were even fun. *Them* you wanted to emulate.

The group wondered about what it takes to create a classroom that works as a community. From there, it didn't take them long to speculate what is required to create a communit of colleagues who are also genuine allies. Whether among one's students or colleagues, this raises the question of how sufficient trust can become established. It is hard to cultivate, the group agreed, when, at the same time, conflict cannot easily be expressed.

"We talk about community, but unaddressed conflict and competition are what we know."

Some people reflected on the issue of wanting to be the best teacher they could, and the fear, alienation, and even despair they felt when they looked at the gap between what they hoped to be and what they felt they were. They talked, too, about the expending of energy in teaching—the difference between being exhausted but satisfied, versus feeling drained and depleted. And it takes courage to *talk* about teaching, they agreed. Courage, in this case, is not the absence of fear, but the act of going beyond that fear. The two can be in constructive tension in which both are present. It helps to feel one has allies; some fears are easier to manage when you don't feel alone with them.

Underlying some of the fear, the staff said among themselves in their meeting that afternoon, are the complex and multiple dimensions of evaluation and assessment. You grade your students. They evaluate you, and so does your department, and both forms of evaluation have implications in the process of tenure review. There are also evaluations of the curriculum and the department as a whole. How, then, to discuss the dynamics and problems related to all these different pieces. In addition, how to model such a discussion as it might take place in a larger class?

The staff decided to prepare and enact a brief theatrical piece within a department. There would be three scenes: the first, between an older and a younger member; the second, between two younger, untenured peers; and the third between two tenured faculty. Each scene would present a dialogue involving various facets of the evaluative process in the fictitious department, with the overall aim of illustrating how all of them are interconnected. And this time, they demanded I take a role in the skit, resisting any suggestion that I retain my posture as a neutral observer. Following these scenarios, the larger group would then divide into smaller ones and spend twenty minutes each discussing the grading of student work, the kinds of evaluation related to tenure review, and various approaches to the assessment of courses and course activities, curricula, and departments.

Planning the session took up most of the afternoon. This was one of those times when each person on the staff would look at his or her watch and say, "You know, I really want to get in a swim this afternoon . . . but now about that part of the scene . . ." It became sort of like planning a surprise party, which is why nobody left to take the swim. Embedded in the experience were, perhaps, some of the most important elements in doing a team project in a class—namely, opening up the mind to the multiple ways in which material can be presented, and doing so with the objective of making it as engaging as possible. This process itself then has the potential of involving everyone in thinking through the complexities of the material itself, so they can also figure out how to present it clearly. In the process, the team engages. It was hard to imagine a team having a better time unless, of course, it was that same team when they got together again the following day.

Day Five: Thursday, June 23

Following the enactment of their three scenes, the staff divided the group into three sections.[24] Today, however, there was a different spin to the division. Instead of going off on their own, the groups took turns sitting in the middle of the room, surrounded by the others. Each one took on a topic, discussing it while the others

---

[24] For this session, the group had been asked to read: Heather Dubrow, "Teaching Essay-Writing in a Liberal Arts Curriculum," in *The Art and Craft of Teaching*, Margaret Morganroth Gullette, ed. (Cambridge, MA: Harvard-Danforth Center for Teaching and Learning, 1982), pp. 88-102; James H. Foard, "Writing Across the Curriculum: A Religious Studies Contribution," in *Beyond the Classics: Essays in Religious Studies and Liberal Education*, Frank E. Reynolds and Sheryl L. Burkhalter, eds., (Atlanta: Scholars Press, 1990), pp. 203-17; Keith Hoskin, The Examination, Disciplinary Power and Rational Schooling," in *History of Education*, vol. 8, no. 2, 1979, pp. 135-46; Christopher M. Jedrey, "Grading and Evaluation," in *The Art and Craft of Teaching*, Margaret Morganroth Gullette, ed. (Cambridge, MA: Harvard-Danforth Center for Teaching and Learning, 1982), pp. 102-15; and Karen J. Warren, "Toward an Ecofeminist Peace Politics," in *Ecological Feminism*, Karen J. Warren, ed., (London; New York: Routledge, 1994), pp. 179-86.

listened. At a set point in time, the larger group would enter the discussion for a few moments, providing commentary on what the small group had said. Then, a new groups would go into the center. What follows are overviews of these discussions:

On Grading

In the commodifying of education that appears to be invading a fair number of schools in North America, students sometimes come into a class expecting that so long as they work hard, all good things will come to them. Some equate the expenditure of energy in a course with doing good work, and don't always understand the difference between the two. Expecting that, if they work hard, they will get an A, when they don't, a second aspect of the culture kicks in—namely, the litigious self. The student may quibble, finagle, or quarrel to try to raise the grade to the one they feel they are due.

In addition to the distress various people in this workshop group felt over having to grade anyone else's work in the first place and in trying to figure out fair ways to go about doing so, there was thus also the issue of how to clarify one's standards and expectations from the beginning. A second issue involved defining the extent to which students play a part in determining their own grade. In both cases, the common elements involved the expectations presented by the professor and the degree to which the student met or did not meet them.

From there, any number of other variables could enter the picture. For example, one can hand out a summary of what constitutes an A, an A-, a B+, and the like. This gives the student a sense of the tasks that must be done well at each level, and the choice of which ones to try to accomplish. It does not, however, insure that the student will necessarily understand what one means by standards like "critical thinking" or "a carefully reasoned argument" or, for that matter, "well written." To be fair, the professor must also explain and/or point to examples of what each of the tasks corresponding to a particular grade looks like in practice.

A second example, which increases the students' involvement in defining the outcome, is the contract. In this case, students are given a similar list of criteria, but determine at the beginning of the course which of the various grades they want to earn. They contract with the professor that they will carry out at very least the amount and quality of work corresponding to that grade. To get an A, for example, they may have to come to every class, do more writing and do it better, and engage at a more sophisticated level. The "A" option may also include several occasions for revising one's work which, in practical terms, also means doing more writing.

The standards must be clear. Even with the contract system, there is no absolute guarantee that the student will get the grade he or she contracts for—or, therefore, that he or she won't challenge a grade. But when the standards are, indeed, made that clear, then students can no longer assume that the amount of time spent was the point. Likewise, the professor has to justify giving a B-. This approach does, however, help students to realize more explicitly how they can influence the grading process. When the criteria underlying a grade are made explicit, they also allow the professor to specify more precisely the differences between how well the student has conveyed information and how well he or she has met the particular task—which may be something different.

On Tenure-Related Evaluation

As an untenured person, one wants to build a network with other untenured faculty and with people outside the department in order to get a sense of the larger institution. It is also helpful to talk with others who have been through the process. They are more likely know the requirements for one's own institution, helping one to understand the ambiguities embedded in the politics and policies. ("It's known," said one person dryly, "as girding your loins to cover your ass.") One should keep a paper trail of every sort of evalutation of one's work. If any of these evaluations is not clear, one should insist that it be made clear—and then get a copy. Finally, one should seek a mentor among the tenured faculty, who can help one to understand the inner workings of the department and who will also advocate on one's behalf.

None of these broad suggestions touches, of course, on the part of the process which often feels fear-driven, making it difficult to remember that the people evaluating one's work—and even criticizing it—may be offering useful suggestions to which one should actually listen. What can complicate the process is when the standards are not clear. This is particularly the case when mixed signals are given about the relative importance of research and teaching. Usually one can get some handle on the research expectations, but teaching is more often devalued in the actual review process, even when an institution may perceive itself as committed to a high quality of teaching. It can be harder, therefore, to get a handle on the criteria by which one's classroom work is judged. One can also request that clear criteria be institutionalized.

There may be class evaluation forms required by the institution. These may or may not be detailed and precise. Where can one exercise some influence? Given that student evaluations figure in the assessment of one's work, one can try to insure that these evaluations include enough specific questions relating to the different aspects of a course that they are likely to be more accurate. ("Did such-and-such a film help to make the nature of that culture clearer?") One also has to be sure to tell students what these are being used for and especially that they will be looked at by someone else. Finally, it sometimes helps to read other people's evaluations. It can help put your own in context.

On Assessment in General

The discussion of assessment was less focused, probably because there are so many directions into which it can split off. It also seems probable that, as untenured faculty, the assessment of the department and of the curriculum may not have been as immediate a concern. In any case, what interested the group more was the subsequent of the process in which they had just engaged, particularly because it brought back memories of the fishbowl thought exercise they had done the year before. Through the experience of sitting on the fringes of the center, they found themselves better able to discern the process of whichever small group was going on. Sitting at the center themselves, they were also aware of being back in a fishbowl, and found the process of making eye contact a more complicated business.

Last year, however, they had found the fishbowl exercise uncomfortable; this arrangement had gone more smoothly. It had taught them something about learning to listen to people differently, given that they couldn't interrupt the ongoing discussion in the middle. Also, it so happened that the quieter people had ended up together in the center, which meant that everyone had gotten to hear more from them—or had had to listen to them more carefully, depending on how you looked at it. The other reason everyone probably found this exercise an easier task was that, at this point they had now known each other for going on a year.

By this time, people were feeling the intensity of the week. Having the afternoons off if they wanted helped, but the workshop experience is, in general, an intense one. To vary the rhythm and allow people to step back from the steady succession of meetings, it had been decided that the group would go to Seneca Falls, a site that combined both matters of gender and non-textuality as the setting of the Seneca Falls Convention in 1848. Organized by Elizabeth Cady Stanton, Lucretia Mott, and several other women, the Convention produced the Declaration of Sentiments and Resolutions, a formulation of women's rights as envisioned in nineteenth-century antebellum America. There was the museum to see, and the memorial to the women of the Convention. Through this visit, the discussion of gender was relocated into the context of American women's history.

The group went out that night. During the previous weekend, the weekly schedule had taken to announcing "dinner at an exquisite restaurant"—one of which had turned out to be run by the Hare Krishnas, preceded by a tour of the ISKON temple itself. This night, however, it was to be an upstate winery *cum* restaurant. It was also Peter's birthday. To celebrate in style, several of the participants turned him into a package closely wrapped in colored ribbons. They perched party hats on his and everybody else's heads, and sang happy birthday to him. And it did, after all that, turn out to be an exquisite restaurant.

Riding home later on, the sun had just begun to cast its light at that certain slant, and the heat had abated somewhat. Cruising through the countryside, the fields wide open and green, old

Grateful Dead tunes coming off the radio and old stories from the sixties rising up out of our memories to make everyone laugh, it can only be said that the rest of the world sure did feel far away.

Day Six: Friday, June 24

A certain parable tells of the young woman who had been given the task of teaching an introductory course. Never having done so before, she took a six-week long workshop on how to go about it. By the end, she had learned one thing: "It's possible—and it's hopeless."

Having returned once again to the subject of the introductory course, the group was inclined to agree, this having been a matter with which each of them had wrestled.[25] This time they split off in dyads, with each person getting five minutes to think out loud as the other person took notes.

As the group came back together, they posed themselves the questions: "What is an introductory course about? To what are we introducing our students?"

"To college work—critical thinking, a more advanced level of oral and written expression, the types of skills relevant to the study of human beings."

"To a comparative method and approach. To a global approach that will help them appreciate other values."

"The 'stuff,' the 'data.' We're trying to convey that these things matter, at the same time as we try to figure out how to give them life and meaning."

"To the question of what other people's beliefs and behaviors might have to do with *them*."

"To uncanniness, to how a transcendent, ultimate reality has been experienced and expressed—and to what differentiates this from other social sciences."

"To the idea that there are ways of looking at the world that are good and complete in themselves."

---

[25] For this session, the group had been asked to review the essays in *Teaching the Introductory Course in Religious Studies: A Sourcebook*, Mark Juergensmeyer, ed. (Atlanta: Scholars Press, 1991).

"To suggest a vocabulary of the field with which to organize their thinking, with a bibliography, as an academic discipline."

"To explore the question of what it is to be human and what, in that connection, it is to be religious."

In comparing what they understood their own intro courses to be doing in comparison with those of other disciplines, almost everybody had the feeling they were dealing with the study of human beings through comparative methods that relied on various tools of the trade, guided by particular meta-questions. There were also important multidisciplinary dimensions to many of the approaches. But they also agreed that the problem in the intro course resides in the unresolvable tension between going for depth or for breadth, insofar as it is not possible to do both. None of the intro textbooks has resolved it either. One can organize the course around certain key questions that one might bring to each tradition, but with so much to cover it still requires being all the more conscious about precisely why each issue, is being included. In such cases, part of what one is modelling are ways to learn widely.

In figuring out how to introduce primary texts to students, one can at least keep pointing to them as specific voices speaking about specific issues. One is also up against the ways the various traditions perceive each other, Christian understandings of other traditions being only one of the possibilities. ("Right," said someone. "How do you get your students to see that from the perspective of some people in some of the other traditions, what Christians are about is the worship of a dead body on two-by-fours?")

One of the primary problems, when it comes to insuring that multiple voices are included, is the tendency to conflate those who are different into a homogenized view of a given tradition. Systemic issues get lost, as do the ways in which a given system shapes the voices of different groups quite differently. A second challenge involves not falling into one reductionism or another. We all have ideological positions, and all of our teaching is political and ideological. That is to say, the questions one asks and the information one presents are structured by these positions. There is, therefore, the risk that of unwittingly adopting a schema that speaks in liberatory terms but whose effects are anything but that.

For example, to put women at the center of what one teaches—to keep asking, "What was/is going on here for the women?"—is a radical move. But if one does define one's pedagogy as liberatory, then one must be clear about the motivations for raising questions concerning gender, asking whether one is doing so with a tranformational intent or in ways that ultimately do nothing to challenge a status quo. In doing all of this, as one contingent in the group pointed out, the seriousness of the project can get deadly. It remains important to create an environment in which both humor and a spirit of play are possible.

With only one more day to go, the staff tweaked the schedule and gave everyone the afternoon off, moving an afternoon discussion to the following morning. Guessing that there were those among the participants who would put this time to use in coming up with final ceremonies, the staff resolved to be prepared with a few awards of their own, such as:

> C., whose courses in myth and ritual are wildly popular among his students, has become an animator for the *Myth America* series to be shown by PBS. In the first episode, he introduces us to "Satyrs and Bacchanales I have known and so should you."

> M., the noted feminist, has just finished a book called *I'm O.K./ You've Got Testosterone*. She currently chairs the Men's Studies Department at Wabash College.

The particapants had composed their own set of awards, in turn. As in previous cases, the importance of humor became apparent once again. However lighthearted the awards themselves, they represented the ritualizing of relationships through the exchange of gifts and jokes.

In looking back over the week, the staff agreed that it had been pedagogically oriented, with its focus on different small-group strategies and approaches to discussion. They recognized that they had modelled liberal pedagogy as opposed to a more radical approach. It surprised them somewhat that there had not been more conflict. Still, in thinking about whether or not to ask the group if anyone had learned anything about community that might be useful back in their own institutions, the staff acknowledged the limits of the community that had been created through the workshop. They could see all the questions that remained unresolved.

"In some ways we haven't built one," concluded Sharon. "But we *have* done some extraordinary work together, and a lot of friendships and respect have been formed."

"But," said Mark, "that's why it's crucial for the workshop to have older faculty so the younger ones can see that those issues *don't* all resolve. They never do become fully clear; we just do all we can."

Day Seven: Saturday, June 25

The discussion of the introduction of business models— particularly those deriving from "Total Quality Management" (TQM)—was brief.[26] People were tired, there was an evaluation to do and, perhaps because it was such a painful point, people couldn't quite find the wherewithal to go into it deeply on the last morning. Almost everyone had experienced some aspect of the trimming down of teaching staffs, the result being that faculty now do a great deal more of the grunt work in their jobs. Downsizing never means less work; it just means that everyone has more to do, with little by way of corresponding increases in pay. In the parlance of labor organizers, it is known as "speed-up."

An older "faculty-driven" model now intersects with this newer one, further complicated by the fiscal crises many schools increasingly face. In some settings, administrators assess their faculty in terms of enrollments, with budgets informing curriculum

---

[26] The readings that had been assigned were: William R. Darrow, "Dearth in Venice," in *Beyond the Classics: Essays in Religious Studies and Liberal Education*, Frank E. Reynolds and Sheryl L. Burkhalter, eds., (Atlanta: Scholars Press, 1990), pp. 221-35; Frank Lentricchia, "The 'Life' of a Humanist Intellectual," in *The Academic's Handbook*, A. Leight Deneef, Crawford D. Goodwin, and Ellen Stern McCrate, eds. (Durham: Duke University Press, 1988), pp. 29-35; Mike Parker and Jane Slaughter, "Beware! TQM is Coming to Your Campus," in *The NEA Higher Education Journal*, vol. X, no. 1, Spring 1994, pp. 5-30; George W. Pickering, "Rethinking the Humanities for the 1990s: Redressing the Balance," in *Beyond the Classics: Essays in Religious Studies and Liberal Education*, Frank E. Reynolds and Sheryl L. Burkhalter, eds., (Atlanta: Scholars Press, 1990), pp. 63-74; Robert Sessions, "Education is a Gift, Not a Commodity, mss.; and Nancy Warehime, *To Be One of Us" Cultural Conflict, Creative Democracy, and Education* (Albany, N.Y.: State University of New York Press, 1993).

decisions in ways they never had before. Quantifiable assessment tools have been introduced to "measure" how much students have learned, privileging the transmission of quantities of information. The framework, it was agreed, is one that commodifies education, leaving little or no room for religious, ethical, or moral positions.

It was time to end. The group filled out their evaluation forms and took their leave of one another. It might be summer, but everyone still had a lot to do. At a tri-regional meeting that fall, they would all come together for dinner, and some of them would go on to write and publish together on matters pertaining to pedagogy. Perhaps the more lasting effect, however, as one person put it, "Is knowing that there's this group of people out there, and I can call any one of them up when I'm stuck with anything at all in my teaching. And I never thought I'd find *that* in the Academy."

IV

Teaching Religious Studies in the Southeast

Introduction

It has been well documented by historians and sociologists and has been given narrative power by the region's novelists. Judging by such accounts, religion has played a prominent role in determining the social, cultural and political agenda of individual and community life in the South. While the South has always enjoyed great religious diversity, including some of this nation's largest and earliest Jewish communities, as well as Native American and imported indigenous indigenous traditions, Christianity has dominated the religious landscape with its own distinctive character as a predominantly Protestant, conservative, and biblical tradition. Though the range of Christian beliefs and practices are also exceedingly broad, Southern students—no matter what their own religious tradition—tend to bring to the classroom distinctive perspectives and questions influenced by this "Bible Belt" heritage. Their classmates from other regions of the country are oftentimes unaware of the cultural context that influences the religious studies classroom.

Further complicating the traditions of Southern religious life is the recent transformation of the region implied in phrases like the "Sun Belt" and the "New South." As the national economy moves from an industrial to a service base, a continental shift from North to South has been occurring. Besides this national migration, the South has experienced a tremendous influx of immigrants, especially from Latin America, South Asia, and Southeast Asia. All these newcomers

bring their own religious beliefs and practices with them—
beliefs and practices which both modify and are modified by
Southern religious traditions.[1]

When the Lilly Endowment had first agreed to help support the
AAR Teaching Workshop Program, it had stipulated that, although
full funding would be provided for the first two series, the AAR
would be responsible for raising matching funds to cover half the
costs of the second two. One of the practical consequences of this
decision was that the AAR—rather than extending an open-ended
call for proposals to the different regions, as it had with the first two
series—would instead become more engaged in designating the key
issues to be addressed by the two current proposals and in locating
the two directors, who would, in turn, recruit staffs and develop
more specific plans. These would all then be folded into the larger
proposal for a matching grant which, it was hoped, would be
provided by the National Endowment for the Humanities (NEH).

One of the AAR's long-term objectives was to insure that
workshops be held in each of the ten regions. Yet the workshops, till
then, had not had an explicitly regional focus. The prototype group
at Wabash had been drawn from around the country; the other two
groups, despite their participants being recruiting primarily from
within region and having explored the question—to a limited
degree—of who their students were, had not focused on what it
meant to be teaching the study of religion *in* their particular regions.
Indeed, in the original proposal to the Lilly Endowment, there had
been no mention of making regional issues the focus of the
workshops at all.

The first round of proposals submitted by the different regions
for the earlier two workshop series had included one from a team
located in the Southeast and one from the Southwest. Although this
particular proposal had not been accepted in 1992, the interest
expressed by its writers in directing a workshop—along with the
strength of their own expertise—drew the attention of the Workshop
Committee of the AAR.

---

1   "Academic Teaching of Religion in the South," AAR Proposal to
the NEH matching fund program, pp. 1-3.

As Barbara DeConcini tells the story, it happened like this: she, Warren Frisena, and Raymond Williams went to meet with a representative from the NEH. The three of them knew that they were interested in finding a way to bring the Southeast and Southwest regions into the workshop circle. As they started talking about what they wanted to do with the workshops, nothing seemed to be catching the interest on the other end. As she recalls it:

> So, on the spot, together we generated the regional focus out of whole cloth. No one of us individually could get the credit for that idea. We made the case that we wanted to do two workshops, and we had these two regions in the South. How about funding us to do 'Teaching Religion in the South?' We would include racial and ethnic diversity, the South as the Bible Belt—we began to think all these things out loud on the spot. The person with whom we were speaking became very enthusiastic. The whole conversation turned around. After that, we had to go back to the potential directors, and ask them if they could add this dimension without losing the integrity of what *they* had proposed. Each of them was enthusiastic about the idea, too, so then we all had to shift gears and modify the proposals. But we pulled things together, sent in a fresh draft, and the funding came through.

Carl, who was to be the director of the workshop, later remembered it as having been an assisted effort.

> My recollection is that Warren Frisena and Barbara DeConcini made some suggestions based on the critique of our first proposal. We rewrote it, putting those things in place. It was mostly Jack and I who worked on it at that point.
>
> Our initial proposal had all the staff coming from one school. It was recommended that we change that, so we invited Mariko. She was in the region, she was a woman, and we wanted someone who knew about theories of religion. It helped that she was from another culture, and that she was teaching at a school that was different from ours.
>
> We had also originally planned to hold all the sessions at one place, but ended up redistributing the locales throughout different parts of the Southeast. We contextualized the content, regionalized it, and resubmitted it.

In one sense, the questions addressed by the workshops had not changed; at the same time, in these two new series they would now be examined through a more specific lens:

> The American Academy of Religion (AAR), the major learned society in the academic study of religion, proposes to conduct two teaching workshops that will help pre-tenured faculty improve their teaching by examining the relationship among *where* they teach (the Southern United States), *what* they teach (religion), and *how* they teach.[2]

Region would no longer be the neutral background; instead, it would become the explicitly examined setting. This approach had its roots in a pedagogical assumption:

> If good pedagogy in the humanities starts from students' questions and seeks to uncover their presuppositions, this is especially the case in the study of religion. Students often bring strong personal convictions to the "Introduction to Religion" and "World Religions" classrooms. Developing in students the dual capacities of appreciation and criticism requires, in the case of the academic study of religion, a rigorous interrogation of the familiar and an exposure of the unfamiliar which are oftentimes delicate and difficult . . . . By maintaining a focus on issues that are specific to teaching religion in the South and at the same time providing opportunities to explore more general pedagogical issues, these workshops take a holistic approach to helping a total of thirty faculty become better teachers.[3]

The more explicit centering of the workshop focus in regionally-shaped student realities represented a shift in stated emphasis; the previous grant proposal, for example, had emphasized the refining of teaching skills, the developing of confidence and self-esteem as teachers, the relationship between pedagogy and the study of religion, but little had been said about the specificities of student populations. Even though the New England/Maritimes group had included the question of "who we teach" in its own proposal, this had been the area least addressed. At the same time, it had also been the case that the staffs of the earlier workshops had all, with some range

---

[2]   "Academic Teaching of Religion in the South," AAR Proposal to the National Endowment for the Humanities Matching Fund Program, p. 1.
[3]   Ibid., p. 3.

of difference, taken seriously a student-centered pedagogy, of which this proposal now was one example. The other core aspects of the series would remain the same: the fifteen pre-tenured teacher-scholars, the staff of four experienced faculty teaching in the region, the four meetings wrapped around the academic year, and the teaching project.

The second new element among the stated goals for these two workshops was that of establishing "an ongoing, regionally-based community of scholars who know one another *first* as teachers and who are committed to helping one another improve their teaching skills."[4] Through the earlier workshops, it had become apparent that one of the most meaningful dimensions of the experience to be reported by the participants was precisely that of community. If the original proposal had defined as one of its goals, "to continue refining the workshop model which will influence future workshops and initiatives in other regions of the AAR,"[5] the adding of the regional focus represented one such refinement.

The revised proposal also retained a focus on teaching religion in the context of the liberal arts—an issue explored by earlier NEH workshops held in the 1980s[6]—but added to it the objective of enhancing "the understanding and visibility of the teaching of religion in the settings of academic cultures in the region."[7] This, in turn, was related to another AAR objective, namely to promote the recognition of the influence of religion on virtually every area of

---

[4]   Ibid., p. 3.

[5]   "AAR Grant Proposal to the Lilly Endowment Inc., requesting funding for the Lilly Workshops on Teaching Religion for Young College and University Teachers" (1992), section 1A, p. 5.

[6]   These workshops resulted in the publication of three volumes of essays on teaching the study of religion in liberal arts settings: *Tracing Common Themes: Comparative Courses in the Study of Religion*, eds. John B. Carman and Steven P. Hopkins (Scholars Press, 1991); *Teaching the Introductory Course in Religious Studies: A Sourcebook*, ed. Mark Juergensmeyer (Scholars Press, 1991); and *Beyond the Classics: Essays in Religious Studies and Liberal Education*, eds. Frank E. Reynolds and Sheryl L. Burkhalter (Scholars Press, 1991).

[7]   "Academic Teaching of Religion in the South," AAR Proposal to the National Endowment for the Humanities matching fund program, p. 9.

contemporary life—an objective which, it recognized, could not be achieved without also promoting effective teaching.[8]

Like the New England/Maritimes proposal, that of the Southeast detailed the complex mixture of schools in the region. Here, the mix included:

> . . . small church-related colleges (Protestant and Catholic), large and medium-sized state university campuses, traditionally African-American colleges and universities, and single-gender colleges. Some institutions are long-established, others represent post-war and more recent origins. Some are in small town or rural settings, while others are in the center of major metropolitan areas.[9]

Curiously, with the exception of traditionally African-American colleges and universities, one could make essentially the same statement about many of the other regions in the country, including New England. What, then, made this same blend distinct when it came to the Southeast? This question they hoped to address, through discussions within the workshop itself, by looking closely at the "character of academic cultures in the Southeast" as represented by the different staff members and participants.[10] They would, in the process of forming a community of teachers, share with each other "how the teaching of religion is carried on in those cultures." They hoped that this experience would lead everyone involved "to develop a new level of expertise on issues of teaching in ways that are appropriate to and effective in the cultural and institutional environments of the Southeast."[11]

They would include many of the issues that had been part of their original proposal—aspects of the culture(s) of the liberal arts and the place(s) of religion in that culture, discussions about the classroom as an environment for learning about religion, comparative studies and multicultural environments, religious texts

---

[8]   See "AAR Grant Proposal to the Lilly Endowment Inc., requesting funding for the Lilly Workshops on Teaching Religion for Young College and University Teachers" (1992), section 1, p. 4.

[9]   "Academic Teaching of Religion in the South," AAR Proposal to the National Endowment for the Humanities matching fund program, p. 9.

[10]   Ibid.

[11]   Ibid., pp. 9-10.

as objects of study, conducting fieldwork studies on religion, and the teaching of narrative films in religion courses.[12] They anticipated that, by the final week, the participants would "take greater responsibility for topics and presentations."[13] They also expected that the sessions would take place at two of the larger universities in the region. This part of the plan would later be modified, so that only the first week's meeting would happen at one of these schools, with the other sessions being held at the locations where various participants were teaching.

The staff would be directed by Carl, chair of his department and a professor of East Asian religious traditions. He had played a part in developing the new curriculum and major for the Religion Department at his school, and had been a consultant to a number of departments. Jack had worked for years on education in church, public, and academic contexts. Louis taught courses in areas of African-American religious traditions. He consulted to academic and civic groups on issues of race relations and multiculturalism. Mariko taught in the areas of the history, and religion and culture. Although it was the first time that a staff had consisted of three men and one woman, it was also the first time one had included an African-American and an Asian-American.

The First June Meeting

The Planning

As the other directors had discovered, Carl soon realized that publicity about the workshop in *Religious Studies News* had not been sufficient to reach the various constituencies the workshop intended to address. Indeed, so few applications came in that the deadline had to be postponed. He decided to write directly to the chairs of the different religion departments and to the presidents of the African-American colleges and universities in the region. It was then that the applications began to arrive.

The applicants had been asked to send a statement about why they wanted to be part of the workshop, along with a description of themselves as a teacher. That, a Curriculum Vitae including courses

---

[12]   Ibid., p. 10.
[13]   Ibid., p. 11.

they had taught, a description of the project they were proposing to carry out during the workshop, and two letters of recommendation completed the application. From the beginning, those involved had to begin to define themselves *as* teachers.

The staff went through two steps in choosing the participants. There would be room for twelve untenured faculty. Carl had sent them copies of all the applications, along with a rating sheet. In his instructions, he wrote:

> The criteria we need to keep in mind are: overall excellence of the candidate and project proposal, field of candidate, type of institution, teaching environment (e.g., religion department, competitive general humanities program). We need to finish at the end of the day with a seminar that has participants from large universities, small colleges, institutions reflecting distinctive characteristics (e.g., women's colleges, African American colleges, etc.); geographical distribution across the region, demographically diverse locations (e.g., small towns, large metropolitan areas). No single criterion should dominate all others in every case. Imagine the sort of mix you would like to have around the table in terms of what they will be able to contribute out of their experience and institutional setting to the theme of the workshop. The success of the workshop will depend on our being able to draw out their contributions more than anything we might transmit to them.[14]

The graduate student applications would be reviewed separately. The staff members were each to rank the applicants and send their tallies to Carl, who would then set up a conference call in case there were any candidates requiring further discussion. The group they finally assembled:

> . . . ranged from a small church-related college in Appalachia to small women's colleges to a large traditionally African-American technical and vocational university in Florida. Participants are located in institutions in Georgia, Florida, North Carolina, Virginia, West Virginia, Tennessee, Alabama and Mississippi. Some are native Southerners, others came from other parts of the country; some did their graduate training in the South, others in the North, Midwest, and West Coast. We

---

[14]   Director's memorandum to the staff.

had a good mix of women and men; African-Americans and Caucasians.[15]

More specifically, there were eleven men and four women; including the staff and myself, those numbers changed to thirteen and six. Three of the participants were of African descent—one man and one woman who were African-American, one man originally from the West Indies. The others were Caucasian. One of the participants was Jewish, one a Buddhist, one was interested in a Hindu-based American meditation practice; the others either belonged to Christian denominations or were now unaffiliated.

The staff came together for the first time in April. (Carl's memorandum inviting them ended by saying, "I've enclosed a copy of the final proposal in case you don't remember where you put yours.") What they had to work with was the preliminary schedule that had been drafted for the proposal to the NEH—a schedule which had proposed using the three hours in the morning for seminar-like meetings, the afternoons for informal discussions, individual research and meetings with the staff, or an excursion to a local historical museum, and evenings left open, except for one session on teaching with films. Two group dinners had been planned; other than that, the participants would be on their own each day once lunch was over. Everyone would be eating lunch together in a common dining room; the other meals would take place in the university food court and people would have meal cards. It would be up to them to find each other if they wanted to get together either for breakfast or most of the dinners.

Originally, the morning sessions had been planned to focus on regional identity and religion, race and class in the South, and gender and the construction of Southern culture. Two days would be dedicated to discussions of the teaching projects. The staff also decided to drop one of two sessions on race and add, instead, a morning on institutional contexts for teaching religion in the South. Carl and Louis would each lead one discussion, Jack and Mariko another, and the staff as a whole, the remaining one.

---

[15] Director's report to the AAR, the Lilly Endowment Inc., and the National Endowment of the Humanities, p. 2.

Much of the afternoon went into sorting out the readings and roughing out the broad strokes of the content for each session. As they thought about the layout of the week, they decided not to wait for the final week to set up optional field trips to local religious sites. Instead, they would set up visits during the first week to the Martin Luther King, Jr. Center for Non-Violent Social Change, the Ebenezer Baptist Church, and the APEX Museum of African-American Arts. Those who wanted to might go to see the Coca-Cola center. There would also be visits to the Oakland Cemetery and Stone Mountain. The idea was to illustrate how one could draw on the resources of a local setting in the planning of field trips to religiously-related sites. It would also give the participants a chance to see the surrounding city for themselves.

Realizing that the schedule as originally designed ran the risk of leaving everyone adrift once lunch was over—the plans for optional field trips notwithstanding—the staff recognized that this could undermine the objective of building a sense of community. Carl would therefore see to it that there was a common room with refreshments and a video monitor. A five o'clock social hour would be scheduled each day, allowing people to congregate and coordinate their dinner plans. Should they choose to do so, they could also come back after dinner to watch the movies from which they would have seen excerpts during some of the morning sessions. The group would go out to dinner one evening.

It had been a long day, and the staff wound it down by going to dinner. The three men knew each other pretty well; Mariko and I were the newcomers. Over dinner, the group got into a discussion of their individual religious odysseys—certainly a different sort of introduction to each other. In the two previous workshops, these issues had never particularly been discussed. I wondered whether putting the subject out on the table had something to do with being in the South—just as I had been surprised to have a local cab driver open up a discussion about race. Coming from the North, I hadn't often run into either religion or race as breaking-the-ice sorts of topic, whether you were talking about academic gatherings or taxis.

The first meeting was to be held not in August but in June, as one of the staff had to be out of the country later that summer. Carl sent letters to everyone a month before, informing them about the logistics of housing, meals, arrivals, facilities, mail, schedule, weather and clothing, excursions, and my role. The letter was clear, and full of instructions. A week later, packets of all the readings would go out, with the request that they be read ahead of time.

Everyone would be living in one of the dormitories. There would be air conditioning to offset the heat, and use of the libraries and exercise facilities. One of Carl's letters to the group had stated up front that "All members of the workshop, staff and participants are expected to stay together on campus. That includes participants who live here in the city!" One or two of the latter may have gone home for one or two nights that week, but if they did, they were quiet enough about it that nothing ever became an issue. Carl would be bringing along his youngest son, who would camp out for the week in his room, spend the days in tennis classes and other activities, and come along with the group for many of the breakfasts and dinners. It is unusual to have a father caring for a child during an academic meeting and, if anything, it would, over the week, be positively remarked on by others in the group.

Day One: Sunday, June 11
A reception had been arranged, sponsored by the AAR, Lilly, the NEH, and the university's Religion Department. Although the instructions had directed everyone to dress casually, people were still feeling each other out; they all showed up looking ready to step into a classroom. By the next day, many of the men would quickly relax into shorts and T-shirts; the women, however, kept up the level of their style even when they did, occasionally, wear shorts. The interpretation of the clothing code varied to some degree with each workshop, but generally it was the men who more promptly and thoroughly took up the invitation to look casual.

The group went in to dinner. As all the lunches were to be, it had been catered by the university with the idea of giving people at least one fine meal a day together. When they had eaten, Carl drew them into a large, crooked circle that wove its way in between the tables, and invited them to talk about the kinds of courses they had been teaching, their research interests, and the questions they were bringing to this discussion. People spoke freely—these were familiar sorts of opening questions.

What quickly emerged as a general demographic feature of the group was that only six of the fifteen participants were actually from the South. (Of the staff, there were two.) It was precisely because they had come from other parts of the country and were now teaching in this region that the other nine had applied to this particular workshop, figuring that it would help them better understand the religious and cultural worlds into which they had moved. The implications of this configuration would gradually unfold over the following year.

Day Two: Monday, June 12

"What," said Carl, "do you find to be the defining characteristics, stereotypes, images, moods, social conditions, and ideologies that constitute 'the South' in your experience? What are the semantic ranges of 'the South'? In what ways is it an environment, a state of imagination, a site of contention, the focus of a mythology?" Standing next to a large pad of paper on an easel, he looked at the group sitting around the large table, bright morning sun filtering in through the plants hanging in front of the high windows surrounding the room.[16]

"I'm teaching in Tennessee—that's the *mid*-South, and I'm thought of as being in *middle* Tennessee. The subdivisions within the South get pretty specific."

"It's a sense of gentility, like a finishing school in Kentucky."

"The students express a lot of deference to authority—they say, 'Yes, sir,' to me. It's not like California, where I'm from. They're

---

[16] In order to frame general issues about the South, the following readings had been sent out in advance: Charles Foster, "A Selected Bibliography for Teachers of Religion," mimeo; O. Kendall White, Jr. and Daryl White, eds., *Religion in the Contemporary South: Diversity, Community, and Identity* (Athens, GA: University of Georgia Press), 1995; Raymond Williams, "Class," in *Keywords: A Vocabulary of Culture and Society* (New York: Oxford University Press), 1976, 1983; Charles Reagan Wilson, "Review of Eight New Works on Religion in the South," in *Religious Studies Review*, vol. 16, no. 3, July, 1990, pp. 205-10.

not trying to subvert that authority or make the classroom more egalitarian, and they're not altogether sure they want *me* to, either."

"I'm not from the South, either. As a female, I find my students are suspicious of a female teacher. They associate me with Mom or their grade school teacher. I'm different from the female students, and they're not sure they want to be like me."

"I come from California, too, and I see traces of the Confederacy alive and well here. There's a Confederate flag at the State House and one of the fraternities at my school celebrates the Confederacy and the image of Robert E. Lee."

"I grew up here," said Louis, "and even as an African-American I internalized a lot of the ideals of the Old South. Even if I was formally excluded from them, the ideal of chivalry and of a humane and nurturing culture—all the romanticized dimensions of the South—these were powerful images and I longed to appropriate them, at the same time as this was enormously complicated for me."

"That reminds me of what's known as the 'Gentleman's Rule' at some Southern men's colleges. It's assumed that a real gentleman has no need for it to be explained to him. The question is, what allows a person to be recognized as a legitimate owner of the rule?"

"As a Southerner, I'd say that part of the region's sense of itself is based on antagonism with other regions."

"I'm a Southern woman, and I see the external perception of Southerners—like on T.V.—as being stupid."

"I agree," said one of the men. "When I'm in an academic setting, say, at an AAR conference, I turn off my Southern identity and try to speak a blander academese. It's almost unconscious, now, but I do it because of the assumption that anyone with a Southern accent must be stupid."

"Ah," said Carl, who had been busily noting down the key issues on the large pad, allowing the group to track what had been said, "what if we play with the word 'accent' for a while?" Different people responded.

"There's a difference in the rhythm of speech, here. 'Heey, how ya *do*'in?' That's usually how students greet me. It's like a cultural cue. When I talk with people from the North, I feel as though I'm listening to verbal aerobics."

"My accent is a benefit in the classroom, because I sound like my students. My reaction to the sense of being put down as a Southerner is to have consciously kept my accent."

"I'm not from here, and I can tell that some of my students change the way they speak in class, probably to hide their accents."

"I'm from the West Indies, and my black students say to me, 'You have an accent!' Which is their way of saying they don't have one. Of course, to me, they do."

"Accent is very much related to identity politics," said Mariko. "I found that, in learning English as a Japanese woman."

"It's also related to how people got here," added someone else, "and to where they came from, and whether they were prisoners, slaves, indentured, or so on. There are the differences in how people survived the Civil War and reconstruction. 'South' is not just about a compass. A lot of the African languages don't have the sound 'th', or the words end with a vowel sound. That transformed the English they and their descendents spoke."

"Then there's the added issue of voice for Southern girls and women, as in 'a lady doesn't argue.'"

"Oh, but there have always been strong women down here, and once they have permission to voice what they think, some of them do. Others don't want to. Some look at their mothers, who've been divorced, and they don't want to go through what they think of as the 'punishment' for being strong. Some of them buy into Rush Limbaugh's equation of feminism with being a 'feminazi.'"

"Women students in the South—although it's not just in the South—in class will say, 'I'm not a feminist, but . . .' They don't want to be ostracized. It also has to do with the characteristics you need, to survive in a particular region—and I'm talking, here, about women who define themselves as Southerners."

"At my school," said one person, "there's the reputation that students are wealthy. That's not true any more, but the school has an ethic of service, so sometimes even though students have to work at jobs to help pay their way, they're also required to do work in the community. We see them burning out on service, which comes out of a religious and a class ethos."

"I think it's part of the institutional history of Southern colleges," said another person. "There has, historically, been an upper-class clientele, so at my school there are hundreds of service organizations. I didn't see that so much in California."

"How much," said Carl, "do your institutions identify as Southern, and if they do, how so? How does that play into the reality of the students who go there, the administration, being in the study of religion, and so on?"

"Mine was originally related to the Southern Baptist Convention," said a third person, "although there was a divorce in the eighties. But it's still seen by the public as a religious college. The students are middle and upper middle class, predominantly white, mostly Protestant, even though it's in an area where there's a lot of . immigration from all over the country, as well as from Latin American and the Caribbean. There aren't many Jews, not many Asians. There's a genteel southern atmosphere, a spirit of accommodation within the department. It's very much perceived as having a regional identity, even though the faculty are trying to broaden that. The biggest challenge is that some of the students come from wealthy Republican backgrounds—they're really into law and order. Then there are the Evangelical, charismatic types. But there are also people whose parents were hippies. It's a mixed population, in that sense."

"Virginia Baptists aren't the same as Southern Baptists," said someone else. "In 1979, the Fundamentalist elements took over, and for them, compromise is a dirty word. My school is independent, so they can't take that over. So if you're going to be a Southern Baptist, Virginia Baptist is the best thing to be! Half the students there are Baptists, and out of three courses in Old Testament, New Testament, and Intro to Philosophy, everybody has to take two. We're that way partly because of where we are, but also because we like being that way, as part of a traditional program. About half of the faculty are Baptist and so are about half of the students, but we also have Lutherans, Catholics—it's fairly ecumenical. The Jewish community helped to get the school located where it is. Chapel services are still required, but the rabbi was invited to speak along with the priest.

"But it's also very difficult to get my students to discuss things. They prefer that I'm the authority. I have to know them for a while to get them to disagree with me. I try to get them not to proof-text, and to teach them that the Bible is a dangerous text! Some people are there with a lot of misinformation; some students say you're going to hell; and others say, 'The hell with you!'"

"So," said Carl, "a number of these schools are similar in seeing themselves as being *in loco parentis*—which includes the moral, religious, and spiritual formation of the students, along with character building."

He turned to one of the women who taught at an all-women's college. "What about your school?"

"My school is affiliated with the Baptist Convention, and in its charter it's recognized as a Christian school related to character and values. I think because it's a woman's college, it's been overlooked by the denomination. We have some authority in appointing trustees, but they have to be Southern Baptists.

"The students, on the other hand, are no longer a majority of Southern Baptists. They're only about thirty percent. Now it's a real mix. But they're all required to take six hours in religion, so we have something of a captive audience. About fifteen to twenty percent are women coming back to school. They're more outspoken, so they fulfill what's often the 'male' role in the classroom. There are issues because of that, between the older and the younger women—the younger women don't want to be like that.

"And even though it's a women's school, we have a male president." The new speaker was a second woman, an African-American, who also taught at the same school. "There's a lot of camaraderie there; it's a more protective environment for the students. Some come because of tradition—they're the second or third generation in their families, and there's a family thing about the ceremony with the white dresses. 'My mother was a graduate,' they'll say, 'and my daughter will be, too.' Me, I see a plantation. If you come on campus, the president is white, most of the students are, too. Cooking and cleaning? African-Americans. The grounds? Hispanics. Repairs? Those are mostly done by white people. People hear about these jobs by word of mouth. In the fall, the faculty will be going to a workshop on diversity."

"Is tradition contested at all?" said Carl?

"In certain ways," said the first woman. "There are also a lot of East Asian and Southeast-Asian families coming in. They want a single-sex education for their daughters, so most of the classes have two or three students from these backgrounds. The faculty is sixty percent women, trying to be a leadership model for these women in their communities. As more and more women are expected to support themselves, some of the traditional programs, like Child Development, are growing."

"Lest anyone think," said Carl, "that just because a place is small, it's not complex!"

"At my school," said one of the men, 'the religious studies department has a good reputation, and we have about a dozen people on the faculty. It's not centered in Christianity; we also teach courses on Judaism and Islam. But it's a drop in the bucket, compared to the relative weight of any of the rest of the faculty. The university used to be considered regional and is now trying to become more national, with mixed success. You can't imagine the importance of the football team.

"The majority of students are white, and Baptist or Church of Christ or Pentecostal. Lots of them are born-againers. They listen politely to what I say, and then discount it, probably as something sent by Satan. It's the issue of deference. I thought some of the students I'd taught in the mid-West were not so good; the preparation of these students is substantially worse. It's a strong working-class background, for the most part. Many of the students are working many hours each week, just trying to get out. I've had a fair number who want to know how to do the minimum to get a D."

"Your state is especially rural, with a lot of power still with the locally elected officials," someone else said. "The state policies don't work their way down too well. Like, the state requires two years of another language, but the local areas don't necessarily teach it."

"Right," came the reply. "It's an instrumentalist ethos, to get one step further up from the working class, to the middle class. These different factors make some of the students not terribly engaged in the actual process of education."

"Having grown up in your state," said another person, "I can say that the attraction of that school *was* the football team. If an anthropologist were to study the South, they would see sports as a religious phenomenon."

"That's right. The football stadium is in the center of campus, and you can't find parking on the day of the games."

"One thing that strikes me about some of the contrasts," said Carl, "is that here you have a large department, that self-consciously teaches religious studies, with less foregrounding of the 'nurture' than at some of these other schools, yet in some ways the type of students may not be so different."

"I want to go back to the issue of voice," said Mariko. "The thing that strikes me is that the United States is very into regions. We see regionality in the styles of pedagogy, and people make a lot of assumptions about other styles. I notice the emphasis on getting students to talk, for example—along with the stigmatizing of silence. This is very different from Europe, where professors are supposed to *profess*. The Japanese university system was modeled after the German one, so that it's only when you get to a more advanced level—say, a seminar—that the students expect to have to speak more. Silence is not necessarily a sign of passivity. There is a cultural model here that assigns meaning to it."

"That can be related to the question of what is the *work* of the classroom," Carl replied. "There's a therapeutic model at one end, which is embedded in the ideal of character formation—of taking a person through late adolescence into early adulthood and building a certain kind of citizenship in relation to traditions that are assumed to be taken seriously, even as they are critiqued. For others, all of this is ancillary to the effort of upgrading their lives, social mobility, and professional training. We assume the idea that the discussion mode is more important, but how does that idea get constructed?"

"It all gives rise to a philosophy of education," said an African-American graduate student, who had been listening silently to the conversation until now. "What does it mean to speak and teach in one's *own* voice, or to learn in one's own voice? To what extent do people unconsciously mouth what a dominant culture says, like ventriloquists? What would it mean to teach in our true voices?"

"What does a 'true voice' mean?" said Carl.

"Beginning with a regional accent, I'm asking how we've been shaped by a dominant culture. How much has it been subjected to this ventriloquist phenomenon? How much do we teach students how to subvert that?"

"That's tied in to the issue of 'professing,'" added someone else. "We supposedly bracket that. But how much does—or should— my true voice inform my teaching? If it doesn't, why not?"

"Mariko, you brought up the issue of silence in the classroom. I also think there's a question of engagement. It includes not only talking, but writing."

"Right," added another person. "I assign a lot of in-class writing. Often the written responses are more thoughtful and allows students to develop an authorial voice in class."

"There are a lot of different silences," said someone else. "The silence of thinking, of not wanting to be there, of being overwhelmed by something. Both voice and silence have so many different meanings in a class."

"Just like they express so many things about learning," said Jack. "You know, I had a shocking experience in graduate school. We were required to read a book on learning theory. It happened, by the way, to be extremely dull. But it described twenty-one different theories of learning (this was in the sixties), and they were all grounded in research. And you know what? They *all* work."

The time for the session was up, and Carl moderated the formal discussion to a close. It was clear, by that point, that his style was one of prompting other people to speak not so much to him, but to each other which, by the end of the session, they were actively doing. The group commented, as they closed, on how talking about region makes anecdotes inevitable, because of the specific variations in which each person found him- or herself or because of how each person experienced a subject like voice and accent.

What was also already becoming apparent was the degree of difference in how various participants identified or did not identify with the region itself. This surfaced, for example, in talking about the ways in which the South is alternately stigmatized and romanticized. Both men and women participants from outside the region had described their experience of being perceived as outsiders suspected of trying to undermine core values and beliefs, at the same time as their students often expect them to play the role of the authority in the classroom. Those who favored a more egalitarian classroom dynamic found this difficult. Participants from within the region, on the other hand, were able to point to less consciously held images of the South that were being expressed, and to describe how they themselves feel compelled, at times, to compensate for these in their own academic lives.

As was usually the case at the workshops, these questions spilled into the conversation over lunch. There, for example, one of the professors from the women's college who was Southern born-and-raised, described the ethos of politeness instilled in Southerners, particularly women. The white dresses worn at graduation, for example, are a remnant from nineteenth-century women's schools (the same, I noted, held true for the women's college I attended in the North). She talked about her own identity as a Southern woman— how these different values continued to influence her, and which ones she had found herself rethinking.

When the staff met toward the end of the afternoon, they were delighted by how well the morning's discussion had gone. They felt that already people were asking questions they might not be able to ask elsewhere, and even taking a chance on putting themselves in the more vulnerable position attending on some of these self-disclosures.

They then turned to the next day's session on race and the South, which was to be led by Louis. In what would become part of their working style together, they listened to what he, as discussion leader, had in mind, and offered suggestions. While not precisely an instance of team-teaching, it afforded the front-man (in this case, Louis) the occasion to get input from the team while still being the person responsible for the session. How, he was thinking aloud, would he use the materials he had in mind—particularly a number of film clips—to link the issue of one's own race with one's teaching.

"You're employing different kinds of voices," Jack observed. "Not Dubois, and the like, but voices from pop culture, ethnographic voices. It raises the question of *whose* voices we attend to."

At the same time, Louis thought, it would be useful to integrate a number of small-group strategies. After some discussion, the team decided they would have people count off into groups of three and four, giving each small group two or three questions to head off outside and discuss. They would then all come together again.

Over dinner, several of the participants asked Jack and Louis about the possibility of developing support teams to help each other with their teaching projects. Could everyone be given information on what everyone else was doing as soon as possible, so they could set up these kinds of teams for themselves and meet on their own? Jack and Louis agreed to pass the request on to Carl who, when he heard it, went into gear to compile everyone's project summaries and get copies made, to pass out the next morning. The team, as they talked about this later, agreed that the move itself was clearly an initiative from some of the participants to appropriate the workshop in all the best ways; it should therefore be fully supported.

Two points bear noting. First, the staff had clearly succeeded in creating an environment in which the participants found it possible to propose an initiative of their own. This, in part, had to do with the personalities of the participants themselves and, in part, with those of the staff. Second, the staff's willingness and ability to be light on their feet in responding to this request—as they would be to others— meant that participant suggestions were folded into the planning for the week almost as quickly as they arose. Either that, or it was made clear how and when they would come up for discussion at a later point. This, I suggest, meant that there was never any particularly felt need for a Rebellion.[17]

---

[17] Ironically, one of the original ideas discussed and then discarded by the staff had been to have a session on "triumphs and tragedies" in the classroom—an equivalent to the session on best and most embarrassing teaching moments that had been attempted in New England. There is no way of knowing how it would have worked in this particular group, however, as the staff decided against it.

That evening, a group gathered to watch *Daughters of the Dust*.[18] The film, set in 1902 on one of the sea islands off the coast of Georgia and North Carolina, shows an African-American family— particularly their women—and the final ceremony being held prior to some of them leaving to journey to the North. Among other things, the film portrays the integrating of Christian and African religious practices and understandings.

As they waited for others to arrive, people sat somewhat stiffly around the room, still in the mode of making conversation with each other. I was asked if I would be writing an evaluation of the program at the end—a notion which, not surprisingly, came out of one description of my role as an evaluator. The very idea appeared to make a number of people uncomfortable, and illustrated the pitfalls in terminology, particularly insofar as it can jeopardize the possibility for trust within a group. (In a subsequent conversation, one of the participants noted to me that she, too, had found this to be the case in a different project. The term "evaluator," she thought, had put people off and made them a little afraid of her.) I quickly explained that this was to be a thick description of the experience which, it was hoped, would allow other planners in the future to replicate what seemed best about the whole experience. I also made a mental note to myself to suggest the term be reconsidered.

Day Three: Tuesday, June 13
The group had reconvened, this time in the large-windowed seminar room where most of their gatherings that week would take place. With some of them sitting around the seminar table, and the others in a surrounding ring, they began the session.[19]

---

[18]   Julie Dash, *Daughters of the Dust* (New York: Kino on Video, 1992).

[19]   The readings assigned for the morning's session were: Julie Dash, *Daughters of the Dust: The Making of an African American Woman's Film.* (New York: The New Press, 1992), pp. 84-7; Jack Epstein, "Ancestor Worship in the Deep, Deep South" in *U.S. News and World Report*, May 29, 1995; Matthew Glass, "Producing Patriotic Inspiration at Mount Rushmore" in *The Journal of the American Academy of Religion*, vol. 62, no. 2, Summer, 1994, pp. 265-83; Wardell J. Payne, ed., *Directory of African American Religious Bodies: A Compendium by the Howard University School of Divinity,* (Washington, D.C.: Howard University Press, 1991), p. 131, 133 (on Black Jews and Black Hebrews); Tex Sample, *Hard Living People & Mainstream*

"This morning," said Louis, "I'm going to do a couple of new things—I haven't done them before, but I'd like to try them out and I hope you'll bear with me." In that singe stroke, he legitimized both experimentation and the taking of risks, at the same time as he recruited the group's support. (They, after all, were not the one's who would be on the spot.)

"We're going to take a look at some comparative iconography through images of two sites—Stone Mountain, and Mount Rushmore; then at what I call "Heritage and Quest," through some images of black syncretisms, retentions, and adoptions; and finally at some connections between new immigrants and class. Along the way I want to introduce the concept of what I call 'strategic self-disclosure,' and think about how that can play a part in what we do in the classroom." Now, everyone knew—or could imagine they knew—what lay ahead for the morning.

He directed the group to count off in pairs, and to review with each other their particular ethnic and class backgrounds. The risk was diminished by having to name things to only one other individual. Suddenly, personal histories no longer hung invisible over each person in the room, but began to take on ghostly form as people fleshed out these parts of their lives. After a while, he called everyone back together.

"I'm going to ask all the people with Irish heritage to stand up." Eight stood. "Everybody clap for them," he said, beginning the round of applause.

"How about French heritage?" Most of the eight sat down, as others rose to their feet, looking a little sheepish amidst applause.

"Scotch?" he said. The clusterings so far did not follow mainstream stereotypes, in that most included both black and white members of the group. One by one, Louis worked his way through

---

Christians. (Nashville: Abingdon Press, 1993), pp. 44-60; Merrill Singer, "The Southern Origin of Black Judaism," in Hans A. Baer and Yvonne Jones, eds., *African Americans in the South*. (Athens, GA: University of Georgia Press, 1992), pp. 123-38; Gayle White, "Black Hebrews find stability after twenty five years" in *Atlanta Journal-Constitution*, August 13, 1994; Charles Reagan Wilson, *Baptized in Blood: The Religion of the Lost Cause, 1865-1920*. (Athens, GA: University of Georgia Press, 1980), 37-57; 100-18.

different groups, eventually asking for help to recall those he might have overlooked. Each group was met with applause.

When he had come to the end of the list, he explained that this was an exercise drawn from diversity workshops he ran. It was intended not just to name these aspects of people's backgrounds, but to celebrate them and their survival against the odds. Without the celebration represented by the applause, the disclosure of ethnicity or class background could collapse into a negative piece of one's identity through shame and invidious comparisons growing out of cultural conditioning. This way, however, it created subtle possibilities for alliances between unlikely people, through the recognition of common roots where one might not have thought to find them. The exercise as a whole was intended to further an environment of openness and association at the same time as it gave a positive spin to difference.

Stone Mountain was a monument to the Confederacy and to the romanticized past of the South. Carved into the side of a 1,686 foot high domed granite mountain in northwest-central Georgia by Gutzon Borglum, later the sculptor of Mount Rushmore, the huge carving depicted heroically huge figures of Robert E. Lee, Jefferson Davis, and Stonewall Jackson riding gallantly by on horseback.[20] A whole state park and tourist center had risen up around it.

Louis passed out tourist brochures and turned on a clip from a promotional video. The film rounded the bend into a reconstructed plantation manor, the guide to which was a white woman in period costume who explained the details of the rooms. A few scenes later, the camera went down into the kitchen, where an African-American woman in a dark-blue polo shirt and slacks was making cornbread. She said nothing and she didn't look up at the camera; a voice-over explained what she was doing, and continued explaining as the camera went outside and looked at the slave quarters. The scene then quickly shifted to a woman in a bikini and sunglasses lying on one of the Georgia beaches.

The group, jarred by the switch, talked about these three representations of women. Who had a voice and who did not? Had

---

[20] Borglum himself did not live to complete the project, which was not finished until 1970, by others.

the sexually charged scene been slipped in to undercut the possible effects of thinking back to slavery? How did history get milled in ways intended to bury the pain? How to use these kinds of materials to help students become conscious of the manipulated dimensions of historical presentation in their own back yards?

The group had been asked to read a piece on "the politics that necessarily shapes religious landscapes"—a treatment of conflicting ways of seeing the memorial carved by Gutzon Borglum into the side of Mount Rushmore in the Black Hills of South Dakota.[21] This provided background for the next excerpt, a segment from a PBS special, *The Way West*, showing discussions about the memorial, which had been occupied by Native American activists during the summer of 1971. The Lakota people interviewed in the documentary talked about their experience of stolen place.

Someone in the group raised the use in classrooms of texts like *Black Elk Speaks*—a text written by a Catholic and subsequently translated into English.[22] Different people contributed what they knew about the book. They wondered together about how one might elicit these kinds of interactive observations in a class. How, too, to prevent student from completely relativing the sacrality of a text, assuming its inauthenticity, or rationalizing that "my way is real religion, and that isn't"? How to introduce a certain existential vertigo without leaving students alone in their vulnerability?

"I think it may be by disclosing your own vulnerability in this regard," said Louis. "Otherwise, the text is vulnerable and so is student, but you are not. The real challenge lies in inducing and supporting a tolerance for shared ambiguity, while we avoid students' experiencing *us* as watching them fall. The issue is how to create a community of solidarity."

Then, the group continued, there were other issues of meaning held around different monuments for different groups. The Lakota had talked about how Mount Rushmore, for them, symbolized not a

---

[21] Matthew Glass, "Producing Patriotic Inspiration at Mount Rushmore" in *The Journal of the American Academy of Religion*, vol. 62, no. 2, Summer, 1994, p. 265.

[22] Black Elk, *Black Elk Speaks; Being the Life Story of a Holy Man of the Oglala Sioux*, as told through John G. Neihardt (Lincoln, University of Nebraska Press, 1961)

glorified past but the hope of reclaiming lost lands. It was an emblem of what remained to be done, raising the issue of how to detoxify a site and detoxify the history. How, for example, could descendents meet in ways that didn't perpetuate the polarization? How to address the reality of living among the descendents of the victims and the perpetrators?

The group discussed how painful these issues are and how one has to take great care that people, in the process, not go numb. For themselves, there had been the relief of taking a break, but maybe having a class go into twos or threes to talk might allow a similar release. They recognized the importance of anticipating that point and attending to it. It all had to do with the necessity of helping students unlearn a world-view and re-order their sense of things, coupled with the necessity of creating a space within which this could take place. It paralleled what happens for some students when studying the Bible.

This led Louis into the next segment—the exploration of African practices layered under Christian consciousness, not yet retrieved or in the process of retrieval, remembered as fragments of a heritage. He showed a clip from the film *To Sleep With Anger* , a story about an African-American "toby," or "conjure man." He handed out a few pages from the screenplay for *Daughters of the Dust* and showed the corresponding clip from the film, talking about the pieces of tradition and language that had come together—like the way the Bible was simultaneously a Christian book and a conjure text. In a scene showing "the Root Revival of Love," a religious ritual of spirit regeneration, the strong old conjure woman, Nana Paezant, takes a "hand" she has made, wrapped in a chain with a St. Christopher's medal, and places it on top of a Bible. She holds it out for the others to kiss as, she says, "It is full of *me*."

Both excerpts, it was noted, thematized touch. Nana holds the power of the Bible bound with roots; the pastor, in *To Sleep With Anger*, also holds the Bible, but his wife is the one with the herbs and the ability to touch. Here, there are different understandings of the soul being represented. The film illustrated some of the ways in which there are no pure deposits of tradition; rather, all traditions are amalgams. The work of culture here, as elsewhere, is one of bricolage. How, then, to see the ways in which things are perpetuated and sustained?

The discussion to this point had been an illustration of how to mix film clips, texts, and self-disclosure deliberately undertaken.[23]

"I've probably tried to do too much this morning," said Louis ruefully, "but let's go on next to the final piece for this part of the discussion on heritage and quest, the article on the Black Hebrews."

Founded in the 1960s, the Black Hebrews are a group of African Americans who understand themselves to be the descendents of the lost tribes of Israel and, therefore, Jews by birth. Identifying with the Hebrews instead of the Christians, they are a case of the biblical story of freedom from slavery not taking a Christian direction. They understand this as resistance to the adoption of an oppressor's religion, and retention of their own. In contrast, a work like Martin Bernal's *Black Athena* pulls together image of Greeks, the mid-nineteenth century Indo-European hypothesis, Aryan mythology, race theory, and anti-Semitism.[24]

"Both of them represent the issue of having historical status in the world, and of origins," said Louis. How to deal with this in religion classes?

"I tell students, 'Let me help you make your case stronger,'" said Jack. "I provide counter-arguments against which they can test their own, so that they have to look at where they hold up and where they don't."

---

[23] Readings suggested during this segment of the discussion included: Emily Apter and William Pietz, eds., *Fetishism as Cultural Discourse*, (Ithaca, N.Y.: Cornell University Press, 1993); St. Clair Drake, *Black Folk Here and There: An Essay in History and Anthropology*. (Los Angeles: Center for Afro-American Studies, University of California, 1990); Robert E. Hood, *Begrimed and Black: Christian Traditions on Blacks and Blackness*. (Minneapolis, Minn.: Augsburg Fortress, 1994); Zora Neale Hurston, *Moses, Man of the Mountain*, (Urbana: University of Illinois Press, 1939) and *Mules and Men*, (Philadelphia, London: J. B. Lippincott Company, 1935) (The latter is about Hoodoo, African American songs, the formulae of hoodoo doctors, the paraphernalia of conjure, and the prescriptions of root doctors.); P.K. McCary, interpreter, *The Black Bible Chronicles*. (New York: African American Family Press, 1993: Theophus H. Smith, *Conjuring Culture: Biblical Formations of Black Culture*. (New York: Oxford University Press, 1994).

[24] Martin Bernal, *Black Athena: the Afroasiatic Roots of Classical Civilization* (London: Free Association Books, 1987).

The final section that morning would briefly touch on the question of new immigrants and class, particularly in the overlay of ethnicity and class. The reading had come from *Hard Living People & Mainstream Christians*,[25] a collection of life stories told by the hard living, and interviews with pastors of churches who sought to minister to them. How did the two experience each other?

"How does your own institution hurt and displace students," said Louis, "especially the ones from working class backgrounds?"

"*The Hidden Injuries of Class*[26] talks about this," one person said. "It describes the resentment, envy, and awe experienced by the lower class toward people with the leisure and resources to craft themselves, and how these feelings sometimes lead to violence, like the bombing in Oklahoma City, or the targeting of abortion clinics."

"I come from a working class background," said one person, with tears in her voice. "This is not a topic I can come to without a great deal of pain."

"My father always used to talk about how my grandmother worked as a domestic, cleaning at my university, " said Louis, "and here I was a professor at the same school. He was so proud of that. But I always felt a kind of shame for having advantages that my grandmother never did."

"My grandmother was a domestic too," said someone else. "But I always admired how she had been able to do so much. I used to wonder at her ability to provide so much for her family."

It was time to end the discussion.

"I think in the future," said another person, "that this kind of strategic self disclosure requires us to make time before we end a class—I mean, *we* need room not just to end, and that has to be true of a class, as well."

"I'd like to leave you with three questions to think about," said Louis, nodding at her comment. "First, how does your own class and/or ethnic background interact with those of your students, with your teaching setting, and with your subject matter? Second, whose

---

[25] Tex Sample, *Hard Living People & Mainstream Christians*. (Nashville: Abingdon Press, 1993), pp. 44-60

[26] Richard Sennett and Jonathan Cobb, *The Hidden Injuries of Class* (New York, Vintage Books, 1972).

voice do you select and value in the materials you use? And third, how do you use such materials optimally (however you define the term) in your particular setting?"

With that, the group recessed. Louis had succeeded in modeling the use of a range of commercial, documentary, feature, and artistic films, all strategically excerpted, and the integration of these with a spectrum of texts—articles from academic journals and newspapers, chapters from books, tourist brochures. He had illustrated issues of content and of group interaction in thinking about the construction of sites, identities, and religious traditions, as well as introducing the issue of strategic self-disclosure and its use in the classroom.

That afternoon, many of the group went on a field trip to the Martin Luther King, Jr. Center for Non-Violent Social Change, and to the Ebenezer Baptist Church, and then to the APEX Museum of African-American Arts, all sites that complemented the morning's discussion. Some went from there to the Coca Cola museum. By the end of the afternoon, the professorial personae had softened further, and the people behind them come out a little more. By the time they got together to watch the full length of *To Sleep With Anger* that evening, you could see it in they way they were sitting around with each other, and cracking jokes during the movie. The solemnity of the night before had disappeared.

Day Four: Wednesday, June 14

The staff hadn't had a chance to meet the day before, but they had already pretty much decided on the format for the morning session, which was to focus on gender in the South. They would, themselves, become a panel, with each of them saying something about the question from the perspective of his or her own work.[27]

---

[27] The readings assigned for this section were: Judith Butler, "Subjects of Sex/Gender/Desire," in *Gender Trouble: Feminism and the Subversion of Identity.* (New York: Routledge, 1990), pp. 1-34; Joan W. Scott, "Experience," in *Feminists Theorize the Political*, Judith Butler and Joan W. Scott, eds., (New York: Routledge, 1992), pp. 22-40; Donna Haraway, "Ecce Homo, Ain't (Ar'n't) I a Woman, and Inappropriate/d Others: The Human in a Post-Humanist Landscape," in *Feminists Theorize the Political*, Judith Butler and Joan W. Scott, eds., (New York: Routledge, 1992), pp. 86-100.

Carl talked about the history of his department and the influence of gender studies on his own research and writing. He talked about how, particularly with the help of women colleagues, he had learned to think about the issue of gender construction as a motif working its way through an entire course. Like race and regionality, it was something that permeated our entire identity.

For Louis, gender in the South involved an irony. It had long been a familiar idea to him that people of color were not the only ones to have a race, although white people sometimes seemed to find it more difficult to think about this idea in connection with themselves. It had taken him longer to internalize the idea that women were not the only ones with a gender, and that there was some point to there being a men's movement in which men were also the subjects of liberation. His own work on the issue of diversity had led him to think about men as socially conditioned into being agents of domination, and increasingly he had been reflecting on the idea of men falling along the range of gendered existence.

In a larger context, he thought, the work of the men's movement to reclaim manhood in American culture—however much it had come under fire from some feminists as the pursuit after an earlier mode of dominant virility—seemed to him more accurately to be about learning to think about multiple dimensions of male identity. There was the identity to be found through rituals of manhood and initiation and, for him, rituals coming out of his African heritage. The movement had also been a part of his own thinking about issues of violence and abuse, and about how men learned to be the agents of both. Southern manhood in particular, he argued, had experienced a loss of virility after the Civil War, and had been refashioned into a myth of a lost cause merged with constructs of Arthurian chivalry, a Greco-Roman heritage, and Christian images of the crucified South. Out of the defeat had arisen a sense of emasculation, a lost Southern manhood, a pathos, all of which had led to a need to vindicate and reclaim the idealization of that manhood. Cycles of violence and oppression had resulted. In the course of it all, women had been rewritten into vessels of purity.

What would lead the way out of that captivity, that nexus, without polarizing it further or reifying the toxicity of the system as a whole? Could men of color, and women from the different races, participate in deconstructing how they and Southern men had been conditioned and victimized by that experience, in ways that could lead them to experience reconciliation?

Jack, steeped as he was in theories about how people learn, had thought about the question from a different angle, and had thought about it in relation to the group's first discussion about of the voices of students. How did we experience these voices, he wondered, whether as silent or soft-spoken, and how could issues of learning be talked about from the perspective of gender and its influences on knowing? He had found the work of both Bill Perry and Mary Belenky particularly helpful in talking about silence, although almost none of the people writing about gender had said much about the influence of culture as a significant variable. It was also useful, he found, to draw on a developmental perspective, and to assume that there was a gender factor in how people learn at different stages in their lives. Men often focused on the aspect of abstract, absolute knowing, as Carol Gilligan had pointed out, whereas women seemed to move more readily into a contextual take on things. Any classroom will include such a range of student ways of knowing.

If the patterns of pedagogy reward only one style, and recognize only one type of student as absolute or independent knowers, then the other kinds of students have to respond to that model at the expense of their own strengths. If the course is an elective, these other students self-select out and go, instead, to courses where their own styles are better rewarded. It is possible to design a course that identifies and rewards all styles, just as it is possible to formulate guidelines aimed at teaching other modes of knowing. And, he added, although we usually forget it, we bring a mode of knowing of our own that colors how we understand everybody else's.[28]

---

[28] Books suggested in connection with this discussion included: Mary Field Belenky, et. al, *Women's Ways of Knowing: The Development of Self, Voice, and Mind*, (New York: Basic Books, 10th anniversary edition, 1997); Carol Gilligan, *In a Different Voice: Psychological Theory and Women's Development.* (Cambridge, Mass.: Harvard University Press, 1993); bell hooks, *Teaching to Transgress: Education as the Practice of Freedom*, (New York: Routledge, 1994); William G. Perry, Jr., *Forms of Intellectual and Ethical*

Mariko, as a historian, added a different spin. There are, she suggested, two frameworks in which to consider the subject of gender, sex, and sexuality—the three of which, she felt, could not be altogether separated. Gender, first of all, is a matter of identity politics, as is race. Second, it is part of a larger project of learning to recognize the process by which present-day formulations have emerged, particularly those which now seem self-evident—like the idea of being men and women, as biologically based in the body. The alternative involves coming to see such ideas, instead, as the outcome of documentable, historical processes. People did not, for example, necessarily think as we do about such things in the eighteenth century, although ideas developed in earlier centuries may persist in different forms. (Just because a particular construction arose in the nineteenth century, it doesn't just go away.) In reference to pedagogical issues, it means trying to get some sense of how disciplines like Queer Theory are important to heterosexual people in understanding the broader constructions of gender. How does one bring such theory into the classroom, when identity formation in general is such a volatile issue?

There are parallels between race and gender as structurally similar problems, she went on. If we see both categories of difference as parallel and concurrent, even as they are distinct, then we recognize some of the ways in which a person's identity is composite. There are pitfalls here, too. When we talk about "a non-white woman" or "a bi-sexual black," underlying these descriptions is often a heterosexual white male as the unmarked category. Furthermore, all such categories are composite. A black heterosexual woman is not one thing; neither is a lesbian white woman. Each expresses multiple dimensions of identity which are interrelated, parallel , and all historically conditioned and intermeshed. The issue is to recognize race and gender as interrelated categories.

The deeper objective for her, said Mariko, was to discern the ways in which these categories are not universal, but historical and provincial, and represent deeply vested interests. They have, in other words, a political character. For example, both race and gender have

---

Development in the College Years: A Scheme, (New York: Holt, Rinehart and Winston, 1968).

been biologized as ways of distinguishing people, as though both were pre-culturally "real." We take them to be natural, as simple biological realities. This strong appeal to positivity masks the vested interests behind the categories and hides the politics they represent.

"I resort to history," she added, "not to make something go away, but to put the present in context."

One of the participants, interrupted her, "But to say that race and gender are not biological terms—to argue that there is *no* underlying biological reality—is also to make a biological claim."

"Yesterday," replied Mariko, "we talked about differences between people as though they were pre-culturally determined— inner tendencies manifesting in the peripheries of the body, like skin color, the shape of a nose. These kinds of thinking are related to nineteenth-century ideas of criminal types."

Descent, she went on, like bloodline had, until the nineteenth century been the privilege of the aristocracy. It was related to laws of inheritance, purity, and privilege. These kinds of purity issues were built into theories of race, which were also tied into developments in philology (which, like theology, was deeply implicated). During that time, the idea of a "purebred" came into the picture. But this was not at all "natural." In fact, the state of nature, from a "purebred" perspective, is mongrel. Therefore, the recognition of these constructions must make us all the more suspicious of the ways we think about a topics like gender or race.[29]

With that, the panel brought their presentations to a close. Carl said, "We've opened up four different ways of getting at the issue of gender. We're going to divide into small groups now and give you a kick-off question to talk about: in your own institutional setting, how are these issues having an impact on your teaching and on how you formulating your courses?"

When they came back together, each group reported on its discussion. The first group talked about the authority attaching to

---

[29] Books suggested in connection with this part of the discussion included: Henry A. Giroux, ed., *Postmodernism, Feminism, and Cultural Politics: Redrawing Educational Boundaries*, (Albany: State University of New York Press, 1991); Thomas Walter Laqueur, *Making Sex: Body and Gender from the Greeks to Freud*, (Cambridge, Mass.: Harvard University Press, 1990).

what a professor says. Even if one states that an idea represents a current theory, it is hard not to make what students take to be truth claims. Students often have difficulty with the idea of rhetoric as the statement of a position, which may not necessarily be making a truth claim. They worried about developmental theory, for the ways in which it is not only descriptive, but also prescriptive. What kind of "development" is favored, they wondered, and who is left out? They also compared notes about their experiences with some of the men in their classes, confessing to their difficulties.

"You know, I've never talked with anyone about this before, but the students I have the hardest time getting to talk in class are the men," said one man. He laughed. "So, I guess that's a piece of strategic self-disclosure."

Where had the other groups gone with the discussion? One had puzzled the question of whether you make every category a variable at the same time. In addressing questions of difference, we are in a language game, to which we try to state the operating rules. But if we recognize this game, then which game should *we* be playing? In doing so, how do we work for change? There is, they thought, a practical need for the students in a class to be clear about some of their own contexts—what we, for example, expect from them, what the academy expects, what the professional world expects. At the same time, there has to be a critical bracketing of these expectations. We may use a particular term, but use it provisionally even as we work to find ways to subvert it.

The third group had come up with two major issues, both of them spin-offs from the constructedness of gender, and related to the question of pedagogical style. In an introductory class, they wondered, how do you go about deconstructing things when the students are not yet aware that they even exist, much less matter? How to bring a subject to the point of even being at stake? In thinking about teaching styles, they noted how difficult it can sometimes be to get men to talk in a class, particularly when one tries to promote a more "open" or "safe" teaching style and classroom environment. Does this approach, they wondered, somehow undermine what these men expect in a classroom, and is the very image of a "nurturing environment" one that even feminists are entirely comfortable with? How to foster a setting in which students also learn to tolerate discomfort?

Finally, the fourth group suggested, they had focused on certain situations in the classroom, their questions sparked by Louis's previous presentation: how, in other words, to talk about class in relation to these other issues of race and gender? That had been one theme. Another had been the tension between nature and nurture, and the risks of essentialism. Why, they asked themselves, did it need to be so either/or? They had played out these ideas in thinking about different classrooms: how, for example, might one talk about gender in a group where feminism has become a dirty word, or about AIDS in one where any discussion of sexuality is an explosive topic? What about interracial marriage in certain settings? The challenge, it seemed to them, was to figure out how to balance the specific and particular on the one hand, with the abstract and analytical on the other, without sacrificing the latter.

As representatives from each group made their reports, Louis noted their central points on the large pad of newsprint. At the conclusion of each report, the other members in each group nuanced and supplemented what had been said, and he added notes from their comments. Before the next group began, he tore off the sheet and taped it to the wall, allowing the group to see its discussion all at once. Increasingly, during their subsequent remarks, people pointed to these earlier comments, drawing comparisons, and synthesizing the discussion as a whole.

Some of their questions spilled over into an optional gathering that afternoon, which focused on challenges people had run into in the designing of introductory courses. All of the staff attended, as did seven of the participants. Going around the room, each person spoke about his or her own particular concerns. How well, for example, does a traditional model for an introduction to the Bible really serve students and what they want in establishing a relationship with the text? How to get around an increasingly consumer model of education? What to privilege in the designing of a syllabus?

"What is it," said Jack during the discussion that followed, "that you want them to be able to *do*? What skills, in other words, is the course designed to teach? Are they learning how to read, for example, and if so, then what? The syllabus is your statement of intent about such things."

"The site of the religious is not only beliefs, but also texts, practices, social realities, and bodies," added Carl. "I'd say we're trying to figure out how to introduce them to the reading of each of these things."

"If you think of a syllabus as a contract," said Jack, "then you include a statement of purpose. You can set up a contract for grades with your students, explaining carefully what each grade means. Used as a teaching tool, this can be useful."

"I do something like that," said one person. "In a course of thirty or forty students, I design three models for how they can do the course. They can contract to do one of these. It's also a way of dealing with the diversity of the classroom, and with the differing ranges of experience."

Jack nodded. "You can negotiate the syllabus, too, asking what they would like along the way, and making notes of that in your own copy. It's also a good idea to tell them as you go what *you* are doing, so they know how their thoughts are being factored in."

In the staff meeting, the four noticed that there had been no signs of a revolt. Having been led to expect one, they thought nevertheless that, unless they were about to be caught completely off guard, there seemed to be little evidence of anything brewing. Why was that? They speculated that it might be due to the lack of hierarchy they had tried to establish, and to their efforts to create a collegial environment. Each of them had also engaged in various conversations with different participants from the start, and had been reporting whatever critiques they had heard. These conversations allowed the team, as a whole, to have a sharper sense of occasional individual difficulties. Particularly where they wondered if various participants might be having a hard time with some aspect of a discussion, they agreed that one of them would make a point of checking it out.

The staff, in turn, had tried to incorporate suggestions as quickly as possible into their planning. This had the effect of creating a different paradigm for allowing the participants to influence the workshop and make it their own. Moreover, this process had begun within the first day or two. The fluid, behind-the-scenes interplay between the staff contributed to the generally informal atmosphere they had succeeded in creating within the group as a whole, making it all the easier for people to raise ideas and suggestions in the plenary meetings. Consequently, there wasn't a great deal against which to rebel.

It was now mid-week, and the staff had figured that everyone would be ready for some time out. Carl had thought a Moroccan restaurant would be conducive to conviviality. The food was good, he said, and there was a belly-dancer.

It was a chancy move. There were a number of more conservative religious folks in the company who might have been made ill at ease by the latter, not to mention the possible repercussions among some of the women in the group. Carl simply remembered it as a fun place and a setting, as he would later write, in which "each person got to experience being an outsider."[30]

The van ride over, which seemed to wind on, block after block, dissolved many of the riders into laugher. The restaurant itself consisted of large rooms, dimly lit with brass lamps, the floors covered with carpets. Because it was the middle of the week, the place was nearly empty. The group was led a corner recess ringed with low brass tables and slightly raised, carpeted platforms to sit on. The tables, which were small and side by side, split most of the group into pairs.

It was a long, languid evening. The food at breakfast and, for most people, at dinner, had so far been indifferent—a detail which had not escaped them. They were therefore ready to enjoy an evening of different fare. When the belly dancer did come out and make her circles round and round the floor, one or two people quietly kept their backs turned. Still, another of the more conservative was heard, at the end of the evening to chuckle and say, "I'd give that dancer *my* car." It seemed to have gone all right.

---

[30] From a director's report to the AAR, the Lilly Endowment Inc., and the National Endowment of the Humanities.

Day Five: Thursday, June 15

Jack, Carl informed the group, had been awarded a small grant for some of his research.

"Well, guys," said Carl, who was wearing an Indiana Jones T-shirt that read, "The Adventure Continues," "if we run low on funds, at least we'll know where to dip into!" Jack's grant quickly became a running joke in the group.

Jack laughed, and said, "This morning, Mariko and I are going to talk about the emergence of religious studies as an academic discipline and about changes in its curriculum, as a way of locating ourselves and our institutions in these broader trajectories. We hope that it will help us identify some of the forces that assist and limit our vision of what we are teaching." The two would give presentations for roughly forty-five minutes, there would be time for some questions, and then the group would split into smaller discussion sections as they had the day before.[31]

"I would like," said Mariko, starting out, "to focus on three moments. First, the birth of the modern university in nineteenth-century Germany, as a site and center of intellectual life of a kind that had not existed since the high Middle Ages. Second, the nineteen-sixties and seventies, when religious studies as we know the field came into being in American universities. Ours has been the great century of departments! Third, is the present, as we who have lived off the legacy of the sixties and seventies, now feel something shifting and perhaps even falling apart."

In the nineteenth century, she continued, the rise of the university as a center was also the birth of the modern university. It was a German model, one that rode on the emergence of the new

---

[31]   The readings assigned for the morning's session looked at issues in the study of religion over the past thirty years: Karl D. Hartzell and Harrison Sasseer, eds., *The Study of Religion on the Campus Today: Selected Papers from the Stony Brook Conference on Religion as an Academic Discipline.* (Washington, D.C.: Association of American Colleges, 1967); William Scott Green, "The Difference Religion Makes" in *Journal of the American Academy of Religion*, vol. 62, no. 4 , Winter, 1994, pp. 1191-1207; and Richard B. Miller, Laurie L. Patton, and Stephen H. Webb, "Rhetoric, Pedagogy, and the Study of Religions" in *Journal of the American Academy of Religion*, vol. 62, no. 3, Fall, 1994, pp. 819-50.

sciences (*Wissenschaften*) and on new understandings of human life. It was an entire *geist*.

"The delineation of this," she went on, "and here I'm relying on the work of Immanuel Wallerstein, was the rise of the five disciplines of the social sciences—that is, the human sciences. The first three of these included the new disciplines with which to study the West; the other two were to study the rest. These first three demarcations were in line with a liberal ideology and its understanding of modern society: political science as the study of the political process, economics as the study of economic processes, and sociology, which included everything else that didn't fit into the first two. For the study of the rest of the world, there were the other two disciplines, ethnology and anthropology—that is, the study 'primitives' and 'preliterate' people, using ethnographic methods to write about those who did not write. Those who *did* write, but who were not thought of as 'modern,' became the object of Orientalist study, and were examined primarily through their texts.

"This Orientalism put Western scholars in the position of claiming to recover or reclaim lost ancient written traditions. This allowed them to define their role as a variation on writing for others who somehow could not write for themselves. Instead, these others were redefined as being dependent on Western scholars. Along with this went the valorizing of texts which, in the context of their own traditions had perhaps previously not been very important. In India, for example, the most 'Aryan' texts, such as the *Vedas*, were privileged. Yet the pandits who translated them became invisible.

"Religion as a topic was floating around in all these disciplines. As a discipline in its own right, it didn't exist, but it was being looked at through sociological and anthropological studies, in order to examine what was disappearing. It was assumed to have been eliminated from politics and economics, but to be that which defined the rest. It wasn't until the nineteen-sixties and seventies, 'religious studies' came into being, as distinct from 'religion.' That is, it became a field and, sometimes, an academic department. In Santa Barbara, in 1968, the University of California was hiring sociologists and political science professors, and in some cases theologians. For example, they invited Paul Tillich to lecture. The term 'religious studies' was used from the beginning in Santa Barbara."

At this point, the group interrupted with comments about ways in which different departments had shifted their names over the past several decades, and about what these name changes had signified in the politics of the developing field.

"Some of the new departments," Mariko continued, "added the first 'Eastern specialists,' a shift that coincided with the adoption of 'religious studies.' These were non-Bible-tradition scholars. It was also around this time that the newly established religious studies departments began to offer courses on comparative religion, or subjects such as 'Mysticism East and West,' using texts written in the nineteen-twenties and thirties—the works of Rudolf Otto, Gerardus van der Leeuw, Mircea Eliade's earlier work on yoga, Carl Jung, Black Elk, and Evelyn Underhill. In the nineteen-twenties and thirties, the books by these people had not been thought of as textbooks, but as texts responding to the deeply troubled times in which they lived. In the sixties, they took on new significance. Jung's collected works were translated in the late fifties. Later, Yeats and Eliot were championed by the New Critics, who were re-reading them and their contemporaries. People started looking at both of them in terms of their spiritual search, not their politics.

"Certain terms, categories, and assumptions became central, like the primacy that began to be assigned to experience. William James's writings were important in this shift, as James Moore shows, in tracing the concept of experience back through James, Otto, and Bergson.[32] Otto refers to Schleiermacher, but Schleiermacher himself is not the main influence. It would be a later reading backward that would insert his work. Another focus in the sixties and seventies came to be the idea of 'spirituality,' which derives most conspicuously from the work of Evelyn Underhill. She was a British laywoman who thought of herself as a Roman Catholic, although she remained an Anglican. She understood her task as a ministry carried out through letters.

---

[32]   See John M. Moore, *Theories of Religious Experience: With Special Reference to James, Otto and Bergson.* (New York: Round Table Press, 1938).

"One of the most widely taught texts in the seventies was Eliade's book *The Sacred and the Profane*. He provided a kind of theologically neutral language. It looked at religious phenomena in a way that allowed the new departments to say they were cross-cultural and non-denominational. This meant they could argue they were meeting the requirements set by the Supreme Court to keep religion out of public education.

"Now, in the current moment, we are re-figuring and re-imaging what happened in the period we call modernity, particularly the eighteenth and nineteenth centuries when Enlightenment Europe was understanding itself as coming out of religion. The assumption then was that religion, as something visible with more conspicuous forms like ritual, was becoming a thing of the past. That which was essential about religion, it was thought, because of secularization, went underground to permeate the fabric of culture, surfacing in areas of creativity like literature, art, or advanced physics. In other words, the core of religion lost its ritual baggage, and emerged instead in these other places. This is not actually what happened, but it is what was imagined. You see this in the history of the AAR, where one of the earliest sections was on the arts, literature, and religion.

"So, when we engage in religious studies, we must examine and reconfigure what we are doing both in terms of its own history and its history within the university. To the extent that we engage in the study of 'culture,' how long can we go on studying Flannery O'Connor or Walker Percy alone, reading them and identifying their 'religious significance' and assuming that religion is to be located in the form of spirituality as a core, depth dimension?"

She turned to Jack.

"The parallel narrative," said Jack, "is to be found in the pedagogical dimension, in the structuring of curricula and the psychological view of the student. We find the persistence of continuities here, too, with certain elements from eighteenth-century configurations still present.

"If you look at 'higher education'—the college—in colonial and earlier American history, the curriculum historically focused on Latin, Greek, Rhetoric, and Grammar. The issue, or task, was one of equipping people to *think*. The other aspect was to enable them to read the great texts—the Bible, the Greek and Roman philosophers, or writings on matters like citizenship—with the objective of preparing them for intellectual leadership as preachers and governors. In the United States, they added Geography. It was a transplanted Britain, a transitive civilization. The standard method of learning was recitation and memorization, with the proper inflection in terms of rhetoric. A person started in primary school."

"In some parts of the Caribbean," interjected one of the participants, who was from the West Indies, "you still, in high school, learn Latin, Grammar, and French. Then you go 'up' to Cambridge to do the classics.'"

"It's a form of oral tradition," Jack continued, "that is, a literary society engaged in an oral tradition. It still exists in the United States in some of the more conservative Christian colleges, with the emphasis on learning Greek and Hebrew. Then in the late nineteenth and early twentieth centuries, this pedagogy became more aligned with Locke's philosophy of the human being as a *tabula rasa*, or a blank slate, where the teacher transcribes and the student recites, in order to prove that the material has been transmitted. This pattern persists in many of our approaches to testing.

"In the eighteen-thirties, the structure of the curriculum is reorganized around the concept of disciplines. Greek and Latin become departments in their own right. Moral philosophy becomes a department. There is a shift from method to content, with an emphasis on the mastery of content. The change is pushed by a new understanding of the leader. Business, political science, and economics are added. In the frontier, there is the new discipline of surveying. There are also, after 1836, now women in some places.

"This expansion also led to the diversifying of the colleges which were no longer only grounded in the institutions of the church. In the 1860s, the land grant colleges got going. They offered agriculture, engineering, mechanics, and so on. This was the origin of the state universities. The 'normal schools' also emerged, which were intended to train teachers to teach these other disciplines. These eventually became the teachers' colleges.

"The essentialist notion of an accessible body of truth which can be transmitted prevailed. An educated person was one who 'knew' enough of this material, and could use it in a discourse. This led to the idea of gradations of knowledge , with beginning and advanced courses, and then seminars, in which the students came closer to being peers with the instructor. The seminar became part of a mentoring process for those engaged in the act of thinking.

"The universities also gradually appropriated the industrial model, with a director and a board, and classes organized into blocks with a bell. School itself was redesigned on the industrial factory model, with knowledge conceptualized as a commodity. This was radically different from the prior century, and represented a major shift in consciousness, as everything became rationalized, in the Weberian sense. The advocates of this approach were excited by how education would shape the future, and communities were excited by the idea of founding colleges as a sign of progress.

"In fact, all of this was part of the ideology of progress. The patterns of patronage played a part in it as well. The beneficiaries of capitalism plowed their money back into the universities of their choice—as Rockefeller did, for example, with the University of Chicago. This period extended up to and past the second World War. It still represented a Lockean view of knowledge, in which the student does not know, and the professor does. This model, however, became democratized after the war, to accommodate and absorb the returning soldiers, although schools like Harvard and Yale tried to hold on to the older model. The universities increasingly operated within a tiered system, with junior colleges, state colleges, state universities, private colleges and universities, and so on. Many of these expanded to accommodate the Baby Boom and the new surge in the number of adolescents. More and more people began to expect to go to college.

"After World War II, too, the consciousness of the proliferation of knowledge and the creation of new disciplines led to an explosion in curricula in the different schools, without there necessarily being parallel curricula *between* schools. Disciplines with what then seemed like a limited textual base, like Scriptural study, were the last to experience the explosion.

"As teachers now, we confront things that teachers in the past did not. First, it is now the case that no one can teach all that is known about a discipline, unlike nineteenth-century teachers who assumed that you could. This has led to the emergence of specializations, and you have to work your way through to the points of contact between them. The old essentialist notion about knowledge has become dysfunctional, although schools may choose to follow it as one among a set of options. St. John's is an example. Second, we face a radically diverse student body, even in the most homogeneous university. We cannot assume we will know all that would be helpful to understand and work with this diversity. Third, this shifts our thinking about our teaching from an essentialist to an ecological model—that is, an ecology of learning styles and cultural patterns, to help students learn to enter a field and manage within it. This is in clear contrast to the older idea of mastery.

"Fourth, in many institutions we can't assume a common ethos of teaching and learning, so we can't assume that students carry what they learn from one class to another—for example, having a student in a doctoral-level class in philosophy, whose writing doesn't reveal that when they're taking a course in another discipline. People now experience the academy in an episodic way. What does this do to a quarter or a semester, as an artificial design created in the eighteen-thirties and forties to divide a discipline into 'learnable' units? My hunch is that it will lead to a shift in the structure of timing related to learning.

"Fifth, the factory and business models are resurfacing, along with consumer product language. The college which was originally designed to train persons to become leaders and ministers has, since World War II, moved its emphasis to participation in a contemporary society. The character of that society is more and more driven by market forces, so that the content of the curriculum is increasingly coopted to produce consumers and producers in a market economy. All of this leads to growing tensions concerning what liberal education is about. (You might want, in that connection, to look at *The Idea of the University*, by Pelikan.[33]) Key words started coming into the vocabulary, like 'efficiency,' 'productivity,' 'technology'— words that had been seeping through administrative language,

---

[33] Jaroslav Jan Pelikan, *The Idea of the University: A Reexamination* (New Haven: Yale University Press, 1992).

along with the idea that schools have to accommodate to survive. Now this is the language of those who are in charge of the universities. At the same time, the structures of capitalism are changing. Workers now are not necessarily working from nine to five. The administrative structures of graduate education are changing. So are the financial funding patterns.

"My questions to the group are, one, where are you and where is your institution in this pattern? Two, what are some of the forces and dynamics at work in how you locate yourself, that assist and limit you in your teaching? And three, anything else?"

The presentations had been long and—although not reflected in this narrative—frequently interrupted by questions, comments, and discussion from the group. Jack found himself having to omit entire segments of what he had planned to introduce, in order to leave time for the small groups to go off and think over what he and Mariko had presented.

When everyone had reassembled some time later, one of the small groups reported the painfulness of the shift in the field, as their own ideologies have become exposed and the models they absorbed earlier in their training change.

"There is the vulnerability of exposing ideological content we're not always aware of," said their spokesperson, "and of disclosing the conditioned nature of our own performance, as if we were not free agents but simply moments in time. A term gets contaminated with associations that a group wants to abandon. One can't just stare at the word and "see" why it is now bad; it involves the associations that cling to it. In some places, for example, to talk about a Department of "Religion" is now seen as a quasi-confessional statement, leading some people to feel the need for a new term. Older faculty are, in some cases, being displaced or marginalized by the process, and some feel depressed at seeing their assumptions and structures go by the wayside. We ourselves are watching our own re-tooling, even as we speak."

"We are walking among the ruins of all the structures, and have no narratives with which to reassemble them," said another person. "There is a fragmentation, and we lack the meta-narrative of the college."

Others added there thoughts. There is a sense of something being out there, but we are unclear about who we are, as the old models ring false. As scholars of religion, we find ourselves living in the the interstices. To continue to do so is a choice. We assume that our main locus for our identity as professors is the academy and the professorate, but is this really the case? Are there other communities to whom we are accountable? It can be helpful to talk about the vertigo of trying to relate to the two. How many people have an active religious affiliation within the academy, not to mention within the church-related colleges?

"I have one colleague," said Louis, "who describes himself as five days a week an evolutionist, and two days a week a creationist."

We try to make it clear to students that there are religious dimensions to culture, but often we imply that religion plays this role in *other* people's cultures in a way that it does not in our own. For example, we describe our involvement in conflicts in the Middle East as being about politics and economics—"Take the oil and run"—and not related to religion, instead of disclosing how all these forces are present in our country's own involvement in different situations.

We face the issue of trying to edify students without jeopardizing our own popularity. Students who come into our classes on a personal quest expect something spiritual to happen. The academy doesn't recognize how many people's interest in general is focused on the occult and on New Age readings of spirituality. That is where the broader public attention is currently found. Yet there is a tremendous resistance on the part of institutions and their faculties to recognize and interpret these interests, or to recognize their interplay with thinking going on in the academy.

"We have to look at these things for other reasons, too," said one person. "Feminism has gotten short-circuited by a lot of the New Age and Twelve-Step stuff, because both of them have the effect of stopping leftist movements. Socially, they tend to be very conservative influences."

"A good question to ask," said Jack, "is 'What is the Utopia that informs your own classroom practice?'"

"The other complication for me," said someone else, "is that I may be moved by a vision, but that vision is located within some tradition which, itself, is being reshaped by what's happening now. Everything is shifting."

It is a time of genre meltdown. How do we clarify our own teleological visions in order to understand where we are each located, both personally and historically? If we make students somehow "wrong" within that framework, how do we engage with them? How do we define ourselves as advocates at the same time as we struggle to respect our students' initial positions? We want to encourage them to think about and see things differently, without annihilating them in the process. How much of these hidden agenda do we divulge?

"I'm one of those people who was influenced by Paul Tillich," said Louis, "to assume that there's always a religious depth under culture and the religious and institutional forms are culturally defined. So, I thought, the reading of culture disclosed embedded religious dimensions. This is different from the institutional forms. I've thought of both as parts of our field, each informing the other. I feel convicted affectively!"

"Tillich *is* a paradigm of this," said Mariko. "And I don't mean to reduce current forms of religious studies to his model—but it does inform and give moral support to the project. The difficulty is that when you point out that the subject 'religion' is a discursive formulation with a date of origin, some people respond by saying that the basic reality was always there—that this is just the current name. I don't agree. I think that the *phenomenon* has been formed by the name and its politics.

"What does that critical awareness do to the study of religion?" she continued. "The analogy is to the study of English literature. In the past, some version of *reading* English literature existed, but historical-critical analysis has shown that the curriculum called 'English literature' came into being in the nineteen-twenties in England, as the English educational system changed with a large middle class going to the universities. This was new. English literature, as part of the curriculum, was the poorer man's and woman's Greek or Latin. That's how it begins. Even before that, in India, it was part of the civil service examination. My argument is that to see these layerings exposes the political stances behind them."

The time had run over, and came to a close. The staff debriefed later that afternoon, before joining the group for the five o'clock social hour. Both Mariko and Jack commented on the dilemma of having their presentations punctuated by questions and observations from the group. They had intended to complete their presentations and then turn to discussion. It was, Jack acknowledged wryly, a lively indication of people's engagement and their sense of sharing the authority for running the session. The staff had, till then, created an expectation in the group that discussion was expected and valued. Clearly it had become a group norm. At the same time this did, on occasion, derail some of the staff's own plans. Should they do more to regulate when and how the discussion took place? They were operating with the objective of trying to build a community of people who would increasingly take on the shaping of the workshop. In the balance, they agreed, the dynamic emerging around the discussions was a fruitful indication that this second objective was, indeed, coming about. They should do little to constrain it. If anything, they should recognize it to be part of the nature of the group and, for that matter, of the general personal disposition of the staff, and make efforts from then on to factor it more explicitly into their own planning. It was a minor but significant moment in the refining of the culture of the workshop.

The team then turned to the question of how to manage the project presentations. They discussed how earlier workshop groups had found it difficult to devise a method that didn't make the presentations feel endless, however interesting they might have been in their own right, how to get all of them in and still have time for discussion and suggestions? The team decided that they would first tell everyone to re-read the project descriptions handed out earlier in the week. They would also notify the group that anyone who had other materials they wanted to circulate—say, a syllabus—should turn these in to Carl that evening, so that he could have copies made. Instead of having to describe the project itself, the presenter could then focus on stating the particular areas in which he or she was looking for help.

The staff also decided to hand out sheets to everyone with the presenter's name. Each person could then write down his or her ideas, critiques, references, and questions, so that if these didn't come up in the course of the discussion, they could all still be given to the person at the end of the presentation. The participants in earlier workshop groups had often found it difficult to listen to suggestions and write them all down, resulting in much useful advice falling through the cracks.

Finally, one of the staff would keep strict time. (It so happened that Louis had a small pocket alarm.) Each presenter would have no more than ten minutes to state his or her questions to the group. Newsprint and markers would be provided ahead of time, in case anyone wanted to prepare lists, charts, or the like. The group would then in turn have only ten minutes to respond. Hence, the usefulness of the personal notation sheets as a method for gathering up all the group's ideas about a particular project. Finally, the participants would be asked to present in reverse alphabetical order, to confound any sense of inevitable sequencing.

Day Six: Friday, June 16

Carl explained the proposed strategy, which would organize that morning and the next. The group liked the idea.

"For the project presentations, Louis has agreed to be our Draconian time keeper," he announced.

"And if he needs help . . ." said Jack, holding up a big stick.

"In Zen practice," said Carl knowingly, "they call that the stick of mercy."

The strategy devised by the staff not only worked; it compressed the collective attention into the fruitful sort of brainstorming that one would hope to elicit from a support team. Moreover, in the course of talking about their particular projects, different people raised questions that were, at one and the same time, more broadly applicable. To suggest several brief examples, the first project involved a course in Native American literature.

"Literature, as Mariko pointed out yesterday," said the presenter, "is one of the places where one does archaeology, where discourses and history clash. Native American literature is a re-mythologizing of an oral tradition. It is also about loss, and about storytelling, both constructed over a loss and encompassing that loss.

The question is, how to express our own self-consciousness of our positionality in relation to the Native American traditions? Because there is no ground on which to stand that is not politicized, I want the course to look at different positions toward these traditions, including the issue of what I call 'cannibalization'—the taking on of 'otherness'—that has been one piece of white identity. I think this is especially important in a history-of-religion course that's apt to be one arena where students seek some form of spirituality."

A second person, when it came her turn to talk about a course on the Bible, described her dilemmas over the question of allegiances.

"I have an allegiance to the content," she said, "although the exact meaning of that becomes less and less clear to me. I have an allegiance to my department and its ideas about what liberal Protestants need to know. I also have allegiances to the different institutional constituencies. The English department, for example, expects students to have some preparation in Biblical literacy. And then there's the administration, who want to market our courses to students as consumers as products. Each of these bears its rewards and punishments, and the content of what I teach is affected by each one of them.

"I ask myself whether what I want is for students to be able to go and get graduate degrees elsewhere and do well professionally, or whether I'm more concerned with my own growing feeling for issues of empowerment for women. I'm influenced by Martha Nussbaum in thinking about how literature and philosophy help foster moral development. But trying to do it all makes it hard to do any of it well. I'm trying to figure out which parts are non-negotiable. So, I'm asking myself—as Jack puts it—what I want my students to be able to *do*. I know that I want them to be able to read a text with comprehension, and to reflect on it. I want them to be able to contribute to the public and the confessional discourse. I want them to be able to recognize varieties of appropriation and performance that are both confessional and public, and I want them, as women, to be able to feed themselves."

"I, too, ask myself what I want my students to be able to so," said another person, who was planning a course on religion in the South. "I want them to know—this is a Santa Barbara phrase—how to do 'religion on the ground.' I want them to know how to study *lived* religion. There is such unsympathetic language in many of the writings about the South, and I'd like them to go in there for themselves and see what's really at work."

"I want to make a case for men's studies," said one of the next people. "Rather than just criticizing traditional religious studies for letting the male-oriented aspect of many traditions go unexamined, I want to look at how it affects what we do in the study of religion if we pose this question explicitly. I also want to raise the question of masculinities of different kinds, and about how these have shaped and been shaped in different traditions. I'd like the course I'm planning to include understandings not only of how men's studies have looked at violence but also at pain in the defining of masculinities—like initiatory rituals, for example."

"My course will be on popular religion in the United States," said the last person for the morning. "That's going to include the demographically prevalent phenomena, like going to church; it also includes the folk practices, the mass-mediated versions, and the counter-cultural and counter-hegemonic groups—the oppositional ones. Then, of course, that leads into the question of who defines the multiple hegemonies, and how those definitions shapes what is presented as oppositional."

That afternoon, there were various excursions, among them a visit to the Atlanta History Center, where there was an exhibit on the history of the Jewish community of Atlanta. Some went to see Stone Mountain. Later, a well-known Holocaust historian had been invited to talk with anyone interested in teaching a course on the Holocaust, as were several in the group.[34]

---

[34] The books suggested during this discussion on teaching a course about the Holocaust were the following: Lucie Adelsberger, *Auschwitz: A Doctor's Story*, trans. Susan Ray. (Boston: Northeastern University Press, 1995); Yehuda Bauer, *The Holocaust in Historical Perspective*. (Seattle: University of Washington Press, 1978); Christopher R. Browning, *Ordinary Men: Reserve Police Battalion 101 and the Final Solution in Poland*. (New York: Harper Perennial, 1992); Ian Buruma, *The Wages of Guilt: Memories of War in Germany and Japan*. (London: Vintage, 1995); Lucy S. Dawidowicz, *The War Against the Jews, 1933-1945*. (Toronto; New York: Bantam Books, 1986); David P. Gushee, *The Righteous Gentiles of the Holocaust: A Christian Interpretation*. (Minneapolis: Fortress Press, 1994); David A. Hackett, trans.

"It's useless to get into a discussion of comparative pain," she said, "or to try and see one phenomenon or another as somehow 'worse.' I tell students that it's all right to be upset, but I also use a 'less is more' approach. You don't need to *tell* them it was awful, or have them convince you in their papers that it was awful. The issue is, what led up to it and how did it happen? That means looking, for example, at how Christianity was a necessary, versus an insufficient, condition for the Holocaust, or at how the New Testament allowed a Justinian to happen, as well as blood libels, the Crusades, and Martin Luther.

"There's nothing so popular as studying about dead Jews. But a good course on the Holocaust is not about memorializing the cadavers. Teach, instead, about the world that was destroyed. Ask how it was that the Holocaust started in the country where Jews were the most assimilated. Who were the people who *were* destroyed? Present them not as some 'other.' It's the pictures of the boyfriend and girlfriend on the motorcycle, or the child in a ballet dress, or the postman. Find *those* kinds of images. Bring in a survivor, if you can.

"It's important to teach comprehensively—about victims, perpetrators and bystanders, and those who engaged in resistance and rescue. There were Jews who resisted, but they had the hardest

and ed., *The Buchenwald Report*, (Boulder: Westview Press, 1995); Raul Hilberg, *The Destruction of the European Jews*. (New York: Holmes & Meier, 1985); Ernst Klee, Willi Dressen and Volker Riess, *Those Were the Days: The Holocaust as Seen by its Perpetrators and Bystanders*, trans. Deborah Burnstone. (London: Hamish Hamilton, 1991); Eugen Kogon, *The Theory and Practice of Hell: The German Concentration Camps and the System Behind Them*, trans. Heinz Norden. (London: Secker & Warburg, 1950); Deborah E. Lipstadt, *Beyond Belief: The American Press and the Coming of the Holocaust, 1933-1945*. (New York: Free Press), 1986, and *Denying the Holocaust: The Growing Assault on Truth and Memory*. (New York: Free Press; Toronto: Maxwell Macmillan Canada; New York: Maxwell Macmillan International, 1993); Carol Rittner and John K. Roth, eds., *Different Voices: Women and the Holocaust*. (New York: Paragon House, 1993); Art Spiegelman, *Maus: A Survivor's Tale*. (New York: Pantheon Books, 1986); U.S. Holocaust Memorial Museum, *Liberation 1945*. (Washington, D.C.: United States Holocaust Memorial Museum, 1995); U.S. Holocaust Memorial Museum and Michael Berenbaum, *The World Must Know: The History of the Holocaust as Told in the United States Holocaust Memorial Museum*. (Boston: Little, Brown, 1993).

time doing so, because of other partisans, who turned them in. The risk in glorifying resistance, in this case, is of having students lose sight of the historical realities and conclude that the only worthy victims were those who fought back."

It had not generally been the practice of any of the workshops to invite in outside experts. There had been the sessions at the technology resources center and with Frances West in the New England/Maritimes group, but these would prove to be the exception. The feeling from the beginning had been that the community-building aspect of the workshops required the possibility of forming a fairly close-knit group, which the entry and departure of outsiders might weaken. By locating this particular discussion in the late afternoon as an optional session, the Southeast staff translated it into terms analogous to the other excursions, thereby setting it outside the frame of the plenary sessions. These various optional outings and meetings allowed both the staff and participants to feel there was a certain amount of play in how they spent their afternoons, which reduced the likelihood of the "group" dimension becoming oppressive. For some, it had been a welcome occasion to work on their teaching projects. Nevertheless, the occasional counter-sentiment surfaced, as in the regret later expressed by one participant that the trips *had* been optional. The cost, she felt, had been a more fully shared frame of reference.

In their debriefing late that afternoon, the staff addressed the complex range of perceptions about the South that had risen to the surface over the course of the week. There were those who identified with the South, in contrast with those who were suspicious of it and seemed to feel a need to fix it. This had been off-putting for those originally from the South; they had not appreciated their turf being seen as a problematic region. For one or two, the difficulty lay in feeling that they themselves were perceived as conservative Christians in a group many of whose members were more conversant with post-modern discourse. How could they not feel out of place, for example, when the group's discussions problematized religiously conservative students and implied that one's agenda should be to change them? It left some participants occasionally silent and ill-at-ease, wondering whether they really belonged in the group. Was there a place for people strongly committed to the Bible and to a relatively more conservative allegiance to the Christian tradition—people who, in their own circles, ironically enough, were frequently seen as the leftists?

It is perhaps worth pausing to compare this particular tension with the one described earlier in connection with the Eastern International workshop. In each case, the focus of the tension was, in certain respects, directly related to the themes of the two workshops. In the first, it involved an eruption around issues of gender in particular, as well as race. In the second, although the tension, to some extent, went unvoiced, it nevertheless was related to the ways in which one dimension of Southern identity was sometimes problematized in some of the discussions—namely, that of the more conservative Southern Christian.

In both cases, the dilemma never fully worked itself out. Nevertheless, those who felt the differences more keenly made enough of a place for themselves to feel it was all right to stay. Here is where the importance of the informal time spent hanging out, watching films, sitting around after meals, and trekking to different sites together made a difference. It all added up to relationships. The staff doubted that people had gotten over all of their subterranean differences, and suspected these would come up again. The saving grace, however, was that sufficient trust and mutual liking appeared to have taken root that the native-born Southerners could occasionally admonish the others in the group when the latter spoke out of their stereotypes about the region.[35]

Finally, that day, the group met to discuss what they had done during the week, and to think toward the weekend in October. They agreed they would like to spend more time on syllabi. Carl turned to one person and said, "Jack made the comment this morning that your syllabus seems dense and cognitive. But your actual style seems quite different. Maybe we need to look at how to make these kinds of things more congruent. Of course, in the end, it's still *you* who pulls it all together—your consciousness, the point of power, and the and synthesis. But what makes who you are line up more clearly with how you teach?"

---

[35]   For further discussion, see Chapter VI.

"One issue for me that has come out," said someone else, "is how to draw from the insights of performance studies. How do we understand our relationship to space, to the people we're addressing? I'm a better teacher if I have ten minutes of silence before I go in. What things help us, and how do we become aware of them? It might make sense to cluster a session on the instructor as performer in a performative context. We could trade ideas."

"If students are primed to prefer entertainment modes," said Louis, "there's a way to accommodate that, but also to introduce other modes that are more intensive, like getting excited about close textual analysis and, in that connection, doing with a video what one does with a text—a thick reading of the visual or the architectural. This gets us back to the question of the kind of literacy that should evolve within the academy. It could be that we show each other different ways we think things can be read."

"The conversation raises for me the question of the public role of the teacher in the academy, particularly with respect to the production of knowledge. What social ecology are we trying to contribute to? In becoming more aware of the socially constructed nature of knowledge, in what directions do *we* participate? Which brings us back to the question of teaching in the South. To which South are we contributing?"

It was inevitable with this group that planning for a next meeting would head off down a road of rumination that circled back, around and around, to re-examine its own offshoots and cross back over itself. From the beginning of the week, the staff had led discussions by keeping running lists of who was in line to speak next. When possible, they had tried to allow those addressing the immediate point at hand to move up in the line, doing what they could to sustain as tightly integrated a conversation as possible. This could not altogether prevent a point from getting left too far back in the dust for someone to feel it was worth going around to pick it up again, but by and large it countered the tendency to the scattershot fragmentation that characterizes some seminars.

One person seemed to speak for many of the others when he said, "Every year I get acutely depressed and usually I'm on overload by the national meetings. Now I'm looking forward to them. We'll have a bond that I don't feel with many people in the academy. It's the advantage of having people committed within the region. You don't see the usual intellectual arrogance."

Day Seven: Saturday, June 17

"The course I'm going to be doing is related to research I'm working on about a leading Southerner during the Civil War." One of the participants, himself from the South, looked up from the syllabus he had handed out.

"It's a course on religion and racism, and the relationship between the two.[36] The constraints I'm up against are that the school where I teach feeds my children. This person exhibited some of the worst expressions of racism and anti-Semitism during the nineteenth century. And because he donated a great deal of money to the school in the past, my work has the potential to embarrass the college. So, how far do I go in exposing this side of who he was? But the other issue is how to approach this man with the proper humility. He suffered a great deal in his life and was pastoral in much of his giving to others. There's a lot to admire and a lot one hates. How to handle what one hates?"

"How," said Louis, "to construe Southern white men as complex victim experiences, themselves crying out for reconciliation? Buber said that only part of a person can be hated. The whole being cannot be hated."

"Half of the course is related to Christianity and anti-Semitism, and half to religion and racism. My stake in this is the question of whether religious belief is a cause of racism, a mitigating factor, or both."

The group talked about what it means to teach and write about figures with whom one feels both a sense of identification and profound distance, and about how much of this, in one measure or another represented an autobiographical project.

"My father grew up in Germany during World War II," said the next person. "I write about white supremacy. It's a way of being

---

[36] The following was suggested in connection with this discussion: James William McClendon, Jr., *Biography as Theology: How Life Stories Can Remake Today's Theology* (Philadelphia: Trinity Press International, 1990).

true to my father, by working against the elements that constrained his life. The course I'm planning is going to be about the meaning for students of religion, culture, and spirituality—that is, personal meanings with historical roots, shot through with questions of power. I also want to get them to think about class. I'm going to have them examine their family trajectories—their locations, their religious affiliations, their class backgrounds—going back three generations. This is to help them get a grasp on modernity as it has played out in their own lives, and to look at what they inherit. I want to question the assumptions often made about pluralism as a matter of free choice in a market economy—to look at how these things have been negotiated within our own families.

"One of the case studies I'm going to have them look at involves skinheads. I want to do that, because some of them listen to White Power music, rising out of reggae and ska. I want them to examine the economic forces structuring this, and to look at what these forces look like as someone's life story. But one of the questions I'm facing is how to deal with the conflict that may arise in the classroom. Do I avoid it, or slide through it? When it gets up front, how do you deal with it?"

The group pondered this question. Louis's involvement in training workshops about diversity gave him one working model; others were less certain they had one. They talked about having him present some of this work during the final week. It would be useful, in the workshop, to learn more about addressing issues of conflict.

Another course being designed would be on African religious traditions. The person presenting put up a large, brightly colored map of Africa and stepped back. What did people in the group associate with this map, if they were fully honest with themselves? Fascination? Strangeness? Enormity?

"I'm going to be teaching this course at a predominantly African-American school. As much as anything, I'm trying to address a fundamental question from the philosophy of education—to articulate epistemological presuppositions in designing it. In this case, I think the subject matter determines the pedagogy.

"The religions of Africa are often associated with the aboriginal, the archaic. There's a historical framework to this attitude. I want to challenge these kinds of gut assumptions. The students I'll be teaching are young men, and I want to help position them in terms of the professional identities they will be trying to develop. Many of them are also Christian. I want them to be able to assess where they stand in relation to these traditions in relation to their own identities, and to do this at an institution where Afro-centricity is crucial. My goal is that they learn the capacity for critical reflection—that they wrestle with questions of existential appropriation, not simply a romanticized, sentimental glorification."

None of the courses being described were ones that anyone had gotten stuck teaching. They didn't reflect a different piece in the experience of religion faculty—that of being expected to teach subjects about which one knows little and, on some occasions, for which one feels even less. Even in the cases where people were preparing otherwise required courses, they were doing so in ways that allowed them to raise questions of their own. This was one of the keys to the vital energy people brought to the workshops.

The October Weekend

The Planning

As with many of the weekends, there was little planning beyond the logistics, which in this case were undertaken by the participant at whose school the meeting was being held. The weekend was to be dedicated, for the most part, to progress reports on the teaching projects. Beyond that, there would only be time for a trip to a few local sites later on Saturday afternoon, and for some additional planning. Carl wrote:

> As you think about your progress reports, consider the following questions: (1) who are you teaching? (2) how are the Southern locale and your institutional setting factors in the presentation of your project? (3) how do you address the issue of religious identities (the students, your own)? (4) how have the issues and discussions joined in this summer contributed to the shape your project is now taking?

Day One: Friday, October 20

It took over an hour to drive from the airport to the school where the meeting was being held. People had hooked up with each other to carpool, some driving in from other states; others had flown down. As they arrived, they drifted in to the courtyard lounge area, clustering to catch up with each other. There was a buffet off to one side, and they wandered over to graze. As tired as they were after a day of teaching and traveling, it was good to sit down and find out what had been going on over the past four months.

Day Two: Saturday, October 21

The point of the day's work was to see where everyone had got to, up to that point; thus, it held a retrospective function. The other was to plan how to use the week the following June. This time, the participants were each given half an hour—fifteen minutes to report, and fifteen minutes for responses from the group. Again they used the method they had devised the previous June for turning in written comments. Some of them were already teaching the courses from their projects; others would not begin doing so until the spring. Many had found that, once their semesters had begun, they had had little time to do much further work on their projects. The demands of their teaching and departmental work were too steep. It had been frustrating, although not altogether suprising.

Through the course of discussing the various projects, they found themselves turning to broader questions, such as how to evaluate student work with which one disagrees. Suppose, for example, that a student wants to exclude women from speaking in the church, and decides to make a biblical case for it. Do you challenge the idea itself, or do you evaluate the work on the basis of the skill and intelligence with which the argument is formulated? How to address the whole question of moral stance?

"We are not explicit," said one person, "about our own ways of indoctrinating students, but we still do it—like when we focus on process over content, or emphasize 'critical thinking.' These are ideological biases in their own right."

"Also to be seen as energizing the passive," said another person dryly.

Most of them agreed that they were now teaching students whose public school preparation was not always strong and who were, indeed, more passive.

"But our classrooms are not value-less. We have to make those values explicit. Like, no one can make racist statements, or wear T-shirts denigrating women."

"It's destructive to many people's conceptual categories to teach religion in the South," someone added. "Like the things their grandparents told them—there are highly charged emotions involved. In my course on religion in America, I asked my students to locate themselves back to their grandparents in religious terms, and to identify where they now saw themselves with regard to the American mainstream."

"Of course," another person interrupted, "that also involves questioning the meaning of 'mainstream,' as representative of a certain cultural, moral hegemony, along with examining the politics of what it means to identify within or outside of that mainstream. A lot of them don't question it."

"Yes," the other person replied, "but we *are* indoctrinating people into the belief that large categories are dangerous, problematic, and not to be trusted. It's easy for them then to slide into relativism and inaction. On the other hand, as a Southerner who came out of a conservative background, I am the best example that there is life after the study of religion. I still believe in things, fight for things, stand for things. What is destructive can also be constructive. There *is* a point after the destruction."

"I worry," said Mariko, "that we are not attending enough to the historical dimension of things. We have some myth of the free agent here, some idea of the individual, and this individual is supposed to pursue his or her spirituality. But how much of this itself comes out of a certain very historically conditioned indoctrination? None of this is innate. People in the past have not fought for identity as we do."

"On the other hand," replied someone else, "my concern is how we view student change in our understanding of our teaching. What *are* we trying to bring about? For example, a lot of people read Tony Hillerman's fiction about the Navajo. Do we assume that this will change their understanding of Native Americans, or is it just a woven into a larger web of preconceptions? I'm fascinated by the way that the same text can take some people to a liberative perspective and others to a conservative one. Can works like Hillerman's lead students to become aware of ambiguities or to think of their own experience in that way?"

"There are any number of justice questions involved," another person added, "and sometimes our more conservative students don't necessarily know the full story of their own heritage here, to know how to read their own history. For example, one of the unheralded groups in the Civil Rights movement were the white church women, who made radical decisions about how they would *be*. In settings where students may be hearing conservative, racist messages elsewhere, I think the task is not necessarily to show that Hillerman is wrong, but to show that there are different ways to read him."

Carl had asked them think about how they addressed the issue of religious identities, whether their own or their students'. The question led them into these other areas of what it meant to be preparing students to live within the culture and the world. It was untenable, as one person put it, "to act as if we do not have a point of view about what it means to be a citizen." Implicit within this were their own visions for the culture. Toward the end of their previous gathering, Jack had asked, "What is the Utopia that informs your own classroom practice?" He could also have asked, "What is the Utopia toward which you hope to be educate your students?"[37]

Late that afternoon, they all headed out to a local museum of early Native American culture and, from there, to a museum commemorating Harriet Tubman. Neither visit had been designed as part of a training in how to run a field trip. Instead, both seemed

---

[37] The group, during this discussion, and the one the next day, suggested the following books in this connection: Morris Berman, *The Reenchantment of the World*. (Toronto; New York: Bantam Books, 1984); Paul Berman, ed., *Debating P.C.: The Controversy Over Political Correctness on College Campuses*. (New York, N.Y.: Laurel, published by Dell Publishers), 1992); Jacques Ellul, *The Betrayal of the West*, trans. Matthew J. O'Connell. (New York: Seabury Press, 1978); Pervez Hoodbhoy, *Islam and Science: Religious Orthodoxy and the Battle for Rationality*. (London; Atlantic Highlands, N.J.: Zed Books, 1991); Roger Kimball, *Tenured Radicals: How Politics Has Corrupted Our Higher Education*. (New York : Harper & Row, 1990); Nel Noddings, *Educating for Intelligent Belief or Unbelief*. (New York: Teachers College, Columbia University, 1993); and The "Opposing Viewpoints" series published by Greenhaven Press.

more intended to take advantage of being in different locales in the South. At the same time, they focused the group's attention on the range of local religious worlds that coexisted in the region.

They had dinner that night in the campus dining room, a rather dimly lit, cavernous hall ringed with large paintings of former college presidents. By then, people were tired, and the conversation flagged. The weekend sessions were crucial in consolidating a group, but they also made for fatigue. The evening ended with a brief review of the idea of teaching portfolios, a topic to which the group agreed to return.

Day Three: Sunday, October 22

After a few remaining presentations, the group found itself going back to the question of what each of them was really trying to bring about in the classroom, and of how this objective existed in tension with their scholarly lives. How to negotiate, as Carl wrote later, "the conflicting claims of teaching—especially the broad introductory courses one is expected to teach—and scholarship, which often demands more specialized expertise than can take place in the teaching environment?"[38]

Furthermore, as one woman put it, "We're moving into a time when our teaching has to be absolutely flexible, but our writing cannot be. There is less encouragement for interdisciplinary scholarship. It's out of touch with the job market."

The group returned to the question of ethics and student development, particularly given their awareness that they often encountered students who opted for an unqualified relativism.

"It's an unhappy outcome," said one person. "I support tolerance, but *this* kind of relativism doesn't promote critical thinking. In one of my classes, we discussed creationism. I tried to suggest some of the problems inherent in it, but they didn't hear it."

"I've been thinking about the ethics of course readings," said another person. "I'm seeing that I can choose readings—like the predictive statements in the prophets—and talk about how such

---

[38] Director's report to the American Academy of Religion, the Lilly Endowment Inc. and the National Endowment for the Humanities.

things lead to outcomes with profound ethical issues involved, like pogroms, or the Holocaust."

"When students resist talking about something," said Jack, "another question to ask is 'What is the basic fear at work?' It's one way of helping students address what's really at stake."

"There is another question we haven't talked much about," said someone else, " and that is the issue of engaging our own faith commitment in our teaching—the issue of how to locate our work in relation to our own religious identity."

"How much do your students know you as a religiously commited person," said Louis.

One of the participants, a Buddhist, said, "I try to show that my commitment is important to me, just as I hope their's is to them."

"It's ironic," said another person, "that I use rational discourse to tell students that affect is important. How *do* we convey the importance of the affective and the ecstatic?"

"Part of the problem," said someone else, "is that they get hit so heavily with affect in the popular context, without any critical awareness. So, that makes part of my job the removing of blinders."

"How," said Jack, "do we understand the function of teaching religion in the liberal arts? When I was in college, we thought the task *was* the removing of blinders—to become more intelligent participants in our own religious communities. But when people from Mississippi went through that, they then moved North. I'm intrigued by how, even among those who most identify with traditions in the South, there is still a cynicism, an *anomie*, that skews what we mean by 'removing the blinders.' The social location of the enterprise has shifted."

"But if we think about the bigger ethical outcomes," said someone else, "then do we not have to be willing to let the students adopt creationism?"

"I try," said another person, "to ask, 'What do you know about X, and what is the source of that knowledge?' I also try to bring into the discussion how the popular imagination gets created, especially by the media."

"But we're still talking about *anomie*. Students still come in with minds formed by T.V. Their passivity worries me even more than their intolerance."

Then there was the question of the growing tendency for people to have identities that represent the mixing of traditions—what one person referred to as "hyphenated religious identities." A person could be active in the Presbyterian church and be taking yoga classes. We don't, it was agreed, have adequate language for these mixed religious identities. We teach religious traditions, often, as though such mixtures are the exception when, on the ground level, they may be far more common.

It was proposed that one issue the group might take up during the final week could be that of the activist teacher and the passive student. A variation on that might be the ethical dynamics of teaching in the South, integrated in some way with related developmental challanges. It would also be useful, one person suggested, to include something on how to converse with academic officials who do not share one's views on advocacy in the classroom. With that, another piece of the wish list for the following summer had been drawn up.

The February Weekend
Day One: Friday, February 9

In an advance letter to the group, Carl defined the agenda for the weekend, saying:

> There is considerable interest in focusing on the issue of teaching: its evaluation, its relation to research, and negotiating the conflict between meeting the curricular needs of our departments that require we teach broadly, and the rewards of scholarly writing that often take us into topics in depth. We will also take up the issue of teaching portfolios and building networks of support in our institutions.

The format for the weekend was to resemble that of the previous one, with the group staying in a local inn this time. The evening before, there had been a buffet, referred to by one of the participants as the group's *soiree*, and an evening of checking in with each other. People talked about how their courses were going, about the politics in their schools, about family events. It wasn't a working session *per se*, but work was being done.

Day Two: Saturday, February 10
The next morning, the group caravanned over to the campus of a traditionally African American college. There, they were welcomed by several of the faculty in the religion department, who had also asked to sit in on the morning session. It was one of the only times that non-workshop participants or staff had been—or would be—included in one of the regular sessions.

The updates on the projects were more informal this time. It had been agreed that this was enough, for this meeting, and that more detailed accounts could be rendered in the June meeting. Following the project updates, the group was to discuss two topics: first, the conflicts between the research rewards recognized by the national and international guilds on the one hand, and the teaching and service expectations of one's local school culture on the other. Second, they would explore ideas for transforming departmental cultures in ways that made teaching more visible.

As it happened, both topics converged in one of the project reports, leading the group into the broader agenda. One participant described having proposed a revision to his school's core curriculum, based on the experience of the workshop. The faculty, a traditional one, would be moving toward a team-teaching approach in which each discipline would be expected to put its content in relation to that of another. A religion professor, for example, might team up with someone from the biology faculty in a course on origins. There would also be a rhetoric seminar, which would address issues of reading, writing, speaking, and research methods. Each of these elements would, in turn, be worked across the curriculum to attend to the demands of the various disciplines. The objective would be to show the interconnectedness of different fields of knowledge, and to model the making of those connections for the students.

"How did you propose this, as an untenured faculty person?" asked Carl.

"I was the only one with interdisciplinary training. There was a real conflict between the 'body of knowledge' people and someone like me, who is trying to bring students into different discourses. We emphasized that we can't teach without bringing in bodies of knowledge, but these would be set in relation to other bodies. Additionally, it became a way to differentiate ourselves from another college in the area. It also results in an increase in actual *reading* of the Bible. We're now putting the Bible in relation to other disciplines. The old curriculum offered no reason for reading the Bible."

The description prompted a conversation about how to influence the curriculum in one's school. The year before, there had been news of the closing down of a religion department in a major university. The safeguarding of the departments was, therefore, on people's minds. The group talked about different strategies, including team teaching and, more importantly, the tying in with other departments, in order to enhance the perceived value of religious studies in a given school. In schools where religious studies departments could not take their existence for granted, it became all the more crucial to find ways to make their work indispensable.

"The experience of teaching often involves the accommodation to working in isolation and, thereby, to powerlessness," one person said. "More collaborative stances may help us in periods of crisis, particularly under circumstances when trustees and other figures in power try to exploit that isolation."

Part of what complicates the matter, as another person pointed out, is that the reward system in the guild is based on detailed forms of knowledge production whereas, in our teaching settings, we often have to teach outside of our fields. The assessment of our work doesn't necessarily follow these contours. The matter becomes all the more difficult when one works in a small, teaching-and-service-intensive school. (One person there *was* the faculty at his school for all non-Christian traditions.) Often, such faculty receive little if any financial support or confirmation from their schools for their efforts to participate in national and international meetings and to stay engaged in the guild discourse. This makes it all the more important to forge connections with colleagues outside of their institutions.

Over lunch in the President's Dining Room with the Chair of the Religion Department and other colleagues from the college, talk turned to the recent Million Man March and its impact on the students at the school, especially those who had chosen to participate. The discussion continued, as the group was taken to meet with the dean of the chapel, followed by a tour of other parts of the campus. When the group reconvened, they moved over to a discussion of teaching portfolios, particularly with respect to how these can be used to influence the evaluation of one's work in promotion and tenure review.

What frequently gets blurred in such discussions is the distinction between performance review for promotion, and review for improvement. The two may or may not coincide. The selection of what goes into a portfolio is necessarily informed by whether it is intended for professional development or the assessment of one's current work.

"A lot of the motivation for teaching evaluation in the academy is judgmentally driven, instead of being about professional enhancement," Jack said. "All this talk about the measurement of teaching—what does that really mean? It measures a particular ideological perspective on the teaching enterprise!"

"It's also based on rising costs and parents' wanting to know what they're buying," said someone else.

"Yes," another person replied. "And lately the exposure to technology is often related in parents' minds to the sense that their kids are getting more. The more you incorporate technology, the more you're seen as progressive. But people haven't necessarily set this in the context of higher goals. Another factor is the externally imposed set of assessments some of us now have to deal with. You have to provide documents that 'prove' you've done what you said you'd do. But how do you prove moral content?"

"The irony," added someone else, "is that religious studies is one of the roots of liberal arts education. If we're teaching in a liberal arts college, perhaps we can remind people that they may be undermining traditions we cherish."

"The shift," said Carl, "seems to be first in the direction of globalization, such that we need to be teaching both western and non-western traditions. The other is in the direction of emphasizing skills, over content—for example, the reading of a text. The problem, too, is that the faculties can no longer agree on a content. Hence the culture wars on the campuses. The question is, can the religious studies departments in any way mediate?"

"Part of the problem," said Louis, "is that we're taught a hermeneutic of suspicion and a compulsion to judge—and we all know that compulsion."

Some of it, the group agreed, spilled over into a tendency to lack respect for people not doing the same thing as oneself, making it hard to have open dialogue. Did this come, someone wondered, from the inculcation into classical models of pedagogy rooted in Platonic and Aristotelian modes of thought, with their notion of hierarchies of truth? If so, how to bring our methods more into line with the newer contents we teach?"

"We have really thin skins and insecurities," said one person. "We get territorial and defensive."

"So," said another person, "how do we model appreciation and generosity without seeming soft?"

"Sometimes the younger faculty get brutalized by the older ones," someone else said. "There's a kind of hazing, sometimes a sort of jealousy. It's a predatory culture."

"Well," said Carl, "maybe it's about committing oneself to creating this other kind of culture and to making it happen."

"I think we're bringing some of that about in a faculty reading group I'm part of," said someone else. "It's almost like a revolutionary cell group, in that it's both small and broad enough to have an impact on the rest of the university. It functions as a setting within which to build camaraderie."

"I found," Jack said, "that in our faculty, for the senior members to recover their joy in teaching, it began around the discussion of our syllabi. It was amazingly candid, in terms of our struggles and our joys. A lot of us are facing a whole different kind of student, and don't necessarily know how to retool our courses for the way the students now approach the learning experience."

Day Three: Sunday, February 11

They would have to come back to these issues in June, they agreed, as they began to think their way toward the final week. Maybe they could give some attention to some of the emerging technologies, learning how to create a Web page. For that matter, maybe they could set up a Web page for the group itself. Perhaps there were panels they could do at the AAR regional meetings. In a discussion that occupied them for the rest of the afternoon, and which they continued the following morning, they proposed talking further about how to modify their organizational cultures. They might also, they said, think about how to state their own teaching philosophies. How would each of them define what was non-negotiable about what they did, and cared about doing?

They also wanted to come back to the matter of how to do all of these things in the South. There was still the question of what the South *is* and, within that, what the Southeast is. Was the region unique, or was that a myth? Either way, was the myth at all useful? How were pedagogical practices to be negotiated in the South? That is, were there teaching strategies people could share that might be related to the region more specifically—strategies that might help students challenge more traditional patterns of deference? How could all of this be translated into a syllabus? And, as Carl later wrote, they wanted to continue to give "some descriptive density to the notion of 'South.'"[39]

The Second June Week

The Planning

"The planning for the final session of the workshop," as Carl wrote in a subsequent report, "turned out to be more abbreviated than would have been optimal. One staff member was out of the country at the time of the planning and we did not have the budget to bring the participant-observer to Atlanta for the meeting." Having reviewed his notes from the previous meetings, he put together a number of topics, ran them by Jack, figured that the staff would work out the remaining details once they came together in June, and trusted the rest to the spontaneous capacity for creativity on the part of the group.

There are, David Kantor's work suggests, three general types of systems, these type defined by the nature of the relationships

---

[39]   Director's report to the American Academy of Religion, the Lilly Endowment Inc., and the National Endowment for the Humanities.

between their members. The first is the *closed* system, characterized by the hierarchical ordering of relationships, with strong authority structures and clear chains of command from the top on down. Roles and responsibilities are clearly defined, precedent and stability are valued, and conflict is carefully controlled, because it is perceived as a threat to the system. The military, and some corporate structures are good examples of this system type.

The second is the *open* system. Here, relationships are expected to be more egalitarian, and agreements get negotiated through a process of give and take. Those who favor this type of system expect to engage in discussion and joint problem-solving, examining their decisions together along the way to see if they need to adjust them. When there is conflict, it is supposed to be brought into the open and discussed, based on the assumption that disagreement can lead to creative problem-solving. The group is expected to work cooperatively according to a vision they have formulated together. Authority, in such a system, tends to minimize its power as much as possible, operating instead as the facilitator to these processes.

In the *random* system, independent initiative and creativity are the most highly valued qualities. These tend to shape the approach to problem-solving. The members of a random system are free to introduce modifications, and may do so frequently, particularly since the needs and interests of the individual are—if one had to make the choice—more important than those of the organization. Things get done because people feel inspired to do them. Conflicts tend to be perceived as an expression of individuality. When outside challenges arise, the system favors change and innovation. Communication may be sporadic and there are few if any formal channels or processes for it to take place. The system relies, instead, on the generative power of spontaneity. Those in charge (to the extent that there is such a thing, in a random system) are expected to create an atmosphere for everyone to act freely and independently.[40]

---

[40]   Drawn from "The Constantine Organizations Paradigm Scales Form E" (1990), pp. 1-3, and David Kantor and William Lehr, *Inside the Family*, (New York: Harper & Row, 1975).

Generally speaking, everyone has a preferred system type, just as there is at least one type with which they are likely to have a hard time. People who feel most at home in a closed system tend to find a random one tantamount to complete chaos. They may have difficulty even with the structures of an open system, wondering where the person in charge has disappeared to. Likewise, those preferring either an open or a random system may, to differing degrees, experience the closed system as authoritarian and stifling. Those who like the open system may be able to appreciate the intentions of a random approach, but may also find them frustratingly open-ended in practice.

These preferences affect people's experience of a group; they also influence how planning takes place. The approach to the planning for this particular session was, in part, affected by the constraints Carl described. But it was also influenced by Carl's own preferences for a more random style, and his expectation that the creativity of the staff both individually and collectively would spontaneously generate interesting refinements to the plan. What remained to be seen was whether the other members of the staff shared this perspective, and whether they would be able to act according to Carl's hopes.

Day One: Sunday, June 9
The group was to stay in two campus dormitories this time, each of them a two-story brick bungalow housing ten people. It was the most communal the group had gotten to date, particularly around the bathrooms which were quickly labeled as the men's and the women's. (Since there were only six of the latter, the usual public-facility lavatory shortage was, for once, reversed.) Less felicitous was the recent paint job in one of the dorms, which left a few people with off-and-on-again headaches. There was some good-natured grumbling, but since not much could be done at that point, everyone figured they could queue up for the bathrooms, prop a door open to let in the air, and not mind it too much if their feet hung over the edges of beds designed, it would seem, for a great many short undergraduates. Still, there was common room in each building, and a kitchenette. Carl, who had taken on the job of

foraging for social hour provisions, saw to it that the fridgewas as well stocked as if some unseasonable meteorological event were about to cut everyone off from the rest of civilization for a long time.

The group reconvened over box suppers. They used that first evening to check in with each other and to think about how they wanted to elaborate on the plans for the morning sessions. There was some sense, on the one hand, of winding down and, on the other, of gearing up.

Day Two: Monday, June 10

The morning's session, held in a faculty lounge, had been organized around a new configuration. Rather than starting out with a plenary discussion, the group was divided into smaller teams and given the task of talking about their goals as scholars and teachers of religion. It was a warm day, and the groups went outside to sit on the grass. It was one of those occasions where relaxation and intensity combined.

In the first group, one person raised the distinction between her own self-defined goals and the goals she presented to her institution: she saw herself not only as an academic and a scholar of religion, but also a leftist and a Christian. What she thought she was setting out to do was to enable her students to be more active, self-critical citizens. This led her to promote service learning. It was more difficult for her to figure out what kind of writing she felt she should do—should it, for example, be directed to a seminary audience to whom she felt accountable, or to some different group whom she had not yet fully defined?

"For me," said someone else, "I have to believe there is room for a public discourse that does not separate theology and ethics. It's not easy to separate the study of religion from being religious. I don't see why it's perceived as being so dangerous. I have consciously started to look for different kinds of positions—some of which could end up being outside of the academy—that would allow me to work as a public intellectual. I'm looking at the costs associated with a teaching career."

"I assume," said the next person, "that everyone in my class is engaged in developing a world view that includes the relationship with the sacred. I assume they're in my class to become more empowered in this, and to see something they haven't seen. I'm trying to help my students find their own relation to the sacred. So I think of myself as a facilitator. I use words like tolerance and respect, and I talk about developing the critical capacity to look at our own traditions. I'm coming into all of this after fourteen years of being part of different spiritual communities." Laughing, he added, "I think of what I'm doing as being a kind of undercover agent."

This group agreed that they had difficulties with divisions like "faith" and "intellect." It was troubling to use these terms for heuristic purposes and then to leave them divided. The solution, it seemed to some of them, was to model the integration of the two. But being the solitary undercover agent wasn't enough; there was also the question of community. How, otherwise, would change take place within the institution? The issue was, what were the costs one was willing to pay, and how then to bring about change? They also recognized that, in their classes, there was the overlap between personally compelling questions and the vocabulary and content of the texts they were using.

"Some of our goals may be informational," one person commented, "but at that very moment the students also may be undergoing some kind of eureka experience. How do we build in the feedback mechanisms so that eureka can happen *and* they still get the information we're trying to teach them?"

The second group had focused on how to make what they were each doing regionally relevant. How, they had discussed, to present the different ways that religion has mattered in the Southeast, and how to do so within the discourse of particular institutions, faculty relations, and student responses? These questions were affecting how some of them were beginning to think about their own identities as potential shapers of the field. For some, this might mean chairing a program, for others, working to help develop a department's curriculum. Others of them had found that the more effective they were at mainstreaming what they were doing and at getting colleagues within their institutions take them seriously, the more the identity of the faculty in their departments was shifting within the larger context of their schools.

"Our discussion dealt with several themes," said the spokesperson for the next group. "One was how our personal teaching goals get played out in the classroom, and how to handle things like self-disclosure. As individuals, we went into teaching with different goals, vocations, and personal hopes, and there is the difficulty of living these out within the limitations of our institutional milieus. Another theme was the issue of our own authority as teachers, especially in positions that are radically different from our own with respect to confessional issues. We have this desire to divest ourselves of that authority, at the same time as we secretly like some of it insofar as it allows us to present students with certain agenda we think they should think about."

The conversation within the fourth and final group had focused on those moments when one's identity as a scholar and a teacher becomes a big issue—when one has the option, for example, to change jobs or go up for tenure or be involved in the hiring of another colleague. And even when one defines oneself strongly as a teacher, who and what is one's audience? Is it possible to sustain a genuine scholarly interest while, at the same time, talking to a larger audience—without necessarily wanting to become a popularizer? As institutional conventions exist, by definition the more popular one becomes and the wider the audience one reaches, somehow the less valuable one's work is often considered to be within the academy. There is a price to pay either way as, for example, in choosing a press with which to publish. And if one creates a certain cachet for one's work, one can be trapped within it by institutional standards which can then prevent one from doing something else.

There are, in addition, all the incidental factors that shape the direction of our identity as teachers and scholars—factors such as where we are able to get a job. These do, in fact, become an important part of our development and identity. We are sometimes reluctant to acknowledge serendipity for its role in our work, going even to the lengths of reprocessing it so that nothing looks merely incidental. Yet such factors do, in reality, become an important part of our development and identity.

"I want to comment on the process of this discussion," one person said, suddenly, turning to the reporter from his group. "Since you reported on our group, I've been thinking that what you said in no way reflected *my* experience of that group—but it also made me see how these personal things can't be schematized." His question, as he thought out loud, was not only a plea for a more personalized dimension to the discussion, but that the group reflect on what happens in small groups. What, he wondered, is the purpose of the general reporting back? It makes what had been a thick narrative drop out of the picture, with the account becoming far more abstract.

The comment served—and was taken—as a mildly cautionary note for all that gets lost in the telling.

There were no further sessions for the day. Indeed, the afternoons and evenings during most of the week had been left open, and no arrangements had been made for dinners. Fortunately, the presence of the common rooms allowed people to find each other easily during the afternoons, and to converge later on to go off on group treks for dinner at local restaurants. Gradually, the groups going out together got larger, as people sought to spend more of their evenings in each other's company. They did, in fact, get to do so in a range of local spots around the campus, and were free to join up with whomever they wished. That was the more random nature of the system at work.

Day Three: Tuesday, June 11

Some of the participants were puzzled by what appeared to them to be a lack of planning. What about all the time they had spent in previous meetings racking up lists of issues and topics they hoped to cover? Moreover, the evenings had, before, been given over to watching films together and to thinking about how these might be useful in the classroom. What had happened to continuing with this? While they didn't want to spend all day and every evening in working sessions, their previous meetings had led them to expect something a little more intense. During these first few days, occasional comments slipped into the informal moments prior to the working sessions, and Carl took a certain amount of ribbing for the ultra-casualness of week's scheduling.

That morning, the topic was to have been syllabi; the turn it took, instead, was the planning. Carl told the group to think of the week's plan as a syllabus that they all played a part in shaping. He pointed to the discussion that had taken place the day before and to what the group had learned from going into smaller groups.

"What are your expectations when you plan a syllabus?" Louis said. "How does the syllabus deliver that?" The different members of the staff commented, responding to the question.

"Well *I*," said one of the participants, "would like to have heard this discussion on Sunday, about how the planning happened."

"When we met in the spring," said Jack, "I brought three things: issues we had identified in past sessions, e-mails from some of you talking about what you were hoping for and, finally, a personal concern about the congruence or lack thereof between our own ideology and what we espouse on the one hand, and what we teach on the other."

"Can you explain that further," the person persisted.

"It's the gap," Jack replied, "between the ideas we profess, which may be non-hierarchical, and the methodologies we use—or which our institutions impose—which themselves are hierarchical. Students live with that mixed message."

"Tomorrow's workshop on diversity will be more interactive and experiential," said Louis. "It's an attempt to do something more than just the textual, which is part of my own hope. What happens Thursday and Friday can reflect some of that integration."

"My task has been somewhat interpretive," said Mariko. "I'm thinking back to February. My overwhelming impression was how rare among professional peers it was to have this kind of sustained connection, in which we are free to be confrontational but with the time to work it out, without being personally aggravating. We have been able to discuss issues that concern us the most, professionally, that we can't necessarily talk about even with family members. I came in with a certain sense of urgency from a personal stake. This 'syllabus' I liked, because it was not overly structured, and left things open. How else can we have this kind of community?"

"In the planning for last year," Carl said, "we sent out lots of stuff. I could have circulated the syllabus for this week earlier, and asked for feedback ahead of time."

"But there's also the benefit of just creating this space over the year," said someone else. "There's the value of the one-on-one conversations here. It's the space and time to do that, and the things that happen between the planned activities, like on a retreat, that have allowed us to be reflective about what we do."

"We have a kind of charmed community here," said Louis. "The question is, why can't it be more normative? We have to be careful not to squander it."

It was clear that there were multiple takes on how the week had been organized. I suggest that these different perceptions of the planning process can—to return to Kantor's interpretive framework—be understood as a case of different systemic expectations. Carl, it turned out, was a more random sort of person than the earlier meetings would have suggested. Some of the others on the staff preferred more definitely structured, if open, approaches. This time, where Carl had taken on more of the planning, he had had freer rein to play out his assumption that the individuals in the group would generate the necessary initiative and introduce creative modifications along the way. This had also been an expression of his assumption that, by the final week, the participants would be increasingly engaged in defining the contours of what went on. What might look like sloppy planning from a different perspective was, from his side of the table, a formula leaving plenty of room for inspiration. It explained the open-ended afternoons and evenings.

If anything, he was chagrined to discover that others were not quite as enthusiastic about this approach, and was later relieved to hear that some of the disparities in perception might have to do with differences in the type of system various people preferred. Putting the matter in those terms assigned a certain measure of legitimacy to how he had gone about the whole thing and, while it didn't quite solve what to do in the open time, it enabled some of the others to see that their frustration had just as much to do with their own difficulty in tolerating a more random systemic type. So, having engaged in this fairly minor skirmish about the planning (nothing warranting the title of a rebellion), the group returned to the issue of syllabi.

"A syllabus is a text," said Mariko, "an instrument, a contract. What makes it a pedagogically effective and integral part of a course? In the context of your institutional culture, who else reads it aside from your students? Those who assess you, for one. It's also a text of your devising, making it a matter of intellectual property which could be plagiarized. There is some issue of ownership."

After going into small teams to talk further, the group reconvened and reported in. The different groups had raised such issues as how departmental and institutional cultures have an impact on one's syllabi. A given school, for example, may have certain policies on grading, or may favor the use of a single textbook for a course. There may be unstated caps on the cost of the books one can assign, or the amount of reading one can require. Insofar as a syllabus is conceptualized as a contract, what is the nature of the relationship it is intended to effect? How to make it an effective pedagogical tool to give out on the first day of class?

"The contract articulated in a syllabus has to be culture-specific to a given school," one person noted. "What's in it and how it's laid out depends on where you're teaching. Both aspects have to be accounted for. For many students, for example, having things spelled out is what they need."

"Most of my students' lives are different from my college life," said someone else, "particularly in the number of courses they have to take, the kinds, the work they have to do. What does my course look like to them? For a lot of them, I'm not sure."

"I use mine as a blueprint," another person said. "It gets fairly detailed. If I get behind, then it causes static for them. I want to build in as much collegiality and make it as collaborative a process as I can. The more open-ended I make it, the less of a straight-jacket it is, but it can also be more confusing."

"You know," someone said thoughtfully, "I'm wondering just what a course *is*. Why fifteen weeks? What have we done in that time? Can you know any of the real outcomes of what we've done at that point, or only later?"

"One of the things I liked about a syllabus on varieties of American religions that we looked at in our group," said Louis, "was that it laid out a landscape of religions in America. The students have to choose field assignments early on, and do presentations scheduled to complement the readings. They also have to do a critical review related to that tradition. The course, it seems to me, is a collaborative achievement."

"I worry about the issue of literacy," said another person. "Is there value, for example, to foregrounding Biblical literacy? I struggle with trying to figure out the right balance between critical issues and the kind of literacy you could assume in an earlier era. I think there's some value to orienting people to broader issues, even if you can't cover them comprehensively. I put it to them in terms of the student-as-citizen. I'm working to help them find things, so they won't be intimidated by those who claim to be authoritative, particularly about the Bible."

"I try to show them how the Bible is all around them, in American culture," someone else added. "That is, how infiltrated the culture is with it."

"Coming back to the contract issue," said Carl, "once you give it out, you don't know exactly what the students will do with it, but at least it's an attempt to say something about what's trustworthy about the instructor and the course. Who owns it? Is it the instructor, the institution, the guild? I suppose all of them, in some sense. In our department, I look over my colleagues' shoulders to see if the style reflects that of the department. But there's always the question of where structure leaves off and where it can become stifling. You can give too specific a set of directives and extinguish the possibility for novelty and surprise."

"With the increasing complexity of the student body and the field of teaching," said Jack, "it makes this document all the more important." With that, the group disbanded for the day, reminded by Louis to meet the next morning in time to start promptly at nine.

Later that afternoon, the staff met to discuss the issues that had come up during the morning session. They recognized that some of the people in the group were task-oriented, and had wanted things more clearly spelled out. For others, it had to do with ambivalence about having things too controlled.

"What do we do with this?" said Carl. "It will come out in the evaluation—do we do anything? Last October, and in February, for example, we talked about how to use this particular location as a context, and we didn't follow up on that. I think we need to listen carefully tomorrow to determine our plan for Thursday. We may want to talk more about the impact of ourselves on our courses—the issue of self-disclosure and the self-consciousness we bring to the teaching environment. How does a syllabus reflect who we are? I can see that more stuff has to be spelled out."

When he came to evaluate the workshop the following month, Carl wrote that, in thinking back, more sustained planning and greater inclusion of the participants would have been a good idea. It might have helped to have articulated more explicitly a set of tasks and assignments, and to have done more groundwork draw on the local area itself as a resource. The insufficient planning, he concluded at that point, had not been "a fatal flaw . . . but it is clear that more effort in this direction would have been appreciated."[41]

The staff's discussion wound its way from there into reflections of their own on syllabi—on questions of content, the possibilities for a course to be a case in co-learning, the unrevealed assumptions that get played out. They went back over some of the morning's discussion on "the syllabus as a text, archive, canon, and statement of pedagogical commitment on the part of the instructor."[42] It was an illuminating look into the reality that these questions confront not only newer faculty, but those who have been at the project of teaching for some time.

Day Four, Wednesday, June 12

The day's session, as Carl would later write:

> . . . was a departure from previous efforts. In an attempt to get at the deeper issues of identity of the teacher and student in the classroom the Workshop called on Louis to present a day-long version of his Prejudice Reduction Workshop. . . The Workshop is an intense effort to make people feel safe to acknowledging the ways in which they are both participants in and victims of prejudice (racism, sexism). The format for the Workshop involved a certain level of risk-taking and self-disclosure.

---

[41]   Director's report to the American Academy of Religion, the Lilly Endowment Inc., and the National Endowment for the Humanities.

[42]   Ibid.

In the course of a series of exercises, the group was asked to disclose earlier experiences of discrimination in their own lives about which they continued to hold anger and hurt. Rather than simply talking about these feelings, they were to recall them vividly, and to speak out of them, in the company of a partner, before the group. Using the metaphor of "the beloved community," Louis created the context for emotionally charged and frequently raw sequences, with the intention of generating potentially cathartic effects.[43] In their subsequent discussion of what had taken place, the staff talked with each other about the implications of this kind of work. How had it affected everyone? How was it likely to be frightening to power structures? What questions did it pose as to where to make interventions in the life of an institution?

"There is a kind of terror toward the implications of this kind of freedom," said Carl, "especially once the barriers erected by a system are exposed. It's analogous to certain Buddhist moves aimed at awakening a person to the conspiracies of language, conceptual habits, lifestyles designed to keep us asleep. To wake up is to re-enter the project as an agent of transformation, to yield to a world that is radically transformative.

"You have given permission for us to look at and assess the epistemological assumptions that inform our approaches to teaching, such as that the primary goal in our syllabi is to help students develop an appreciation for the academic study of religion as a *feeling* objective; to help them develop the competence to participate in the public discussion of religion, which means taking seriously the biases and commitments we bring to the classroom. So, what kind of space must we create for our students to engage at the feeling level what our objectives talk about?"

"I think," said Louis, "that our vision of transformation is in great conflict. There is not a consensus. The predominant agenda in religious studies is the pressure for ecumenism, toward unity, making it dangerous to question that."

"In this group," Carl added, "we don't have a classicist or a theologian in the old enlightenment liberal tradition. The one strong

---

[43] Because the exercises are part of a copyrighted program, they will not be described here in detail.

voice in religious studies these days is that of essentialist ecumenism, minimizing the differences between the different visions of transformation posited by each of the traditions. There's the idea that there's something good about religion—the sense that one has to assent to that idea. In my career experience, I haven't had discussions about whether religion is 'good' for people or not."

"Here again is where a historical perspective is important," said Mariko. "It's where the real work starts, as we look at how these ideas have come to have power over us. What kind of power is that, and how does it work on us? Disclosing the historical frame helps us see these things more clearly."

"We know enough about religion," Louis replied, "to be terrified of its toxic dimensions. We don't always yet know the way to get around that."

"You started out by asking who participated in religious formation when they were young," said Jack. "It would be interesting to add to that another set of questions on how many would identify their background as fundamentalist in some way. I'm always struck by the number of people in religious studies who have a love-hate relationship with a religious community that sometimes comes through in their—or should I say our?—teaching."

"Will everyone formed in either a more evangelical or highly liturgical tradition please stand up?" said Carl, laughing.

"How many people became converts as Buddhist monks— Americans, that is—and then professors of Buddhist studies?" said Mariko. "A lot of people seem to experience ambivalence about their own background. It affects their identity as teachers and scholars. Here, even the converts to Buddhism didn't necessarily remain monks in a community; instead, they became professors of religion *a s* a resolution. This didn't pertain in the same way with European scholars who studied things like philology with an Orientalist approach. But the question itself makes me feel like a minority—it is not my quandary."

"What I long for from my colleagues," said Carl, "is the safety to express this puzzlement, and for such people to feel safe enough to talk about their own. For me, whatever Hinduism I would convert to doesn't exist. To go inside would be more inauthentic for me than to go inside the Anglican tradition I'm part of, with all the density and elegance of the ritual that I find compelling in Hinduism. It creates a space which feels more workable to me than becoming the disciple of some swami."

"I think sometimes it's a kind of displacement," said Louis. "If you can't find the real thing, in its real context, then you become something else."

"A something else which can also be a figment of one's imagination," Mariko added.

"Not necessarily," said Louis. "There is a certain despair within the Christian community over the possibility of creating what King called the beloved community—that as a tradition, we could not create a loving community that would persist over time. We still have all the rhetoric, but the tradition did not give us the resources to pull it off. At least the early church hadn't expected it would have to last all that long.

"Our disappointment in the inadequacy of our practices gets us looking at other things so that we don't have to look at the inadequacies. Some people figure they can impose other things to simulate the fulfillment of the tradition—like 'if we could just get gays out, and women out of the pulpit,' through the coercive use of the state and a fabricated version of the tradition, in place of really enacting the loving community. Religious transformations that are displacements out of despair are not able to pull off what the tradition really espouses.

"Our historical trauma around religion is sometimes so toxic that we experience despair over religious formations that are so contaminated. The implication of the workshop model today was that this is one way to retrieve the authenticity of the traditions. What, in other words, is benignly human about the traditions? It may be a fabricated universal, treating the tradition almost as something that needs to be recovered, but that has also been the spirit of many a reform movement."

"We need now to think where we're going with this tomorrow," said Jack. "So far, we've been talking about different ways we find ourselves in American culture. The first day was about where we are and why we're doing this. The second was about the syllabus and who it's for. Today, we looked at who we are in the classroom in relation to the subject matter we teach, especially as the demographics of the classroom change. We've also been using small group discussions a lot more, to create a different forum for talking about broader issues."

"I think we need to find ways to reflect on how we can be agents for the students in our classes to celebrate who they are," said Carl. "and to empower them to locate themselves in their own formations. Also, to ask how we operate to perpetuate stereotypes."

"There has to be a feedback mechanism built in to correct for that," said Louis.

"But some of this is built into the academy," Mariko said, "as in very construction of 'religion' as a category. We should take into account the way that teaching religion is, itself, a construction of the academy, as is the way the discussion of racism takes place. We need to keep looking at the involvement of the academy as an institution."

After further discussion, the team agreed to set up five groups the following day, and to pose five questions:

1) What do your pedagogical strategies say about what you (and your institution) value?

2) Drawing on the day's workshop experience, what possibilities and limits to teaching students about self-disclosure are present in the course?

3) What does the syllabus and the course reveal about the kind of learning community we are trying to create in and beyond the classroom? (And, in that connection, what kind of social capital are we building up for the transformative community? What do our answers say about what must be unlearned, what must be surfaced and brought to discussion?)

4) In what way does the course contribute to that which has been oppressed, or celebrate that which has been recovered? How much does it lead to the empowerment of ourselves and our students to locate ourselves in relation to that which has been recovered?

5) What positive or negative "recordings" about ourselves and others does this course perpetuate, through the way we focus on the subject matter and the practices of our teaching and learning?

They agreed that the changes in the week's agenda had come about in a more organic way than had been the case in some of their previous sessions, and that part of this had been due to their own daily meetings.

"How does *that* process get back to the group, as a model of planning?" said Jack. It occurred to them that this might serve as one illustration of how goals can change over the course of a year, and how one—as a teacher—can also change.

Day Five: Thursday, June 13

Jack posed the questions to the group the next day, proposing that the they might split into pairs at first, as a way to illustrate one approach to take with students. The objective of the discussion would be to work toward further understanding of who *we* are in the midst of our teaching, as the one enduring element in all that we do. As one person put it, "Wherever you go, there you are."

"But wait a minute," said another person. "I'd like to take some time for us to process our experience yesterday, either in the large group or in smaller ones."

The interruption was unexpected. The staff looked at each other. This hadn't occurred to them, but now that the point had been raised, they realized it made sense. Jack immediately reconfigured the morning's first session, proposing that the group take time to discuss the previous day's events, followed by a break during which a group photo had been arranged, and then come back to engage the discussion questions.

"Why not start out by going around the room," he said, "and say something about what you found good or useful about yesterday, and what you found hard or challenging." No one was prepared for what followed, as the first person began to speak again.

"I was furious," he said. "I felt coerced into a project about which I hadn't known a lot, and there was no escape. First of all, it was a theological model—the ideal of the beloved community—that I utterly reject, and I was being asked to buy into it, without being asked whether or not I wanted to do so. Secondly, we were being asked to expose a lot of pretty heavy stuff. In my opinion, it was not a safe space to do that. It's true we formed a preliminary bond last summer for looking at parts of ourselves we're not comfortable with or that we might fear being rejected. But I didn't feel we were given any warning that that's what was going to happen yesterday, and in that sense, I didn't feel we had a choice. We had to submit to it, and were being challenged without preparation."

"I agree that the voluntary component was missing," the person next to him broke in. It might be an extremely valuable exercise in some settings, but here we were all *expected* to be a part of it. The presupposition was that this was a model we would accept for teaching. That point needs a lot more discussion."

With those two statements kicking off the discussion, others in the group began to voice their own perceptions of the previous day.

"I was asked to recall a moment of injustice," one woman said. "I was surprised by the rage I still had about it. I also know that from the age of two on, we tell male kids they don't have permission to cry or show much feeling. In a setting like this, the idea is that the guys will open up the way that we, as women, are more permitted to do. I'm not sure how easy that is."

"I had a good idea of what this would be like," said another person. "Personally, I didn't feel coerced, although I can appreciate that feeling. But I did feel rushed, in terms of the emotional pace. I spent a lot of the day trying not to cry in public."

"I'm really not sure about using it as a teacher," said the next person. "There's a time issue. In a lot of women's studies courses, there are all kinds of emotions there, but you only have an hour to teach the class. I find the model appealing, but I also feel cautious about it, and am asking myself where it fits in the classroom."

"I was angry," said the first person, coming back to the original argument, "because we had agreed *not* to do the expert model—but then we did it anyway. There was no space to be collegial, and it was done in the name of creating an emotional model and bond. It almost assumed that we ourselves didn't know anything about issues of diversity. But the fact is that a lot of us have already tried to draw things into our intellectual work. We didn't get to talk about *that*."

"I think it did cut across our intellectual work," someone else said. "It was one of the most important conversations we've had. Even though it was structured this time, it *had* been requested from last summer. It's sort of like the way a syllabus is imposed, and made us get at the way we do create an environment, which we need to bring to the surface. What happens to our students and their issues of identity? What we did yesterday made all of that surface for me."

"I'm finding this a remarkable moment," said another person suddenly. "Yesterday I said to myself that I wasn't looking forward to this." Turning to the person who had begun the discussion, she said, "I want to thank you for instigating this. Had you not done so, this would have escaped us."

Louis had been listening to the different statements. Finally, he spoke. "One of the things I said to the staff last night was that the metaphor of this process is more that of a journey than a program. It's one of stopping places, and what we make of what happens."

"I'm frustrated by some of the resistance," said someone else. "I went into the thing looking for a transparency of relationship. At the same time, bracketing out the intended goals, it's the first time something we've done has really created conflict with substance. Not addressing conflict is a regional issue, and one that I associate with Southern upbringing. I think the most beneficial thing about this is engaging in the conflict."

"Well," said Louis, "the ethos of our guild is that feelings are dangerous, as opposed to what is normative. That's the most alarming thing to me."

It was time for a break. The group drifted out and down to a local coffee shop, talking in twos and threes along the way. When they got back, they were rounded up for a group photograph. The anger that had been expressed seemed in no way to interfere with their engagement in this. When everyone came together again in the faculty lounge, Louis went on.

"One of you suggested during the break that I tell you I also do these diversity workshops as something of a research field, so that my stance is one of learning with you about what all this means, and about what's possible. I haven't found the Grail, the real transformative thing, but I'm on the trail more than people who are only writing about it. I think a real colleague is one who pushes back, and that having feelings about each other is not a disconnect—that we hold on to each other beneath those feelings. The question is, how to do that without abandoning anyone?"

The group thought about what it meant to say that something was coercive. As one person pointed out, there is always a coercive dimension to what went on in any classroom. Louis's exercises had only raised a number of elements that were, to some degree, invariably present, albeit embedded.

"One of the differences for me," said one person, "is that I share this particular commitment with Louis. Many of us do have different commitments and convictions, although we have some similar goals, and we may also have different self-understandings as scholars. But I've learned the most when others talk about their own commitments." In the academy, they agreed, fighting usually becomes a win-lose matter; this was a different kind of fighting. There was, they knew, a risk in conflict, the potential of a bomb going off, of a wreck, with the group possibly being polarized and there not being enough time to do anything about it.

"You were talking about beloved community, yesterday," said someone else. "My beloved community doesn't include Nazis. And there are neo-Nazis in the extended families of some of my students. What if part of a group isn't on board with the vision of a beloved community? I came up through neo-conservative religious people. They silenced the left by accusing us of laying a guilt trip on them about not being academically sophisticated enough. That's not *my* idea of community, and those tapes play for me."

"Well," said Louis, "but what is the beloved community? How do we find the common goal? Can something be formed? I myself have tried the combat mode—'I'll defeat you and *then* I'll talk to you'—but I need to go beyond that, for myself."

"But 'beloved community' is not my language," the first speaker said, in frustration. "'Coalition' is. That's what I'm trying to say. As long as I'm not forced to accept this particular model, I can live with it. But if I lose the idea that this is not my language, or how *I* hold a fork and knife, then I end up feeling like the hidden Jew in a Christian setting."

"The term 'beloved community' comes from Martin Luther King and from Howard Thurman," said someone else.

"My ignorance is such that I didn't know that. But my difference is also with the language of 'healing' that you used. And any move for me to accept it feels like a coercive push to pretend there isn't a difference here, or a potential conflict. It's like the way the head of a department can't tell me we should build a department in which he or she doesn't exercise undue power—because in reality, it's not so. It masks what the power structure really is, but doesn't allow me to say that. I'm not questioning the intentions here, but certain kinds of blindness to power."

"That," someone else interrupted, "speaks to a lot of my issue with yesterday. What pisses me off about the model is that it operates as another power structure that doesn't recognize itself as such, but seeks to perpetuate itself. I come out of an evangelical background, and I felt right back there. It all felt too Christian, in presenting itself as a transparently true way, without being attentive to *us*. Like, wait a minute, have we all been heard that we're not all Christians, or are Christians with a different view?"

Louis was clearly beginning to feel beleaguered. "I said specifically," he reminded the group, "that this is a model developed by a Jewish woman. I see it as a secular humanist model, to which I said I had added some things of my own which are, to be sure, Christian aspects. I made explicit disclaimers which were not heard. This is not a 'liberal' model. I won't hide my own theological convictions, and I'm not afraid of naming power."

Carl would later write:

> On Thursday, the initial time we had devoted to processing the previous day took the whole morning, a good example of a "teaching moment" borne out of a desire to address what some took to be undisclosed ideological commitments within the Workshop, including an implicit theology of self-disclosure as a practice of liberation. The discussion was intense, highly productive, and the most self-involving of the discussions the group had experienced.[44]

But did the group survive it? Even as the morning's time came to a close, it was apparent that part of what had made the conflict possible was the very bond which had formed among the different people there. Ironically, those who most rejected the methodolical

---

[44] From a director's report to the AAR, the Lilly Endowment Inc., and the National Endowment of the Humanities.

concept of self-disclosure were laying out their own reasons for the rejection with considerable candor. When it was pointed out to them that this, too, was a version of the self-disclosure Louis had been talking about, they became even angrier, protesting that they refused to be forced to stand under an umbrella which they had not elected and which neither of them felt covered their own ways of seeing and defining things.

This was, in some respects, a Rebellion; in others, it was not. There were real differences of opinion among the participants over how they had experienced the Wednesday session, and the disagreements had been as much among themselves as with Louis or the others on the staff. At the same time, their appreciation for each other had become strong enough that they could tolerate this. The group began to realize that it could, in fact, enter into the thick of a full-pitched fight and come out the other side still somehow connected to one another. This was to be the only workshop group in which this happened to this degree.

In the staff meeting later that afternoon, the other members of the team worried about the effects of the morning on Louis. They had borne only a minor part of the heat; he had been the primary target. He reminded them that he had done these workshops in far more hostile settings than this one, and that part of the work in doing them involved a certain amount of emotional preparation. What was more frustrating for him was his recollection—one that proved to be shared by the others on the team—that the group had, at the end of the first week, explicitly requested that he do something from his diversity work. Why, then, were some of them now talking about having felt coerced into doing it? It was a telling instance of how people may think they know what they are about to engage in and be caught up short by some dimension they had not expected.

Without dismissing the specific concerns presented by different members of the group, the team slowly began to untangle some of the other elements they speculated had been at play. It was clear that for one of the participants, the Christian elements that seemed acceptable enough to some of the others, were alienating and, probably, too reminiscent of being forced to assimilate once again into a dominant culture—which, of all things, in this group should not have happened. For another person who had reacted bitterly, comparing how the exercises had made him feel with certain aspects of a rejected evangelical upbringing, it had also seemed too Christian, but for different reasons.

There had been no way to anticipate these particular hot spots. They just happen. Moreover, there were, indeed, an agenda and a theology to the work Louis had done. It was therefore not altogether surprising—especially in a group of religion scholars with the language to talk about it in those terms—that the work might have prompted a range of reactions. The question, as the staff had discovered again, was how to translate the experience as a whole into an occasion for teaching.

Day Six: Friday, June 14
The group had been thinking about what had happened, and brought it up again the next morning. Clearly there was more they wanted to say, and the staff decided to let the topic for the morning—"Department curriculum and its cultures"—float loose for a while, focusing instead on the matters at hand. These had to do with the personal consequences and emotional responses which material in a class can arouse for students. What is the nature of the professor's responsibility? Some simply didn't feel responsible on that level. Neither counselors nor therapists themselves, they didn't want in any way to walk through the therapeutic door.

"Whenever the word 'suicide' comes up, I'm on the phone," said one. "I don't want to live with that one, and I don't want to mess someone up."

But, it was pointed out, there may be a false dichotomy here: was there not an important difference between having feelings in the classroom and being confronted with a therapeutic encounter? Also, was there not the risk of again perpetuating the indirect message that no feelings, no emotional response, was tolerable? Describing a class she had taught on women in religion, one person talked about how, in reading about the restrictions placed on women by one tradition after another, there had considerable emotion among some of the students. She could not, she thought, have taught some of the conceptual material without that level of affect.

"I don't want to run for cover from feelings that keep them from hearing each other *and* the conceptual material," she said.

Another person, describing his own teaching setting, talked about its being the university's housing office that dealt with any and all matters relating to the students' emotional lives. The faculty, in contrast, had little involvement at all. On the other hand, both he and many of the others also remembered being undergraduates for whom classes had sometimes stirred up all kinds of upset, often without there being much recourse to anyone for help.

"I think," he said, "we need to be aware of what we stir up, and to respond and refer what we can't handle, but to try to talk about what we *can*. I feel my students need to see that I exist on that level. *My* teachers were irresponsible in stirring stuff up and not dealing with it in class. We may be the first person who's allowed them to talk about these things. If we don't respond, we leave them stuck out there alone with it."

Aside from the reality that academic culture tends to suppress the full spectrum of a person from expressing itself, there is a separate issue, which is that as a teacher, one doesn't have to everything in every course. Nevertheless, the corresponding reality of academic life is that faculty often abdicate from seeing the whole person of the student, relegating it instead to a campus-life staff. Thus, students' affective needs—even when directly related to course material—may get farmed out to another professional guild.

A second, developmental issue involves what may be the new experience for many undergraduates of being treated like an adult.

"It's very important, I feel," said one person, "to make sure that I do this. Age differences, hierarchical structures, and gender differences all make it harder for me to respond to some of my students as adults. What bothers me is an over-emphasis on being empathic which can sometimes lapse into an approach that underestimates or infantilizes the other party."

"In my class on alternative religions," said someone else, "I figure this may be my only shot at teaching non-majors about religion. Whether I teach about the Klan or about the Nation of Islam, media recordings get tripped off. I try to promote an awareness of how those recordings influence us, and to link it up with what it means to be a participant observer. Or I may point to what is said about cults in encyclopedias, and ask how this compares with anthropological or history-of-religions accounts."

One of the only people in the group who had also had training as a family therapist suggested that much of what students were really looking for was simply to be listened to. It was fine not to have answers for them when they found themselves confused and even distressed by materials from a class. If anything, acknowledging and thereby legitimizing the confusion and distress were often enough.

"We're institutionalized to separate the affective life and reason," said Carl. "In my graduate career, we learned to inhabit these ideologies in our practice. We divide ourselves between our interpretive, analytic skills and our affective life, which is seen as necessarily personal and private."

"This spills over into the issue of mentoring," said someone else. "Suppose I teach a course on death and dying, and I'm aware that death has touched each one of my students in different ways. Suppose I set up half an hour each week for that course, and another half hour for a different course, where I'm available for students to come and talk with me about anything they don't feel they want to bring up in class. By the end of the year, I've spent, say, thirty hours doing that. Then I get told I haven't published enough.

"Now, as I think back, I wonder why my mentors didn't to that for me, so I wouldn't feel so insecure about doing it now. Louis's paradigm shows not so much anyone's being at fault, but it does illustrate the way in which time is a unit of exchange with value. The question is, how we allocate it, and what leads us to say, '*That's* a worthy thing to do—let's add that one in.' It's where a department chair has to exercise some influence over the process of evaluation, and to assert that being actively present to students *is* doing part of the work of teaching."

"Well," said someone else, "I feel that for most of my adult life I've been trying to unlearn what I learned as a kid about being an adult—not to feel, not to cry, not to complain or have irrational thoughts or feelings. I don't want to pass those things on to anyone else, whether they're adults or not. I want my students to learn it's okay to be an adult and to have an irrational feeling, or to say 'I failed' or 'I can't do this.'"

Emotions, a number of people agreed, were not problems to be solved. Where it got more complicated for them, as religious studies faculty, was that, as one person put it, the nature of our subject entails the cognitive, the volitional, and the affective. But in this connection, many of them had experienced other faculty who had, essentially, said "I don't have anything to say about the emotional thing you're going through."

"We all get different challenges at different times," said one person, "but I wouldn't wish what happened to me on my own graduate students."

"I understand that people are complex wholes, and that you can't separate reason and affect, but *I'm* not here to deal with their emotional or spiritual development," said someone else. "But wait a minute—actually, it's hypocritical of me to say that, because on an existential level that *is* what I'm trying to do. Of course I sit and listen. I'm a pushover." The group talked for a while longer about the nature of listening, and then Carl proposed they take their break and come back afterwards to the discussion of department cultures and the curriculum.

What they returned to, instead, was a point raised earlier in the week by a participant who had talked about the personal experience of coming from a working-class background and the class-based nature of the academy—the difficulty of the things one has to learn to leave behind, in order to be socialized into it, for example, and the pathologies that accrue in the process. But in the current scheme of things, where do academics fit in the class structure of the culture?

"The hidden injury of class for me," said one person, "is the need to work so hard. Privilege, for me, is to work on what I call 'strawberry pie.' There's a radical insecurity I live with, because we're not part of the elite or the upper class; we're employed by it." Strawberry pie quickly became the group metaphor for the things one most loves to work on, regardless of the reward.

"The strawberry pie part is right," said someone else, "but under what conditions? There are instructors who are now making only twenty-five thousand a pop, even with their doctorates. We don't talk about instructors' situation at the AAR."

"I resonate with that," said someone else. At the last annual meeting of the AAR, I experienced one of my national moments of hilarity. There, in the program, was a paper on being a fairy cross-dresser. In itself, that's okay, but there was not one paper about our own economic condition, our own social anxiety, our fear. We were all absolutely silent about it. Ten years ago we could talk about class—that is, if we were talking about working class. Now we don't want to talk about our own downward mobility as an institution. If we did that, think about the blow-up it would produce! The reality of the insecurity many of us feel is palpable. And yet we're unable to talk about our own institutional conditions over the past decade."

"One way I've thought about this," said Louis, "in terms of myself and my colleagues as members of the middle class, is that we are also agents of domination for students. We're at the service of a corporate culture that says you get these people ready according to certain standards of English, punctuality, accountability and so on, to fit into the economy. We're in a machine doing *that* to our students by our structures. On the other hand, because we're at the paid beck and call of the system that's doing that, we're also its victims. We're in a crazy situation, hurting because it's done to us and also because we see the pernicious effects of what some of what we're doing. Our own pathos lies in seeing this, just as our own emancipatory energy also comes out of seeing it. Likewise, we are caught between trying to find a way collectively to dismantle the machine, and yet facing the terror of what that could mean not to have the machine."

Somehow the discussion shifted back to the experiences on Wednesday. What had been the most significant learnings to have emerged? For some, it had made them ponder the question of coercion on the one hand, and how far to enfranchise their students on the other. It had forced them to reflect on how coercive an instrument a syllabus can be, and made it easier to think about possible resistances it might arouse.

For some, the diversity workshop itself had been an exercise in submitting to an alternative practice with the willingness to see what insights might come of it. For others, it posed the risk of discovering that one does not, after all, speak for others, however good one's intentions may be. What kinds of ecumenism can one live with, and which kinds are more difficult, however great the more idealistic longing for coalition?

"One of the most powerful insights I came away with," said one person, "was that Louis had presented us with one explicit model of education as transformational practice. The reality is, we all have a transformational practice built into our teaching, but we don't put that up front, and we're usually not strategic about it. So, I think we have to be clearer about that."

In the main, they had also, they thought, experienced a fruitful use of anger.

"So long as it's not aired, owned, discussed, you can only go so far," another person pointed out. "You're stuck in a certain degree of superficiality till then. I see it throughout the academy, but especially in the South. It's part of the culture here. You don't tell people directly what you mean."

Would they find a way to continue their discussion after the end of the workshop? Did they want to? Should they try for e-mail, and aim to sustain something of a virtual community? Would there be ways to keep getting together? What was the nature of their relationship, and to what extent should they try to continue? Should they get a T-shirt made? ("It should read, 'May I have some more strawberry pie, please?'" someone quipped.)

It was clear already that there was no consensus. Some people wanted to continue discussions online; others fought the idea of having to buy into the idea of being a "group." They might keep up connections with particular individuals, but had no other interest in trying to hold the group, as such, together. It was, however, generally felt that holding some sort of closing exercises would be a good thing. They could agree to let a small team work out the details.

In their meeting that afternoon, the staff thought back over the past several days. They had not, they agreed, quite known how to bring the curtain down on Wednesday's aftermath. At the same time, they felt that both the most difficult and the most fruitful discussions had happened over the subsequent two days. There would have been no way to plan for it, and perhaps part of it came out of their allowing themselves to be caught off guard. Ultimately, they thought, they had done the right thing in hanging in with the topic. Whatever dissonance they had experienced as a result, it had taken some people's reacting negatively to get the group to recognize and listen to the different experience of the same event. It also showed them that there were voices who wanted to be heard not just in an affective mode, but in a more cognitive one as well.

The one outing that had been planned for the week was a trip to the Grand Ole Opry. It had been Carl's idea, and went along with his own exuberance and sense of leaping into popular culture for the fun of it. The group car-pooled their way out to the mega-parking lot, those who had arrived first sitting on the porch of the entry-way watching the crowds stream in.

For those who haven't yet been to the Grand Ole Opry, the theater seems large beyond reckoning and—at least from the third or fourth balcony seats (that high up, one starts to lose count)—the figures on the stage, glittering, fringed, and small. There is a great deal of red velvet, and countless clusters of loud speakers spread across the rafter heavens, which didn't include the larger-than-life speakers at either side of the stage.

Few of the stars of Country MTV were on the program. It was, instead, mostly an older set of singers, some of whom would at one time have been cronies of straw-hatted Minnie Pearl and her dangling price tag. Most of them sang out of bluegrass and old-time country, the kind one hears echoes of in the new cross-over music. None of them could have been confused with soft rock. The fans were devoted, each performer drawing his or her own to stand on the ground level along the stage, waiting for the artist to reach down and shake a hand.

The jokes were vaudevillian, the sentiments unambiguously evangelical and nationalistic. The participants from the North were brought to recall, as they listened to the patter surrounding the songs, that the accents in which the performers were singing were no affectation. Most of the workshop participants who had grown up in the South recognized the names of even the older singers; those from outside the region did not. There were a number of both who became nostalgic and had a grand time, and a number of both who found the event amusing for a while and then uninteresting. It was not altogether clear to them why they had come, except that they were in Nashville and so was the Opry. Some left early. If only because it prompted such different responses, it proved an ambiguous note on which to spend the final evening together.

Day Seven: Saturday, June 15

There was this one morning left. The group took the first part of it to talk about the curricula in their departments, returning again to the example of the interdisciplinary program that one of them had designed at his own school. The rest of them had, in other settings, seen two tendencies at work. The first was more conservative, retaining the traditional sense of disciplines working in cooperative relationship. The other was more radical, where it was not just a question of coordinating the contributions of different disciplines but of questioning those very allocations of knowledge. The objective, in this case, was the deep interrogation of one set of knowledge bases by another.

The first was the more common. It was safer. Much of the resistance people had witnessed arose against the second, because it challenged the very definition of their areas of specialization. Who was willing to have their field questioned by another? It was often younger faculty who pushed for such an approach, their allegiance to a particular discipline being, perhaps, more fluid. At the same time, there was often a great deal of identity tied up in a given curriculum.

Jack pointed out that whenever changes of this nature are made, there will, in all likelihood, be a backlash within three to five years. It is wise, therefore, to think strategically about how to anticipate and respond to such a backlash as part of one's planning. When a curriculum seems to be running out of gas, it can be because the problems it once addressed no longer exist in the same way. One could aim for about a five to seven year life cycle for a curriculum, and it should be presented in this light.

Before ending their discussion, the group turned for a while to thinking about how, at both the regional and national meetings, to pass on what they had learned through the workshops. Finally, it was time to wrap things up. The committee entrusted with designing the closing rites had a couple of things planned, the first of which was, as the sheet they passed out put it, a "Traditional melody; c. 19th Century," otherwise recognizable to most as the tune for a well-known jingle.

> "Teaching: It's the Real Thing"
> Lyrics: Anon.
> *Chorus*
> It's the real thing,
> South or North,
> Great students, colleagues,
> It's the real thing.
>
> *Verse:*
> I'd like to teach my guild to teach
> in perfect harmony.
> I'd like to learn just how to earn
> while avoiding class envy.
>
> *(Chorus)*
>
> *Verse:*
> I'd like to be a Ph.D.
> and have myself a job,
> and sit me down
> in an endowed chair
> of Enlightenment and Peace.
>
> *(Chorus)*

There were a few skits, which included a satire of a staff planning session. "None of the staff escaped without a good deal of lampooning," wrote Carl.[45] And with much laughter, the workshop came to an end.

No grand theories defining the South had emerged. "For some," Carl wrote, "the issue of regionality diminished as a compelling topic to be replaced by issues of pedagogy, strategies for professional survival, intellectual nurture, community within one's own institutions, and maintaining lines of networked communication."[46] In a more overt sense, this was indeed true. At the

---

[45] From a director's report to the AAR, the Lilly Endowment Inc., and the National Endowment of the Humanities.

[46] Ibid.

same time, the settings being described and brought into the discussion each day had been Southern. Thus, it was through the focus on the particularities of their own teaching worlds that the complexities and multiples meanings of the South were sustained.

V

Teaching Religious Studies in the Southwest

Introduction

In 1992, the AAR received a proposal from a team in the Southwest region. They were interested in running a teaching workshop, and proposed to follow the general structure of the Wabash model in virtually all respects. The proposal was turned down in favor of others more thoroughly developed in terms of their planning, schedule, and objectives. One point did, however, stand out, and may have served as a seed for the eventual focus on the South: Among their objectives, the writers of the proposal included the development of "the special skills needed for teaching religion in the 'Bible Belt.'"

When it became clear to the AAR officers in the national office that they would need to organize the proposals the following year as part of their larger funding request to the NEH, they approached the regional committee in the Southwest and asked them to rework their earlier proposal. As had been the case in the Southeast, a preliminary proposal was drafted, critiqued by Warren Frisena and Barbara DeConcini, and rewritten in the interest of composing a program that would address the distinctiveness of the Southwest.

The person from the region who had drafted the original proposal remained part of the process for a time, but difficult personal circumstances eventually required them to withdraw from the project. How, then, to find someone to direct the program? Sarah, who was on the regional board at the time, recalls, "They told me, 'We need to have someone's name on the proposal.' 'All right,' I said, 'but don't expect me to actually *do* it.' They got all the way to receiving the funding, and then said to me, 'But you've *got* to do it.'"

Thinking back and laughing, she said, "I went in kicking and screaming. I said, 'On one condition—that you let me co-direct it, and I want Augustín—that's Gus—Martínez. Then they let me pick the other folks, too. But I thought Gus was especially important, because he's Latino. We went into the writing of the proposal knowing that if we got it right, it would happen. It wasn't an open call. It *would* be in our region if we re-did it, and honed it and honed it and honed it. The first couple of times what we wrote wasn't satisfactory, but we got to do it over again, and to polish it to make it more compelling than it had been at the first pass." By the time they had pulled it together, the proposal stated that:

> The purpose of this workshop is to explore issues of teaching religion in the Southwestern United States. Southwestern religious practices carry their own distinctive assumptions, many of which have persisted from frontier days to the present. While it would be wrong to make too much of the Southwest's unique blend of Protestantism, German, French and Mexican Catholicism, and Native American religious practices, these traditions do form the background against which contemporary Southwestern religious life continues to be drawn. Coupled with broader cultural themes that draw on Southwestern agricultural and ranching patterns, it is clear that the Southwest is in many ways more West than South.[1]

In addition to the structure and general objectives that had defined all of the workshops, the drafting team came up with five that were regionally specific:

> 1) equip participants to deal with issues relevant to teaching religion in the Bible Belt by helping them to develop a deeper understanding of the questions, issues, and expectations that are likely to be found among students in the Southwest region;

---

[1]   AAR Proposal to the National Endowment for the Humanities, p. 1

2) develop an awareness of the influence of the Southwest's expanding cultural diversity on the teaching of religion;
3) become more attentive to the historical and contemporary background that is currently shaping the religions of the Southwestern region;
4) foster an understanding of and some facility in using non-textual materials and methods for classroom use;
5) explore and develop proficiency with a variety of teaching methods and skills.[2]

As in the case of the Southeast proposal, this one also stated the intention of creating "a community of scholars who knew one another *first* as teachers and who are committed to helping one another improve their professional skills."[3]

To carry this out, the planners figured that morning sessions would be dedicated to seminar-style discussions about general pedagogical issues and regional contexts, for which the staff would put together "a common reading list of historical, literary, and sociological texts, along with texts devoted to specific pedagogical themes."[4] They expected to set up a list-serve as a means of communicating with the participants.

> The goal is to create an atmosphere where participants feel welcomed into a community that is open and interested in exploring innovative ideas with one another. Those participants who do not yet have access to electronic mail will receive help in getting "on-line."[5]

Taking seriously the goal of giving greater attention to pedagogy at the regional level, the staff planned to hold the spring weekend session in conjunction with the AAR's spring meeting which, in the Southwest, is always held in Dallas. The point of doing so was to encourage the participants "to participate in those meeting sessions that seem most appropriate to the workshop's goals."[6]

---

2   Ibid., p. 3.
3   AAR Proposal to the NEH, p.14.
4   Ibid.
5   Ibid.
6   Ibid.

The First August Week

The Planning

Of the four individuals who would eventually constitute the workshop staff, Sarah and Gus had been the only two involved in drafting of the actual proposal. Some time after that that, Jerry and Roger, the other two staff members, were recruited. Gus and Roger were Bible scholars; Sarah taught theology and women's studies. Jerry's field was East Asian Buddhism. The staff, now complete, met together for the first time at the regional meeting during March, 1995. They agreed to send out applications to all the schools in the region. The original announcement of the workshop in both the Southeast and Southwest in *Religious Studies News* made no mention that the participants would each receive a stipend and, when the team announced it in the regional newsletter, they duplicated the original, thereby repeating the omission. Responses were sparse.

The team worked hard to increase their numbers. Sarah, describing the process, wrote:

> When we figured out what was wrong, we sent letters to all academic departments of religion in the area, soliciting applications. The number rose from 9 to 13 at this point. The four of us directors directly solicited institutions by phone for nominations and extended the pool to include seminaries as well as undergraduate and graduate institutions. We ended up with about 25 applications total and picked the strongest 15, plus 3 alternates. [The selection process was carried out through a conference call between the members of the staff.] These break down as follows: 2 ABD's, 2 seminary professors with interests relevant to the study of religion, 1 medical ethicist teaching at a medical school, 1 adjunct faculty member in the state system, and the rest standard academic study of religion types. (Unfortunately for us, one of our strongest applicants got a job outside the region; so, we lost him.) We think the overall professional variety is an asset and should produce some lively discussion.
>
> The process of having to work so hard to get applicants, however, was very sobering. Among other things it made us aware of the following: 1) how much SBL (the Society for Biblical Literature) dominates this region; 2) how few institutions in which religion is taught there are within the region, compared to some of the other regions (the prohibition against teaching religion in the public system, unless it looks

like philosophy or history, really works against us in Texas); and 3) how few new faculty are being hired, such that the region itself may soon be "tenured in."[7]

As her letter illustrates, regional variables influenced the workshop even before it had actually begun. A more ominous note also hovered over the project in the form of the reductions in the hiring of new people. This uncertain job future increasingly confronted those coming into the job market, as departments compensated for straightened budgets by not replacing their retiring members.

The staff met again in mid-June, at which point they took the original schedule they had sketched out for the funding proposal and, in light of new, pertinent publications—particularly the Winter 1994 issue of *The Journal of the American Academy of Religion*[8]— revised their plans. What had changed encompassed:

> ... workshop subjects, including order, focus, titles, and the reading list, though we have not departed from the overall goals or substantive focus. Gus is currently working on a "syllabus" and a list of additional resources for the first session . . . We have kept the required readings relatively few and short so that we may discuss issues in depth, but we have also developed an extensive bibliography of additional sources. We've also divided up responsibilities for the sessions and set up a schedule that we hope is both disciplined and flexible.[9]

Lest it not have become clear even at this early point, and had the title not been spoiled from being previously assigned, Sarah would have well deserved the designation "the great communicator." Throughout the workshop, one of the tasks she would take on was that of insuring the dissemination of necessary information, coupled with a strong sense of the process of things.

By the end of June, a letter from Gus had gone out with the schedule of the activities, the bibliography, and some logistical information. In general, he and Sarah either alternated in writing these letters, or signed them together. It was the first of these workshops to have this sort of joint directorship, and their

---

[7] Personal correspondence, June 15, 1995, p. 1.
[8] *Settled Issues and Neglected Questions in the Study of Religion*, *JAAR*, vol. 62, no. 4, Winter 1994.
[9] Personal correspondence, June 15, 1995, p. 2.

communications made it clear that this was how they understood their working roles. Following a string of missives, one last-minute letter went out in mid-August. It advised everyone further about the readings and suggested that those who worried about dietary restrictions not being adequately addressed (although the staff would make every effort to do so) might choose to bring their own stash of snacks. With that, and with the request to let them know everyone's travel plans, the staff was ready to begin.

Day One: Monday, August 7

The participants had been asked to arrive by the afternoon, so that they would have time to settle in before dinner and the following meeting. They would be staying in campus dormitories, in two-room suites. Their meetings and meals would all take place in a large, old elegant old house that had been purchased by the school and restored to serve as a conference center. As one entered, to the left, there was a large room which may, at one time, functioned as a reception room, but which now served as a dining room, its elaborately carved moldings all freshly painted. Straight ahead was a sun room where lunchtime buffets were laid outby the waiters, who also served the evening meals. In the front hall itself, a grand circular stairway—the type down which one envisioned a Texas belle descending in full ball regalia—spiraled its way upstairs. The group itself would be meeting on the third floor.

It was August, that first day, and hot in a dry, breathless way that hit you when you stepped in and out of the air-conditioning chill. Early in the morning, the sprinklers would go on, keeping the campus, at least, a green time out from the browning, dusty lawns in some other parts of town. It was an older private school, and a central boulevard lined with old homes running down its center, served as a reminder that it had come from gracious beginnings.

That afternoon, as people entered their dormitory rooms— brick barracks, with desks and shelves built in along the walls, and twin beds in just about the only possible remaining arrangement— they were met by fruit baskets put together by Sarah. (She later joked about her frantic scramble to assemble the twenty baskets the night before.) She, too, had taken to heart the encouragement to make the participants feel welcome from the instant of their arrival, and had labored mightily the night before to insure that everything would have the right touch.

Once the group had mingled over the reception and dinner, they went upstairs to introduce themselves more formally. The staff had originally thought to have everyone discuss their most memorable teaching moment and what they had learned from it. As they thought about how to foreground the regional dimensions of the workshop, however, they had decided instead to have people describe their teaching projects—which they would be asked to sketch out in their briefest contours—and the schools and departments where they were each teaching. The title would be "Who Are We, and Where Are We Coming From?"

Gus opened the conversation by saying that this would be an occasion for everyone to begin the process of bonding (as I recall, he made a passing reference somewhere in there to Super-Glue) followed by Sarah, who said, "This is Sarah, who sitteth at the right hand of Gus." In that dry quip and chuckling follow-up, the nature of their teamwork, expressed in their earlier letters to the participants, began to come alive as a working reality.

Sarah was another shorts and T-shirts person; so was Jerry. Gus and Roger were not. The participants ended up being a similar blend. Some were located at relatively liberal church institutions, others at a number of larger private universities. One taught in a small school where, as she put it, "I *am* the religion department," and was expected to generate her own enrollments by placing ads in all the local media. Then there was a big state school where, as the person said, "In my larger lecture courses, I have students who can't remember what my name is." One person taught at a school where the students were primarily fundamentalist Christians, and where he was expected to prepare them for preaching careers in the ministry. The two who came from a seminary said that it lay out in the backwaters, and they had little access anywhere nearby to research resources, meetings, or other colleagues. To use a larger library entailed hours of driving and usually a visit of several days.

Eight of the participants considered themselves to be from some part of the South, although not necessarily from the

Southwest; five were originally from other regions of country. Two of the men were from Africa. There were no African-Americans; nor were there any Latinos. Five participants were women. Twelve were Christian, some more conservative than others; one was Muslim; the other two were not affiliated with a formal tradition, although one had engaged in meditation practices for years.

The concerns they raised relative to their teaching environments included questions of how to teach about differentiating one's personal religious life from materials in a course, the ethnic and religious diversity of some of the schools in particular (and the lack of it in others), and how to undertake some of the remedial work required by some of their students' lack of preparation. Even before the conversation had gone around the table, people were beginning to draw comparisons between their different teaching worlds. This focus on setting would remain a constant throughout the workshop.

Day Two: Tuesday, August 8

"What we're trying to do morning," said Sarah, as the group settled in around the open rectangle created by four long tables, "is not to address your projects in detail but to raise general issues about teaching in this region. We'll focus the weekends on your projects."

The team had decided to divide the morning into two thematic sessions, the first entitled "Feed Their Minds' or 'Cure Their Souls?" and the second, "The Place of Theology in the Teaching of Religion."[10] Jerry and Roger would start out; Gus and Sarah would pick up after the break. Jerry and Roger would begin by laying out positions in disagreement with one another. Roger went first.

"What is the difference between critical reflection and teaching about one's own commitments and tradition? Some people have said they feel that the most important thing is to teach critical analysis, and we're all concerned with that. But should personal commitment

---

10 The readings for this session included: Delwin Brown, "Believing Traditions and the Academic Theologian," in *JAAR*, vol. 62, no.4, Winter 1994, pp. 1167-79; Sam Gill, "The Academic Study of Religion," *JAAR*, vol. 62, no.4, Winter 1994, pp. 949-75; Susan Thistlethwaite, "Settled Issues and Neglected Questions: How is Religion to Be Studied," *JAAR*, vol. 62, no.4, Winter 1994, pp. 1037-45.

be kept entirely separate? There is an emphasis on objectivity in the academy, to avoid being accused of running Sunday Schools. So, there have been pragmatic reasons for people in religious studies to emphasize objectivity and critical thought, to appear to be dispassionate, ant to play down the issues of personal identity. It's ironic. If we were teaching a course in philosophy, we would want to present the option for students to become Platonists or Aristotelians.

"In the case of the Bible, it isn't really studied because it's an interesting artifact, but because it is a set of living scriptures and bodies of precedent that have shaped both Jewish and Christian cultures and communities. At my school, I take the approach of setting these precedents alongside each other and looking at the choices they represent. I've done that because the students there are more centered in these things and because my department takes seriously that this is a church-related institution. Hence, my courses include using texts for 'curing souls.'" He turned to Jerry.

"I'd like to start out with the mission statement of the AAR," said Jerry, who proceeded to read it aloud:

> The American Academy of Religion is a learned society and professional association of teachers and scholars in the field of religion. Through academic conferences and meetings, publications, and a variety of programs and membership services, the Academy fosters excellence in scholarship and teaching. Within a context of free inquiry and critical examination, the Academy welcomes all disciplined reflection on religion and seeks to enhance its broad public understanding.

"We are part of a Western intellectual, academic tradition," he went on. "I argue that there are many resources within our culture to deal with personal and developmental issues, but not that many for doing critical, reasoned reflection. Our job is to introduce students to the latter in relation to religion. Sam Gill's article on the academic study of religion puts it well, I think:"

> The academic study of religion . . . has not enjoyed adequate development. As an academic discipline, distinct from the religious study of religion, it has failed to advance any sustainable body of theory, any cadre of religion theorists, and substantial body of literature. The inability to articulate the academic study of religion and the unsatisfactory defense of the place and role of religion studies in

the modern academic environment have placed departments of religion at a low level of budgetary priority and at risk in many colleges and universities.

In contrast, what has thrived is the religious study of religion, that is studies in which the scholar is studying her or his own religion or a religion other than his or her own primarily for the purpose or purposes stipulated by the religion studied rather than the purpose or purposes stipulated by the academy. In other words, the study of any religion—whether one's own or another—in order to find God, to transcend desire, or any other reason that religious practitioners have for their religious practices, including study, is a religious and not an academic study. These religious studies have long American traditions and intellectual heritages spanning centuries. However, it will be contended that the success of these kinds of religious studies has likely contributed to the repressed and retarded development of the academic study of religion.[11]

Looking up from what he had been reading, Jerry continued, saying, "If we address personal concerns too much in our classes, we neglect something else that our students don't get elsewhere, which is the discussion of religion as an academic discipline. The readings for today make the case that our courses can help breed tolerance and a reasoned approach, as an ethical, moral project, which an emphasis on personal inquiry might not. This would argue for a greater emphasis on feeding their minds as one way to cure their souls."

Was it so absolute a distinction, one participant wondered. Another responded that, in his experience, it was unworkable both theoretically and practically.

"What are we telling them?" he said with some indignation. "Forget your existential problems when you come into our classes? Forget that your parents are getting a divorce?"

"If you don't," said Jerry, "then what do you spend your time in class *doing*?"

"We're examining things that have existential relevance," the other replied. "These are not objective parts of our existence."

Sarah interrupted. "No one is using the term 'objective'; we're talking about a difference in models. Sure, we're talking about people claiming that God became flesh in Jesus, and people who said Krishna did the same thing, and both in the same class. If I were

---

11   Gill, "The Academic Study of Religion," p. 966.

taking an anthropology class, I wouldn't necessarily think it had a bearing on my parents' divorce, and I wouldn't expect the professor to address it. In religion classes though, it is a different question as to what extent we're getting students to integrate their lives, and to what extent they're supposed to put all that aside when they come in. There are political and economic ramifications to our choices, too, because in some places we *are* thought of as high-class Sunday School teachers, and our departments are getting cut."

Someone else wondered whether part of the task was, indeed, simply to describe what others did somewhere else far away, or whether it was to show how these other traditions represent real models of selfhood which might potentially be meaningful to one's students. One would present them with scholarly rigor, but not necessarily stop there.

"If you can have feminism in the classroom, why can't you have these kinds of questions?" he said.

One of the issues at stake is the authority of one's own background. Does this have any legitimate place in the classroom?

"However we approach the study of religion raises questions about what's legitimate," said one person. "Do we understand that we can't take a more universal stance, but invariably speak in some way out of our own commitments? This is so, even when we say we are speaking in a reasoned way. We have to locate our perspectives, because even then we are speaking out of the rationality of particular perspectives. The thing is, religion scholars become embarrassed about 'religiosity', so they try to talk about religion as a means to some other end."

"It is partly an issue of how we draw comparisons, too," said someone else. "Do we succeed in presenting something about the coherence of a given tradition and how it holds together, or do we engage in that most pernicious of American habit, namely picking, choosing, and borrowing segments because it's more comfortable to do so and we are less likely to have to confront the difficult dimensions of different traditions?"

What we present in the classroom, it was suggested, creates an authoritative text about what religion *is*—one that may, wittingly or unwittingly disclose our own struggle. This is all the more the case insofar as we present certain materials sympathetically and others less so, whether it be those that are somehow "other" or those that are closer to us which receive the more critical judgment.

"As a footnote to that," said Gus, "we all realize that the academy is an establishment with its roots in the history of the West. In our field, what is exciting is that previously excluded people have come into it—women, for example, and others with personal histories going back to before nineteenth-century colonialism."

It was also pointed out that for some of those present, their teaching settings complicated the project by expecting from them a more conservative and even confessional stance in the classroom.

"In my school, for example," said one person, "there's a tension between trying to be more rational on the one hand and the strong church connection on the other. That has pushed the graduate Sunday School emphasis to convert these students, which disgusts me. But it also raises for me the question concerning my ethical responsibility, given that I've taken a job there and have agreed to a exercise a certain profession."

The academic inquiry of anything, one person observed, involved looking at things critically on both phenomenological and existential levels. If religion can be understood as saying that it is a source of something along with a human way of being in the world, cannot both of these aspects be examined with rigorous methodologies, in order to understand better how they function?

"Or," said someone else, "it's like an image from an exhibit on the Americas—a sculpture of a shaman with his arms thrown out and his eyes wide open. You can see him as either someone offering a vision, or seeking to grasp one."

They took a break. When they came back, Sarah and Gus segwayed the conversation into their own topic, with Sarah commenting on the number of people in the group who, in one way or another, defined themselves as theologians. Only two, however, were teaching in seminaries. So, where did theology belong?

"The question," she said, "is often posed as 'religious studies versus theological studies versus where do you put Biblical studies?' Our department is loosely affiliated with the Presbyterian Church. We take the tie seriously as a school, but don't think that means we should be doing something other than the academic study of religion in our department. This becomes more crucial as a discipline in the time of budget cuts and challenges from the extreme right. It makes the issue of where theology belongs in relation to the study of religion all the more important.

"I think theology *does* belong in my department, but that it also depends on what you mean by theology. It's the most important of the things I do, especially insofar as it gets students to imagine worlds and selves other than their own. I teach about theology, and understanding oneself as a theologian. This is at the heart of my own theology, the outward trajectory of which is toward the stranger, the other, the enemy, and the neighbor who don't agree. I do all of this from an academic stance. Of course, it helps that the school, because of its religious affiliation, has a clause making the religion department the only guaranteed department in the place."

Chuckling, Gus said, "In her department they've had serious questions for years about what she does." Sarah turned and looked at him over her glasses. "But more seriously," he went on, "the point here is that the traditional way of looking at theology has for years contrasted it with the academic study of religion. It does require a specific stance; there is no generic theology. Of course, by extension of the name, there is necessarily Hindu theology, and so on.

"To remind you of the obvious, the systematic theology of the past sees itself as the exposition of a particular religion. Christianity doesn't concern itself with explaining how anybody else sets up the world, but gives it its own particular spin with its own particular set of intellectual tools that have originated in the West. That kind of theology is dependent on a particular faith tradition. Another definition—that of Gustavo Gutierrez—describes theology as a *praxis* of Christian communities. This is also not a generic theology, but clearly a Christian and, more specifically, Catholic one.

"If the academic study of religion must not depend on a particular point of view or religious tradition, and given that there is often a resistance to the expression of theological views, it is possible that we have an unsolvable problem with teaching theology. I, too, went for a while priding myself on the fact that my students didn't know I was an ordained Presbyterian minister. I used to get a bit of a thrill when a kid said at the end, 'You're not Jewish?' I still don't teach the Hebrew Bible in a Christian way, because I've gone in a direction that allows me to bypass that. But the tradition in my department is that the closer you get to theology, the closer you are imagined to get to a sectarian position, which brings a series of problems. Sarah, on the other hand, has redefined theology as a way to encourage students to imagine worlds and selves other than their own. That fits in the classroom, but is it theology?"

"Actually," said Sarah, "in the economics department you may have various schools of economics all calling themselves a science, and they can do that. The question for me is not why there are multiple perspectives, but why Christians have theologies in the first place. I teach courses on public policy, law, the family, and so on, in the midst of Christian pluralism and different Christian understandings of these things. I use lots of materials from anthropology and sociology; I also teach a lot of Christian responses to these things as well. Of course, some people might not recognize this as theology."

"I tend to be more open about my own location now," said Gus. "I let students know, as a matter of honesty. But last year, an interesting thing happened. A lot of Muslim students take my courses. They've been pushing to get a Muslim students' association started, and they asked me to be the faculty sponsor. Even when I went on leave, they kept me on."

"I don't understand the problem you set up, Gus," someone said. "Certainly there is no generic theology or ritual or religious practice. Everything is specific to a particular community. Likewise, so is Sarah's a specific construction. I think it's a misleading practice to take a particular form of openness as somehow less particular."

"It's not a dichotomous problem," said Gus. "It's more of a spectrum. When I came here to teach world religions, I replaced someone who had been a missionary and who, when he reached the end of each segment, would compare each tradition with Christianity. That's one way to bring a particular theological position into the classroom. Actually, my own theological position is quite close to Sarah's. I have a serious problem with the one-way, exclusivist claims that so many people make who teach in this field. I can't possibly make that part of my personal beliefs or teaching. But there are a lot of Christian theologians teaching who do."

"Maybe I'll put what I'm about to say in a provocative way," said another person slowly. "Maybe it's not surprising that you'd have a similar theological approach, or a coincidence that people in academic settings have similar perspectives. We don't entirely protect the First Amendment. We *do* have an establishment in secular institutions, and give a certain privilege to certain understandings. But in making a case for theology, it involves certain assumptions, themselves rooted in a religious tradition. I don't see why theology should be excluded from the academy as an interpretive or analytical lens."

"I agree," said Sarah. "The problem isn't that; the problem is the legacy of Christians beating people over the head, but that's not happening in the same way. The question is, when you have so much pluralism and such scarce resources, where will you put your money to reflect the pluralism most genuinely? In a department, do you weight things to reflect the pluralism of the culture, or in the direction of the Christian and Western traditions?"

"In fact," said Gus, "even giving priority to theology is really a Western Christian fact already. Other traditions don't. In the cases of Islam or Judaism, it would be the study of law."

"So," said Sarah, "part of the debate is over just how Western we're going to be."

"We can't escape our history," said someone else. "Gus has described his experience here. Where I teach, my work is to get people to see that there's a world other than the one they come from, with a broader context—to get them out of the theology they were raised in. But I can't break them out of that theology without doing it theologically. The academy made great gains in the sixties, seventies, and eighties,but the world is now calling for expressions of faith. The population is saying, 'We need help.' Our history has brought us to a new place."

But was there not, another person speculated, an important difference between not requiring a particular point of view and excluding a particular point of view?

"In my classroom," he said, "I see a lot of diverse people, but a strong segment wants a generic theology. They're often not satisfied with an exclusionary Christian theology, but are crying out for some faith position. In the class on world religions, they're sometimes not so much learning about others as they are searching for options for themselves. On the one hand, part of my job ends up being to help them wrestle with the strangeness of other traditions; on the other, in a loose way, it's about creating a history-of-religions theology of some kind."

The church-related schools, it was pointed out, had been intended to prepare young men in pre-theological training, and to fit them out for a seminary education. This makes the place of a religion department in such schools quite different from the one it might hold in state institutions. When we talk as if all solutions were equal, it does our colleagues a disservice, because of the great disparities between their teaching settings.

"I want to come back," said someone else, "to what seem to be the differences between Jerry's position of trying to help students develop a sympathetic understanding of other traditions, and what was just said about giving them the tools to develop a generic theology. On the surface, these appear in stark contrast. Yet my guess is that, in class, both of them may do quite similar things.

"I would appeal, in our teaching, to the phenomenological method, with its suspension of beliefs. My objective is probably more like Jerry's, out of a commitment to my profession. I want my students to have a tolerance and appreciation for others—to see the world as a great and vast place, without condemning others. I'm now thinking about how one does that. Do you have them engage in imaginative exercises where the objective is to develop an understanding of the other? When we do those kinds of things, don't we have to point out not only how it's an interesting project, but also how misappropriating it can be, and how much we can thereby end up *failing* to understand?"

"But you already have a theological statement in that stance," another person pointed out.

"No, teaching religion is not, itself, a religion. I have a commitment to a multicultural approach, but that's different from a religious commitment."

"I will argue that it's not," the first person replied. "It makes statements about our existence. In the context of where we're teaching, *that* becomes theological."

"One thing that impresses me more and more as I age," said Jerry, "is the 'otherness' of the other, and how one goes about doing justice to that."

"With regard to tolerance for those kinds of differences," said someone else, "there are given commitments that can be viewed as religious, or as part of a broader set of commitments. I think it legitimate to say that the understanding of tolerance, as one way of relating to other traditions, can be thematized as arising out of a given set of religious commitments."

The question remained one of how to move back and forth between sameness and difference. But, as one person noted, there is no way that students do not be reflect back on themselves somehow.

"In the West," someone responded, "we first understand something and then we apply it. But Gadamer said that in the very act of understanding, we already apply something. As students encounter the material we give them, that application is a necessary part of the act of understanding."

They could go no further, as the morning had come to an end. By mid-morning, Sarah had begun making lists of those who wanted to speak, asking them as much as possible to follow whatever happened to be current thread of discussion, otherwise deferring their comments until a given thread had run out. In some cases, the thread had so wound its way beyond an observation someone had wanted to make that he or she simply dropped it. Nevertheless, this approach served to weave things more tightly, lending greater integrity to the conversation than one often finds in seminars.

After lunch, as the staff reviewed their first morning, they agreed that even when the dynamic had become more confrontive, an underlying good will had not gotten lost. They speculated that this had something to do with everyone's being there due to a shared commitment to teaching, and because they were not being ranked against each other. Thus, people were neither pulling status nor competing with one another. The emphasis on the particularities of each person's teaching setting also allowed everyone an authority that grew out of these experiences. Moreover, Sarah noted, there was a strongly democratic spirit in the Southwest, which tended to express itself both in the governance of the regional AAR and in the enormous energy in the region itself. It was also generally more acceptable to be open about one's own religious allegiances in the context of being an academic.[12]

At the same time, the staff remained aware of underlying differences that could result in some participants not being sure of where they fit—a Muslim participant, for example, or one person teaching at a conservative Bible college who was uncertain about the effects of being perceived as a more conservative Christian. How were they, as a staff, to insure that no one ended up feeling marginalized? In one sense, Jerry suggested, the workshop itself was almost like enacting a fantasy of what teaching and collegiality could actually be like. In another, even this did not eliminate differences among the participants. Would it happen that, so long as such differences were not brought to the surface, they would result in less overt and even unconscious acts of silencing?

In thinking these things through together, the staff found themselves replicating concerns they faced in the classroom. While they came to no clear resolution, they determined that they would try at least to remain attentive to what was going on in the various sessions, and to look for indirect ways to intervene. They also found themselves facing the reality that there would be limits to what they could do to ensure that everyone felt equally at home. The significant element, therefore, was their awareness of the dilemma and their concern with arriving at ways to address it.

That afternoon, a library tour had been scheduled for those who wanted to take one. Otherwise, people were left free to explore the campus, work on their projects, meet with members of the staff,

---

12 This is in contrast to regions like New England/Maritimes, where such issues went virtually undiscussed in the group that met there, even though it became clear over time that this same group consisted of people many of whom had strong religious commitments and affiliations.

or head off to the city. A few probably took naps. They did not, after all, have to come together again until early evening.

After a dinner liberally sauced with jokes, the group moved over to a large conference room in one of the nearby classroom buildings, where they were to discuss the issue of "Liberal Learning and the Teaching of Religion."[13] As had been explored a decade earlier in the NEH workshops in teaching, what now was the role of religion department in liberal arts colleges? Various participants described how, in their schools, it was religion faculty who had raised the level of concern about the value of civil discourse and of reasoned analysis.

"We are often generalists and liberal arts people," one person said, "and we teach our students in that vein. I'm not so sure that liberal arts people are being graduated in other fields. In our school, it's been the job of the religion department to teach the larger faculty how to do that. It's who we *are*. In studying our field and how to teach it, we're also talking about influencing our colleagues."

"If you were only listing the characteristics of a liberal education and what a person who has one can do," said Gus, "these skills, in the history of our department, have been influential in the larger university. It's been our people who have had the interest, the vision, and the linguistic capacity to put these things into words. People don't look down on the religion department here; we can produce the evidence that we can do what we say liberally educated people should be able to do."

"What we call the study of religion has been born in our own lifetime," said Sarah. "That is, our own methods, as well as the birthing and making of our field. It's still not accepted by everybody; natural scientists don't necessarily think what we do is knowledge."

"But one of the ways we reach into other disciplines," said another person, "is through students who come from them into our

---

[13] For this discussion, the group had been asked to read: American Academy of Religion/ Association of American Colleges, *Report on Liberal Learning and the Religion Major* (pamphlet); William Scott Green, "The Difference Religion Makes," in *JAAR* vol. 62, no. 4, Winter 1994, pp. 1191-1207; Jonathan Z. Smith, "Narratives into Problems: the College Introductory Course in the Study of Religion," *JAAR* vol. 56, no. 4, 1988, pp. 727-39.

classes, who enter a liberal arts inquiry in that way. We then send them back out into a dialogue with their other professors."

"You know," said someone else, "I'm hearing a concern over the disparagement and exclusion some religion faculties face, and our own reaction over how wonderful we are as a beam of light to our institutions. Our need to emphasize how unique we are is related to our feeling excluded. I'm just not comfortable with that kind of effort to assign ourselves a special place. My experience of my colleagues in other departments is that they're just as gifted."

"I don't think we're God's gift," said Sarah, "but I do find an inability among some of my natural science peers to explore their own assumptions. It's not necessary to their being able to do what they do, because what they do 'works', and what we do doesn't look like it works. That's part of the political reality we're up against. So, sometimes instead of crossing barriers, we defend them."

"I teach in a state university," said another person, "and there is a crisis, at least at the state level, in justifying the humanities or a liberal arts education at all. It doesn't have a practical end vocationally in terms of giving you as many chickens or big dairy farms as the legislature thinks it should. We fight that battle every day to convince the powers that be that we're going to produce marketable skills. I've also been told I can't cross-list history-of-religions courses with history courses, because I'm not a trained historian. There's a real resistance to anything having to do with the department of religious studies."

"The problem with trying to build relationships across disciplines," someone else replied, "is that historians, for example, do have their own canons. We all know that the process of education is a socialization into a way of seeing. It goes back to the concern with what should be done in religious studies. It would seem that there should be something uniquely religious about our approach. If that is, indeed, the case, then it's not just about more training in critical capacities. It would have something to do, instead, with the tension between some 'modern' way of seeing the world and what is imagined to be a 'religious' way—with the latter assumed to be somehow distorted.

"This is part of a resistance to religion and religiousness that one finds especially among many scientists. It goes back to Galileo and Belarmine, and has been replayed on many fronts. For that matter, we're not the only discipline that feels it's not being taken seriously or appreciated *as* a discipline. Listen to psychiatrists— 'We're not seen as being a *real* science.' So, there are questions at a number of different levels here. There are those facing every department in terms of its own standards of socialization and what each one requires for entry, and then other factors having to do with the unique status of religion in the unique march of secularization."

"But Jonathan Z. Smith also points out that we're not necessarily training students to enter *our* field," said another person. "We are interdisciplinary, with multiple canons (even though Gill seems to think that's specious). Out of all the majors we have, how many are planning on going into our field? Not that many. So how do we justify our existence? By appealing to the qualities that a liberal arts education is supposed to be giving them?"

"In contrast," said one of people teaching in a seminary, "things get flipped around at my school. Those who are over and against me are not the other faculty, but the students, who themselves marginalize the liberal arts aspects of what I'm trying to do. One student said to me, 'Don't teach me anything *you* think I need to know; just teach me how to use the things I already know.' I'm up against a resistance to learning anything about the humanities, to getting young white males to acknowledge that there might be any validity to feminism. I find that they regress as soon as they get to the parking lot. At least in the divinity schools in this region, there tends to be an anti-intellectual bias."

"The basic dichotomy between us and our students," said someone else," is that we got into some course along the way that clicked for us. But for ninety-nine point nine percent of the students, it's a hoop they have to jump through to be ordained or get a job."

"You know, if we are doing something religiously, then our place is going to stay tenuous," another person said. "If we're asking for any sort of epistemological privilege or saying that what we do is unique, and somehow at the direct service to a tradition or a religion, then we're at odds with the free university of which we are a part. There's a tension with our colleagues in our asking to be part of the liberal arts, because we are also perceived as maybe somewhat unfree—that is, as having a hidden agenda. It's seen as asking for a special status for our knowledge."

"But religious studies *is* a different way of knowing," said another person. "If we don't make a case for that, then we lose what makes religious studies unique. It's like the Sunday School point. We can't really escape our own perspective and what is significant in what we teach, which does involve conveying another approach to knowledge. The places where it gets problematic are when you assume faith, or are trying to legitimate a particular position. A better approach would be to say 'Let's talk about what is illegitimate in the classroom.'"

"We've been talking about the diminishing of our discipline," someone else said. "But I don't experience that so much as a weird mystique people attach to us. I'm wondering what we do to play into or promote that. I think my colleagues are baffled by what I do."

"People aren't malicious," said Jerry, "but it's true that they just don't know what we do. There *is* a level of theory to it. It's one of our strengths that we're amorphous, but that's difficult to communicate to outsiders."

"As an outsider to the culture," Gus responded, "I find that the American attitude toward religion is tinged heavily with individualism. If you ask what someone's religion is, you're asking a private and almost improper question. To say what you believe becomes the limit. We run into that with our students and with our colleagues in the field—who are just those students grown up. One source of that prejudice is people's thinking we make it our business to question these things."

"But," said someone else, "one of my roles is to challenge the cognitive imperialism of scientific secularism about why we're here and what we're doing—the things that are never challenged by some of my students—and to present a sophisticated alternative. This may be my one and only chance, and I'd better make it good!"

"In what you just said," Roger replied, "I heard a kind of generational difference, perhaps marking the beginning of an end of some part of the Enlightenment. Many of our older colleagues were trained in an Enlightenment perspective. What you just said undermines some of that. If one is to take seriously that an emergent assault on the Enlightenment in religious studies is on its way, then our role needs a lot more discussion."

"That realization occurred to me the other day," said someone else. "There's a post-modern thrust critiquing the Enlightenment, and questions about the limits of reason and rationality."

"Feminist theory does an effective job at it in some ways, too," said Jerry. "It's also not a coincidence that Buddhism has met with receptiveness in the culture."

"All of this is wonderful," said someone else, "and it scares me to death. The resistance to intellectual life that was described at the seminary—I feel that bias in the culture. The local newspaper has a regular pontificator against intellectuals and professors. But we're also among the underminers."

"I don't think the Enlightenment is over," said another person, "and I urge us to be careful with the idea that it is. We're simply challenging certain tenets of the different positivisms. Remember that feminism comes out of the Enlightenment."

"But the community at large does not recognize what we're doing, because it's seen as a lower level service department. The question in my mind is how to raise up what we're doing."

The evening was coming to an end. Within the one day, the group had raised some of the questions that would persist throughout their time together—questions, for example, about their own identities as religion scholars, teachers and, in some cases theologians, both within their classrooms and their larger teaching settings. What did, in fact, locate them squarely in the liberal arts, and what made them different from their colleagues in other disciplines? *Was* teaching religion in itself a quasi-religious commitment or necessarily a kind of theology in its own right? And at what point does the study of religion become embarrassed by the issue of religiosity? They had touched on the issue of experiential exercises conducted in the classroom, and about the advantages and risks of drawing on such exercises to convey something about another tradition. They had sat down to what Sarah would come to call their "intellectual feast."

The group left the classroom building and walked back together to the dormitories, twos and threes of them still talking about the issues they had just been discussing. Even after they got back, they continued, pausing on the stairways to the second floor outdoor walkway, sitting on the steps, pieces of their conversations rising and falling quietly over the whirring of the lawn sprinklers, in the middle of the din of the night-time insects.

Day Three: Wednesday, August 9

In thinking over the dilemmas faced by religion faculty in general, the staff had hit on the issue of teaching about traditions other than one's own, giving it the topic the title, "The Upside and Downside of Inside and Outside: Judaism, A Case Study." They hoped to focus on how regional factors further complicated matters. This would be the morning's first session, and would be led by Sarah and Jerry.[14] The second, led by Gus and Roger, would begin a discussion the team expected to continue over to the following day, in which they would ask "Whom Do We Teach and Where Do They Come From? Teaching Religion in the Bible Belt."[15] By team-leading each of the sessions during these first few days, they hoped to model teaching as a forum for discussion and, potentially, disagreement.

But before going into these topics, they first asked the group to give thought to how they would participate in the AAR regional meeting in the coming Spring. It was proposed, given recent events at the David Koresh compound in Waco, that this be the focus of one

----

[14] The readings assigned for this first part of the discussion were: Judith Plaskow, "Transforming the Nature of Community: Toward a Feminist People of Israel," in *After Patriarchy: Feminist Transformations of the World Religions*, Paula Cooey, William R. Eakin, and Jay McDaniel, eds. (Maryknoll: Orbis Press, 1991); Chaim Potok, *The Chosen* (New York: Fawcett, 1967); Richard L. Rubenstein, "Person and Myth in the Jewish-Christian Encounter," in *After Auschwitz: Radical Theology and Contemporary Judaism* (New York: Macmillan, 1966); Huston Smith, "Judaism," in *The World's Religions* (San Francisco: Harper, 1991).

[15] The readings for this second section were: Kathleen C. Boone, *The Bible Tells Them So* (Albany: SUNY Press, 1989); Samuel Hill, *Varieties of Southern Religious Experience* (Baton Rouge: Louisiana State University Press, 1987); Ada María Isasi-Díaz, "The Bible as Mujerista Theology," in *Lift Every Voice*, Susan Brooks Thistlethwaite and Mary Potter Engel, eds. (New York: Harper & Row, 1990).

panel, and that another be organized around issues directly involving different participants' understandings of their own pedagogy in their particular teaching contexts. It was the one case in which a staff made conference presentations by the group a structured part of their involvement in the workshop. Rather than leaving things to chance, this immediately put into practice one of the workshop objectives, namely that of strengthening the involvement of untenured faculty at the regional level.

When it came to teaching about traditions often perceived by her students as "other," given their own frequently Christian Protestant stereotypes, Sarah found that one of the greatest challenges was the tendency to assume that all traditions are belief systems, and that all of these "others" believe in God. She taught a course on Judaism, she said, because it often appeared to her students to be the most familiar. She used writings by a mixture of insiders and outsiders, some of them sympathetic, some of them— including those by insiders, who were critical.

"I tell them these are little tastes," she said.

She had also found that her students often thought of religious traditions as frozen in time. They sometimes resisted the idea that a person could really be part of a tradition and, at the same time, have strong reasons for wanting to change it.

Jerry, who taught courses on Buddhist traditions, agreed, and added that, for him, an added complication grew out of any attempt to speak for those others—a complication that necessarily arose when teaching about "other religions."

"I can't *not* speak for others, in that case," he said, "but how legitimate is it? I'm a pluralist and a humanist who thinks that religions are largely socio-cultural constructions, so I'm part of the religious studies orthodoxy—which is a far cry from a Buddhist orthodoxy. That means I'm doing a different religion."

How to make these traditions sufficiently accessible while, at the same time, retaining a sense of their differences? How to address the ways in which women and many of the vernacular traditions have gone unmentioned? During the nineteen-sixties, a quasi-Sunday-School model had been useful, insofar as it presented these other traditions as compelling religious worlds. But, argued Jerry, this was no longer, however, a viable approach. The matter was further complicated by the tension between one's own reluctance to present oneself as an authority and students' wish for the teacher to be just that.

"Would the ideal be to have a practicing Hindu come in?" said one person?

"The ideal for teaching in an American university would be to have someone who grew up as a Buddhist and who trained at a cutting edge American school," Jerry replied.

"Let's say that's our ideal," said someone else, "that only an insider can present the tradition. But let's take the teaching of a foreign language as an analogy. Job descriptions often say 'near native fluency expected.' Yet we do hire people for whom it's a second language. Part of what we're trying to teach people is not just about Buddhism or Daoism or Confucianism, to take an example. In my classes, I'm also modeling a person who is not any of these things but who loves and respects them and their cultures as worthy of being engaged with."

"I also think that sometimes the outsider can present the continuum of a tradition," said someone else, "whereas sometimes the insider may represent the particularity as standing for the whole of the tradition."

"I have a question," said one person. "If we say that only insiders can understand a tradition, it boils down to a kind of racism, and means that we are limiting the knowledge of a tradition to that group. As a Muslim, when I see what has been done in Islamic studies by some Westerners, it illuminates things for me. We need people able to present things from both sides."

"I have faith," said Jerry, "that religious studies is going in the right direction. In the sixties, you'd have someone in religious studies who had been to India, but had no language skills. That's no longer sufficient. We're working toward the equivalent of a passport or a visa into the study of other cultures. You are a better teacher for an American school because you've come to the West and done a Ph.D within Western cultural orthodoxy."

"Of course, when I teach about fourth-century Christianity," said someone else, "I can't bring in a real informant. There's some sort of assumption that we're closer to these primary sources, but that's not necessarily the case."

"As a historian," said another person, "it's my job to present the views of people that are other than my own—say, Athanasius's *Life of Anthony*. I have to try to explain why someone in the fourth century would go out into the desert to live in a tomb and fight with demons. That's pretty other!"

"Oh, not necessarily," said someone else. The group laughed.

"I tell people that I want them to be outsiders even to their own traditions," said another person.

"The difficulty I have with Jerry's ideal of the sympathetic insider educated in a Western setting," said one person, "is that this individual might still have a hard time communicating with the fundamentalists within his or her tradition. There's the issue of communicating with students. I come out of a conservative Christian background, and teach in a conservative school. That's one of the difficulties I face."

"I want to push at the strategy that was just mentioned," said Gus, "of being the total outsider. How do you do that? I can't imagine the students allowing it. How do you deal with the inevitable desire to relate and get inside?"

"The adjectives I use for the outsider are 'empathic' or 'sympathetic'," the other person replied. "We have to recognize our own role as outsiders trying to understand how an insider does view the religion. I didn't mean it to sound as antiseptic as maybe it did. Some students change their opinion as to what I am, each time I introduce a new tradition."

"At the beginning," said someone else, "it seemed we had a paradox, or a struggle, between the insider and the outsider, as if that would be the case for all traditions. For example, suppose we're talking about a tradition, or a denomination within a tradition, that allows for certain doctrinal statements independent of an individual's will, something of that nature might lend itself well to an outsider's perspective. But if you have an esoteric position that rejects the affirming of a given dogma, then it seems more difficult to do justice to the inner workings of that position without being an insider. It may be that the more esoteric you get, the more having an insider there is important. Then you have to look at what it means to have both an insider and an outsider present."

"At least fifty percent of the people in the Buddhist section at the AAR are engaged in Buddhism," said Jerry, "whereas that's true of only about ten percent in the Hindu section."

"Going back to the question of those of us who work as historians," said someone else, "we read our texts within mega-theories and interpretations, which cloud, confuse, and skew our interpretations. I can think of one scholar, for example, who has ruled for decades on the Transcendentalists, and in a lot of ways, he's wrong about a lot of things!"

"I'm perturbed by how sanguine we seem to be about the very categories of insider and outsider," said another person. "When I teach about world religions, I tend to err on the side of a more sympathetic presentation of other traditions, and a more critical stance toward Christianity. That's because I feel like more of an outsider to certain forms of Christianity, like fundamentalism. I lived in a neo-Hindu community for some time, and now I'm not sure where I fit. I've studied *tai ji* for seven years, and have been part of men's groups who've undertaken sweat lodge rituals. Am I an insider or an outsider? I don't know. I wasn't raised in these cultures, but does that assume they're hermetically sealed with electric fences rising up to the heavens? So I'm an American. Does that mean I really know America?"

"This ties in with a serious problem that I think we've skirted around," said Gus, "and that's the boundary we've drawn around the world religions as though they're somewhere far away. There's a Hindu temple in El Paso, and all kinds of other religious traditions have entered other American cities. We have people from these different traditions *in* our classes. There was a time when Christianity was a Jewish heresy and, later on, Islam a Christian heresy. These distinctions we make in saying 'the world religions' are not out there anymore. These are sometimes now the kids down the block."

"We set up this session," said Sarah, "because so many of us end up teaching as generalists. This, for me, is about a kind of sensitivity. One thing we have not discussed, that we may come back to, is the issue of how political and social power interact and lead to categories like insider and outsider. It's problematic for me to presume to be critical of a tradition that's not my own, when there has been a long history of outsiders being critical in order to justify dominating somebody else. As a feminist for whom reason is important, I try to teach these things rationally, because however authoritative that experience of a tradition may be, if I can't get you white men to imagine it, it will never get anywhere." With that comment, she wrapped up the session and the group took a break.

The second part of the discussion would explore the question of students in the Bible Belt. Roger began to speak about his own ethos of teaching in this setting, recognizing that even the term "Bible Belt" means different things depending on where one teaches.

"But the evangelical fundamentalism that is very much alive here affects the climate of study for all of us," he said. "Maybe it would be useful to be somewhat autobiographical. I've taught at the same school in Texas since 1967, during the winding down of much of the public phase of the civil rights movement when we were looking at a lot of social questions. By 1969 or so, I began to realize that more people were turning inward and experimenting with drugs. But other students were starting to ask me if I taught the Bible historically, or as the word of God. I began to realize that I would have to deal with this. One day in a class, we were looking at the Garden of Eden narrative and at the serpent's portrait of God as petty and jealous. I asked, 'Did the snake correctly portray God, as far as the story is concerned?'"

"A conservative woman said, 'I don't think so.' She was using a passage from the New Testament to make her point. I said, 'Isn't that like using Hemingway to interpret Shakespeare?' She said, no, that it was a systematic whole.

"I said, 'What if you see contradiction? Either there is one or there isn't one.' She said, 'I just pray to God and ask him to tell me what it means.' I thought to myself, 'If she's praying to God about what it means, and I'm supposed to allow her academic freedom, where does that one go?' In the process, she got very upset, and I began to realize that I was going to be dealing with this kind of situation more and more. I would either be up against a kind of warfare in the classroom between different positions, or would have people from that tradition not taking classes with me—or, I would have to find a way to deal with it. I decided on a different strategy, which I began to use and which seems to have worked, at least in our kind of situation.

"Fundamentalist students are a significant minority in our context, but they are there. I decided to make it very clear, partly by how I treated them and partly by talk, that I loved them. I believed in doing that, anyway. I tried to make it clear that I was drawing on a virtue from the tradition we both believed in, and that I was operating out of that framework. It was natural to me and, I think, appropriate in a church-related institution, that I take the Bible seriously as addressed by God to me. I also decided to become more of a questioner and facilitator of discussion, rather than a pronouncer, so that I could represent different positions.

"I talked about the development of different guilds of scholarship, making it clear that I was part of this, without fully endorsing it. I did so to show that I could treat the whole thing with a lot of distance. It was also an attempt to get them to examine what it was like to see things with some distance. For example, I said things like, 'Nobody would think God was literally a shepherd. So would they necessarily think God was literally male?' I also avoided a sense of closure about any subject, to avoid imposing some official imprimatur, and I was careful to provide alternative models."

"We're talking about two dominant cultures here in the Southwest," said Gus. "The one is Protestantism with a fundamentalist core, that influences the other Protestant denominations. The other is Catholic culture, along with the drastic changes in that culture since Vatican II, *mujerista* theology, and various forms of liberation theology, insofar as these have gone to the level where our students live. One question I want to raise involves the students who actually get into our classes, and the ones who stay away because they're being told we're hopeless. I have no idea what to do with that self-selecting factor."

In the small group discussions that followed, the participants compared notes about their teaching settings, finding that some taught introductory classes with thirty students, while others had over a hundred. They talked about the different ways they learned about who was in their classes—index cards or questionnaires, for example. In one group, they quickly turned to their students' religious lives.

"I say, 'My job is to be where you're not," said Jerry. "I rather arrogantly say, 'Here are some presuppositions: one is that you believe as you do because you were brought up that way; the second is that you're reasoning from your assumptions."

"If I were a born-again Christian," said Gus, "I'd say I believe the way I do because I was touched by God. The problem I keep running into is the different way the word 'believe' gets used. You're talking about it as an intellectual construction; some of the students use it as an expression of accepting the Lord Jesus Christ. Wrapped up in that package is a certain view of the Bible and how to read it."

"I find," said someone else, "that more students who want to be preachers or teachers are not excited about being identified as fundamentalist. They're aware of how their upbringing helped them to read the Bible, but they don't buy the precise fundamentalist language. So it gets more dangerous, because now you think you have them tagged as evangelical and not fundamentalist, but they're actually still really very fundamentalist without necessarily realizing it. Like, they aren't going to deny the virgin birth. The issue is one of students for whom fundamentalism forms a total world view. I know what it's like, because that's the world I come out of. You continually meet it in the field of rational discourse and in classes in religion in America. That is, students who give in to Pat Robertson, who says we started out a pristine Christian nation, but we've gone downhill, led by professors, and funded by an international cartel of bankers. So, as one student told me, I couldn't talk to him because he knew who I was. The fact that I denied it merely proved it."

"I've known many people with that perspective," said another person. "They're quite intelligent, but they set those boundaries. *They* know intuitively, and because people tell them, that 'If you take certain classes, you're faith will be taken away.' And *we* say we're here to do critical inquiry. Our task is figuring out how to be tactful, to understand the special circumstances this person is in, and how to get a wedge in."

"A lot of it comes out in class, as other students challenge them," said someone else.

"I say that everything is a point of view," said Jerry, "including 'everything is a point of view.' I say, I am willing to have you think I'm condemned to hell and that I'm bringing others down with me. You can think that, but that's not the world view supported here."

"At my seminary, things take a different shape," said another person. "These kinds of encounters are minimized by an admissions policy that weeds out people who couldn't live with us. The shape it takes now is the power issue of women in the church. It's the largest problem for conservative students, who realize over time that you can maintain a conservative theology and be somewhat socially liberal—that is, for example, around women clergy. My colleague here is the only full-time woman with Ph.D. status, so she's immediately labeled a radical feminist."

"I bifurcate," said someone else. "I say, this isn't Sunday school. We're not doing this devotionally. I'm not teaching you to pray. I'm trying to distinguish these things from academic study, and I'm not giving them any tools with which to bring the two together. I say I've *chosen* to privilege one approach."

"I have to confess that part of my frustration," said one person, themself a Southerner, "is my real bias against Christian fundamentalism for which I have a disdain and a distaste—even as I try to be sympathetic to fundamentalists in other traditions. It doesn't always make sense. And the other thing is that I'm in Louisiana, which is and is not part of the Southwest."

"I find that I'm more critical of things coming out of Western tradition than I am of things from other traditions," said Jerry. "The other thing I notice is that there are things I can get away with saying as a man, that get heard differently when some of my colleagues who have the reputation of being feminists say them— like, that a text was 'written by men for men.' I have one colleague who talks about the arena of faith and the arena of academics. She then characterizes each one, and makes it explicit that she privileges the latter."

"I worry," said Gus, "when I'm teaching about Judaism or Christianity or Islam, about the comments that are not made or voiced. The other thing is my own honesty. It becomes a matter of where to draw the line—when to defer or sidestep for the sake of not having an argument, and when to stand up for pluralism."

"One thing I do," said another person, "is to talk about language as analogous, so that *no* term can encapsulate God. That leaves some opening for me not to be burning in hell!"

The groups came back together and discovered that much about their discussions had overlapped. They recognized the danger of addressing these religious differences with sarcasm and disrespect, even when they themselves felt besieged in their own classes. Part of their struggle entailed finding ways to model disagreement among scholars—to underscore that each person's opinions are worthy of respect, without implying that these same opinions will, therefore, never be challenged. The question was, how to do so in a way that also allowed an opening to happen.

"The important thing to recognize," concluded one person, "is that the Bible is an intimate thing. For some people, it's like their mother. Also, there are differences between different fundamentalist perspectives. When you really get to know someone personally, usually you find they're wrestling with all kinds of questions."

In the subsequent staff discussion, Sarah voiced the feelings of the rest of the team, talking about how well it all seemed to be going. The group was excited by their discussions, and that excitement had spilled over into the lunch-time conversation. It was striking how quickly the group had developed an effective seminar style of discussion. There were no grandstanders, nobody monopolizing the floor. People had already got into the practice of referring back to earlier comments, catching up and sustaining earlier pieces of the argument. They had some difficulty sustaining a focus on single points, on the one hand, but on the other, this seemed to be offset by the frequently repeated phrase, "in my experience"—what is sometimes referred to as the "I" statement. The legitimizing of various points as rooted in particularity helped to keep any sense of confrontation to a minimum, while still making room for differences of opinion. Each person was speaking about the specific context out of which his or her style had emerged. This allowed for the establishing of parallel points of authority.

In the light of Gus's comment about the things that went unsaid in a class, it occurred to the team that it might be useful somewhat later in the week to ask everyone to write down what they had *not* said or asked, as well as a reason for not having done so. Still, it seemed to them so far that an authentic respect and even liking were taking form.

Both were tested that evening. The staff had decided to dedicate two evenings to watching films which they had found useful in their own teaching. The first of these, *Tender Mercies*, was about a down-and-out country singer, Mac Sledge, trying to make a comeback, with the love and help of a widow and her young son. For some of the members of the group, the world portrayed by the film came close to home to the worlds where they, themselves, had grown up. They all but knew the people in the story and were left almost without words. Sarah, herself a Southerner, talked about her own sense of the women in the film and about how she didn't like the way they were kept in passive, supportive roles. It was clear that she was moved.

Maybe it was because the group was tired. Maybe it was because Sarah had left herself vulnerable. Maybe she had stepped on one of those landmines that might, under other circumstances, have gone undetected. Whatever the reason, one the participants spoke up in the midst of the discussion and undertook the task of analyzing why she had responded with such feeling. Visibly upset, the person spoke of having perceived the leading female character in the film as a Madonna figure, and wondered if Sarah wasn't imposing her views on her students.

"I think you're not being a very good teacher," they said, "and that you're doing damage to your students."

Sarah later recalled that, in the moment, she had felt so unexpectedly under attack that she had become silent. In fact, she doubted anyone had realized just how angry she actually was. After a moment, she spoke, making it clear that, in her opinion, this difference in perspective was not her problem. Others also quickly stepped in to mediate.

"That's not fair to Sarah," said someone else.

Another said, "Sarah comes from that background. She's speaking from the authority of her experience."

Later that evening, Sarah fell apart, and several of the other staff members comforted her. A few of them were amazed that she had not retaliated. Yet up until that session, although the different discussions had included some strong disagreements, these had all been civil. Indeed this civility had been the tenor of the workshop to date, with no one resorting to *ad hominem* attacks. Sarah had therefore been unprepared for such a possibility. Still, the support from the others on the staff had allowed her to articulate her anger behind the scenes. In the end, she let it go.

"I decided it was not incumbent on me to resolve the situation," she said later. "It worked itself out, and we didn't let it interfere with the rest of the workshop."

It was a case of a conflict that dissipated through deliberate design. Had the cause recurred, it might have required a different resolution. Had the staff not supported Sarah's perceptions, she might have been left feeling estranged from the group. What mattered to her was that the incident had not been left at her door, and that she had been permitted to walk away from it.

Day Four: Thursday, August 10

The Southwest, Gus began, and Texas in particular, presented strong issues of regionalism. Slightly over half the population in the area was Hispanic and the territory had, at one time, belonged to Mexico. The current dominant culture is, therefore, a latecomer, and prior cultures remain a significant presence in the area. Despite the impression held by many Anglos that Hispanics continually enter the region as outsiders, the facts of culture, geography, and history give lie to that idea. The student population in the region has been shaped by that presence and that history. Even so, until now, Hispanics have been practically absent from academic religious studies, although this is beginning to change. Of course, Gus added, when one sees the word "Hispanic," one has to remember that someone, at some point, made a decision to use this as a comprehensive term which in no way reflects the complex differences between the different groups covered by it.

In this region, the major culture is Mexican-American. Although evangelical Protestantism was beginning to take a hold, it is still a region flavored by a Catholicism centered in places one might not necessarily expect. It might seem, for example, that this should be the church, but in recent years the church itself has been trying to reappropriate elements of popular religious culture and bring these back into its own orbit.

The blended aspect is an important one in all Hispanic traditions. Indeed, Gus was convinced that all cultures are mixed. In this particular case there are, he thought, two ways to look at it. You can deny the mixture, even when presented with the evidence of another culture's presence, or you can recognize and celebrate that same presence. *Mestizaje*, this mixing, is one of the central concepts in the awareness of Hispanics as to who they are culturally and religiously. The Roman Catholicism of the region reflects this mixture as, for example, in the veneration of ancestors one encounters during the *Día de los Muertos*, the Day of the Dead, which comes out of Native American tradition but is practiced by people calling themselves Roman Catholics.

The introduction of Protestantism in this culture began in the nineteenth century, with the more conservative to fundamentalist style of the time very much in competition with the Roman Catholic majority. In the heart of these tensions and the religious forms that have descended from them, blendings have still taken place. Older traditions have asserted themselves as, for example, when girls turn fifteen in the Presbyterian Mexican-American churches and have a *quinceañera* service and party. In the United Methodist book of worship, for example, there is now a ceremony for it. Although the original practice came out of Spain, and was reinforced in the Americas by parallel emphases among the Native Americans as the tribal recognition of a girl's availability for marriage, even the Spanish Roman Catholicism that came over is now itself a mixture at the level of popular religion. Moreover, he added, students have become increasingly aware of their roots, and will find it peculiar if we think that Roman Catholicism is a standard textbook type without a regional flavor.

One example of this is the Virgin of Guadalupe. Originally part of an evangelizing strategy developed by the Spanish Catholic church in Mexico, the Virgin was deliberately introduced as a symbol. Although Guadalupe was a place in Spain and Our Lady of Guadalupe a well-known icon, the competition between the native-born Spaniards and the Mexican-born *criollos* led the latter to appropriate this version of the Virgin. Eventually, she became a symbol for a number of Indian rebellion movements and, by the eighteenth and nineteenth centuries, a patron of the little guy. Now she is everywhere, from car washes on the west side of San Antonio to murals with Juan Diego—the Indian who is said to have first seen her—kneeling before her. Even gang members who spray graffiti on any other wall will stay away from murals with the Virgin, or risk severe reprisals. More recently, the Virgin has undergone a certain debunking by those who argue that the Juan Diego story never happened and that it represents, instead, the composite creation of a legend based on an earlier goddess figures associated with the same hilltop at Tepeyác. Nevertheless, Guadalupe has become a pervasive figure, and one who illustrates the particular nature of Roman Catholicism in the region.

The Spanish roots of Catholicism have also merged with Native American healing practices, through the *curanderos*, or healers. More recently, *botánicas*—shops where the candles, herbs, oils, and figurines associated with the practice of *santería*—indicate that some of the Afro-Cuban traditions have entered the local religious world as well. The latter attract not only the poor, but also professionals, such that the meaning of "popular" traditions is undergoing a change in the area.

The university where he taught, Gus added, tends to be perceived as the Anglo school in the area; two others are seen as the Catholic schools, and more of the Mexican-American students to apply there. At the same time, there are more of these students even at his school than people often realize. They are, as he put it, "inconspicuous," however, because of their fluency in English. It is among the buildings and grounds crews and the cooking and cleaning staffs that one is more likely to notice the disproportionate numbers of Mexican Americans.

The other dominant religious influence among Mexican-Americans in the region, as well as in Central America, has been Pentecostalism. These groups, some of whom receive support from the United States, have experienced an enormous explosion in numbers. It is not yet fully known how much right-wing political groups have been involved, but the growth of these numbers has caught the older-line Protestant groups by surprise. Many of them also push a fair amount of anti-Catholic rhetoric

As the group went on to discuss, such religious tensions, woven in with ethnic differences, give this region a particular character unlike that of others in the country. In this they could speak with some authority because, unlike the group in the Southeast, fewer than half the participants were not originally from the Southwest. The ratio of "locals" to "outsiders" was therefore higher. Their students, they agreed, were more likely to speak about their faith positions in the classroom. Likewise, it bears noting, the issue of individual faith stances entered more consistently into the group's own discussions than it had in the other regions. For example, some of the participants who saw themselves as having moved away from a more conservative stance reflected on difficulties they now confronted in teaching Bible study to conservative students who resembled their former selves.

The staff's original proposal for the workshop had observed that the role of the Bible and biblical interpretation in Southern Christian religious beliefs cannot be underestimated. Even though the Southwest differs in significant respects from the Southeast, faculty in both regions discover that they have to be familiar with Southern biblical hermeneutics, and to recognize the ways in which such hermeneutics inform how students perceive other religious traditions and texts.[16] The discussion that took place during these several days underscored the importance of focusing on the regional dimension in these cases, as well as on the particular teaching settings within the region, as a way of getting at broader trends and significant differences.

---

[16] Preliminary proposal for the Southeast/Southwest Workshop Series, mss., p.4.

As one person who taught in a large state university pointed out, the concerns of faculty in the religion department differed from those of people teaching in the church-related schools, insofar as the two settings viewed the importance of teaching the study of religion very differently. What, then, did they have in common, and how were their differences represented within the larger AAR? For that matter, did this group replicate some of these very same power relations as they were perceived to express themselves in the national organization?

"People from schools with a denominational affiliation are more likely to ask these questions," one person pointed out, "and are more likely to feel marginal." Ironically, it was noted, as the AAR conference structures at the national level attempts to represent increasing diversity, people are less and less likely to talk across disciplinary boundaries. It was, they found, pedagogy that was bringing them back together.

What also surfaced in the discussion were anxieties related to being untenured faculty in the region. In some cases these anxieties were due to being at smaller, isolated schools with few resources to support one's scholarship; in others, to not feeling certain about how to find one's way into the power structures of the AAR. Because of the geographic distances separating many institutions in the region, the organization serves a function different from the one it fulfills in some other parts of the country. In the southwest, it is active precisely because it becomes a vehicle for networking that may otherwise be missing. It is therefore also correspondingly more important to untenured faculty to find ways to register their own presence within it, so as to become better known to their regional colleagues. Not everyone felt certain of how to do so.

Sarah quickly made it clear that one of the central reasons she had agreed to co-direct the workshop was in order to promote involvement within the region as a whole around issues related to teaching. As she had begun to observe herself moving into more of a senior role, she was struck by how she increasingly understood her role to include a responsibility to mentor younger colleagues. The workshops had provided one way for her to do so. Still, it was less obvious to her, initially, how these colleagues might find it difficult to make their way into the AAR.

"But some of us see you who are running it as a power elite," one person said. "It's like we're getting off the boat and you give us five dollars and a shirt. We don't want to offend anyone. There's a political dynamic going on here, and no one has talked about the power issues."

"It's impolite," said someone else. Everyone laughed.

Gus spoke up. "I'm being cast as part of the power elite," he said, "but the basic idea behind our relationship here is that we're colleagues. By virtue of who set things up, of course there is a power structure. For heuristic purposes at times we organize ourselves as students and teachers, and sometimes as colleagues sitting around and talking. What does the AAR get out of our doing this? Hopefully the benefits from networking that empower all of us as we do work in the region."

"I don't feel as though we should be insecure about what we do as untenured people," said someone else. "I don't want to be in a position of fear and vulnerability."

"Yes," said Sarah, "but some of us *are* insecure, and the earlier comment was a pragmatic one. I think people are asking 'How do *I* get involved?'"

Power, as someone else went on to note, however, has subtle ways of expressing itself. Those who begin by feeling well placed in a region are more likely to feel confident speaking. They may feel they have greater access to finding out how things work, or have a better chance of knowing others who play significant roles. This can leave some people feeling alienated, and more at home remaining within specialized organizations.

"It's an unavoidable tradeoff between diversity as it's expressed in certain ways, and inclusiveness," said one person. "As some people are included, others are excluded. For example, the more other areas grow, the more limited the sessions dedicated to traditional areas of Christian studies become. People in these areas feel there are fewer sessions they can go to, like in church history, so they're less apt to come and talk about issues of power at a meeting like this."

"The powerful," said Jerry, "never feel their power like the powerless feel the lack of theirs."

The staff, nevertheless, encouraged the participants to get more involved at the local level, using the workshop as an entrée. Work with others on common tasks, they suggested. Get elected as program chair, and from there work to hold higher offices. Get grants for the region, or nominate oneself for tasks. It is more possible than many people realize to play a role in the given region.

What was striking about the discussion as a whole was the degree of candor with which the participants voiced their uncertainty about how they fit into existing structures of power, and the degree of responsiveness with which the members of the staff responded. The congruence between the assertion that this was a gathering of colleagues on the one hand, and the actual fact on the other, may not have reduced some participants' sense that they themselves felt out of joint in the region. It did, however, contribute to what most set the workshops apart from other experiences in the professional academic world, where it is difficult for untenured people to speak candidly about multiple degrees of vulnerability without feeling dangerously exposed.

"Let's reflect now on what we just did," said Sarah, in a move to meta-reflection that also characterized this group. "What are the parallels between what goes on between us, the way you're describing it, and what goes on in a classroom?"

"There's always the issue of how much power students give me," one person answered. "I want power deflector-shields! It drives me nuts!"

"You must be a sensitive person," Jerry rejoindered. "I want to give you more authority for that."

"I try to be clear that yes, I've got more power than they do," she said, "but I want them to take responsibility for their own, too."

"I walk into the room," said someone else, "and the students are sitting there without enough light because none of them had turned on the switch. No one empowered them to do it."

"I try to take a Freirian approach," said another person. "I say, 'As a community of learners, I give you the power to challenge me at any point, and to enter a dialogue with me.' If I don't get a response—which I don't always, at first—I call on individuals, and then call on other individuals to respond to them: 'If you were to disagree with what so-and-so has just said, what would you say?' By the end, I don't have to call on them to get a response."

"There is an added dimension to the power we exercise," said Gus. "One of the onerous ways we do so is through the control of time—like in how we set up a syllabus. It's the economy of time in the classroom, where time is power, and we have to be careful in seeing whether we structure it to be oppressive or democratic."

In thinking later about this discussion, the staff reflected on the importance of creating a context in which those who felt more at risk could say so. Yet what had been equally valuable had been the process of stepping back to explore the implications of those same dynamics in relation to everyone's own teaching. It had allowed for immersion in the more immediate dimensions of susceptibility and, conversely, engagement.

Days Five and Six, Friday and Saturday, August 11 and 12

The staff had learned about the method developed in the Southeast for the presenting of individual projects, and decided to try it out for themselves. Once again, it worked well.[17] For two days, the participants discussed each other's proposals, for which they had already read summaries, and offered their suggestions. As one person later put it, "You can't begin to describe to someone outside of here what it's like to have a roomful of your colleagues all paying attention to something you're trying to figure out in your teaching, and doing so in a way that really supports you!" It is a relatively rare experience in academia to find oneself among a group of colleagues with whom one is not in some form of competition and, therefore, with whom one can leave one's guard at the door. Although certain imbalances in power unavoidably remained even in the workshops, the collaborative dimensions were what stood out.

This did not mean that everyone agreed with respect to their approaches to teaching, and some of the disagreements led to argument. One of the more intense points of disagreement, for example, arose over the issue of how far to go in incorporating

---

[17]   For the description of this approach, see pages 212-13.

experiential exercises in the classroom. To what degree, for example, might students feel indirectly coerced to participate in something they might privately find off-putting, disturbing, or offensive? How much do such exercises risk misrepresenting the traditions which they are intended to illustrate? For some, the experiential dimension provided a point of connection to other traditions for students who might otherwise be inclined to dismiss them; for others, they represented unacceptable practice. The dispute, although heated, remained open.

On Saturday night, there was to have been a concert out of doors at one of the old missions, but the threat of rain led to its cancellation. Those who went, only to find this out, poked around the huge mission enclosure as Gus explained the hydraulics of the *aséquias* --the old irrigation system—and the historical circumstances that made the missions possible in the first place. It should be noted that as much as the group's daily discussions were bent on exploring the specific characteristics of the region, this kind of outing did so as well, albeit from a different direction.

Day Seven: Sunday, August 13

"An unevaluated event is not worth having," said Sarah, as she wrote a series of questions on the board.

"I think Plato said that," Gus informed the group sagely.

"No, actually, it was Socrates," said Jerry, "before Plato changed it."

Sarah threw them each an exaggerated glare, then cracked a grin. "Okay," she continued, "so we'd like to know what you all liked, what exceeded your expectations, and to ask you to be as specific as you can. What suggestions do you have for what we might do differently, less of, or not at all? What were you expecting or wanting that hasn't come about yet?"

"T-shirts," someone said. "We want group T-shirts!"

The group took its time responding to Sarah's questions, after which she gathered up their answers. As a brunch was soon to follow, she drew things to a close by commenting on her own sense of pleasure at feeling that she had gotten old enough and now had sufficient experience to be helping to pass along a tradition. What people of Gus's and Roger's generation had done to mentor teachers like Jerry and herself they were all now doing with this next generation of teachers coming along.

In reviewing the feedback later on, Sarah noted that the criticisms were "minor and infrequent, and included a request for fewer desserts, a request for a little less verbal dominance on occasion by some of the staff, and a request that time be set aside on Sunday so that participants could visit various worship services afforded by the diverse religious communities in the area."[18] On the other hand, the participants had also felt that the workshop succeeded in introducing them to a broader pedagogical context, at the same time as it had given them a network of colleagues who shared similar concerns, reinforcing their affiliation with the AAR and affording them resources with which to carry out their own projects more effectively.

The staff concluded with preliminary sketches of what they would do together during the coming two weekend sessions, recognizing at the same time that the very brevity of these sessions made it difficult to do little more than reconnect, review the progress on the projects, and give some thought to future events. As Sarah would write to everyone the following week, the staff agreed that "we feel exhilarated, exhausted and energized at the same time, and sure that we have had a wonderful and productive experience."

Some of this, they agreed, was due to the setting and their own preparation, but it ultimately it also involved the commitment invested by everyone there. They had begun to see that one of their own strengths lay in their ability to be responsive to the abrupt surfacing of new issues. They had discovered their ability to make impromptu adjustments when something didn't work, and to factor in concerns raised from within the group. Moreover, people were able to voice their individual uncertainties over how well they, *as* individuals, fit in, thereby addressing openly the differences among their respective stances.

Often this took the form of explaining to each other how what worked for one person was not applicable in a different institutional

---

[18] From the Director's Report on the Southwest Region AAR/Lilly Teaching Workshop, p. 4.

setting. Such comments remained unthreatening, insofar as they were essentially descriptive. They served, instead, to allow for more precise discussion of these different environments and how one's teaching had to fit the specifics. How, for example, did an untenured person go about teaching a substantive course grounded in the academic study of religion in a small religiously conservative denominational college with an explicit evangelical mission? How, on the other hand, did someone else navigate the uncertain future of the religion department in a large state school?

The combination of the staff's flexibility, combined with their providing an outlet for these softer versions of challenge, were such that the group never felt the need to engage in a rebellion. The particular rapport between Gus, Sarah, and Jerry served to invite the participants to enter into a challenging intellectual dialogue in which, at the same time, it was legitimate to laugh at oneself, to tease others, to articulate frustration, confusion, and doubt, and to raise one's more deeply felt questions. Roger brought a quiet, gentle, and probing presence that further contributed to these possibilities. Together they generated an environment in which the personae usually brought along to academic conferences were—to everyone's expressed relief—left hanging in the closets at home.

The October Weekend
The Planning

The group would be meeting in a hotel this time, as classes were in session at the university and the dormitories were in use. The participants were reminded that, due to reasons of cost, they would be sharing rooms. Much of the meeting would focus on project reports, for which each person would have half an hour.

"We look forward to hearing from each of you just how well things are progressing," wrote Gus and Sarah, "but of course if you are encountering problems, we will all be glad to try to help." Time would be set aside, as well, to discuss an article, and to plan for the Pedagogy Section of the Spring regional meeting, with which the workshop would coincide. The participants would be in charge of organizing the session, including choosing who, from among them, would lead different parts of it.

"We tested the food at the hotel on your behalf," the letter went on to add. "As you know, we'd go to any lengths for you! We found it quite up to the standard we set in the summer."[19]

Days One and Two: Friday and Saturday, October 13 and 14

They would not have much time together. Forty-eight hours, after all, only allowed for a few intensive discussions and the occasion to reconnect. But already by the time they came together that Friday afternoon it was apparent there was celebration to their welcomes. The bond formed in a preliminary way back in August became a thicker, living thing with this reunion. Sitting around a large rectangle of conference tables punctuated with little bowls of hard candies (and jokes about picking out the licorice-flavored ones either to hoard or discard them, depending on the bias of the particular speaker), the group finished its initial greetings and brought each other up to speed on events over the past months.

"We became aware in August," wrote Sarah later on, "that a large number of participants had felt isolated and powerless in the community of scholars at large, and we had emphasized that they could assert themselves—and support one another—in gaining places for themselves in various program units of the AAR, particularly at the regional level. As the October meeting opened, it was gratifying to see that a sense of ownership of the community of scholars was beginning to manifest itself."[20]

Jerry had proposed that they then proceed to a discussion of "advocacy" rooted in an article by Louis Menand.[21] Menand, after puzzling through just what it is that the term actually means in the context of teaching, concludes that it comes down to the question:

> Should professors attempt to put across their own point of view about the material they teach in the classroom? Is this really a serious question? Of course we should. What else could we do? It is because we have views about our subjects that we have been hired to teach them.

---

[19] Directors' Memorandum, September 26, 1995.

[20] Final report on Southwest Regional American Academy of Religion Lilly Teaching Workshop, p. 1.

[21] For this discussion, the group had read: Louis Menand, "The Advocacy Trap," in *Lingua Franca*, July/August, 1995, pp. 57-61, 72.

> Our ethical constraint is only that we teach what we honestly believe the significance of the material to be.[22]

Quickly pointing to the distinction between teaching texts ideologically and teaching ideology, Menand goes on to argue that multiculturalism has become the operating paradigm for many disciplines. In that connection, he suggests a certain "disinterestedness," by which he means not the "absence of strongly held views" or the "willingness to give equal weight to every view," but arrival at one's views "uncoerced . . . by anything but the requirements of honesty." It is such disinterest that allows for independent thought and debate.[23]

One of the challenges, the group agreed, involves training students in how to make a good argument by showing them how to make a strong case for at least two different positions. The very act of doing so can, in itself, be construed as a political position; nevertheless, this is one way of getting students to learn how to recognize where they stand in relation to the data they are studying, and to understand how and why they hold the positions they do.

"All disciplines have orthodoxies," said Roger. " For example, in teaching Biblical studies, I don't know many people in scholarly societies who would go at it from a Freudian perspective. So, I point out where the discipline is and is not at that time."

Nor does the acknowledgment of multiple perspectives let one off the hook from seeing that there are practical outcomes to each of the positions represented in a discussion. Disinterest, in this sense, may be more a matter of trying to hold all interests in view, drawing the distinction between advocacy and fair representation.

"Going back to the earlier point," one person said, "I don't think, if I were presenting Christian theology, that I would be constrained by the positions represented by the students. There are all kinds of heresies that don't have a church anymore, and there is a way that the discipline establishes a constraint on what goes into the classroom. On the other side, all of this has to take place in an atmosphere in which a real dialogue with the students can happen. It

---

22   Ibid., p. 58.
23   Ibid., 72.

bothers me when it all remains 'rational' argument. That can get very Western."

"In a class I teach on Religion in America," said someone else, "I lecture on liberal Protestantism in the late 19th century, partly to try to get them over their hatred for the word 'liberal'. I also spend time on Darwinism. They ask me what I believe and I refuse to say. Then they ask me, 'You teach about things you don't believe?' and I say, yes, I do, and that I do so in a way that refuses to advocate for one position or another. The second example, on the other hand, comes from my teaching about the 'other' in Jacksonian America, which brings up some discussion of the Mormons and the angel Moroni. On one occasion, a student said, 'Leave off the i, why don't you.' At that point I had to advocate. So I see myself playing different roles, depending on the situation. The thing I do find interesting, however, is that it's acceptable in academia to advocate for post-structuralism, or neo-Marxism, or post-modernism; but it's not okay to be an advocate for any version of Christianity."

One of the individuals who was teaching in a conservative Bible college spoke up. "I struggle with how to be the disinterested advocate. The more I try to express positions other than fundamentalism and to do good liberal education, the more I find myself characterizing fundamentalism disrespectfully. I then have to try to balance things, which leads me to subvert my own advocacy position for a more open perspective and undermine what *I* care about. I haven't figured out how to resolve that."

Roger nodded. "I'm trying to get students not just to think through things about the Bible, but to come to some self-awareness with respect to the material. I don't think I can refuse to discuss my own views."

"I agree," said Gus. "All my life I've struggled with this. When we teach, the most important thing we teach is respect for other people's strongly held religious convictions. If that's part of what we're teaching, at some point we do have to let it be known what we believe. We're not just teaching a subject, so we have to structure in these attitudes and be open about it. As I think I said the last time we met, my predecessor used to teach a course in comparative religion, in which he compared each religion unfavorably with Christianity. That stopped when I started."

"Is it even possible to avoid self-disclosure?" someone asked?

"Well," said Jerry, "I want my students to engage in a mental migration, into the world I'm presenting, which is oriented by a liberal humanism—which, I get the sense, many of us share."

"I'm not so convinced about the openness of that approach," replied another person. "Liberal humanism tends to be self-congratulatory about its own openness, and represents other positions as oppressive. I find that the PC positions it tends to promote can have the unintended consequence of shutting down genuine inquiry and of hardening people's positions in a way that can become tyrannical in its own right."

This discussion served as a bridge into the review of the individual projects. In some cases, people had begun teaching the courses they had begun to plan during the summer; in others, the courses would be taught either that spring or at some later date. (This was particularly the case for the two graduate students, whose job prospects remained uncertain.) Either way, each report was met with questions and suggestions, some of which included non-traditional resources such as specific films, literary works, pieces of art, and field trips.

Again the differences in the participants' institutional settings surfaced, making it increasingly evident how these informed each person's approaches to teaching. Through this process, the group succeeded in conveying to its various members—including those who taught in the more "conservative" institutions—that neither they nor their schools were, as Sarah later expressed it, "backwater" or "second class."[24] If this recognition came as a surprise to any of the participants, none of them expressed it; for the faculty from these colleges, it opened up a sense of possible connection with the AAR which had, before then, been tenuous at best. Furthermore, in the course discussing each other's projects, there were frank acknowledgments of explicit borrowings from different aspects of what others were doing. Far from provoking resentment or anxiety,

---

[24] Final report on Southwest Regional American Academy of Religion Lilly Teaching Workshop, p. 1.

these cross-fertilizations were taken as part of the purpose of the workshop itself, illustrating the fruits of this kind of collaboration.

Once again, the debate over how far to go in incorporating experiential exercises into classroom work surfaced with some heat. By now the group had gotten fairly good at arguing with one another, that same heat not going so far as to make anyone lose their cool. While some of those engaged in the debate were sympathetic to efforts aimed at cultivating student sensitivity to religious practices, they nevertheless worried about the risks of trivializing or, in a facile manner, appropriating these same practices. Would this not amount to "using" isolated elements in ways that failed to recognize the integrity of traditions as a whole? Clearly not everyone agreed in full; nor were the differences reconciled. Indeed, later, in their evaluation of the session, a number of people pointed out that the places where they all, as a group, had some of the strongest disagreements were in connection with issues of advocacy and distance.

Day Three: Sunday, October 15
On the final morning, the task at hand was the planning of the Spring workshop and of the Pedagogy Panel for one of the plenary sessions at the regional AAR meeting in March. The staff had taken seriously its own objective of using the workshop to strengthen the position of untenured faculty in the region, and therefore presented this not as an option but as an expectation. As the group began to think about what they might want to do, they found themselves returning to some of their discussion the day before.

"It sounds like many of our comments are about where we are as instructors," one person noted. "My concern is that we may be addressing students as if trying to disabuse them of their religion. This ties in with the issue of being either an insider or outsider."

"But what's also both striking and moving to me," said Jerry, "is to watch the kind of respectful dialogue going on here. I want to go back to the idea of insider/outsider, and to have the panel let others watch the sort of discussion we've had going on here."

Others suggested also handing out a sheet with teaching tips, based on their own suggestions, as another contribution to the region. They wanted to find a way to bring together the conceptual issues they had been discussing and the practical strategies, recognizing that there was an interplay between the two. They also felt it would be important to avoid presenting themselves as some sort of elite cadre.

"Does everyone agree that theory and practice can be combined?" asked Sarah. Essentially, they did.

A title was proposed by one person, who said, "Well, I'm willing to be the opening act for this road show, and I'd like to throw a suggestion on the table for a title: 'Cheerleader, Midwife, or Commander Data?: The Role of the Instructor in Teaching Religion.' We'll have people from different teaching environments speaking to some of the issues that come up in their settings, and talk about how we've been influenced by each other. It could be about the issues of location and the involvement of the students."

They wanted to convey, too, their own excitement about what they had been doing together. It was agreed that, because the dynamic of the workshop itself had avoided the tensions of an "us" and a "them," this should be the style of the panel. The point would be to do everything possible to enable those present to participate.

It took them a while to figure out who would speak, to represent them, although they each agreed to be present whether they were on the panel or not. They decided, too, that those speaking would hand out the summaries of their projects in order to illustrate the classroom skill they were trying to discuss. Finally, their moderator was to keep them on track with respect to tying these issues into what it meant to be teaching in this particular region. And with the resolution of these matters, the session came to a close.

The March Weekend[25]

Days One and Two: Friday and Saturday, March 15 and 16

Unlike any of the previous workshop weekends, this one would be piggy-backing on the meeting of the Southwest Commission on Religious Studies in Dallas. This meant that, in some cases, there would be absences from the workshop sessions as a given staff person or participant had to be present at some other panel or meeting. The participants were instructed to send in either copies of the proposed syllabi for the courses they were working on, or an extended progress report.

After gathering for lunch on Friday, the group spent the next two days reporting to each other about the state of their work. This was therefore the third occasion on which they had been given public time to discuss this work. It was clear that where there had been rough drafts in October, there were now more fully defined formulations. Although there were, in fact, a number of absences along the way, for the most part the group remained together.

The segway into the Southwest Commission meetings took place first with the AAR plenary session on pedagogy in the study of religion. The title, "Cheerleader, Midwife, or Commander Data?" as Sarah explained it, encapsulated what the group had identified as common concerns and challenges as teachers of religion, voiced in the following questions: Do we rally our students as we lead them through new material and then onto victory at final exam time? Do we offer aid and assurance as our students give birth to new ideas, insights, and experiences? Or, do we act like mechanical dispensers of information, walking encyclopedias of the tremendous and the trivial? The task the group had set for itself and its audience was to explore the role of the instructor in teaching religion.

The participant who had so strongly advocated experiential or participatory modes of teaching spoke on the value and potential problems he had encountered in using this approach. A second

---

[25] Due to the death of her sister, this was the only set of sessions at which the author was not present. The data comes from interviews with some of the staff and participants, and from selected documents (The Final Report on the Southwest Regional AAR Lilly Teaching Workshop by Sarah, the conference papers for the group's panel on pedagogy, and a memo written to the participants by Jerry).

participant spoke about the struggles and rewards of teaching philosophy of religion in the context of a confessional Christian university—a presentation which faculty from his school came to hear. A third person discussed the challenges besetting faculty in large state universities where "a talking head is what they want." This drew considerable response from the audience. The fourth addressed the importance of the mission of a university, college, or seminary in shaping the context for one's teaching.

The panel was well attended by scholars not involved in the workshop, including more than half the total number of members registered for the annual meeting. Sarah noted afterwards that this was one of the highest levels of attendance there had ever been. It was, as she said, "very *us* in spirit."

Day Three: Sunday, March 17

On the final morning, the group gathered at a panel entitled "Koresh and the Classroom: Teaching about the Branch Davidians." The point of having the participants attend this workshop, which had been organized by Jerry, was to gain both pedagogical and theoretical insights into how to teach about this event which had occurred within the past year in Texas. As Jerry described it in a memo to the group:

> Images of the charred remains of David Koresh's compound are indelibly imprinted in many people's memories. The battles, verbal and physical, between the Branch Davidians and various government agencies brought much attention to issues concerning the relationship between religion and American society. One of the most disturbing parts of this confrontation was the marginalization of experts in our field on these matters by government authorities. In addition, most of us who teach religion (but do not specialize on this group or on church-state issues) were asked in and outside of class for our views on Koresh's or the FBI and ATF's actions.
>
> As one of the participants in the workshop for religion professors in the Southwest, I thought the confrontation and its aftermath would be a good topic for discussion. Unfortunately, the workshop participants are not experts in this area. Therefore, this panel was put together to introduce all who are interested to some issues which the presenters, authorities in some dimension related to the Davidian situation, feel are central, and

perhaps insufficiently recognized or addressed, when this matter is discussed.

The workshop members heard presentations on church-state issues raised by the confrontation, and on a series of teaching strategies designed to encourage student reflection on the subject. The issues the presenters raised included how to define terms such as "cult" and "brainwashing," uses of the Bible, the role of the media, and the relationships between government, religion, and violence.

The objective of involving members of the workshop in the region proved a successful one both in the specific events and in the increasing move into regional offices and chairs by some of the participants. In its subsequent evaluation, the staff celebrated that, with respect to the workshop's serving to strengthen the region, "What we are doing is working."

The Second August Week

The Planning

The actual workshop would not take place until August, but all four staff members came together in June for a final planning session. Their purpose was to assess the spring meeting, review the suggestions submitted by the participants for the final week, and design this last program. Other logistical details would be left to the co-directors and the school's conference office.

One of the elements that created a sense of shared task in the workshops was the requirement that the participants engage in formulating their teaching project. Because of the original design of the workshops, one of the constants—however much the individual programs might vary—were these projects. Therefore, the different staffs had tended to take it as a given that the group should find ways to foreground the projects at each meeting, dedicating a significant amount of time to progress reports and related discussions. Yet, by the spring meeting, it often became clear that the participants were generally feeling less need to use large blocks of their time together to talk about this part of their work.

During the March weekend in Dallas, the staff in the Southwest had invited ideas from the participants toward the final week. Whereas they themselves had generated the content of the

August week of the previous year, they were mindful of a deeper pedagogical objective structuring the rhythm of the year—namely, the process of looking for ways to make the workshop increasingly the creation of the participants, with themselves less the organizers and more the facilitators of that program. They decided, therefore, to revise their original plan drastically.

The informal list, put together by Jerry, represented the clustering of ideas from the participants:

> What is your *real* agenda in class?
> What was your most memorable teaching experience (either successful or unsuccessful)?
> Student developmental issues and learning styles
> A continuation of advocacy and representation issues: teaching pluralism as proper vs. hegemonic
> Who is the "other," and how many "others" are there?
> Teacher-student relationship, the different roles of the professor, pastoral issues
> Classroom as public/private arena, self-disclosure: when, how much, and why?
> Pedagogy styles: how are we alike, how are we different?
> Assessing learning, tests and evaluations
> Classroom exercises, multimedia, computer journals, field trips; syllabi exchange, good texts, reasonable demands and assignments
> Our discipline and social presence, as in our relationship with media and government
> Institutional expectations and personal views, especially if the latter change
> Group process: should we break into small groups sometimes?

As they discussed how to reconfigure this list into a workable series of sessions, the staff found itself adding some of their own questions to the list, such as "How to address the relationship between one's spiritual life and one's teaching?" and "How to stay fresh over the course of one's career?" They thought about including some discussion of the tenure decision process, and of surviving course evaluation and learning assessment.

The staff had also originally planned to focus on the use of non-textual, multimedia resources in the classroom. The differences between the participants' institutions ran the gamut from being fully equipped to lacking such services almost altogether. For some, having a session on multimedia technology would, therefore, be of little use. The staff decided to revise their original plan, making the topic available on an optional and voluntary basis. In part, this reflected an accomodation to the realities of the participants; it also allowed them to meet a commitment in the original grant proposal, which had said that the program would, in some way, include multimedia-related methods. In addition, as the letter to everyone reminded them, the group had already done some work with films and a library tour the previous year. Still, there was no getting around the real issue, which was the clear inequities between the different schools, and the related constraints these created.

Having agreed to these changes, they set to work on figuring out how to design headings under which to group the suggestions they had received, and ended up with six, which they organized in relation to the issues of one's own agenda in a variety of contexts:

"What is Your *Real* Agenda?"
"Agenda and Practice"
"Teachers and Students: Fluid Role Models"
"Margin and Center: Agenda and Context"
"Agenda and the Politics of the University"
"Public(s) Responsibility"

Sarah and Jerry would each lead two of these sessions; Gus and Roger would each lead one.

They set aside an additional session during which the participants would be asked to reflect on the significance the workshops had had for their individual projects. They also decided to reserve a session at the end for what they would call "loose strings"—those various topics and stray issues which, by virtue of sessions coming to an end, had remained under-addressed. Roger would keep track of these during the week and lead the session on them at the end.

In keeping with the focus on thinking about how to integrate issues concerning the region into one's teaching, they planned a session on "Pedagogical Uses of the Local Environment," which would include a visit to the Alamo, Mission San José, and Mission Concepción, which would be followed by an evening discussion of "Vision, Revision, and National Identity." Both of these would be led by Gus. And finally, they would leave time for a "closure" session to be planned and led by the participants.

In the letter that went out to the participants, the staff also laid down the deadlines for the final written reports on the projects and the evaluations of the workshop. This was always a slightly touchy point: with each of the workshops the concern was that, once the series was over, it could prove difficult to gather up all the final reports. In general, therefore, these were linked to receiving one's closing stipend. It made things simpler, and got the reports in on time. Finally, along with lengthy instructions on all the facilities available on the campus, Gus and Sarah promised that there would not only be new things to read, but also be a sumptuous menu (although this time, *sans* fruit baskets).

They would not have quite as many days together this time, as the dormitories and other facilities had not been available any sooner. This meant a more tightly filled schedule in the effort to have roughly as many working sessions together as they would have, had they had an additional day or two. They figured, too, that, by now, the participants were less likely to need time to work on their projects. The schedule of events was also formulated a little differently. Accompanying each session, the staff included an explicit goal. For example, the goal for the discussion entitled "What is Your Real Agenda?" was stated as "getting down to the nitty gritty of what we are really trying to accomplish in the classroom and in our teacher/student relations as advisors and mentors." The participants were asked to prepare a one-paragraph response, written in advance but not for distribution.[26] The formulation of the assignment was in keeping with the stated content: the issue of agenda—a question to which the group would return in a number of ways over the course of the week.

Day One: Tuesday, August 6

Much of that first afternoon was given over to coming back together again, figuring out the interest groups that would be

---

[26] This and all subsequent descriptions of the goals and preparation for this week-long session are drawn from the Schedule of Events.

meeting together, and heading down for a reception. It wasn't until after dinner that the question of agenda came up.

Jerry began with his. "I teach Asian religions," he said. "I see this as the only opportunity most students will have to engage with another—that is, Asian—culture. To the best of my ability, I want to help them understand this other in its *own* terms. This is a liberal humanist agenda that favors pluralism and liberalism, and that wants my students to more become tolerant, more self-conscious of their own world view, and to able to develop a social-justice agenda for themselves."

"Why," someone asked him, "do you want to reflect on the understanding of others in their own terms?"

"It's related to a deep sense of a certain kind of dialogue with the other," Jerry replied. "It's not just to understand the idea, but to understand the other. It's almost, for me, a religious conviction that this will lead to tolerance, as a moral good."

"But isn't that also undergirding a self-consistent, self-sustaining view of reality and of the university?" said the other person. "Is that so different from a fundamentalist school teaching a religious agenda?"

It proved not so easy for some to formulate a single agenda as the "real" one. For another person, for example, the agenda in her work seemed both multiple and, in certain respects, contradictory.

"For me, it has to do with self-knowledge and values transformation, and the human skills of empathy. But I'm also teaching them to question individualism—and, by implication, liberalism, even though I promote liberalism."

"My assumption," said another person, "is that you *can't* have just one agenda. But then the question is, is one better than another, and when do I promote the one or the other? Do I make them explicit or do I hide them?"

One of the participants who was teaching at a conservative Christian college nodded.

"I'm struggling with a nice liberal, tolerant agenda versus the moral education valued in a Christian school," he said. "My hope is for students to understand the complexity of their own heritage, and that others need not be dismissed as wrong—to get them to see that theirs is a perspective *as* a fundamentalist. It's the tension between how to acknowledge the clear Christian identity of my students at the same time as I'm trying to teach a kind of liberal tolerance."

"My agenda," Sarah said, "is filled with conflict over which I don't have control. I'm consistently caught up in how to affirm my students and create an atmosphere in which people can be confirmed for their religious identities *and* their non-religious identities, at the same time as I engage in profound questions. As a result, I'm often teaching classes that include people with whom I profoundly disagree, over issues about which I *most* disagree—especially as I'm trying to think and rethink my own ideas about these things. I guess what it is, is that I'm trying both to affirm and disturb my students. It's not that I want to create conflicts, but that we live in a conflict-ridden world, and I have to help them to take on the responsibilities that go along with that."

"One thing about conflict in the classroom," said someone else, "is that it's related to how society treats the discourse, as soundbites. I see part of my challenge as saying that the real discourse doesn't operate in soundbites or in hurling invectives. This whole year, we've been going to the same drumbeat—the appreciation of humanism, and what someone referred to as the different postmodern problem of understanding that rampant individualism is not a net social benefit. Even though we encourage pluralism, it has gotten equated and confused with rampant individualism. In my classes, I want them to understand themselves in relation to how exactly they make choices, especially if they're from different traditions. For example, is it a choice based on Christian liberty, or religious law, or divine command? What is the root for each one? That is the key for me."

"Do you think Christianity and liberal humanism *are* contradictory?" said Jerry.

"With the Enlightenment," someone else replied, "the place where one discerned ultimate truth shifted from a divine Other to the human. There are Christians who see that as wrong."

"But do we not use a phenomenological method which takes the tradition on its own terms, bracketing the truth questions?" another person said. "Underlying this tension from a Christian view are questions of truth. Is the Dao, for example, either ultimate or true? These questions are not part of the agenda in the liberal humanist tradition."

"That's because strong feelings are involved," said someone else, "and liberal 'tolerance' ducks that."

"It's especially difficult in a more conservative school," said one person, "when you try to make room in the classroom for different convictions. Both students and faculty have a vested interest in a particular commitment. Part of the agenda for me is has to do with working out the relationship between personal faith, different religious traditions, *and* another tendency, which is to look to science for answers."

"I find that I try to dichotomize it somewhat," said Roger. "I say that this—here, the Bible—is a text in which people have a vested interest, and I do too. But now I'm trying to promote a discussion in which people from different backgrounds— fundamentalist, Jewish, or more or less Christian—can learn to listen to the text and to each other. It's some sense of being held accountable to one another."

"To say that teaching religion is in some way dominated by the issue of religion in the classroom," Gus replied, "is not the same as saying that a fundamentalist teacher's teaching is the same as that of a liberal humanist, because putting religion out there as an 'it' is not a religious approach. You can do that with mathematics, but with religion, it's not a natural act. It's already imposing an agenda."

Roger turned to Gus and said, "Well, going by that, when I teach intro to Bible, I don't commit unnatural acts."

"That," said someone in a stage whisper, "is the difference between a Presbyterian and a United Methodist." The room broke up for a few moments.

"Right," said Gus, still chuckling. "I'm a Presbyterian minister and a teacher; sometimes these conflict. I want to help students to discover, explore, and be amazed by the different religious traditions I teach about, and I want them to become tolerant if it helps them struggle with their own religiosity. But I can't deal with my agenda without dealing with *their* agenda. We're dealing with materials that have been sacred and important."

"Gus's," said someone else, "is not a religious agenda, whereas yours"—pointing to the previous speaker—"is. That distinction gets at some of the ambiguities and differences. If it's a non-religious agenda, then is the real force and life of a religion being conveyed from within, or is it made instrumental to some humanistic, non-religious goal? And in a pluralistic context, can you avoid an advocacy with which many people in the academy are extremely uncomfortable, particularly because they fail to recognize the intensity with which they themselves advocate the stance of liberal humanism?"

"I assume," said Roger, "that communities who use the Bible as scripture use it as the precedent for things in their lives. A lot of the debates in the culture wars are about just that. I encourage students to develop the sensitivity to weigh different traditions against each other as a theologian or an ethicist might do. Is that something you would have a problem with?"

"For that matter," said Gus, "at the hear of religion, whichever the religion, is an identification with a tradition that comes to you as the sacred. If I'm presenting Judaism I can talk about the development of the concept of Torah as we know it. I do so from a historical perspective, and present the people relevant to the concept. That's what we're there to do. But that's not what the Torah means when it comes out of the Ark. Likewise, if we look at the Nicenean creed, we have to look at what Athanasius and others were doing, and examine all the possibilities they were confronting. But we can't stand up in church and discuss all that as if it remains a set of open questions, because it's not up for grabs anymore. So, one part of your mind has that information, but at that point, insofar as you are a worshipper, you bracket it."

"So theologians *do* commit unnatural acts?" said Sarah.

"Right," said Gus.

"Which," added someone else, "is why they're so conflicted!"

"It's a terrible confusion," Gus continued, "to confuse theology with religion. One of the great sins we commit, especially with students—some of whom are believers—is to convey the misconception that *no* such unnatural acts will take place in the classroom, and that what we're doing will all be a reinforcement for their faith. My callow youth was spent gleefully trampling on students in this way. As I have gotten older and mellowed, I see that this is a hidden agenda in plain sight, and I have to deal with it. I don't mean that I want to be critical, but that I have to work with it in my own life, to keep clearly in mind where religion is one thing, and the study of religion is another. There's an intimate relationship between the two, but for a time I engaged in the replacement of one with another which, in my opinion, is a bad agenda."

"The distinction between religion and religious practice is a second order of reflection," said another person. "It involves whether the approach taken to the teaching of religion can be separated out from everything else. But what if religion is something one can only study by way of initiation into a certain practice, before being able to engage in a certain kind of second-order reflection? If so, do we not end up having to accept that there are a number of legitimate approaches to the agenda, including even with second-order reflection?"

"I agree," said Gus, "but the alternative—and where I go with it—is that there are certain central things in any religion that are irreducible, that cannot be taught. That is, they can only be looked at and talked about, but not taught, without jumping in. A large part of my reluctance to jump in is out of respect. I know these things are real and important, but I would have to do something I am not prepared to do and change my life in a significant way, to become a certain kind of seeker without a guarantee of its coming to fruition. o mystic ever pursued *that* goal in order to teach it to others. They pursue it for the sake of the Beloved."

"It seems, still," the other person persisted, "that the mystic you're talking about is a caricature for the sake of discussion. In that context, any claim to engage in second-order reflection can only be taken as a falsification. If we take that position, then we cannot teach religion. Do we not distinguish between initiation *into*, and the study *of*?"

"It can also contribute to the trend of privileging the insider account as the only legitimate one," said Sarah. "I don't think that having an experience necessarily privileges the person who has it. In the tradition of William James, it's really important to have the narratives and the insider accounts. But I resist the idea that the only way to understand something is to experience it. I wouldn't say that, for example, about psychosomatic illness."

"One thing I haven't heard, yet, "said someone else, "is that among our agenda might be that of creating a community of scholars. The institutional settings we're in have that goal, if only by default, since American universities have adopted the German system of creating scholars (or, in my state—which has no use for scholars—majors), who can somehow be useful to the state. Either way, have we jettisoned the idea of making better citizens?"

"On multiple levels," said someone else wryly, "of course we assume that what's immediately apparent in what we do is not necessarily the real agenda, any more than we can assume that a student's being in our class is necessarily about wanting the material. After all, is part of my agenda not about getting tenure? We're all trained in a hermeneutic of suspicion, but we don't turn it on ourselves to see how much of what we do is over-determined by issues of tenure, course evaluations, and the ways these affect what we present and how we do it."

"A lot of axes intersect in the classroom," said someone else. "There are conflicts in our approaches and agendas. When I think back on my own college experience twenty years ago and what I remember about it—which seems like not that much—I did learn to appreciate complexity and ambiguity, and that *that* is the nature of life. My agenda is to develop the attitudinal skill of being willing to confront ambiguity and complexity in one's own life and in the classroom. Where I differ from a confessional approach is that if students don't come away with a sense of ambiguity, I've failed."

The time had come to stop, but there was no way such a discussion would not spill over into the conversation across the campus back to the dormitories, or sit out on the stairways later into the night. It was the test of a good question, that. It was also one of the virtues of having everyone in residence for the week, because this wore away the sharper boundaries between meeting times and the in-between times. Although the staff had planned to track the loose threads over the course of the week, bringing these together in a final discussion, many of them continued to weave their way through these other moments, bringing none of the issues to resolution, but consolidating a culture of conversation.

Day Two: Wednesday, August 7

The following morning, the discussion of agenda continued, this time in relation to a different aspect of one's practice in the classroom. The goal, as stated in the schedule, was "To address how we do and don't manifest our real agenda in our course design, syllabi, assignments, exams, and grading policies." To prepare, the participants had been asked to bring samples of their syllabi, assignments, exams, and/or other handouts for distribution.

They went around, reviewing techniques, strategies, explaining what they were trying to do with each one. As they talked, they continued to think out loud about how these methods addressed questions concerning how far they went in bringing in the heresies, the mergers between traditions, the negative dimensions. Did they contribute to the romanticizing (or unwitting falsification) of a tradition or to demonizing it? Did they help students become clear about what they did *not* understand?

The group recognized that their selection of specific materials and details for a course, in themselves, involved the implicit statement of values, and that perhaps one way to counter that was, intentionally, to give multiple statements of the same event through different points of view. With regard to a single tradition, it might mean showing students some of the multiple expressions.

"I want," said one person, "through what I do to present the existential dimensions, for example, of what it means for someone to identify as a Christian in its existential dimension, and to show the ways in which Christian faith is existentially engaging—how it is that a person can't say 'Jesus is *the* Lord' without saying 'Jesus is *my* Lord,' and that there are things you can't learn about a tradition until you sit with someone who is dying."

"I also think that this involves raising up the tension between the faith community and the discourse community," added someone else. "There are different approaches to stating what is perceived to be a truth. How you go about doing that establishes different ways of being a person of faith and different ways of being a citizen."

This particular session illustrated two important features of the workshops. The first was the exchange of practical tools and approaches. To see the reasoning behind others' choice of tools enabled one to think more precisely about those aspects which might prove adaptable, even though, in some cases, these were tied in with courses in areas distant from one's own. At the same time, it also brought into focus the ways in which some of these choices were integrally related to a particular teaching setting and the freedoms it promoted, or the constraints it imposed. The second feature involved the element of the members of the group teaching each other on the basis of their own experience. For untenured faculty—"and not necessarily all that high up on the food chain," as one person put it— this fostered a sense of competence at the same time as it provided a responsive audience.

During their meeting after lunch, the staff agreed that beginning with a reception and then dinner had served to pull people back together again, and that they had not needed a check-in session. Instead, everyone had willingly gone into the post-dinner discussion. They also saw, somewhat to their surprise, that this discussion had unintentionally killed two birds with one stone. Many of the methods people had brought up were directly related to their projects, such that the conversation had constituted a preliminary review of where these stood as well.

Already they were beginning to think ahead about what would bring the week to an effective end. They noted that one of the participants had initiated the planning of the participants' closing exercises, and could sense the beginning of amused, behind-the-scenes plotting. Sarah volunteered her husband to videotape the final session, from which copies would be made and sent out to everyone as a momento. So that the participants could get mileage with their schools out of having been involved in the workshop, the staff also decided it would be important to create some sort of certificate to hand out. This would, they hoped, contribute to elevating the importance of being an AAR/Lilly Teaching Scholar.

For the rest of the afternoon, Gus took a small group interested in visiting a local *botánica* out into the city. A full-sized figure of St. Lázaro stood by the doorway, with signs advising customers that he was neither for sale nor to be touched. Glass cases displayed porcelain figures of saints made in Italy, beads for devotees of the different divine figures in the *orishá* tradition, small images of the Buddha, and candles for *las siete poténcias africanas*, or the Seven African Powers. There were books on *santería*, booklets of prayers to particular saints, and bottles of oils to remedy specific troubles and afflictions. This was all the more striking insofar as the dominant Hispanic religious tradition in the region had historically been the Chicano versions of Roman Catholicism, and not the Cuban, African-derived traditions. More recently, however, the two had found ways to overlap, bringing together the *orishá*-related versions of the Virgin on the one hand, and the Virgin of Guadalupe on the other. (In contrast, in local markets the latter was far more apparent.) Here, the one lived nearby the other, suggesting the changing character of the Southwest's religious world

When the entire group gathered that evening, the staff presented them with their attempt to address a series of questions that had arisen in earlier sessions. To do so, they had grouped together many of the issues that bore some family resemblance:

> 1) What are the different roles played or assumed by professors; pastoral issues that arise; the classroom as public or private arena; self-disclosure (how much and for what reasons?)
> 2) Pedagogical styles: how are we alike? different?
> 3) Student development issues and learning styles (for example, analytical vs. intuitive; the significance of gender, class, ethnicity, and creed)
> 4) Development of the professor (for example, vocational and spiritual changes; aging; the significance of gender, ethnicity, and social class)

To prepare, the participant were asked to bring their most memorable worst and best experiences in the classroom that had reflected or generated changes in their sense of vocation and in their relations with students.

As its discussion progressed, the group noticed that it was focusing on several details which, on the surface, did not seem particularly significant. For example, they spent a fair amount of time comparing notes on how their students addressed them, whether by first or last name. They asked each other about how they dressed in the classroom, along with their reasons for their particular choices. The discussion, when looked at more closely, however, disclosed a good deal about the very nature of the teaching setting. This became most evident in the comment of one participant teaching at a large state university, who said, "A friend who was supposed to meet me, and couldn't, called to have a message left with me. They went to my classroom and asked the students—there were over a hundred of them—'Is this so-and-so's class?' 'I don't know,' is what they were told."

"At my school," said someone else, "you're expected to know students' names. They say hello during the semester they're taking the class, but after that, many of them don't. I think they don't think you'll remember them, which doesn't say anything all that great about their earlier experiences."

What they realized they were talking about was their experience of classroom culture.

"Let me ask a question. Do you all dress informally, or in church clothes?" said Gus.

As they discussed their different styles, and what these conveyed about their roles in their classrooms, they observed the degree to which other messages got encoded in names and clothing, and about the multiple messages included in both. In this connection, they pointed to a number of ways in which gender differences led to different practices. One person gave an analogy:

"At a workshop of the American Medical Association I attended," she said, "one woman talked about the difficulties of women physicians, and about how it was important to refer to her colleagues as 'doctor' in front of patients. A male doctor criticized this position, to which she replied that if she did not do so, then patients—and new doctors—would tend to assume she was talking to a nurse. The male doctor, abashed, said he would never make that mistake again."

Yet one of the male participants found that when he invited students to call him by his first name, he had more students trying to manipulate when they could turn things in, "as if that meant that the bargaining was open."

"We're trying to distinguish between kinds of authority," someone else pointed out. "Having lived in an Asian context, where more respect is accorded the professor, there are disadvantages to it, but also advantages. One reason I'm more formal is as a political statement that this is a position worthy of honor. In Zen, there is no particular assumption that the master is greater than the disciple, but that to get to that position sooner than others implies having certain skills helpful to those who follow. I think the acquisition of self-knowledge and of learning is hard work. It takes discipline, and so I want to create a disciplined atmosphere. I want to be a *task master*, but not as an epistemological claim to being a master."

These examples brought to the group's attention the degree to which, within their particular institutional constraints, they each also meant very different things by the "community" they were trying to create.

"For me," said Sarah, "it's about focusing on certain tasks together, as opposed to a group that has certain feelings for each other. I don't care if they like each other; I want them to be able to disagree, although respectfully. Personal relationships are not at the top of my goal list, but getting them to be able to cooperate is. It's about getting people, for a specific period of time, to engage, in spite of a lot of differences."

Although the questions intended to structure the discussion had been clustered based on family resemblance, the connection between them, in practice, proved to be too loose for people to arrive at a clear senes of focus. The difficulty with family resemblance in such cases is that, in practice it can turn into the kind of family reunion that fills a meeting hall and makes it impossible to do more than nod at most of the people across the room, and then only in passing. The problem lay in the goal itself: "To begin to address a wide-ranging variety of topics that include..." Although there was, indeed, a connecting variable involving the relationship between professors and their students, there were simply too many aspects of that variable to address during a single evening. As a result, the experience, while good in its own right, was not altogether satisfying as an exercise in trying to fulfill a particular goal.

At the same time, the recounting of worst/best experience proved effective for two reasons. First, it came during the last week, by which time the participants and staff had gotten to know each other reasonably well and, indeed, had already been telling just these kinds of stories for some time. Second, the reason for doing so was made explicit. The stories were to serve as clues to oneself about one's own identity as a professor, an issue of real concern to the people there. As the evening continued, the group did tell each other stories of difficult experiences and of good ones, throwing in some of the techniques they'd come up with to encourage students to talk and to engage. The moral of the story? Timing, timing, timing, and trust.

Day Three: Thursday, August 8
Pursuing the question of the relationship between individual agenda on the one hand and some of the variables that influence them, the staff had defined the morning's topic as "agenda and context," or "Margin and Center." Their goal was "To address issues and questions of advocacy and representation, including among others, teaching pluralism vs. hegemony; who is the 'other'; how are *we* 'other', and how many 'others' are there?" The group was instructed to prepare for the discussion through a set of readings,[27] "paying special attention to your own experiences of sameness and otherness."

The discussion took a somewhat different turn, however (as anyone who has taught, and watched in fascination as students capture one's questions and head over the hills with them). The group, instead of talking about the "other" as the topic of their teaching, moved immediately to the question of students who come

---

[27] For this session, the readings were: Molefi Kete Asante, "Multiculturalism and the Academy," in *Academe*, May-June, 1996, pp. 20-3; Samuel Fleischacker, "Multiculturalism as a Western Tradition," in *Academe*, May-June, 1996, pp. 16-9, 65; Russell Jacoby, "Marginal Returns: The Trouble With Post-Colonial Theory," in *Lingua Franca*, September/October, 1995, pp. 30-7; George Kushf, "Intolerant Tolerance," in *The Journal of Medicine and Philosophy* 19:161-81, 1994; Barry Schwartz, "Tolerance: Should We Approve of It, Put Up with It, or Tolerate It?" in *Academe*, May-June, 1996, pp. 24-8.

from other backgrounds, and are therefore less fluent in English and, as one person put it, in "our form of discussion."

This they found to be the case most often with some of their international students, which raised questions on several levels. First, were their schools being responsible in accepting students who might not have the necessary preparation to engage in an American formulation of required work? If so, did the schools not then have a corresponding responsibility to provide such preparation, rather then throwing these students into classes where they ran the risk of not doing as well?

"We suspect it may be economically driven," said one person, "but there is also the moral question of having to choose whether or not to generate a track in the degree program which essentially has a different content, insofar as it gets watered down. Is it then an inferior education, and are these students really getting what they're paying for?"

What complicated matters for some people was the case of clearly bright students who don't read or write as well in English. It then becomes more difficult to know if they are poor writers in general or not. Are they held to the same standards as American students, in which case they may not do as well, or are they assessed differently? And, if they are, at what point does that become racist, an implicit statement that "I don't expect you to achieve"?

Gus talked about his own experience of having been an international student. He had, he said, been able to write reasonably well when he came to the United States, but could not understand spoken English easily for a while.

"But to me," he went on, " one of the best things was that no one deferred to my having to catch up. As a result, I caught up. I wouldn't have expected otherwise. My problem with special arrangements for international students is that it easily slides into racism. At my school, I've had some students say they have trouble with my accent; I don't think it's about that."

"When my students tell me I have an accent," said one participant from Africa, "I tell them that so do they! More seriously, I grew up since the first grade with English. I would hate to see someone who had picked it up later to be penalized for certain reading and writing patterns, and would agree with the idea of English classes to help them break these patterns. I get students to pair up with someone who speaks better English, so that whatever written work they do is gone over, but I also expect to see their first work, to see how much of a departure there is from it. That's more about academic integrity."

On the other hand, someone else pointed out, if you don't take the lack of preparation into account, does that not become a different form of racism?

"My attitude about language," said Gus, "is that it is the core of culture and one of the artifacts we cannot do without. A degree in an American liberal arts program should mean that a person has a high degree of proficiency in American academic discourse. Where does it slide into racism? If a white Anglo student comes out without being able to write English well, we say the university didn't do its job. But if a foreign student comes out the same way, we should make the same judgment. We don't tell students that they should come having first learned English very well. There is no question in my mind that we are devoting ourselves to the promotion of a particular kind of academic culture, and to a particular language, and to the ability to use it. That has to be communicated, which I try to do in teaching by persuasion."

How to convey to students why it was so important to master this ability? As they discussed different reasons, it became clear that there were practical ones—being better prepared to get a job, for example—and broader ones, such as being better able to participate in the larger culture.

"One source of the problem," said one person, "is that when students who have these difficulties come into our classes the university has already admitted them. That's a problem with admissions. Now we have the option of flunking them out, or trying to work with the skills they bring in. Motivation, interest, and good will are not the problem; the problem is the humiliation about being so ill prepared, and the frustration over how to get the skills to perform as a good student. I feel the institutions have a responsibility to help—to let students make revisions and to show that effort, work, and progress are of value, which is part of what the humanities are about."

"That is important," said a second of the participants from Africa. "There is a dangerous assumption that certain people like me are not going to make it—that is, make an A. In such cases, they treat you as someone just to pass through, because they assume you're going back to your country anyway. You can see how a professor appreciates another student and underestimates you. On the other hand, even getting help with such things may not be enough. At the university where I did my doctorate, they tried their best to give foreign students preparation in English, with a lab and a tutor, but I also had a professor who had decided that all Muslims were terrorist animals who would not make it in his classes. He tried to prevent my doing a Ph.D. and, when I did pursue it, he tried along the way to prevent my eventually receiving it. Why should that happen? Do we also assume that someone from another culture describes, thinks, and operates with a different logic, such that we see ourselves as superior and others as inferior, no matter how qualified they are?"

"Call it what it is," said Gus. "It's racism. Wherever it happens we have to identify it, especially in the academic community."

"Yes," said someone else, "and there's a subtext, too. Rationality is not purely abstract. It is nested within particular contexts, such that it may not be perceived as a legitimate mode of discourse in other settings. This creates the need for certain canons. There are criteria. We see that those coming from different contexts have been trained in different forms of rationality. How, then, do we legitimately assess such people? Any judgment we make entails the assessment of different forms of rationality."

"Moreover," said another person, "our Western academic environment, as a context, *has* a culture, language, and set of standards in which we all participate. It provides different normative standards from what one might find in, say, an Islamic setting, or one of the Asian contexts. So, on the one hand, as Gus said, we may have cases of blatant racism; on the other, we are embedded in what our notion of rationality *is*. We then claim to be fair, and genuinely feel we are treating everyone the same way. But our very standard is based on a specific normative structure."

"I think it's racist even to see it as normative," said someone else. I present it as a game with rules, like baseball. I tell them, this is how we play it, and here's how you can, too."

"Yes," replied one of the African participants, "and if you teach me to play the game and I come onto the field knowing your rules, then why I should be treated differently?"

"What was said a moment ago is crucial here," said Gus. "The category of 'Western' is artificial, and creates all sorts of problems. We cannot sustain the fact of 'Western' rationality. It also has Islamic influences, for example, going way back. To say there is a different rationality is baloney. As an outsider, I may sometimes play the 'because I'm brown' game, but what that really means is that I don't like what you're doing with my thought. Our cultural backgrounds are enormously varied, but I don't agree that the human ability to think is different."

"I'm getting at something different here," said someone else. "We say that someone is at a disadvantage in coming here. We take for granted all the subtle ways of how to express an idea, knowing when and how to say something, etc. That subtext is operative. There are different logics—that is, the difference between a logic in an oral culture and one in a literary culture. The logic from the one doesn't map too well onto that of the other. So, it's logics that are not the same for different cultures. What counts as a valid argument in one context does not, in another, because all of them involve learned rules and skills. That's different from talking about underlying cognitive structures, or basic human abilities to think."

"Ironically," added another person, "especially in our field, we study other forms of thinking as significant, but then say that few of these, if any, can actually be used in the academy. That, as much as anything, points to the distinctions between different kinds of discourse, and the kinds of judgments we employ to assign them to different settings."

"I want to come back to the earlier question," said Sarah, "of why a person is automatically written off, even when they learn the rules. Why are they still discredited?"

"That has to do with how we define minorities," replied one of the African participants. "When we talk about minorities, we often mean African Americans. But it is important to realize that for some 'others' this status represents a profound change. There is a proverb in my language which says, 'A king's sons and daughters may very easily be slaves in another country.' It reflects the changing demographics, and accompanying changes in status for different groups, in academic institutions. Who, now, *is* the 'other' in a given point in time? In this region, which is part of the Bible belt, what will the demographic changes over the next twenty years mean?"

"The center/margin relationship is changing," said another person. "The old paradigm of the cultural framework is being turned inside out, and the center is much more multivalent. It's like a Mobius strip."

"I think we have to face it," said Sarah, "that the center is the center for whoever is in it."

"The center does define itself," said someone else, "whether as Eurocentric or Chinese, or Muslim. You see this in people's maps—there's a consistency in that kind of cultural arrogance. Gus said that rationality operates across the board, but people also privilege their own center and its ways of doing things. How do we, as teachers in theory and practice, with a moral obligation, combat a privileging based on such ways of perceiving? And how can we not do so, if that's where the racism lives and operates, in the way we privilege the organizing of certain kinds of information."

"What strikes me also," replied Gus, "is that we need to be aware of the power game constantly being played out in this issue of center and periphery and the question of 'who's the other?' In the United States, I'm considered a Hispanic. But I was never a 'Hispanic' before I came here; I used to be, and still am, my specific nationality. The people who get put under the heading as Hispanics are ones that I always used to think of as 'other', too—Puerto Ricans, Salvadorans, Dominicans—but now we're all Hispanics.

"The bad side of that is when you run into related racism. The other side of it is that—guess what—Hispanics in this country are now developing a consciousness of being 'Hispanic.' 'Look at all the votes we've got!' That begins to shape a different consciousness, so that we do, in fact, begin to buy into the label of 'Hispanic consciousness.' That, in itself, begins to create a different understanding of center."

"I want to return to the subtext of power," said someone else, "which does involve issues of difference and related racism. I'll do so with a benign example: When I was learning German, I went to Germany and found that there were distinctions in the pronunciation of the *umlaut* that I could not hear at first. I had to depend on those who were 'other' to me, to make it known to me that I had not mastered it. I didn't yet have the norm to know if I *had* got it. Some friends of mine there sort of made fun of me, and continued to point to the differences in my speech, even after they were no longer there. You have to defer to that kind of authority over whether or not you've gotten something, because *you* can't yet recognize it.

"A power structure comes with that. Once you master the differences, then to a degree you do away with some of the power differences. What gets more complicated, however, is when you *really* master certain differences and find, as was said earlier, that you haven't eliminated the power differences. Then you find that these may, in fact, be based not only on mastery of certain rules, but on other factors altogether."

"It is also related to what it means to acquire a cultural fluency," said Roger. "In the past, for those with access to a university education, that meant something much more homogeneous, so that you could say that learning such things was important for students to understand their heritage and their identity. But what heritage means has now changed, as we have a greater sense of a shrinking world."

"When in doubt," said Sarah, "bring the problem and the complexity into the classroom, as part of the effort of living in in-between times."

"You know," said one of the African participants, "when I go back to my university, two thirds of the students are women. Even though, in one frame of reference, women see themselves as marginalized, such examples make me question the term 'post-colonial.' With everyone saying, in one way or another, that *they* have been marginalized, it becomes a way of self-defining that is really trying to marginalize others. Therefore, the power questions operate on a number of levels."

Gus looked up. "We agree that the ability to master language is a universal trait," he said," although languages are structured differently. That doesn't mean we can say, as the ancient Greeks or the Chinese did, that whoever does not speak a particular language is barbarous, somehow tying it in to being less than human."

"You can do all kinds of things with language at the cultural level," said another person. "I've found with many Asian students that they come from cultures where power relationships between teachers and students work against their being critical of what I say. When I try to work with that, I'm working against ingrained cultural patterns. It doesn't have to do with a different rationality, but with an acquired way of organizing power relationships."

Again, the time brought them to a close. Later, in their own meeting, the staff talked about ways in which the previous evening's discussion had remained superficial. Even this most recent session, they agreed, had begun on that level. It was when people had begun to talk about their own experiences that a turning point had come.

"Although I want to defend the first forty-five minutes as not unimportant," said Jerry. "Where we started out, with grading and so on, was fine; we just needed to find a way to get off it."

"We didn't get as much into all the different theologies that grow out of differences," said Sarah, "like some of the feminist, womanist, and *mujerista* theologies."

"Well," said Gus, "for that matter, I'm more *mujerista* than you are."

"No you're not," said Sarah, looking rather pointedly in the general direction of his crotch.

"Yes I am," said Gus, looking just as pointedly at the color of his arm.

This kind of joking was a longstanding part of the relationship that had grown up between these two colleagues, who had worked with each other for years. But the very ease with which they said such things to each other in turn informed the staff dynamics, and carried over into the group discussions. It made possible a certain level of candor. Even when people talked over circumstances about which they were, in fact, quite angry, the larger framework of the group held up as challenging, but accepting, consistently tempered by humor. While no group dynamic resides solely in the hands of its leadership, the tone set by the very relationship between the directors themselves creates a model for what can be said and done.

That evening, the topic of agenda was to be set in the context of the politics of the university. These stated goals were:

> To address issues surrounding institutional expectations, for examples, the assessment of student learning (relying on standardized forms vs. developing a teaching portfolio); tenure requirements; balancing teaching, scholarship, and service. We hope to raise questions like: who gets rewarded and who gets punished? What helps you?

To prepare, people were instructed to "Bring your own hopes, fears, and experiences."

Much of the discussion turned to the intense worries experienced by many untenured faculty in relation to the tenuring process. They wanted advice and counsel from the staff, seeing in them a group of people who had successfully weathered the ordeal.

The staff agreed that the first issue was to determine the kind of institution with which one was dealing, and who, in reality, held the power of granting tenure. Was it, for example, an essentially arbitrary process in the hands of a few administrators, or did it have credible faculty involvement? Only after figuring out that part can one then move on to determine what to do. If the institution doesn't have the latter, at some point one would want to work for that to be put in place.

"Of course," said Roger, "having it in the hands of the faculty doesn't necessarily mean it will be a good process. From having watched untenured people agonize, I see that part of the problem can be that a lot of people will tell the person different things. It's well meant, but it may lead to bad advice. Some people end up thinking they have to show up at every coffee with other faculty, or that dinner at the president's house is a command performance. Part of the problem arises when there is not enough clarity on the part of the institution for you to know what is really expected of you."

"How do you find out?" said one person bluntly.

"There *should* be a university document on tenure," said Jerry. "Get hold of that document and look at it. Also, find a mentor. Some departments tell a person, 'You're fine,' but you need a person you can trust who also knows the lay of the land—and be sure to check with others to be sure that person *does* have the lay of the land."

"The written documents, if they exist, should be binding," said Sarah. "They also are a way for the university or school to protect itself against suits. But some departments don't have such documents. Then you may have to make a case for yourself concerning how you've met the school's operating standards. So, keep track of how you spend your time. Note, for example, how much time you put into the different things you do. That allows you to document your own work.

"The other important thing, regardless of whether you're coming up for tenure or not, is to act genuinely like yourself. Be who you're always going to be at the university, independent of this tenure decision, because whatever you do before tenure is what you're going to keep doing afterwards. Be the very best at what you really feel *you* can be or ought to be. Otherwise, you'll be paralyzed. You need to do this to be a *person*. It's also a good idea to set up a box or a hanging file with your teaching evaluations and self-evaluations, labeled with a table of contents, according to your institution's description of what's required. It has to be laid out to coincide with that document."

"At my school," said someone else, "where I've now been for five years, it's qualitative. We have to describe a "research trajectory" and say where we see ourselves along it. It's very ambiguous, and I don't know how to figure out what the real agenda is. And what do you do when everyone on a committee says it's up to one person, to whom they all defer?"

"That's a hard one," said another person. "It wouldn't be out of line, though, as you present your tenure materials, to make it clear how these conform to what the institution expects of you. I'd also suggest documenting everything that you can, from your perspective. Keep an office diary so that you have an absolute record of what you did, who told you to do it, and so on. Also, if you can't get a review from within your department, maybe there is someone outside of it who can give you some sense of assessment."

They agreed that it was important to think about the effect a system had as a whole on what each of them was about. How did one maintain a sense of individual integrity and value under some of those pressures?

"In my case," said one person, "the vice chancellor of academic affairs saw that I was putting energy into service activities like National Hunger Week. He felt that kind of thing detracted from what he thought I should be doing, and I later heard that he'd said I wouldn't get tenure as a result. So, it worked against me in the eyes of someone with decision-making power, even though *I* was carrying out my own vision. The rest of the committee ended up having to make a case for me."

Sarah nodded. "Service is often at the bottom of what gets valued, so you have to be clear about what a department *does* value. Look, for example, at the percentages assigned to each criterion. Then, as someone said a moment ago, document all of your own work in each of these areas with a journal. There is also nothing more important than your own self-presentation. Don't give them more power than they have, and then get stuck reacting to it."

"What really worries me," said someone else, "is that if you miss one chance at tenure, you become damaged goods. I've seen it happen to people, and it's my sense that things have a way of unraveling after that. It's pretty frightening. I always have the feeling that 'I'll do this much—and then I'll do some more, to be *really* sure.'"

"You're right," Sarah said. "But in my experience, unless you're talking about getting publications out that you need to get out, which might make a difference, these other extras don't matter as much as you might think. So, you have to know your field and know your institution and, if you can, find a mentor. And don't think that if you get tenure you can undo years of orienting yourself to others' expectations. You can't become someone different once you get it. That means you have to start taking stands along the way, because next you'll be bucking for full professor."

"This may sound obvious," Gus added, "and is an indicator of how claustrophobic the discussion has gotten, but one of the worst pre-tenure states of mind is when the committee becomes the world. Stay connected with the AAR and your professional society. The way things have been going in the field, they will help as your support, because for a department to make decisions about someone's scholarship, they increasingly have to go outside the field."

"What do you do," asked someone else, "when you find yourself penalized by student evaluations because of making students work hard and grading them strictly?"

"You have to be explicit on the first day of class," said Jerry. "Right then and there you tell them that it's a demanding class, and you make your own expectations very clear—'I'm going to work your butts off here!'"

"You do need to assess who your students are," said Sarah, "and also ask yourself whether part of what they're saying may, in fact, be true. 'Am I the problem? *Should* I cut part of this?' In the best sort of world, you start to attract the kind of students you hope to attract. Also, one of my favorite phrases, having been here for fifteen years, is the one that says, 'In accordance with the guidelines on page . . .' In informal conversation, I can say things like, 'In the guidelines of the AAUP—the American Association of University Professors—it says . . .' By the way, include AAUP membership in your CV. They sanction universities for improper processes, which can stand up as good evidence. They also publish *Academe*, which is another good resource to have."

As Sarah would reflect in a later report about this discussion:

> Participants also faced the politics and economics of their various, specific situations rather directly and soberly. Fully one half of the group present could possibly end up not tenured, largely for reasons having nothing to do with the quality of their teaching or their scholarship. For example, in the case of one person at a Christian university, the school is confronting doing away with tenure altogether for reasons of financial exigency; another, by virtue of teaching at a state university, continually faces the threat of budget cuts to losing his position. One of our participants, hired outside his immediate area of expertise, publishes his research in the area for which he was actually trained surreptitiously, in addition to publishing in the related, official area of expertise he is hired to cover. Two teach

at a seminary that may, any minute, financially go under. Not only is tenure an issue, but hiring is problematic as well. Our two graduate students face more than simply a possibility that they will not find tenure-track jobs. Furthermore, one person must, as adjunct faculty, "drum up" her own students through ads in the local newspaper and spots on the local radio station, in order to get to teach her classes.[28]

What had becoming apparent over the course of these different workshop series was the degree to which untenured faculty feeling increasingly at risk in their professional lives. The specifics described here are only variations on analogous situations in the other regions. Jobs which, it was assumed a decade ago, would be available are, in reality drying up. Cutbacks in departments, the recognition that tenure is being phased out in growing numbers of schools—or that retiring faculty are being replaced by poorly paid adjunct hires—have become a growing reality for this generation of scholars. Indeed, it was with some of these anxieties in mind that a number of people had applied to the workshops in the first place, with the hope that it might help them find jobs or improve their chances at promotion and tenure.

At the same time, the participants recognized that, with little job security, they were not the ones in a position to challenge these changing dynamics in their schools. Many were simply hoping that, if they kept their heads low, their noses clean, and their publication level steady, they'd run this gauntlet with minimal injury and find their way into what, for some, seemed an increasingly elusive job security. The staff were well aware of this. As Sarah was to write, "That together we have become a community of teacher-scholars makes these difficulties, which are characteristic throughout academia, all the more poignant and immediate to us."[29]

Day Four: Friday, August 9

The goal of the fourth morning's session was "To address such issues as what the wider public(s) have a right to expect from the academy ('academy' includes undergraduate, graduate, and professional institutions) and what the academy has a right to expect

---

[28] Final Report, Southwest Region, p. 6.
[29] Ibid.

from the wider public(s) it serves." They were all to prepare by reading two position papers on this issue,[30] and to "think more specifically about the various publics characteristic of the Southwest region, how they do and don't interact and how they come into conflict with one another."

As the group quickly acknowledged, the very term "public" is an ambiguous one, comprising multiple constituencies who influence the university in multiple ways. The relationship is therefore equally complex, involving on the one hand the other scholars in one's field, and the wider non-academic community on the other. Insofar as scholars direct many of their energies to the former, particularly through their publications, they become increasingly alienated from the latter; to the extent that they direct their writing to the latter, they become suspect as scholars by their peers. And yet, if academics abandoned the task of fostering an educated citizenry, democracy was all the more likely to be weakened.

"My impression," said one person, "is that the general public views us primarily as teachers, and doesn't necessarily understand what research or scholarship is about. If they see us doing something else, they get anti-academic. That's one problem. Another is that when we *are* represented publicly, our role in a larger setting gets reduced to soundbites."

"Part of the problem is the low standing given to service in the tenure game," said someone else. "People are really hungry for public talks and lectures, but it takes an enormous amount of time to prepare them. Even if a school does count off-campus talks under the heading of service, it doesn't help much in the larger question of getting tenure."

"I may just be speaking for myself," another person said, "but I feel a strong sense of calling for my teaching to have social utility, and that my work with undergraduates be a form of outreach. Students go on and have an influence in the larger world. So, when I talk about service, I can't separate it from my teaching."

---

[30] Paula Cooey, "The Role of the American Academy of Religion Beyond the Academy," and "The Responsibilities of the Public(s) for Support of Scholarship and Teaching in the Academic Study of Religion," two position papers presented by Prof. Cooey as the AAR delegate to the American Council of Learned Societies.

"Our students *are* part of our public," said Gus. "I see *that* as part of my mission. A lot of my students are not religion majors, but may be going into law or other fields. In all those fields, I believe they will be handicapped by a general lack of knowledge about religion and a failure to comprehend it. So for me, my teaching is one form of public service. The way I see it, after thirty years in the profession, we are in a wonderful situation which is different from when we started, when the academic model came out of Biblical studies. You couldn't get anywhere unless you were analyzing picky points. It was disastrous. Now, we're allowing ourselves to use other models like literary criticism or approaches that are more art-like than hard-science-like, which are therefore more accessible both to other academics and to the general public."

"But there are still holdovers," said Sarah. "How many of you write encyclopedia articles, book reviews, programs for computers related to classroom use, or invited articles for volumes that may be used in the classroom, within textbooks? In a lot of research institutes, none of these things counts as scholarship. So the word 'scholarship' is a floating term. The judges who hire us may define it narrowly, and set theory at the head of it."

"To continue that line of reflection," said one person, "the standards for what counts and what doesn't are not just limited to religion and religion scholars. My university wants to be one of the AAUP research universities, so there are additional standards by which they now judge us. This is leading to a shift away from teaching to a certain model of research."

"These kinds of research models lead to competition for money and deteriorate into turf battles over which disciplines owns which knowledge," said someone else. "But my field, ethics, is a synthetic discipline—an inherent application of moral theory to real situations. The more I hear people's struggles over moral choice-making, it makes it clearer to me that we have failed to mesh principles of moral liberalism with people's faith and with what we have learned as scholars. But the more I try to do that with the application of ethics, people respond by saying, 'Keep your religion out of it—just tell us what to do.' I'm no longer willing to say you can divorce moral choice from the choices you make; you have to know the grounds on which you're doing so."

"Going back for a moment to the related issue of writing for the public," said another person, "I would like to see models for younger scholars on how to do that—things like Sally McFague's work, or books like Cornel West's *Race Matters*. Along with that, I'd like to see the academy honor more collaborative efforts."

"And as for other ways of reaching out to the public," said Sarah, "for those who feel comfortable being in touch with people in the media, if there is a religion editor at your local paper, you can call and introduce yourself. Express your willingness to be a source, or call them when a story arises, especially if you see misinformation being conveyed. For that matter, there's an AAR pamphlet by Mark Silk on dealing with the media. Of course, if you do engage in some of the moral issues facing the country, you can get sensationalized in ways that are beyond your control, and you may get ugly mail. After I was quoted as favoring the ordination of women, I got a used menstrual pad sent to me anonymously."

"Carter Hayward," added someone else, "was told in her first year of ordination by one man that he would not take communion from a menstruating woman." The group was quiet for a moment.

Sarah continued. "Going back to the documents we've read, what is the university's policy about receiving pay for additional services? It may, for example, not count paid service in your tenure review, because the pay is seen as your reward. This can come up, for example, if you do political consulting."

"I wouldn't make that distinction," said Gus. "If you get royalties for a book, should the book then not count? If you have a full-blown consulting business, that's one thing, but if you do a workshop for a church and they pay a hundred dollars, that doesn't begin to pay for your preparation."

"One of the things the public confuses is the teaching *about* religion and religious indoctrination," Sarah said. "But the academic study of religion is distinct from theological studies. Part of the reason for the confusion comes out of the origins of the discipline itself, because it wasn't until the sixties that the two began to be more clearly separated in the academy. It's also related to the idea that there is something underlying all these historical traditions that *isn't* politics, which leads to the privatization of religion as something you do with your private life."

"How would you draw a line of demarcation between what our departments are teaching and what is being done in seminaries?" one person asked.

"The technical line," Sarah replied, "is that the purpose of seminaries which have denominational commitments is to prepare people for the pastorate. They're professional schools, and therefore may have some commitment to the spiritual formation of their students. In the AAR and in many institutions without strong denominational ties, you are not in the business of making people religious, any more than political science is to make people religious. We are not in the field of promoting people's spiritual formation."

"But that raises another part of the relationship with the public that is complicated," said someone else, "because they see us as doing a service. They bring their kids to us to learn about religion, and we don't necessarily give them the kind they wanted."

"I *have* had parents put pressure on their kids not to take my courses," said Sarah, "because they worry that it might make their kids less religious. Of course, even some seminaries are charged with driving people out of their faith."

"But for us to then expect them to support us financially is difficult," said the previous speaker. "The other thing is our relationship with the religious leaders of a community. They use us when they think it will be to their advantage and will promote their agenda, but even then are not so interested in raising money to support what we do."

"Which raises an immense problem," said Roger. "The public and the people who go through public schools are often quite ignorant about religion. In the Southwest, I think the political problems associated with that are enormous. In our Bible Belt town of thirty thousand, two or three years ago the "Gifted-Talented Program" in the public schools became the subject of all sorts of controversy. The churches got into it, saying that the program was teaching New Age religion, so then the school board had to get into it. One local opthamologist said it was New Age religion and that this was psychologically dangerous (he had had one unit on psychiatric medicine in medical school). So even to get people to make the distinction between teaching about religion and the practice of religion can open a can of worms.

"At the same time," said Jerry, "one of the things that we who come out of a liberal tradition have deceived ourselves about is that there such a thing as neutral teaching *about* something, which in fact makes the suspicious justified."

"The prevalence of suspicion on the part of parents," said someone else, "has to do with their perception that religion teachers will undermine faith."

"I don't teach to kill someone's faith," said Sarah, "but I know that people in my classes do change. They may become religious, or religious differently, or non-religious. We're getting at the nitty-gritty of what education *is*, which involves the tension between any wider public and the academy. It can get overplayed, but we are not here to produce the acquiescent citizen or what some parents want—the acquiescent child. We are functionally like some religious institutions that stand in tension with the culture, that is, that both perpetuate and challenge the culture."

"I'd go further," said Jerry, "and say that I'm in the business of undermining certainty—not faith. My understanding of students, developmentally, is that many of them assume that faith *is* certainty. My objective—maybe I should say one of my real agenda—is to undermine that kind of certainty."

"Yes, and *your* definition of faith may run directly counter to some people like Calvin and others," said one person dryly.

"True," Jerry replied. "If we take such an approach, we should not then expect to endear ourselves to the public—though I do find people more willing to entertain the kinds of ambiguities I pose to my students when I raise the issue that their certainties are based on flimsy grounds. But I also think we lose touch with the wider community if we are not on school boards or in conversations with the local dentist or physician or the driver of the dump truck who may also be on the school board. I would say that, as public citizens, we have often failed in some of that role."

"But we also have to be careful not to buy into everything the bashers say about us," said Sarah. "Some of those perceptions are just going to remain, and we have to deal not only with the actualities of who we are, but with perceptions we may be able to do little to change. My own theological understanding of faith is a trust and faith in the faith of uncertainty. And Calvin, by the way, meant something very different by knowledge and faith. We can't lose sight of that either. He meant something more like the Hebrew 'knowing'—that is, a more intimate knowing.

"Sometimes when we talk about knowing, we mean certain kinds of content, and sometimes we mean *knowing*—how do you *know*? My goal is to introduce students to modes of knowing they can use for the rest of their lives, making the content somewhat subordinate to that. They may not have come for that, because they think they already know how to know. For them, knowledge is positivist certainty; faith is affective certainty. I'm trying to introduce them to a process that that understands knowledge as a little more free-floating."

"I want to talk about our seminary public," said another person. "In the local church where we are, people often see us as faith destroyers. 'Why go to seminary?' they say. 'It will wreck your faith.' Or—which is better from their point of view—'Well, I guess it didn't harm you that much after all.' Students in that setting are often told that they can either have faith or social justice concerns, but not both.

"I'm trying to teach them that they don't have to choose one or the other, but that they *can* do both. This leads me to recognize that another part of my public is my colleagues. Local churches want people to be faithful, and not deal with the world; the church wants them to be denominational; some of the faculty want people to be Mother Theresa—without wanting them to go to mass everyday to energize themselves. Some of our students have gone to Promise Keepers, but are afraid to admit it. The real problem are the faculty who want to clone themselves."

"There are a lot of points here where I think we're looking at the same concerns from different sides," said someone else. "I think we have our own dogmatics. There's an analogy to what happens in the training of medical students where, for example, they have to learn to think of a human being as a corpse, or to translate suffering into a problem that can be remedied through medication. That kind of killing off a sense of the patient can take place in a powerful way in the study of religion. That is, we're socialized into killing certain approaches to religion. Then we have our own dogmatics that we try to put in their place. There are good reasons some people being pissed off, because we mess with their heads, and they thought their heads were pretty good to start off with.

"This is not just a question about what people are going to do when they 'mature'," he went on. "Parents have legitimate stakes in their children being socialized into who *they* are, before being socialized into other versions of somebody else. So this is not just about taking our agenda, but about coming into conflict with the agenda of others—like Christian Coalition parents, for example—because we want to socialize their kids in a different direction. Not only that, but we have the trump card, a neo-religious secularism, which is the civil religion of this country.

"Take religion itself. "For some religious traditions, it is most important to provide education not just about 'religion', but about history, done with a religious valence. Part of the function of a religious tradition is to educate (that is, socialize) to see history, interpret texts, and understand yourself in a certain way. In most academic settings, children are taught to understand all these things in a non-religious way through the establishment of neo-religious secularism. This has been done in the name of religious neutrality, and in the name of protecting the establishment clause which, in the 1940s, interpreted the role of education in the direction of establishing a neo-religious secularism. But this is, in fact, in violation of the free exercise clause in the Constitution."

"What do you mean by 'neo-religious'?" someone asked.

"If I were to argue in a summary form what might be meant by 'religious'," the first person replied, "and if we were to see religion in terms of a comprehensive world view, ultimate concern, or something along those lines, then alternative perspectives which compete with that, minus God, and which pervade every part of life, would fall under the heading of what I would call 'neo-religious.'

The 'non-religious' becomes the religion in general, and civil religion is implicit in that assumption."

"If I were to put what you just said into Ricouerian symbolic-world terms," said Roger, "I'd say that through a public school, a person develops a symbolic system such that the world they have is a story without a place for God. There is just no place. In effect, it is a kind of quasi-religion, though it is not said to be that, so that some people end up concerned about what is happening to their children."

"To pursue the idea of the neo-religious a little further," said someone else, "it seems central to the intent to protect people's capacity to live out their commitments, but to prevent the legislation of those commitments when intruded on by the commitments of others. But there are also secular realms of commitments that can be legislated. If we see the Constitution as protecting our capacity to live out our commitments, and if we interpret religion as you do, it will privilege the secular and allow the imposition of legislation on others who make their religious opinions explicit as such.

"Think about it: If you teach history so that all causality is non-religious, when done it a broad way that takes *all* events into account. Then you can't be neutral with respect to these broad approaches to living out commitments to which some people turn. There's a problem—although that doesn't mean we know what the solution is."

They had run out of time, and had to head down for lunch. The conversation continued until, after lunch, they gathered again for a final discussion of their projects, during which they commented on some of the specific things they had derived from the feedback they had received from different members of the group and from the workshop as a whole.

They recessed at the end of the day and went out to dinner combined with a boat tour. It took a while for the boat to arrive, so everyone waited, surrounded by throngs of tourists milling and seething along the waterfront. There was Gus in his cowboy boots, denims, and string tie with turquoise, he a Texan by adoption. There were the kinds of stories you begin to tell while waiting, somewhat distracted, breaking off periodically to make sure the rest of the group hasn't begun to leave without you, forgetting you in the crowd of a strange city. And then there was dinner over the hum of the engine motors, the evening cooled by the breeze brought on by motion, and the smaller circles of stories, even confidences, that the companionship of eating together invites.

Day Five: Saturday, August 10

The staff had assigned Roger to note down issues that had engaged the group during the week, and to bring these together in a final session of "loose threads." He had come up with four clusters of questions and would divide the session into four blocks, each dedicated to one of these:

> 1) how one responds to students in ways that factor in differences in learning styles, educational backgrounds, and gender. This includes concerns about tensions that have emerged about public versus private interaction, particularly in a climate where charges of sexual harassment have become more common;
> 2) how we might develop further avenues related to our own development as faculty, including ways of addressing our own sense of vocation as it undergoes changes over time;
> 3) ways in which the issue of margin and center defines who can speak and about what;
> 4) how to deal with some of the ways in which our various publics sometimes conflicted;
> 5) and, related to the previous issue, concerns specifically related to teaching in an evangelical school.

The group reviewed and accepted this list and, after a few minutes of discussion, agreed to allocate a half an hour to each one.

Interestingly, the first question—although containing multiple parts as originally formulated—was heard and pursued only with respect to its final segment, the issue of sexual harassment. This group of younger faculty were clear that their own professors had not, for the most part, had to worry about such things until more recently, and they wanted to know what those who were more experienced had worked out as a "position." Not surprisingly, the responses ranged.

"A lot of it has to do with age and personality," said Gus. "I never touch a student. On the day they graduate, I give them a hug, but in my office, I sit on one side of the desk and they sit on the other.

If I were to characterize the relationship, I'd describe my side of it as avuncular. I don't want to be a buddy or a brother, or anything too closely related. And sometimes I'll be the Dutch uncle—the one who calls them on the carpet. I discourage students from calling me by my first name, because I don't want things to become too familiar."

"Gender relations are loopy enough these days," said someone else. "The issue of decorum that goes with our title places certain behavioral obligations on us. I never close the door when a student is in the office."

"On the other hand," said Roger, "I think in principle that there are times when it's important to shut the door because the student is talking about something they wouldn't want other students—or anyone passing by in the hallway—to hear. Still, this has gotten much more complicated. My anxiety, with a female student, is that if she were ever to raise a charge and the door had been closed, I could be vulnerable."

"One of the things we rarely acknowledge," said one person, "is the erotic nature of an impassioned discussion. We have all experienced some version of that, I suspect, whether as a teacher or as a student ourselves. There is a particular charge to these kinds of intense engagements, and not because anyone is trying to generate anything sexual. But this can also generate unintended mixed signals, and lead to a number of possible misinterpretations. We have to be careful to correct for that."

"It seems as though there are general rules that appear fairly clear," said another person. "But in individual cases there is more variability than those rules would lead one to think. Some people are more touchy-feely, and their ability to interact with others includes that. For that matter, different kinds of individuals construe the same behaviors in different ways, which means trying to read others carefully. I think, realistically, we have to be aware of the kinds of difficulties that can arise, and step back and clarify the boundaries."

"If you can stay attentive," said Sarah, "it allows for correctives along the way."

"That's true," said someone else. "The only caveat I'd insert is that there are things you can do in a group of two or three that you can not do one-on-one with a student."

"Part of the problem, I think," said one person, "is that power inheres in who we are in the classroom, even when it's difficult for us to imagine this being the case. We can unwittingly be perceived as conveying messages about which we are quite unaware. That can include what someone construes as a come-on, or as an attempt to intimidate or silence. We can also offend students, or hurt their feelings, without ever having known we've done so, and they often won't tell us, because we control the grade."

"We need to shift gears," said Roger, quietly stepping in. "The next thing we wanted to touch on is how to pursue our own development as faculty."

"I'd like to hear from those of you who've been teaching longer about how things have changed for you over time," said one person. "I see older colleagues who've become dead wood, and I don't want that to happen to me."

"I've seen one colleague who has blossomed and expanded as he's aged," said Sarah, "and another whose world is shrinking. Both were really good before. I also watch myself shift interests and commitments. When I first started teaching, I was more into what they had to know and what I had to tell them. Now I listen more. At the same time, I used to take everything they said seriously, like you do with a new baby; now, it's less so."

"My faculty is a small one," said Roger. "When one new person came on, he was a very fine teacher, and he began to draw off some of my students. I had to adapt to that. Some of what you see as dead wood can be because someone has not managed to keep from becoming bitter."

"There is a truism we communicate to our students," said Gus, "which is that when you stop learning, you're dead. Some people stop rethinking their material. They become mentally dead, so that change becomes a threat. I sometimes think that, in our lifetime, the overrated paradigm shift in Biblical studies has at least given some of us new toys to play with, so we don't become fuddy-duddies."

"When I came to my school," said Jerry, "I was very popular. An older professor told me that earlier in his life, *he* had been that popular. So I think it's partly an age thing. I also see it as part of my ego needs at that time—a particular kind of passion I had.

Surrendering that has changed me. I used to do meditative exercises in my classes and that kind of thing. I don't do those things anymore, because *I'm* not there. Every once in a while I'll have a student come back and say that those class exercises were powerful experiences— so I occasionally wonder if I've sold my students out by *not* doing such things any longer. What I *do* know is that I don't want to become one of those people whose world is so small that it's the color of the paint on the wall that engages them."

"If your own world is complex and ambiguous enough, you won't," said Roger. "One friend of mine said to me that the reason he'd gone into this was that it was the only way he could figure to be a student forever. I think that's a pretty good reason."

"But have any of you had points in your careers," someone asked, "when you felt you were going to get out of this?"

"I gave myself an escape route," said Sarah. "I made sure there were other things I could do."

"In relation to that question," said another person, "how do you continue to be a student? Because our school is so small, I havet to teach Intro to Preaching, Intro to Worship, and the Lectionary, on top of my other courses in my own area. I keep trying to give a new course each year as a way of keeping things interesting, but what else can you do?"

"That's a good strategy," said Gus, "or you can redevelop one of your courses each year, so that in a different way it becomes new."

"I know we need to be reminded over and over to draw boundaries," said someone else, "I learned that during my first year. But then I still ended up feeling I had to take care of everyone and everything, and was completely overextended."

"One thing you might consider," said Roger, "is to design a career development plan for yourself, as a way of envisioning where you're going. Look into whether your school has any sort of endowment or other money to support that, too."

"One thing the region could do," said Gus, "is to develop a list of such resources and send it around, because there are certainly schools in the region that don't have officers with this information." Everyone agreed this would be a good idea.

"We have to change topics again," said Roger, "and move on to talk about how the margin and center question defines who can speak and about what."

"Some of it ties in with publication and what gets counted as valuable," one person said. There, a center is defined by what leads to tenure, as are the consequences if what you're doing doesn't quite fit the model."

"It can almost blow up in your face," said Sarah. "I had published both in women's studies and on an early American theologian. My chair sent things out to four or five readers, but dividing the materials according to these other people's specialties. That meant that none of them saw the full spectrum of what I do. So, if you do many things, you need to be sure they get sent out in parcels, and that each reviewer gets the whole thing."

"That has to do with being involved in making the case for yourself," Jerry added.

"Our earlier discussion of margin and center," said another person, "triggered my awareness of how many of our students have to learn other languages, including men and women having to learn each others' languages, African American and Anglo, foreign and native, and so on. I think that one way of helping people to speak is first to become more conscious of all the components that make up your own speech."

"I'd add to that," said someone else, "that we have to be very sure not to assume that everyone else has a gender, class, and race, and that we ourselves have none. We also have to take some responsibility for the translating of what we do. It should not be the case that everyone else has to learn to understand *us*."

"But you know," said Jerry, "what outrages me is how much more I can get away with saying feminist things, without being slammed for it, than women can. I used to try to call on women students about some of these things, but if someone is already feeling awkward, then it gets reinforces."

"Perhaps it might help to have them prepare something ahead of time," suggested someone else.

"Time to shift again," said Roger, "to how our various publics and their expectations can conflict."

The group noted its facility for playing a verbal version of musical chairs. While not allowing them to dwell long or deeply with any of the topics, this format was, nevertheless, letting them revisit issues from the previous week and to bring them together in a concentrated form.

"In the Southwest," Roger continued, "a part of our public is self-consciously religious. In the AAR at the national level, and somewhat at the regional level, there are groups that are now considered along the lines of a protected species—the fundamentalists—out of the notion that it is important to build bridges. When someone on a committee says, 'But they're not academic enough,' someone else will say, 'But they're important, and there has to be a place for them.'"

"Still, there's one difference," said one person. "Harvey Cox brought it up in an essay on modernization theory, where he asks why you don't find as many academics studying Pentecostalism, even though it has more members than other Protestants put together. Why has so little been done? Cox says that, on the one hand, there is a history of reaction against the academy on the part of these groups; on the other, mainstream academics often think that to study them is to fraternize with the anti-academics. So, how to incorporate into the academy those who are anti-academy and who are also sometimes viewed with suspicion from within the academy?"

"Yes," said Sarah. "Cox has said that theologians on the left need to engage with theologians on the right. But you don't see the process-thought people reaching out, the way they did with women's studies. "

"We also have to be careful how we categorize people," said another person. "There are more people associated with evangelical theology who would fight tooth and nail if they felt they were being seen as fundamentalist, or that their scholarship was looked down on. This idea of center and·margin has to develop more of a sliding scale with which to define these terms. Part of the problem is that our categories have become so absolutized that we demonize each other for political reasons and for power in the academy."

"One quick qualification to what I said a moment ago," said the earlier speaker. "I'm not talking about just studying fundamentalists, but about a sympathetic study that comes closer to the idea of fraternizing."

"I'm thinking further about how some of our publics may conflict," said someone else. "I now have two large religious cultures I deal with: one consists of liberal religious Protestants; the other is a more politically active set of conservative Christians. The smaller groups I also work with include Jews and Roman Catholics. I ask myself if I have a responsibility to function as a translator."

"Because I'm in a more religiously conservative environment," said another person, "I've been thinking about using particular issues or events to bring people together. In my context, I *must* help the more politically active conservative Christian community see liberal Protestants as a resource."

"I've been put in that position concerning the civil discourse as well," said someone else. "At least at the political and social levels, I've had to learn all the perspectives. I hadn't read Carl Henry or Philip Marsden till I had students who had come out of that preparation. I don't agree with Carl Henry, but he writes beautifully explaining the conservative theology."

"I've come up against groups who are forming themselves into groups as alternatives to the Christian Coalition," said Sarah, "and they have their own inner tensions as well. The more the Christian right is perceived as a threat, the more these new groups have come together in ways they never did before, after which they find they have any number of tensions and internal conflicts in their own right that they'd never had to deal with previously. The group I'm thinking of hasn't been able to get to formulating a platform, because they're still trying to figure out how to keep African Americans and gay people involved, together with the groups who don't want to ordain women. And yet, as a whole, in the context of this part of the country, these people are moderate Protestants."

"These people feel squeezed between the right and the left," said someone else. "There are a lot of issues they're willing to be progressive about, including racial justice, and in some cases they're willing to at least talk about being progressive regarding the status of women, but homosexuality is another issue for them. There, they're not nearly as ready to move. So they end up suspicious of what's going on to the right of them, and fearful of what's going on to the left."

"But how much does everyone really want a dialogue?" said Jerry. "In some cases, I think there's the sense of being better than other people, so why talk to them? In that sense, people write themselves out of the discussion."

"I've found students who don't want to dialogue," said one person, "because they see that very discussion as premised on secular humanist assumptions which, in themselves, invalidate their own premises. Why, then, should they want to talk?"

"There are normative values assigned to 'right', 'left', and 'moderate'," said another person, "with the embedded assumption that to be moderate is best. Previously, the religious right was apolitical, and had theological reasons for taking that stance. But factors like schools, and other issues, have led to their feeling alienated. More than that, their very capacity to be neutral and apolitical gets challenged, forcing them into the arena. The way the language is used to frame them as marginal has, historically, contributed to the right's current position as a force that now has to be considered."

"But margin/center language breaks down, here," said Sarah. "Ralph Reed has argued that he wants to be left alone. He says he doesn't want to take over the government. What he has *asked* for is a place or voice at the table. Then it becomes important that all the people who want a place figure out how that's going to be. Where the parties don't want a dialogue is a different matter, but with people like Ralph Reed and that request from the 'excluded other', we have to deal with it."

"As far as the difference the AAR can make with Protestant fundamentalists," said another person, "historically the liberal scholars ignore schools identified as fundamentalist. They assume they don't need to bother with the faculty there, which is different from the fundamentalists who say there's no point in dealing with a reprobate. But there's always a reasonable chance of there being a few people interested in somebody's reaching out."

"I'd say more than a few," someone else—who, himself, taught at such a school—said quietly, "like a lot of the junior faculty at these places."

"Something else is going on in the region with the denominational seminaries," said Gus, "and it's not fundamentalism. It's the idea that what the AAR does is not relevant. These faculty simply don't participate, or do so at only a minimal level. Some of that is natural, because the AAR is perceived as university-based and not all that relevant for the seminaries."

"That's precisely the meeting point," said one of the people who taught at such a school. "At the pre-seminary school where I teach, even if you take what you might call a negative theological position, the department at a state university needs the resources that the academic discussion of Bible provides. For that matter, one of the important classes at my school is on cults, and we have to go to AAR-funded research to learn how to teach that."

"Part of the problem resides in subtle little things," said Sarah. "Learning how to use inclusive language, for example, takes some time and support. When someone from an evangelical background makes non-inclusive language statements, or statements based on a particular theological position, these don't fit into the AAR code, and they're given a hard time."

"Maybe that could serve as our link into the other topic we wanted to touch on," said Roger, "which involves teaching in evangelical institutions. Most of the private institutions in the United States were founded on a particular religious tradition, and/or are concerned with the propagation of that tradition. It is useful to disuss what the positive contributions of such an approach might be, and especially interesting to hear about the experience of those of you who do teach in these schools."

"Significant sectors of the society in the Southwest are self-identified as evangelical or denominational," said one person. "The education they get will influence the services and contributions they go on to make. So, it's important for their education to prepare them to make this kind of contribution. At my school, we say to students that we want them to be well-rounded people, fully informed about their own religious commitments but able to related to others in a way that does not diminish *them*. Admittedly, there is a tension between the two."

"They're usually smaller institutions," said a second person. "I think my school and most others like it would say we're doing *moral* education. That used to trouble me; I felt there should be a neutral, value-free university project. But I'm coming to favor up-front mission statements, and to think that maybe it's okay that strongly positioned perspectives help institutions and contribute to society."

"Some of my most interesting students have religious backgrounds or commitments," said Jerry.

"I look at where I went," said someone else, "which was a Mennonite school. There it was argued that we should teach students that even though they were conservative, they had to be aware of liberal positions. At the liberal schools, they don't even try to show students what the conservative position is, except to dismiss or ridicule it. It's as if it doesn't matter enough, or doesn't even exist."

"Concerning what you just said about an evangelical institution's offering a broader spectrum of inquiry," said another person, "the media-driven and secularly-driven parts of this society have chosen to make evangelical theology laughable. The contribution of the evangelical institutions is their presentation of their position as legitimate theological inquiry."

"One thing to consider," said someone else, "is that academic freedom in the European model is not the only model of education. Another model says that you assist students in reaching a deeper appreciation of their own faith or you provide assistance in their own walk with God. When that end directs the process of education, certain academic freedoms are not given central roles, because they are not the function of the institution. That, as a value, should be appreciated, and therefore, these schools should not be judged by only one set of a ostensibly neutral academic standards (which are not neutral at all), but also by their own criteria of self-definition."

What this discussion threw into relief the degree to which the religious character of the region represents some of the complicated tensions in American religious life. That these are also present in other parts of the country is indisputable; the proportionately greater presence of denominational schools in the Southwest, however, make the tensions stand out more clearly. In the Southwest group, a higher percentage of staff and participants knew this side of the region more directly and—more importantly— felt a certain sympathy toward it, at the same time as them were critical of some of its political dimensions.

From this discussion the group turned to preparing for the afternoon, during which Gus would be leading them first to the Alamo, and then to two working missions—the one, the Mission San José, the other, Mission Concepción. In the first case, they were to examine a brochure handed out at the Alamo as though it were a sacred text explaining a shrine of the civil religion and—more to the point—as an authorized text, coming from the shrine itself. At San José, they would also see a slide show of the Mission, the content of which they would analyze. The objective of the trips was, on one level, to get out and see some of the local sites. On another, it was to see places associated with the religious diversity of the region.

A school bus took them from one site to the next. In the intense August heat of Texas, they entered the vault-like halls of the Alamo, and followed the crowds from glass case to glass case. They went to San José, where they could not go all the way into the church itself, because a wedding was taking place, but they could look into the chapel for Our Lady of Guadalupe. They could wander through the rooms of San Concepción, and examine the miniaturized diorama showing the work-day of the early residents, with each tiny work group lit up as its particular part in the larger play was described over a barely audible sound system.

That night, they gathered, under Gus's direction, to debrief. Although it was the experience of the Alamo, in particular, that had most preoccupied them, as Sarah would later write:

> . . . [t]he contrast in overall environment (architecture, upkeep, marketing), as well as in self-defining public narrative, between the Alamo and the other two missions, was particularly effective in communicating different perspectives on sacred space, sacred history, ideology, political power, and so forth.[31]

---

[31] Directors' final report on Southwest Regional AAR/Lilly Teaching Workshop, p. 6.

Both presentations had minimized the degree to which Spanish colonialism had replaced the culture and language of the Cuahualtecan peoples, who had not been as resilient as the Aztec or the Maya. The average Texan, as Gus pointed out, does not talk about being descended from Native American people.

"Or at least they didn't," he went on "until the radicals of the sixties romanticized it. Now there's a restaurant in town with a painting on the wall of the most awful sexist goddess figure left over from that time—sort of a Barbie Aztec. The presentation also showed that the cowboys were Spanish *vaqueros* and Indians, but it didn't show the history of the King Ranch—the kind of literal empire building which became possible when the Anglos came in with cattle, technology, and the opportunity to seize land after the Civil War." The Alamo, in particular, had exemplified the contrast between who owns history and gets to tell it, and who does not.

The group proceeded to discuss how they would work with such a site in teaching about it through a field trip.

"I would address the ways in which the space is manipulated and interpreted," said one person, "in order to ask students, 'Where did you feel you were in sacred space, or in a shrine, and what led you to feel that way?' Did you notice that at the rope, you had to take your hat off? It was like going into the holy of holies that commemorates the long rifles and the independence of Texas—that is, the violence required to maintain freedom. It's portrayed something like the Revolutionary War in which freedom is prized over life, in the fight against the tyranny of the British. Here you have the Daughters of the Revolution of Texas, the keepers of the flame and priestesses of the myth."

"What interested me was how the place had fallen into disrepair and was about to be sold to a developer. The Daughters got it because of the threat to the myth. In fact, the myth didn't really arise until they took over—for years it wasn't valued as highly."

One participant was becoming agitated.

"When I was growing up," she said, "my first memory of the Alamo was when I was eight. I loved it. I read every plaque. I saw it as a history about dying for a cause."

"An *American* cause," someone else added quietly. "Think about how this factors into the ways memory is defined: 'Remember the Alamo,' 'Remember the Maine.'"

"One of Santa Ana's lieutenants said that the military men who were not killed surrendered—including Carl Crockett—and Santa Ana had them shot," said Gus. "Those who survived were women. Santa Ana sent one wife to spread the story, to spread fear among the populace. Of course, it was okay for women to survive, but if men had, they would have been seen as cowards."

"Well," the person from Texas said, "For some people that myth is about 'Let's go get them.' For others, it's about a pure and noble self-sacrifice.'"

"The question I asked myself," said someone else, "is how I would point to the things that combine to create a sense of shrine— at least for one group of people—and why they don't, for other people. I was looking at the toy soldiers in the little diorama at the Alamo, and all the Mexican soldiers were made from the same mold. But the Americans were represented as having three or four kinds of regular infantry men, and the famous figures were rendered specifically—Bowie, Crockett, and so on. The whole packet, by the way, was made in China."

As they talked, the question that emerged was whether or not it was possible for the myth to operate *and* be deconstructed at the same time. Revisionist history, by factoring in the multiple perspectives, dismantled the older myth as it had been. Could any of it survive in a viable way? The deconstruction, too, was not in the service of a neutral historiography, but of an alternative civil myth— also about liberation and freedom, but with different notions of both at stake. The issue, as one person pointed out, was mythic power, and what place a given story had in someone's sense of identity.

Therefore, how would one not only lead a trip, but also guide the appropriate debriefing afterwards? The group agreed that one would need to go first oneself, in order to think through how orient students' attention and direct the subsequent discussion. One might need to prepare study guides and questions ahead of time. The goals, they thought, could not be too heavy-handed. There had to be room, as Sarah pointed out, for not trying too hard to control what happened. As for the myth itself, there might be multiple ways to present it.

"It seems important to critique it historically," said one person. "That is, what are being presented as the *facts* about the Alamo. We have a constellation of facts that is ambiguous, complex, and subject to multiple interpretations. That may be the more important aspect to convey, so that it becomes clear why, to different groups, it can hold deeply different meanings.

"You know," said Jerry, "we're living in a time when we see the importance of deconstructing older myths associated with power. But I think the other question to ask ourselves is whether we are equally willing to say negative things about other traditions. There is something troubling to me about being highly critical and deconstructive about one tradition and not the rest. We have to be willing to look at all of them or none of them, so that we don't end up just romanticizing others and vilifying our own, or vice versa."

"Even saying that we're talking about a myth may be upsetting to some people," said another person. "Here, it's seen by a lot of people as the true retelling of the Alamo story."

"Of course," said Gus. "The Alamo may not ring my bells mythically, but the Dome of the Rock and the Holy Sepulcher in Jerusalem—now *those* do it for me."

"For me," said the person from Texas, "there is a big difference between the myth of the Alamo and the myth of Christianity. I want to hold on to the distinction between the quasi-mythical legend, and the religious myth—or, more specifically, the myth of *my* religion."

"For me," said Sarah, "what does it is Washington D.C.—the power of civil religious sites. For some people, that's why it's called civil religion, because it does have such power. It's an axis for people who are either nominally religious or not religious."

"In listening to all of this," said someone else, "how much is it the business of history to tell the truth—and whose truth? I will never again arrogate to myself a definition of truth."

It had gotten late. There were no resolutions to the discussion, but the experience of having gone to the sites, and having seen how they were represented had effectively illustrated how one place can be read in multiple ways. It had led the group to think together about a place as a kind of text, and about how they might help their students both experience and read such a text. It had also brought to the surface a number of tensions between conflicting perspectives which, they recognized, was also likely to happen in a classroom. What made the trip effective was the combination of direct experience, discussion, and the use of that discussion to show how complicated certain places can be in relation to thinking about history, the construction of myth, and the multiple interests involved in the process.

Day Six: Sunday, August 11

It was time to end. Everyone gathered for brunch, and prepared to grant each other tokens of completion, devising awards for each of the participants in the following style:

"In keeping with the tradition of bogus certificates, we award the following:

"The Jonathan Edwards award to _____, the professor most likely to give a sermon in class and extend an altar call to students who are existentially engaged. Here is a starter kit to create a sawdust trail in your classroom (bag of shavings included)."

"The Socrates Award to _____, the professor most likely to be charged with blaspheming. Here is the equipment with which to construct your own model of God (bottle of glue included)."

"Does that mean he's no longer glueless?" said Jerry. There were loud groans.

"Just for that, Jerry—The Huston Smith Award goes to Jerry, whose long engagement with humanism leads us to award him the means to collect and cut out materials from the different religions to present to his class (pair of children's scissors included)."

"To Roger: Roger served jail time for product tampering when selling Bibles door to door, and it was discovered that he had changed a number of the genealogies. We give him the Mellow Leadership Award"

"Gus, yours is in two parts: the first part is this hat (a miniature sombrero) which has both an exoteric and an esoteric meaning, to reveal to you that even though you attempt to maintain your professional demeanor, you have so impressed us that we have made you our *jefe santo*. When we find ourselves in the blazing heat, this hat is the symbol of the shield from all iniquities, and when we are alone and afraid, we sing this song." (The speaker proceded to sing a badly warbled ode to Gus)."

"Oh dear," said Gus, perching the tiny sombrero on his fingertip. "Just my size!"

"As for Sarah, clearly the only award we could give her was the Rush Limbaugh award for undermining unchanging Christian faith. We also recognize her skill at playing the traditional role of midwife to fifteen fledgling academics. In addition, we give her the "Go Your Own Way" award. As many of you know, she entered women's studies when this was not thought to advance one's career. Moreover, the prestigious "Go Your Own Way award is not just in the academic field. Nor is she hampered by it (just because everybody *else* stops at red lights.) She can go home proudly with this award—just give the rest of us a thirty minute head start."

And after several more awards, and a great deal more laughter, the group reluctantly came to an close—although not to an end. Once the participants had all finally taken their leave, and gone off to collect their things and head home, the staff gathered for one last meeting, to look back on these sessions and on the year as a whole. As they did so, they were struck by many things. It is to some of these thoughts, along with those of other staff members from the other workshops, and of the many participants, that we turn in the coming chapter, to explore what seemed to them to have been most effective and memorable about these experiences together.

VI

What Made Them Work?

The question with which these four workshops began was whether, through diverse and creative applications of a basic structure, a core experience could be re-created. To test the replicability of that core experience, certain variables were held constant, defined by a set of basic criteria. Each time, there would be four staff people who were established teachers in the study of religion, fifteen participants who had demonstrated promise as teachers (and who would include from two to three advanced graduate students), and an ethnographer; the workshop would have a temporal structure, meeting at specified intervals throughout the academic year; while the location might not remain constant, it would generally be away from the participants' home institutions; the focus would be on teaching about religion, with the participants chosen on the basis of a teaching project, which they would work on during that year; and every effort was to be made to treat the participants well, showing value for them *as* teachers.

To be accepted, a proposal had first to pass through this primary set of filters. Yet once these criteria were met, and suggestions for revision worked through, the directors of the workshop program at the national level have then been adamant about giving the four staff members the latitude to design the other aspects of the workshop on their own terms, without interference.

There is thus a strong creative tension between the structural design and core expectations on the one hand, and enormous freedom to experiment on the other.

Three things are particularly striking about the outcomes of this experiment. The first is the number of variations which the staff teams did, in fact, introduce into the basic structure. As the preceding chapters illustrate, despite their common structure, no two series were the same. Second, in planning these different series, any number of times a member of one staff or another would say, "I can't see things working if you were to do X"—which quite often proved to be precisely what another group had indeed done effectively. The third and most consistent, if intangible, outcome, was a certain persisting quality of experience that emerged in each workshop.

This leads to the obvious question of what made this possible. If the model is, after all, so flexible, then 1) which among the constant variables were found to be significant and for what reasons, 2) which among the less constant ones were seen as important and in what kinds of ways, and 3) what presented challenges and even tests to the effectiveness of the workshop?

Six Constant Findings
1. The Formation of Community

The benefit most frequently described by those who participated in the different workshops is the way they took a group of individuals who were, in many ways, quite different from one another and, each time, transformed them into a supportive, intentional community.[1] Many factors contributed to this—indeed,

---

[1]   The basic six findings were presented by Raymond Williams to a group meeting at Wabash College to discuss the prospect of a new series of programs to be developed for teachers in theological education. The illustrations and discussion, however, grow out of the experience of the four AAR/Lilly Teaching Workshops, and from the evaluations submitted by the participants of the original Wabash Workshop, both of which corroborate Williams's findings. In general, the attempt has been made to select representative quotes, rather than presenting a comprehensive reiteration of every version of a particular point.

To locate the comments, the following code will be used: NEM (New England/Maritimes group), EI (Eastern International group), SE (Southeast group), and SW (Southwest group). In addition, it will be specified whether

one could argue, every element discussed for the remainder of the chapter. Nevertheless, those which seem to have played a particularly important role will be discussed under this heading.

Living and Eating Together

> Living together was important. It was also important to have the director and other staff staying there and participating in all that. It conveyed that it was something they were devoting *their* week to, as well. There were the meals together, and sometimes the free time, too. I thought the balance was just right. (SE participant)

Three factors stand out here: first, is the very fact of sharing quarters over a period of time. Second, it generally matters that the staff team make every effort to stay there as well, if the workshop is taking place in a setting where some of those involved also live. The exception to this involves cases in which medical reasons make it necessary for a staff person to stay in his or her home (as was the case in one of the workshops), provided he or she is otherwise present for meals and all the other activities. When staff members do not stay in residence, it may have a divisive effect, even if the staff person is present for all events.

It is also important to try to structure meal times so that the group assembles to eat together. That experience provides one of the most important settings for people to continue conversations begun in the formal sessions, and contributes to building other kinds of bonds that prove central in the forming of community. In the Southeast, where it was logistically not possible for the facility being used to provide dinner, the group compensated by setting up a social hour late in the afternoon. This allowed people to come together and find dinner partners with whom to go out and eat. They also show videos during the evening, which gave everyone a second opportunity to come together. Although not ideal, these were creative ways of offsetting the lack of a shared mealtime.

---

the comment comes from someone on the staff or from one of the participants. The one exception to these various identifying codes will be in the third section, in which challenges to the effectiveness of the workshops are discussed.

The Selection of Participants

> I think our strength (though not always visible) was our diversity in field, style, institutional affiliation, etc., and our common passions and our urge to learn. (EI Staff)

One might imagine that people from different disciplinary areas within the study of religion, and from different kinds of institutions ranging from community colleges to private schools might have little to say to one another, about teaching. The consistent feedback, however, has been otherwise. Participants have repeatedly stressed the importance of retaining these differences, discussing them, and discovering in the process their underlying commonalties, the most important of which is the dedication to teaching. The reason most often given for the mixture of disciplinary backgrounds is that it allowed people to meet others they would ordinarily not get to know in professional gatherings. The diversity of institutions gave the younger scholars the chance to link up with one another. It was also suggested that participants be chosen who showed evidence of being collegial, as this tended to carry over into their interactions within the workshop.

Although the processes of selection used by the four staff teams operated differently, each one represented an attempt to find the strongest candidates with demonstrated excellence in teaching. The teaching workshops are not intended to provide remedial services, but to inspire those who are already outstanding and to create a cadre of teacher/scholars in each region with strong connections to one another. Finally, as one Wabash participant noted, there are more elusive elements—the "spirit" of a particular group that comes out of a serendipitous mixture of people. "It's like a dinner party—if you invite the right people, it will be a success."

The Staff Members

Many of the participants acknowledged how important the staff are to the success of the workshops, and stressed the importance of choosing staff who are, themselves, committed teachers.[2] If they are also well-known scholars, that is fine, but this

---

² There were several quite sincere suggestions in this connection,

alone should not serve as the criterion. (Indeed, some participants critiqued other workshops in which they had taken part, where such scholars had, in some cases, shown little understanding of teaching-related issues.) "Try," as one person put it, "to ensure that staff see themselves as learners, too."

> Move the group from the sense of comprising staff and participants to a sense of being co-learners. To do this, the staff must be willing to be changed, to risk, and to discover, and the workshop itself must model good, cooperative learning and teaching. (Wabash participant)

> The strength of the staff was that they were also often participants. They used their experience to offer very nuanced and wise observations and suggestions. I felt they all modeled excellent teaching. They were also non-judgmental and secure people. Their lack of pretentiousness, I think, set the tone of the workshops. (EI participant)

It was suggested that strong efforts be made to insure ethnic and racial diversity among the staff (all the groups exemplified gender diversity), and that the staff come from different institutions:

> I think it was less than ideal having three people from the same institution. They're dealing with a whole different world than a lot of the other institutions in the region—like, say, the poorer, state-related schools, or some of the religiously affiliated schools. (SE participant)

Participants repeatedly remarked on staff efforts to dismantle a sense of hierarchy. Little cues such as the clothing the staff wears give messages. The more informal it is, the more it conveys a relaxed atmosphere for discussion, and signals to the participants that they, too, can relax. But there are other kinds of signals as well. It was noticed, for example, when staff members made the effort to spread themselves out among the participants at meal times, rather than using these times to hold their own meetings. Even having several staff members regularly together at the same table—especially if seen as consistent with other messages being given—can be construed as an attempt to preserve hierarchy. The crucial

---

from members of the Wabash group, that Raymond Williams be cloned.

component is this: untenured faculty are quick to note when they are being treated as students and when they are treated as real colleagues, albeit junior ones. The former leads to resentment, the latter to deep appreciation.

> I think in every way the staff treated us like colleagues, with no condescension. They should be congratulated for that. They picked up on every suggestion from us—I even thought sometimes when it wasn't any of our business. They couldn't have been more responsive. (SE participant)

The sense of being respected and trusted included being recognized as people who have already demonstrated some measure of excellence in teaching in their own right, and are not entirely novices in the profession. One way that some of the staffs demonstrated this awareness was by encouraging sessions in which the participants taught each other. This cannot be done too close to the beginning of the workshop, as it can make people self-conscious. However, the presentation and discussion of the teaching projects can provide a natural occasion for the participants to show each other things that they do in the classroom.

A less obvious aspect of dismantling hierarchy involves the relationship between the members of the staff, and what this models. One challenge faced by a director, in particular, is how to balance initiative, engagement, and responsibility in ways that don't inadvertently turn into taking over too much of the burden of planning or, conversely, not enough. How the staff models collegiality and collaborative interaction sets the tone, and the participants are quick to pick up on it.

The Bystander

According to systems theorist David Kantor, there are four crucial roles played out in any group: the mover, the follower, the opposer, and the bystander.[3] The mover initiates things; the follower agrees with what has been proposed, and goes along with it; the opposer challenges what has been proposed, and may not agree to

---

[3] For the earlier discussion of Kantor's theoretical framework, see Chapter IV, p. 233*ff*.

support the initiative; and the bystander steps back and observes, sometimes commenting on what is going on. The bystander role extends across a spectrum which ranges from disengaged observation to engagement, the latter including the creation of a setting in which others can step back to let off steam or to think about alternatives to what is proving frustrating.

In practice, any individual within a given system can play out any of these roles at different moments. We take turns initiating things, following other people's suggestions, questioning their ideas, or stepping back and just observing what is going on. At the same time, we also tend to have preferred stances. Kantor suggests that for any system to function well, these four functions must be operative. In particular, a system becomes disabled when there is no one to play either the role of the opposer or of the bystander.

I have come to think that the importance of the bystander in the workshop setting is due to his or her being both a part of the group, and yet not in the same way that others are. Hypothetically, anyone in the group can step back to observe and comment on what is going on, and ideally this does, in fact, happen. At the same time, there is a qualitative difference in having someone assigned to that role who is neither staff nor participant. I found, for example, that I often became the person with whom both staff members and participants would talk not only about the dynamics of the workshop, but often about personal and professional dilemmas.[4]

This is not to say that participants didn't seek out other members of the staff for long and engaged discussions. The staff in each of the workshops cultivated strong relationships with the various participants. But as the ethnographer-bystander, I sometimes became the outside sounding board. When it seemed appropriate, in some cases I tried to filter feedback to the staff, and to suggest to participants that they could and should raise questions with the staff when things didn't seem clear. In this sense, I tried to be careful not to pre-empt dynamics that should have been taking place between staff and participants, but rather to encourage those

---

[4] It may be that my own background in pastoral care and counseling, along with two years of training in family therapy and systems theory, made me more disposed to allow this.

dynamics and to act whenever possible as a facilitator. I also tried to keep opening up possibilities with questions such as, "You might want also to consider..." or "What about...?"

I would go so far as to propose that workshop planners consider institutionalizing the role of the bystander, whether or not that be in the form of an ethnographer. By that I mean planning to have someone play this role at the workshops. To differentiate this person from the staff, she or he could be presented as the representative of the sponsoring organizations. To make it clear that she or he is neither coach nor overseer of the process, the role should continue to be described as that of participant/observer, with the stated objective of helping the central organizations continue to learn about what makes for a good workshop. In that way, each group is allowed to feel that its experience contributes something back to the whole. It also prevents the bystander function from disempowering the members of the staff or the participants.

Defining a Dynamic of Trust

Many participants commented having felt encouraged to be who they were in the workshops, although it may have taken some time in practice for them to do so, and most would say there were still aspects of themselves they kept in reserve.

> I felt I had no expertise or "right" to say anything at the beginning. By the end, however, I felt totally comfortable and free to express anything and everything. The group's acceptance of people for who they are was very high. (EI participant)

> We found that we could be experts, and also ourselves. This had to do with the workshop—it came out of that. I think it also had to do with the relaxed seriousness of the coordinators. So much of it was a matter of their personalities. The informality and the seriousness combined to create a certain comfort level *and* an expectation about what our level of engagement should be. (EI participant)

> I am struck by how ego-free this group is. I don't know if that is a function of the time and space, but I don't feel that anyone is trying to get me to do or be anything. (SW participant)

These comments were not atypical, suggesting that, generally speaking, the staff members succeeded in creating a dynamic of trust. Part of this message came through their own behavior, insofar as this conveys indirect messages about what is allowed and supported.

> The staff's strengths included humor, compassion, vulnerability, expertise, enthusiasm, diligence, directness, and being student-centered. (EI participant)

This encouraged the participants to respond in kind.

Because those involved came from different settings, they could speak about their own experience with authority. This helped minimize attempts to grandstand, and focused the group's attention instead on the specific challenges unique to each person's teaching world. It also reduced tendencies to extrapolate general mandates for others from one's own background.

In addition, the efforts to minimize hierarchy reduced another dynamic which permeates much of academic interaction in ways that corrode trust—namely, competition. Repeatedly the participants expressed their relief at being able to interact with one another in a non-competitive context, corroborating the importance in the workshop of avoiding the creation of competition. It was sufficient to expect that each person do his or her best. This feeling was expressed by both men and women, suggesting that it was not a gendered response for those involved in the workshops. This is particularly striking in light of theoretical work like that of Carol Gilligan, which is often invoked to document what is presumed to be women's preference for more collaborative styles of interaction in contrast with men's preference for a more adversarial style of discussion.[5] Yet I have heard men question this polarized description, saying that some of Gilligan's formulations about a collaborative style apply to them as well. The workshop experiences suggests that at least under certain circumstances, this may be true.

This collaborative emphasis was to stand out all the more clearly several years later. Individuals were selected from the various workshops, and brought together to review essays about

---

[5] Carol Gilligan, *In a Different Voice: Psychological Theory and Women's Development*. (Cambridge, Mass.: Harvard University Press, 1993).

teaching which they had been invited to submit. The initial selection process itself proved divisive in ways that the organizers of this new project had not anticipated. For one thing, it was challenged in the planning stage for two reasons by some of the members from the different staffs of the original workshops and then by some of the participants who were subsequently chosen from the larger pool for two reasons. First, the very selection process introduced a competitive dimension that had previously been absent in the workshops. Second, because only some of the essays were to end up being chosen for publication, this new set of participants—many of whom were meeting each other for the first time—were set in yet another level of competition with one another. This dynamic was one they were quick to point out.

Although the reasons for their being asked to compete with one another were legitimate given the new context, the egalitarian, cooperative ethos instilled by the workshops continued to operate so strongly that the organizers of this new endeavor faced considerable resistance. For example, this took the form of an attempt to bargain for a more collaborative approach which would allow everyone's work to be shortened, revised, and thereby accepted as a part of a larger group endeavor. Ultimately, this approach was not adopted by the project's organizers, who felt bound to operate by the normative standards governing peer review and selection in academic publishing. The participants, in turn, capitulated, explaining that they could not escape the pressure in their larger professional environment to publish. They did so, in a way, however, that consolidated their own sense of unity with each other, because they were able to lay the responsibility at the door of a larger systemic force.

The event brought to a head the difference between the general mode of operation in academia, and the alternative generated by the workshops. It inserted competition into this ethos, and threatened what, for those involved had come to function as a rigorously challenging, but nevertheless safe haven, in which all were to be given the opportunity to improve their work, and all were to be included. The importance of creating this kind of safe haven is incalculable, and was repeatedly commented on by both participants and staff.

Other variables played a part in creating this kind of environment, such as the insistence on confidentiality. For example, even though everyone know that a book was being written about what they were saying and doing, they also knew that their own privacy was assured, and that no one was reporting back to any of the influential figures in their lives. There was also an implicit norm that prohibited *ad hominem* comments. As the earlier chapters illustrate, this did not mean the exclusion of disagreement, but of allowing such disagreement to take the form of personal attack.

The demonstrated willingness to listen to each other also created a context of openness. In some cases this takes work. One person's need to take time in formulating a thought, in the context of someone else's quickness to speak and, sometimes, to interrupt, can leave the former feeling that the discussion has always moved on by the time he or she is ready to say something—leaving him or her without much to do except reiterate the points made by others. The person may become a skilled listener in the process, but may also end up feeling resentful. One participant discovered that it was possible to say, instead, "I'd like to finish that point," or "I'd like to go back to something we were saying earlier." For some people this provided the occasion to understand the strengths and limitations of their own discussion style.

Most of all, the significance of humor cannot be underestimated. While not the panacea, as the earlier chapters also attempt to illustrate, humor does break down barriers and compose bonds. It creates a crucial component in the group's secret code by which they communicate *as* a group, and know themselves to be part of one. A good rule of thumb is to encourage serious discussion, but not to forget to allow laughter—and lots of it.

As central as the formation of community is to the success of the workshops, it must also be done lightly, to respect the feelings of those who do not want to think of themselves as being roped into a "group." Each person must be given the room to envision that group as he or she chooses, and identify with it—or not—as he or she wills.

2. Structuring of the Workshops Around the Academic Year
The Year-Long Aspect

It was an opinion commonly held by those who participated in the teaching workshops that the kind of community that emerged would not have been possible without the structuring of time that allowed them to come together on four different occasions over the course of the academic year.

> I believe that one of the most significant ways in which these workshops diverge from other workshop experiences I've had is that they take place over an entire year. People's pedagogical projects are being tested in the classroom as they are being prepared for the workshops. Participants could ask others about how they should proceed in the face of particular successes and failures. Teaching techniques that were discussed in one workshop were actually tried and reported. When they did not seem successful, we could all discuss why that might be the case. (EI staff)

The year-long structure was cited as having supported the combination of ongoing intensity, relaxation, and a positive mood for learning. It was one variable that staff and participants alike urged not be changed.

The week-long sessions were seen as having been valuable insofar as they provided the context for sustained discussion that could go deeper. It was recognized that, in some cases, a given week had to be shortened but, in general, planners were encouraged not to do so. As one person noted, "Given the opportunities and intensity of a workshop like this one, that extra time is important." (NEM participant) Therefore, these sessions—or what one Wabash participant called "the booster-shot weekends"—were experienced as providing a connecting thread that consolidated a group's sense of its shared undertaking. The fall weekend in particular accomplishes this.

Often, although not always, the weekend sessions were used for reports on the progress of the teaching projects. This introduced a sense of ongoing accountability, and also helped to keep a focus on the practice of teaching. (On the other hand, the New England/Maritimes group used both weekends to explore other topics in ways that those involved also found fruitful.)

The major difficulties with the weekend sessions generally involve the logistics:

> Even though none of us would change this structure, I do need to report that there were severe practical difficulties in getting all of us together for the weekends, because of the distances involved in our region. I suspect that the weekends might be more effective if people did not have to spend such enormous amounts of time traveling to specific locations for a weekend... The distances limited us to four sessions per weekend; perhaps other regions might have been able to have had more. Also, by the time those traveling long distances arrive, they were very fatigued.[6]

That the groups begin on Fridays and go through Sundays during the academic year means that people are taking time out of their teaching. In some cases, their schedules do not allow them to leave their institutions early. In such cases, it can be helpful to have the staff express to the institution the importance of the workshop and the significance of the person's presence.

Finally, although not formally a part of the workshop structure, each fall the AAR has also held a reception at its national conference for the AAR/Lilly Teaching Scholars and staffs. These gatherings have provided a yearly occasion for the participants from the different workshops to meet each other and, increasingly, the chance for reunions that help to keep the connections alive.

3. The Opportunity to Focus on Teaching

Opportunities to think in a sustained and serious way with colleagues about what it means to be a teacher are so rare that these workshops stand out for participants as a signal moment in their professional development. By describing participants first as teachers, the workshops value a dimension of their professional identities that is all too often ignored and even denigrated.[7]

> One of the most valuable aspects of the teaching workshops as a whole has been the gathering of committed

---

6 AAR/Lilly Teaching Workshop in Religious Studies, Eastern International Region, Evaluation Report II, p. 6.

7 Memo for the Wabash-Lilly Consultation on Theological Education, March 13-14, 1995, p. 1.

scholar-teachers who are enthusiastic about pedagogy. In particular, the workshops have not only introduced "young scholars interested in, and committed to teaching, to more seasoned teacher-scholars who have maintained their interest in and commitment to teaching" (Wabash participant), thereby giving the younger scholars important role models; they also allowed these scholars to meet peers who share this commitment. Both reinforce the sense that teaching is a legitimate and significant pursuit, as is one's identity as a teacher. The inclusion of graduate students has mattered as well, "because that indicates a future orientation, and shows that we're perceived as future colleagues." (SW participant)

The workshops give people the opportunity, too, to learn about how their colleagues teach. In the press of one's own life in an institution, this rarely happens. Nor do most department members spend much time discussing or observing each other's actual classroom styles. Rarely do they talk about their pedagogical philosophies or teaching strategies. Most people who care about teaching, therefore, come to the workshops hungry for these kinds of interactions and discussions, and often leave with the hope of being able to introduce some these dynamics into their own institutions.

4. Being Away From Home

The workshop is also the perfect venue, because these people are not our tenure committee. We have a discussion culture, where people are critiquing your ideas, but it's about as safe as it's going to get. (EI participant)

It emerged as a general finding that participants generally feel freer to discuss their concerns and anxieties with peers and mentors outside of their own institutions, particularly in a context where these colleagues are specifically committed to helping them become better teachers. The formation of this provisional, liminal world allows for the release of the identity that ordinarily operates under the constraints of feeling constantly evaluated (with tenuring or promotion questions looming in the background). This in itself creates new possibilities to explore as-yet-unexamined parts of one's identity as a teacher, and permits a far more experimental approach. This, of course, makes it all the more important that staff and participants genuinely encourage such experimentation and risk-taking, with the staff making the effort to model it themselves.

5. Prestigious Sponsorship of a "Class" Operation

In the case of these particular workshops, it has mattered greatly that they are sponsored not only by the American Academy of Religion, but also by the Lilly Endowment. The involvement of both organizations reinforces the message that the endeavor is highly valued and worthy of respect. That the AAR in particular actively supports the workshops, along with related projects that have grown out of them, makes it clear that the society's commitment to foregrounding the importance of teaching is genuine.

From the beginning of the workshops, the mandate was put in place to do everything possible to convey to the participants that they are special. One of the ways this message is to be expressed is through various forms of hospitality, which gives people the sense of being taken seriously.

> The first thing was that we were met at the airport. *There* was Southern hospitality in place. (SE participant)

Then there was the proverbial fruit basket, the tradition inaugurated by Williams at the Wabash workshop, and recommended by him as one gesture by which to indicate a gracious welcome. Although not every group did the fruit basket, some opened their meetings with receptions, and most made every effort to ensure that the food was of the highest quality possible. Sometimes this included being waited on; sometimes, going out to the best restaurants the budget would allow. Either way, being treated as honored guests made a deep impression on the participants.

> The meals were quite exquisite, unlike any institutional food I've encountered. This perhaps became a metaphor for the intellectual feast of which we partook in our time together. (SW participant)

> The food was great—like being on a cruise ship! (EI participant)

The general point to remember is that little touches go a long way, and considerable creativity can come into play in adding these details to the overall plan.

In the creation of this overall climate, setting also matters. When possible, having access to a place that will encourage a sense of being on retreat reinforces the awareness of being away from one's ordinary context. If the participants can spend time out of doors in beautiful surroundings, all the better. It is more important that the lodgings be as comfortable as possible, and that people be given individual rooms. But some access to Nature doesn't hurt. As one person commented, "We had the time, space, and meals to work together—and a lake! It was so unusual!" (NEM participant)

In addition, it is a good idea to set up a common room of some kind where people can gather to socialize. The staff may want to encourage this, should there be access to a refrigerator, by providing refreshments. (A well-stocked soda machine somewhere in the building will do just as well.) A common room can also double as a resource center where people can put books, films, and recordings they find useful in their teaching—although if these are to be left in the room, the staff should make provisions for locking it when it is not in use. The point is to encourage an environment where spontaneous conversations can comfortably take place. When such a space was not available, the participants had little option after dinner but to return to their rooms—"Not having a common room meant that you scrambled in the evenings to think of what to do"—whereas they might otherwise have continued their discussions further into the evening.

It is not necessary that all four sessions happen at the same location. The New England/Maritimes workshop did, but this was not the case for the other three. Indeed, there can be significant reasons for choosing to vary the site:

> I think that there is near unanimity among staff and participants about the value of having the various sessions at different locations. An important part of teaching is physical accommodations and support. Actually holding our sessions in

different locations at different colleges allowed participants to have a greater sense of different teaching environments.[8]

As becomes gradually apparent, some of the variables contributing to the effectiveness of the workshops begin to overlap. Here, for example, we see again the appreciation for encountering the diversity of settings in which one's colleagues teach, this time by meeting on different campuses.

At the same time, there are logistical factors that a director and staff need to take into account:

> There is one downside to holding workshops at various sites: the director has a much harder time coordinating budgets and making physical arrangements. Although some organizing tasks are lessened, others are magnified. For example, I was able to have local restaurants bill the AAR directly; I had to use my own VISA card to pay for restaurant meals in other areas. I also had to do a lot more negotiating with the person on-site to explain budget limitations, while they were making arrangements. Figuring out bills was more complicated, because one had to learn procedures from various institutions. If all of the sessions had been at mine, many of the arrangements could have become more routinized.
>
> There is also considerable work for the person on-site. In our case, two of the participants volunteered to have the weekend sessions held at their schools, and we came up with some money from our budget to give them some extra for their enormous efforts. If various locations are to be used in this way in the future (and I strongly recommend that this be the case), a little additional money should be built into the budget for those participants who do the on-site work.[9] (EI Staff)

Note that despite the complications, this same director still weighed in on the side of holding sessions at different locations, suggesting that the benefits outweighed the difficulties.

Both the staff and participants in all four workshops were adamant about the importance of being given an appropriate stipend for their participation. For some, it provided the practical means with which to take time out of the summer to dedicate to the

---

[8]   AAR/Lilly Teaching Workshop in Religious Studies, Eastern International Region, Evaluation Report II, p. 6.

[9]   AAR/Lilly Teaching Workshop in Religious Studies, Eastern International Region, Evaluation Report II, p. 7.

workshops. For all, it reinforced the sense that teaching was being privileged and rewarded.

Although it was generally expected that individuals' institutions would cover their travel costs, in a few cases, the staffs discovered that some would not. This was particularly true for participants teaching as adjuncts, who could usually count on no institutional support at all. In such cases, the staffs did what they could to allocate small amounts from their budgets to help out. If the region in which one is planning to hold a workshop is a large one, it may be wise to factor such a supplementary fund into the budget from the beginning.

6. The Exploration of Issues in the Scholarly Vocation

Discussions about teaching, when done well, shed light on many other issues in higher education. Though each workshop focuses on teaching, part of becoming a good teacher involves becoming more attuned to and adept at negotiating the range of commitments in an academic life. In a supportive and trusting environment, workshop discussions explore the whole range of rewarding and difficult issues in the scholarly vocation.[10]

The workshop created a context in which both the staff and participants could talk about the implications of focusing on different aspects of the scholarly life. The very example provided by the staff who, themselves, had given significant attention to developing as teachers provided one stepping stone from which to do this. In addition, the participants were able to ask their tenured colleagues for advice in how to balance the different dimensions involved in pursuing promotion and tenure while, at the same time, keeping alive their commitment to teaching.

Further Aspects of Time: Scheduling

One of the common dilemmas that confronts a staff is how to fit everything into the schedule. Here, Jonathan Z. Smith's observation that there is nothing that cannot be left out of the introductory course can be liberating. The temptation is to fill the

---

[10] Memo for the Wabash-Lilly Consultation on Theological Education, March 13-14, 1995, p. 1.

mornings, afternoons, and evenings, leaving little time other than meals for the serendipitous to occur.[11] We know that in our professional lives there is no such thing as a large block of time; it is all the more important in the workshops, therefore, to remember to leave any number of them. When the time gets too tightly packed, it affects the overall experience of the whole, and is generally commented on by participants as one of the least valuable aspects of a meeting.

> I would have enjoyed more time, perhaps consciously structured with the leaders to identify specific issues we each brought. There was little time apart from the planned sessions. The fullness of the schedule meant that there was little time to seek out the staff for individual consultations. That was the only time. If there were a way to build it in as an option and structured time left for that, I think that would be a good idea. (NEM participant)

Insofar as part of their role includes the function of mentoring, the staff are well advised to consider this one of their own assignments for at least a good part of the unscheduled time (factoring in their own needs, too, for rest and exercise). The staff will also need to meet each day, in order to review what has happened up to that point, and to determine whether they need to recalibrate their planning. Having unstructured blocks of time at different points in the day provides them with the occasion to do so.

"Don't change having time to play," said one. "Remember the value of play in creating relationships. There should be time for recreation, walks, bicycle trips." (Wabash participant) Another observed that some of the most effective aspects of the workshop came about extemporaneously during the random conversations that emerged "in the space created for us to spend time hanging out together." (EI participant)

The other point related to the structuring of time involves the teaching projects. The staff must determine whether they expect the participants to work on their projects during any of the sessions and,

---

[11] The Smith analogy is all the more apropos in this case, if one remembers one's early syllabi, and the corresponding temptation to load them up with too many readings.

if they do, allow time for this. Particularly if the session is set at a site with strong library resources, planning in project-development time may be important, so that participants coming from smaller schools can have access to these resources.

> Having three or four hours free in the afternoons seemed crucial to me. "Less was more" in this, as in some other classroom settings. It is necessary time, to allow a bit of exercise, for extended exchange with other participants and directors/staff, and to allow some private time to read and to work on our projects. (Wabash participant)

Generally speaking, it is not a bad idea to leave the afternoons open or, if that is not entirely possible, at least to leave a stretch of time toward the latter part of the afternoon. On the other hand, there is the risk of underscheduling:

> We met for three hours a day. I would have gone in for another after-dinner discussion. This was a week I was taking out to focus on these issues and, while it was nice to have that much free time, I would not have taken it badly to have met for another two hours sometime during the day. (SE participant)

There is no clear-cut template, and there is, of course, no way to please everyone fully. For some people, having unscheduled afternoons can seem like a waste of time. Most, however, like the looseness in this part of the schedule in order to let things percolate. The best general advice is first to design a schedule that has both structure and flexibility, along with open, unscheduled units of time. The decision, for example, of how much to divide the time between plenary sessions and small-group discussions is a difficult call, because the rhythm can change from first week to last. It usually proves useful to consult with the participants about their preferences, unless there are specific pedagogical reasons for designing a given session in a particular way. The point is that the staff needs to find ways to be willing to modify things along the way: "You have a plan which you hold loosely and you trust the process as it evolves." (Wabash participant) This requires a staff made up of individuals who are, by and large, comfortable enough with each other and with this kind of process that they can allow it to unfold.

We think that it is crucial to the success of a workshop to have a very clear view of what the goals are initially, and then be willing to modify them in light of ongoing feedback from the participants as the sessions progress. We found that we were able to accomplish the central goals of our initial proposal, while being very flexible in regard to how we did so. Participant ownership as the ultimate long-range goal can only occur if participants play an increasingly greater role in shaping the workshop sessions over time. (SW staff)

There was nothing set in stone. That's another positive thing. It was composed with everyone present. Even in the first week, there was direction, but it was also flexible. (EI participant)
This kind of flexibility allowed, again, for serendipity or, as one person put it, "a lot of well-done accidents." (SW participant) Here, too, it can prove useful to find out what happened in previous workshops if and when certain things were tried.

One of the underlying objectives set in place during the Wabash workshop was the process of working toward having the final week be shaped by the participants, with the staff acting increasingly as facilitators and coordinators. The ideal is for the participants to own the workshop. Yet this process also needs to get underway even during the first week, and be continued consistently over the course of the year.

There was a slow change through the meetings: from being organized and led by staff to being organized by staff with input and being led by participants. This sense of incorporation...was a real modeling of how to guide "students" to take off on their own. (Wabash participant)

It is our experience that an alert staff benefits not only from past workshops in other regions, but also from past sessions within its own workshop. Redesigning the August, 1996, session in light of feedback on what participants would like to see happen really paid off . . . .
As we progressed from session to session, we as staff noted that, while it is not easy to give up control as a teacher of teachers, in fact, it not only can, but must happen for a workshop as a whole to be successful. By the fourth session, we found that we were actually relinquishing control some of the time and growing more able to flag for each other those times when we were too controlling. We noticed that it was hardest to give up

> control when our own individual, most cherished interests or
> areas of expertise were on the line. (SW staff)

That this staff was effective in its efforts is reflected in the following
comment from one of the participants:

> The staff listened carefully and consistently to the
> participants. Our desires for changes in schedule or format were
> taken seriously. They were committed to tailoring the workshop
> to these participants. It was clear that the leaders were modeling
> excellent teaching. (SW participant)

At its best, the incorporation of feedback is folded into the given
meeting time, or clearly included in a specific later session.
Sometimes the same group can find it easy to do so in one session,
and not so easy in another. As was noted in Chapter IV, for example,
the team in the Southeast was extremely effective at being flexible
during the first week, but found it more difficult to factor the long list
of suggestions from the participants into subsequent sessions.

This is one advantage to leaving open blocks of time, insofar as
it can permit some of these kinds of suggestions to be offered as
optional events. On the other hand, as the New England/Maritimes
team discovered, after they had, effectively, filled up all their free
afternoons during the first week in response to such requests, they
were perceived as having over-scheduled. On the other hand,
Southeast workshop group found the loose structure of the final
week to lack a clear agenda. Either extreme can lay the ground for
resistance or even rebellion on the part of the participants.
Therefore, the more the participants are actively included in the
discussion and review of the planning along the way, the more
felicitous the outcome is likely to be. Likewise, the more their ideas
and preferences—together with those of the staff—are visibly
incorporated into the unfolding design of the workshop, the more
the staff will be perceived as "modeling excellent teaching."

Feedback on Specific Activities
Different Theoretical Frameworks and Teaching Styles

Even though many of us have experienced different styles of
teaching during our graduate school years, rarely were we studying

our professors' approaches to pedagogy. To the extent that those same models may have served us when we began teaching, it is equally likely that many of us had little occasion to explore and think systematically about different teaching styles. Many of our own successes may have a hit-or-miss quality to them. For these kinds of reasons, the participants appreciated discussing multiple theoretical approaches to teaching, as well as seeing different styles in action:

> Don't change the open self-examination that was part of the process by pursuing an agenda that supports only one type of pedagogy. (EI participant)

> I enjoyed tremendously seeing and experiencing a range of teaching styles. A tremendous amount of thought went into presenting options in teaching, through Natalie's approach to lecturing and field trips, Michael's discussion method—laying out different options. I found that very helpful. Though we each have preferred styles and the constraints of where we are, it is important to see the alternatives. (NEM participant)

> My appreciation of different teaching styles wasn't new, but it was heightened. Charlotte brought that out well with her quantifiable results about whether or not you're getting through, specifying that there are goals, and ways of approaching these goals. (NEM participant)

The staff may also want to explore ways to demonstrate different styles in the classroom.

> We became more committed to modeling various forms of interactive pedagogy, even as we discussed particular topics; by the end, the workshop itself had become an arena for pedagogical experimentation.[12]

It is useful, in this connection, to discuss not only how to refine one's ability to draw on different styles, but also the kinds of things that each of them helps one to accomplish.

---

[12] AAR/Lilly Teaching Workshop in Religious Studies, Eastern International Region, Evaluation Report II, p. 3.

The Inclusion of Practical Skills

> If there was one criticism I'd make, it was the assumption that I knew what I was doing in the classroom. I could have used even beginner information, but aside from that, this will permanently change how I teach. (SW participant)

The speaker, in this case, is being modest. Nevertheless it is useful to find out which of the nuts-and-bolts skills participants would most like to have included at some point over the course of the workshop (this can be done ahead of time through e-mail or by hard-copy correspondence), and arrange sessions in which to address them. Here, again, it is extremely important to keep checking in with the participants, as it may happen that the felt need to do one thing diminishes in relation to other concerns that arise during the year. The sessions that do take place may also include some of the occasions in which staff the participants teach each other. This can also happen during discussions of the teaching projects, particularly if the staff make a point of raising questions about hands-on aspects of teaching.

Frequently, the skills that have been of greatest interest to the participants to date have included the planning of a syllabus, lecturing, leading discussions, designing assignments, working with students on their writing, and the evaluation of student work.[13] The latter, in turn, can include methods for assessing student learning while a course is in progress, as well as issues of grading.[14]

> The most significant benefits were that I learned a *lot* of teaching techniques that should really help my students learn, and that I know a bunch of good folks to call if I need to discuss my teaching. (EI participant)

> I now have a storehouse of syllabi from others, along with textbooks, resources, and films, *and* the attention everyone gave my work. (SW participant)

---

[13] This should be differentiated from the student assessment of one's own teaching.

[14] An extremely useful handbook in this connection is still Margaret Morganroth Gullette, ed., *The Art and Craft of Teaching* (Cambridge, MA: Harvard-Danforth Center for Teaching and Learning, 1984).

> When we did the syllabus for the workshop, Matthew said "Come up with three goals." What did I want the course to *do*? It helped me to figure out what I wanted the course to do and what the students should get out of it, so we could negotiate it. I also put things in on how their writing would be evaluated. This helped me to convey the terms. These kinds of things were very useful. (NEM participant)

The inclusion of practical skills keeps the meetings from becoming excessively theoretical or abstract by anchoring them in applied aspects of teaching. In particular, many participants often have minimal experience in thinking about how to use non-textual materials skillfully in the classroom. On the most basic level, rarely has anyone showed them how to organize lectures using visual materials, music, or kinesthetic exercises, even though student response is generally extremely favorable to these methods. The issue goes beyond the increasingly visual and auditory nature of the media with which students are familiar, and includes the degree to which university education has tended to privilege the written text.

> One constant theme that emerged... is that films, slides, field trips, etc. need to be discussed as thoughtfully in the classroom as do religious scriptures and that we must begin to develop a vocabulary for analyzing them with our students.[15]

In planning a workshop, it is therefore advisable to explore the skills and experience available through members of the group, and to factor in regular sessions devoted to exchanging approaches and resources.[16] A general principle with this or any other topic about which the staff wants to try to insure that the participants emerge more confident in the classroom is that one session alone is usually not sufficient.

If field trips are included as part of a workshop, they work well when incorporated into the larger discussion of how to draw on the resources of a region in one's teaching. It is a good idea to include

---

[15] AAR/Lilly Teaching Workshop in Religious Studies, Eastern International Region, Evaluation Report II, p. 8.

[16] Examples in the earlier chapters might also serve as resources.

them as part of the main schedule. This not only conveys their importance in one's teaching; it also insures that everyone goes.

> I was disappointed that visiting the various historical sites was made optional. If the intention was to have that experience, then let's do it together and arrange the time to make it possible. Since we didn't, as a *group* we missed that experience. The trip to Stone Mountain, for example—when I saw the statue of Virtue as a woman and a child, and Valor as kind of a Huck Finn type, it was powerful to show the mind-set, along with the various quotations and *who*, among Southerners, they selected. I got a real sense of Southern civil religion. And since we discussed Stone Mountain during one of the morning sessions, we all should have actually gone to see it. (SE participant)

It is also useful to plan a debriefing afterwards, as was done in the Southwest workshop following the trip to the Alamo, so that everyone can talk about the site itself, how it is presented to the public, and their experience of both. This, in turn, can serve to model how one might do something similar with a class.

Technology

Even though growing numbers of younger faculty are familiar with new forms of technology and uses of the Internet, many still do not feel comfortable adapting some of these to classroom-related uses, although their students are increasingly versatile with these resources. If faculty feel awkward in the use of non-textual materials, they often feel even more so when trying to use technology. Over time, this may create a growing gap between teachers and students, which will be difficult to bridge. This is not to suggest that the classroom be converted into a technological tool time, but that new resources be explored for what they do have to offer to today's faculty in the study of religion.[17]

Although the New England Maritime/Maritimes group in particular addressed the use of presentation software, the making of one's own CD-ROM, and the use of the Internet to carry out library

---

[17] A good example is a website designed by one person in a workshop series outside this study, in which different pages in the site and the use of hypertext present a page of Talmud, allowing one to work back and forth between the different layers of commentary.

searches, it became apparent that one morning—and even one day—is not sufficient to raise people's comfort level a great deal.

> I don't know how feasible it would be, and there wasn't time to take advantage of it, but I would have enjoyed having access to the Internet for more than just one time, to practice learning to access it, and to go for the Telnet sources with people with some common interests. (NEM participant)

In some cases, participants had designed computer-related projects, and then found that the staff had not anticipated the kinds of assistance they might need. The projects then had to be revised to drop the technological aspects.

For today's teachers to develop a facility with computer-related media—including the use of web-sites related to teaching—it would be helpful to have one person on the staff be experienced in these tools, good at teaching others how to use them creatively, and on deck to do so. If the use of technology as a teaching tool in religious studies is going to be included at all, then regular sessions need to be one of the ongoing foci of the workshop. Otherwise, participants end up feeling that they have been exposed to something they cannot put into practice. There should also be thoughtful discussion of when these tools are genuinely useful, and when they do not necessarily add a great deal, so that faculty become more sophisticated in their judicious application.

Moreover, faculty at some of the smaller schools and community colleges still find themselves constrained by the lack of resources, making the use of technology in the classroom a more distant prospect.

> That's another area I'm aware of in teaching—the high tech stuff that Charlotte showed us—we're not at that level of technological support at my school. I'm also aware of the amount of work that has to go into doing an orchestrated show. But for technological reasons and lack of knowledge, I can't do much with those things right now, although I hope to some day. (NEM participant)

For these teachers, older uses of media remain viable, and need to be addressed as well. As the same participant went on to say:

> At the lower technological end, I found the discussion about using slides very useful. It is a technology that is simple but that I can apply right away. I foresee doing that much sooner. I found all of that really helpful. As I have been teaching, these ideas have been going through my head. (NEM participant)

It is also worth giving thought to alternatives to hard-copy correspondence, such as e-mail. The staff may want to consider handling much of its communication with the group through e-mail, especially with specific tasks the group may want to accomplish between meetings.

> I think e-mail could have really helped us do some work before we met each time. Maybe some of us in small or isolated Southern situations have already used it as a part of maintaining ourselves in connection with others. Some of us didn't have it, so it might have been useful to make some funding available for these people, at least for the duration of the workshop. (SE participant)

As this participant points out, however, a staff cannot assume that everyone has access. As several groups discovered, if even one person does not, this approach is not possible. (So far, no more than two people in any given workshop have not had accounts.) If the staff hopes to rely on e-mail in any way, then, as the participant suggests, the means to make this possible need to be addressed from the beginning.

Video-Taping a Class[18]

The experience of watching oneself teach on tape in order to analyze one's work in the classroom is something that most faculty have not done. More to the point, few are comfortable with the idea. Particularly if their school does not have a teaching center that encourages the taping of classes, they are not likely to do so on their own. Therefore, a staff who chooses to include the observing of tapes may face initial resistance to the idea, and needs to have thought through 1) how to persuade the participants to have

---

[18] See Appendix for suggestions on how to tape a class and how to view a tape.

themselves taped and 2) how to help them think through the logistics. If one of the staff has an example of him- or herself on tape, it can also work well to use this as an opener. This can be all the more effective the tape illustrates a number of problems, and if the person involved can discuss what he or she learned from the process of viewing themselves at work in the classroom.

> Seeing Matthew critique himself was wonderful—presenting himself first as the boring talking head. We all know this—you can teach poorly or wonderfully anywhere. (NEM participant)

It is a good idea to advise someone viewing him- or herself for the first time to watch the tape all the way through, at least once, before beginning to work with it. For the purposes of the workshop, the person should also be instructed to select a particular segment or segments with which he or she would like help. (If there is a teaching-learning center at one's campus, it may be possible to work one's way through an entire tape more systematically with a trained viewer.) There are at least four ways to include a discussion of videotapes into a workshop or departmental program: 1) someone on the staff can discuss segments of a tape with a participant, as in the New England/Maritimes workshop; 2) participants can be teamed up to work together in pairs; 3) the entire group can be divided into small groups, as the Eastern International workshop did; and/or 4) the entire group can view segments of each participant's tape, as they did in the New England/Maritimes group.

Many are surprised to discover how helpful the exercise usually turns out to be:

> Although I understand people's reservations about being video-taped, I would recommend it. Years ago, a colleague said to me, "I know you'll be embarrassed, so film yourself four times, and watch it the fourth time." So, I was surprised to find that I was comfortable the first time. It's the opportunity to watch how you do with a class. We're all narcissists, but even so, of course there's a part of it that can be embarrassing. I found out that I sometimes stand with my mouth open (I now close it). We talk about what we do in the classroom all the time, but it's useful, too, to see it. This comes from someone who had real

> reservations about it. I had no intention of doing it, mind you.
> (EI participant)

Therefore, if the staff feels that this is an important exercise to include, therefore, they should hang in, and gently but firmly encourage the participants to give it a try.

Readings

Many of us have experienced either having assigned too heavy a reading load, or readings which never make their way into the class discussion. Students, in turn, find themselves unable to complete the readings, or wondering what the connection is and why they had to do the readings in the first place. Things are not that different in a workshop. In practice, it often proves unrealistic to assume that the participants will have time to do a heavy load of readings either before they arrive or during the workshop itself. Second, when there are too many readings, many go unaddressed.

> The readings were great, but we didn't discuss them.
> Before I came for the first week, I had gotten through only about
> a third of them, and I felt bad. But then they weren't referred to.
> If we were going to do readings, it would have been better to
> have figured out ways to incorporate them into the discussion.
> (SE participant)

As with a class, it is important to indicate the role a set of readings will play in relation to the particular session. If they are to serve as background, but not as the direct focus of a discussion, this should be made clear. If they constitute a set of resources that the staff thinks the participants will find useful along the way, again this should be indicated. Both approaches help in reducing possible frustration.

> There were too many textual materials for the last session.
> I just couldn't get to them all, and I felt pretty overwhelmed just
> looking at them. I am, however, glad to have them, for they may
> come in handy in the long run. (EI participant)

If, on the other hand, the materials are going to serve as the stuff of a session, this in itself can become an exercise in modeling how to use readings creatively.

The Teaching Projects

The basic advice concerning the projects is, as one participant put it, to "take them seriously." As with every aspect of the workshops, this too involves questions of balance—there is such a thing as over-emphasizing the projects. But they should, in some way, be kept active in people's attention over the course of the year, and there should be ongoing discussion and mutual support.

> I felt that I got support for my project in the sense that I received resource suggestions like the discussion of slides and teaching styles. I didn't get much bibliography, but I hadn't expected that. It was more general resources for how to put together a solid course. It helped my project, but it would have helped any project. Often, it would be a sort of mental write-up—it was more by chance. People would drop comments that would be useful. It also could have been done somewhat more formally, like having a sheet of paper for each person to add suggestions, or setting up a notebook to leave messages in, related to other people's courses. (NEM participant)

> I hadn't anticipated how valuable the presentations of the projects would be. The feedback pages were a great idea, because you didn't have to take notes, and getting nineteen perspectives was really useful. (SE participant)

In the experience of the team in the Southwest, the pacing of project-related sessions turned out differently from what they had expected. They found themselves spending more time on the projects in the first three gatherings, while there seemed to be less need for such discussions by the final week. They chose not to have reports, and to ask instead for more a more general philosophical reflection on the effects of the workshop on the projects.

For some participants, it is not the experience of doing the teaching projects that matters to them as much as the experience of the group itself:

> I was far more radically transformed by the general topics and discussion than I was either by my work on my course or by the reports of others on theirs. It was disappointing to me that the workshop resources (primarily in the form of time) were directed so extensively to these reports. (SW participant)

> The group situation far outweighs the project in importance. Doing the projects was good, but the real gains were in what we talked about and the different exercises we did. Some related to my project; some didn't. (EI participant)

For many of the others, however, the projects served as the touchstone that provided them with the occasion to think concretely about how they might apply the many things they were discussing during the different meetings. What reinforced this were the final reports each person is expected to write. This was especially the case when the report was viewed as the occasion to pull together one's thoughts about the experience of the workshop as a whole, with the project serving as the focus.

Potential Challenges

Many variables, as we have seen, contribute to the strength and effectiveness of the teaching-workshop experience; some, however, can operate in ways that may weaken a group's sense of cohesiveness and shared purpose. The very process of forming a group or community prompts not only appreciation for the differences between people, but sometimes frustration and even anger. As each of the workshop groups discovered, these issues can either remain under the surface, or become the stuff of its discussions. In essence, each case represents the potential for different forms of conflict, along with the challenging decision of whether or not to address it—and, if so, how.

Some situations involve differences between personalities, which few groups find easy to address without having the discussion deteriorate into *ad hominem* attacks.

> We steered away from personality things. It's very hard to deal with those kinds of things in this kind of a group.... There are various ways of confronting and challenging how different people are coming across. But it takes so much work and trust, and it takes a good leader. (EI participant)

Others involve political and/or religious differences, many of which have to do with issues profoundly related to someone's sense of identity. Whatever the specifics of the challenge, these same factors can, albeit indirectly, also create the conditions for a group to discover something important about itself and its own resilience.

Absences

People often assume that their absence from a session will either not be noticed or that it will have little effect on the larger process. Rarely do they recognize that not being there can damage the sense of a community in the process of formation. It is therefore strongly recommended that it be made unambiguously clear both to the members of the staff and to the participants, from the outset, that—short of medical emergency, birth or death—full attendance at every the workshop sessions is expected, without exception. Likewise, late arrivals and early departures (unless directly related to one's teaching obligations) complicate the effort to develop a shared experience.

When other conference commitments, speaking engagements, and even family events are accepted as reasons for absence, it signals to the group that teaching, after all, is not as important—the very message the workshops are trying to counteract.[19]

Should an absence prove absolutely unavoidable, the person involved should be asked to discuss it with the group at the earliest possible occasion. If it involves a major absence, the staff should set aside time for the group to discuss its response, rather than moving right on to other topics. It may also prove necessary to return to the subject several days later.

For this reason, it is particularly important to present dates for the entire workshop no later than the time when the first letters to the participants go out, and participants should be advised not to accept a place in the workshop if they cannot attend it in its entirety.

---

[19] It is complicated when someone claims family reasons for missing several days, because families often feel marginalized by the professional pressures of the family member who teaches, just as academics often feel that their professional worlds fail to acknowledge the importance of family in their lives. It is also the case that events can surface after someone has, in good faith, accepted a place in the workshop. Nevertheless, such absences should still be discouraged. In a case where it was allowed, it affected the person's participation such that they were never fully engaged in the remainder of the program.

The Difficult Participant

What to do should there be a difficult participant—the workshop analog to the difficult or disruptive student in the classroom? This is the person who, for example, repeatedly interrupts or attempts to monopolize the discussion, who dismisses the ideas of others or, when offered the chance to make a positive contribution, consistently turns it into a confrontation? In such cases, how might one redirect the frustration and even anger of the other participants and the staff?

How one formulates the dilemma turns, at least in part, on the question of how one defines whose responsibility it is to address such a situation. The staff might, one could argue, leave it to the participants to regulate themselves. Unfortunately, participants also take their cues from those they perceive as directing or facilitating the group. If they see these individuals taking no measures to address the difficulty, they are more likely to feel disabled, not empowered. The chances increase that the situation will deteriorate into the behind-the-scenes venting of resentment or into more explosive public confrontations. Either way, it can absorb considerable amounts of the group's energy—along with staff meeting time—and divert everyone from their focus on teaching

Ultimately, as the set of individuals accountable for directing the workshop and addressing dilemmas, it does fall to the staff, who have a number of options. If the person seems at all responsive, it may be possible to speak with them directly in private. It may be that they are unaware of the effects of their behavior. On the other hand, there may be a case where it seems clear that a direct request is likely to be ignored, or given only lip-service acceptance. The staff might then propose to the group—as an exercise in process—that together they define and adhere to ground rules for discussion. The staff is responsible for leading this process but, in so doing, enables the group to exert its own influence. The outcome conveys that there are rules by which everyone is expected to abide. Should one person not do so, the others are then on stronger ground to bring this to his or her attention.

Tensions Over a Workshop Theme: Two Cases
The Theme of Gender

The focus on gender and non-textual materials proved successful in the Eastern International workshop. There had been some initial concern that the staff's choice to highlight these themes might divert the focus from teaching, thereby obstructing the larger intent of the workshop and polarizing the group. This proved not to be the case. The group's success, however, did not mean that there were no tensions, some of which were never fully articulated. In part, this had to do with some participants' feeling constrained by the strength of other participants' positions:

> The feminist critique was overwhelmingly dominant, often dampening conversation in other directions. I felt uneasy challenging this over the four sessions. (EI participant)

> I sensed this second week that a number of participants—women as well as men—felt marginalized, more along a radical/liberal axis than gender. Again, this is not altogether a bad thing. (EI)

As can happen in the classroom, the hottest topics closest to the trigger-points of disagreements can turn out to be both the focus of attention and the object of avoidance, at the same time.

> I would have liked to have actually discussed the gender issue more. We had reading about it but every time we really started to talk about it, it seemed to get out of hand. It was where the greatest polarization in the group seemed to be, so we avoided it. Since this was one of my pedagogical projects, I found this unfortunate. (EI participants)

> There were differences as we taught and learned from each other, but I would have felt much more freedom in the group if those conflicts were not consistently co-opted by the "we all get along attitude." That attitude disguised *real* agreement or disagreement. (EI participant)

Here is an example where the emphasis on a collaborative dynamic and even the use of humor can end up being used not to resolve differences, but to avoid dealing with the possibility of sharper confrontations. Groups are sensitive to these dynamics, and in general everyone is fairly aware that they are going only so far in addressing the positions that divide them.

As much as the year-long duration of the workshop contributes to a sense of real commitment on the part of those involved, there is also an inverse effect to this time-frame, in that a year is finite. The members of the group know that they will not be coming together again after the workshop ends, except in informal reunions. That can change the stakes in resolving differences, sometimes imposing an implicit sense of limit to how far people are willing to go and how much they are willing to risk. In the case of the gender-related discussions, those for whom these issues were central to their sense of identity and intellectual life did not identify the workshop group as their central community. This informed the degree to which they were willing to invest the emotional energy to take hard topics head on in that particular group. Similar conclusions would apply to each of the groups in which there were strong differences that never got brought to the surface.

In this particular case, however, it must also be said that the shared commitment to teaching, to creating as much trust as possible, and to doing what seemed possible in dealing with tough questions resulted in a process more fruitful than had been anticipated. As one person put it, "What was remarkable was that we could disagree fairly deeply without becoming bitter, polarized, or disengaged." (EI participant)

The Theme of Teaching in the South

> It might have been helpful to have asked as part of the application, "Did you grow up in the South?" Then, if the majority weren't from the South, they might want to bring in somebody from Southern history or sociology to talk about it. (SE participant)

As we saw in Chapter IV, it had not been anticipated that a significant number of the participants in the Southeast workshop would not be Southern themselves. As outsiders to the South, they brought not only their own questions about how to understand their students, but also some of their own preconceived notions about the

South itself—notions which the native Southerners were quick to pick up on as expressions either of condescension or hostility. Some of the Southern participants pointed to examples from the readings which, they felt, expressed such biases; a few noted what they experienced as embedded attitudes on the part of some participants:

> In the group, there was a critical mass of people from outside the South, but who are now teaching there. I mentioned to an administrator at my school that, on the first day of the workshop, the Southerners self-identified. I've lived here most of my life, and I felt the need to stand up for something that was maybe getting shortchanged. She told me about her experience of weathering some Northerners who were speaking like missionaries. (SE participant)

The very presence of outsiders, itself, raised issues related to the reality of the current South:

> Now that there are many Northerners relocating here, how are things changing? What is the mythology of the South, and how do different groups relate to it? Who belongs and who doesn't belong? (SE participant)

Essentially, these differences went unaddressed. Feedback from some of the participants suggests that this had to do with two factors in particular:

> Except for the first day, the issue of being in the South was not discussed so directly, although it came into the other discussions in lots of ways. Also, being non-Southern in a Southern context didn't get worked out that much. We read a lot of articles, but didn't use them as much as we might have. Using them might have helped us focus more on the region, which was the unique part of the workshop. (SE participant)

> The weaknesses of the workshop involved the processing of the vision . . . . There resulted in some sense of incompletion about understanding what difference being in the South actually makes and what we had hoped to accomplish toward that end, especially during the last week of the workshop. Many participants felt that a breakdown in communication occurred as to our purpose, in that there was not as much follow-through

> on suggestions made during our Spring workshop as there
> might have been. (SE participant)

These comments would suggest that one variable here involved the
role of the staff. On the other hand, the staff did not shy away from
addressing the conflict that arose during the final week. The critique
here, therefore, may be more about planning than about the attempt
to avoid a hot topic. I would, instead, suggest that a deeper, but
related, dilemma lay under the surface of this one—namely,
religious differences within the group—although, paradoxically,
these were also widely recognized within the group *as* a potential
source of conflict:

> There are a series of developmental stages to any group,
> and before you get to a true sense of community you have to
> deal with conflict. Every time we came upon a potential conflict,
> though, people backed off it—I know I did—in favor of the
> respectful, humorous rapport we had gained. But it would be a
> deeper experience if we could go beyond that.
> One conflict that's incipient is that some of us teach in
> church-related institutions who are just as involved in the
> academy, but also feel beholden to the churches, and value
> maintaining a dialogue with the tradition. But there are also
> people who see themselves as representing the antidote to this
> idea of teaching religion.
> I think we need to find a way to talk about these kinds of
> conflicts we're embedded in. We might find out a lot about each
> other. (SE participant)

I would argue that the connection between regional and religious
identity *and* experience lay at the heart of this issue:

> I wondered if the people who were from the North
> thought of themselves as coming in to teach *us* about religion. I
> wasn't sure they were coming in with open minds, and in some
> cases I thought maybe they were hostile to religious experiences
> themselves. As the first week went on, my perception gradually
> changed. A good talk with one person on the staff opened my
> eyes: these professional types were sharing on a *professional*
> basis. At times I wanted to respond on an emotional level, and
> felt frustrated.
> If there were just some way for people to acknowledge the
> importance of religious experience, and that traditional forms of
> Christianity have some value, instead of denigrating these

traditional values. Denying people's religious experience isn't going to make them give it up; in fact, it may lead to other things that are not so good, because you model the possibility of allowing other people to do the same . . . .

In one of the group's conversations, they were talking about how students "evolve." I thought to myself, "If you talk to a class like this, why wouldn't they see your real agenda as being to "fix the student"? It seems to me there's a certain arrogance to saying that students have something to say, but when they do, it's crap.

One person said to me that their students ask what religious tradition they're from, because the students can't tell. Because of where *I* come from, my feeling is that it's one thing trying to be objective, and another to look like a case of religious rootlessness. Since we're a generally a strong traditional people here, that kind of person can come in and look sort of like a Martian. (SE participant)

These comments illustrate a number of dilemmas which were present not only in the workshop group, but which also enter the classroom on multiple levels. The question, in a workshop, is how far a group finds itself able to go in addressing such differences, and how much confrontation and conflict it can handle. Ironically, it was in the final week of this very workshop, during the session on diversity, that some of these differences came to a head, and were addressed more directly than had happened previously. In the process, the group discovered that it could weather a major storm.

But introducing the question of how different faith positions inform people's relationship to their teaching is one which, on a more general level, presented a challenge to many of the groups, as one person from the Eastern International group pointed out:

It's very important for the workshops to look at being a person of faith in these settings. There was a reluctance to discuss faith in our group, as though that would belong more in a theology department. There was an additional kind of secular attitude at work that seemed to suggest you can't be professional, rational, or empirical *and* be a person of faith. There's a denigrating of a faith position, as though it were inferior. (It reminds me of textbooks that talk about Martin Luther King without saying that he was a minister or talking about his theology as part of his activities.)

The role of spirituality in all these traditions and its connection to power is broader than just the question of power.

> You can reduce everything to a political question, but what space is then left for mystery and spiritual breadth? That opens up an important question. (EI participant)

With the exception of the Southwest group, few of the groups found ways to integrate such issues into their ongoing discussion. This raises the crucial question of what made the difference. Because every group is likely to face some version of this question, formulating at least a working hypothesis in response becomes all the more necessary.

The Example Set by the Staff

Comments from the different workshop groups begin to shed some light on what it takes to create an atmosphere in which people can talk honestly, accept their differences, and allow for controversy. As the following quotes illustrate, one of the most critical variables appears to be what is modeled and supported by the staff:

> It really helped to set from the beginning a tone of civil and serious disagreement. While we modeled this on the very first day, we only later realized we had even done this and that it had made such an impact on what was to follow. We suspect that what allowed us to do this is the long-standing relationship of collegiality among staff in the region. (SW staff)

> For me, the most effective dimension of the week was the leadership. They're good people, with different perspectives. The openness they conveyed and modeled led to a similar atmosphere by the form of their own way of working together. (SE participant)

> Was everyone's ox gored at some point? If so, then probably everyone was somehow tested along the way. That's not a bad thing. (EI staff)

For the staff to be able to do this effectively, their own working relationship needs to be in good order. In cases where the members of the staff have not worked extensively with each other prior to the workshop (note that, in the Southwest, several of the staff had known each other for years), some of this will inevitably unfold over the course of the workshop. It may behoove the staff, however, to start looking at some of the potential hot spots likely to arise in its own group even before the workshop begins.

> It is a good idea for the members of the staff to meet before the workshop begins to work out whatever intellectual or stylistic differences they may have. (Wabash participant)

When the staff does convey, through their own interactions and ways of responding to differences within the group, that it is all right to tackle these directly—or when it doesn't direct the group to back off from these issues—the outcome is generally perceived to have been fruitful.

> The most valuable thing this week has been the challenges to my point of view from persons I have come to respect immensely over the past year. (EI staff)

> Conflict and disagreement absolutely played a role in the educational process of the group—it kept me awake at times. But it was healthy and instructive disagreement, and also contributed to re-affirming and changing my own stance on specific topics. (EI participant)

Furthermore, the take-away message is that, if it is possible to deal with such matters in the workshop, it is also possible to do confront them in the classroom:

> Getting into a couple of intense disagreements was illuminating. That can be threatening in a class, for example. It taught me I can control and allow that. It translates into some strategies that are still inchoate, but I'm more willing to let it happen, now. (EI participant)

Even when a group feels it has not handled a challenge effectively, what takes place can still prompt everyone to rethink what they do in the classroom. The bottom line, with any and all of the challenges is, as one person wrote:

> Don't be too tense about some failure, because taking a risk may involve stumbling. Trust the group to regroup. Learn from what doesn't succeed. Take advantage of everything. (Wabash participant)

Closing Comments

The fabric of all of these elements is the weave of a workshop. The combination of space, time, particular people, a shared endeavor, being treated as valued persons, engaging in effective activities and rich discussion, tackling potential or actual conflicts, and working to create a climate of trust all contribute to the formation of that elusive entity, "a community." And yet this is perhaps one of the most important contributions that the workshops make, and the aspect that appears to have been effectively created in each one of them. This chapter has explored some of the variables that converged to make this possible. The final chapter will now address some of the implications for the professional and personal lives of those who were involved.

VII

Implications for Faculty Development

A perceptive participant attempted to name the unnamed "ideology" of the workshop, and thereby gave a reasonably good summary of the impact of the workshop: "The workshop provided a critique of liberal individualism in which professors are rational, self-determining, ahistorical, free-thinking individuals, and students are or should be the same. The critique led us to think about institutions, our own histories, and process in our courses. There is a 'kind of grace' in being dependent upon contingencies: freedom to let go, to be open to surprise, to be yielding and responsive. An intersubjectivity is created—boundaries of self and others are blurred, solidarity in learning is encouraged, a shared history is formed, familiarity is valued, and a variety of rhetorical practice results. We are moving toward a post-liberal paradigm for teaching, but it is as yet unnamed. Our language fails us here."[1]

Where does the workshop experience fit, within the larger scheme of a person's professional development as a teacher and scholar in the study of religion? What difference does it make?

"Lilly and the AAR have done something extraordinary," said one person. "They should understand how extraordinary it is." But how to identify what that extraordinary thing is? One way is to point to some of the pieces, the effects about which those involved

---

[1] Raymond Williams, "Final Report, Lilly Workshop on Teaching Religion, Wabash College," p. 2.

were able to say something. This final reflection turns much of the discussion over to them.

The workshops profoundly influenced the identities of the staffs and participants in multiple spheres, in relation to self, to students, and to colleagues. On the most practical level, it influenced people's work in the classroom; in more intangible ways, it affected their sense of relationship to their entire professional world.

In relation to their work in the classroom, participants described a new sense of confidence:

> To tell a story or elaborate—the words will come to me. I never wrote my lectures out, but now I really get rolling and think of things. It's fun. The things in the workshop helped. (NEM participant)

> I also experienced an increase in my confidence about teaching. If something doesn't go well, my life isn't over! I felt better about my ability to talk about what I was doing and felt a lot less anxious, and more coherent conceptually. The students understood what the point was. My pedagogical intent was clearer because I was more confident about it. (NEM participant)

> How has it affected my teaching? At first, I wanted to establish my authority. That changed radically. Now I encourage challenge and, if I don't know something, we all look it up. I now try to create a group identity in the class, because of my experience of a strong group in the workshop, and its influence on the overall learning process. (EI participant)

> I do now put much more emphasis on gender issues in the different religious traditions. Also, I'm more aware of gender differences in the classroom, and of my own interactions with men and women. I also now try to observe myself interacting with different students, trying to see how and why I do what I do. (EI participant)

> It has pushed me to become more daring in confronting ambiguity. I tend to retreat from that, even as I encourage students to enter it! Also, looking at how some people engage in what they teach in a more personal way has forced me to confront distinctions I had artificially set up. I have to learn to jump into the breach and test some of those boundaries. (SW)

On a more conceptual level, the workshops led the participants to think about pedagogy itself—for some of them, a new venture in its own right, for others, a process of expanding on a foundation they had already consciously begun to lay.

> Before this, I wouldn't have read about pedagogy or gone to meetings about it. Now I'm doing both, because I find myself including them in the things it's important for me to do. I'm talking more with other faculty about teaching than I used to, and about what we do in our courses. (EI participant)

> So much of the stimulus and gain remains undefined. As I look at a syllabus or enter a classroom, I have so much more to look for. I had excellent teaching reviews before, but this has changed my own sense of inner resources, along with things to experiment with, and my feelings about experimenting. I'm more willing to do so, now. (EI participant)

> One of the biggest differences it made for me was that it enabled me to step back from my pedagogy in ways I was not able to before. The categories I have to think with were limited to *my* experience of the teaching and discussion of pedagogy. I thought I knew a lot about pedagogy, but what I learned from this was that there are other ways of seeing. (SE participant)

In some cases, pedagogy in its own right was elevated to an entire intellectual endeavor, inseparable from the content of what one teaches.

> What I think may be the most fundamental development may also be the most general . . . despite my sense of its importance. It is simply a change of consciousness, a heightening of pedagogical consciousness. Instead of preparing classes that involve either something that is basically lecture or basically discussion, I now face my planning time with a great (and what feels like a healthy) skepticism about how I am limiting myself through laziness, a comfortable habit, a cowardice, or a failure of imagination. Frequently this notion comes into my mind: "I'll bet the best way to engage this topic hasn't yet been thought of; what might I try that would break through convention and explore new methodological terrain?" In short, I am feeling more willing to take risks, more convinced that convention embraced unconsciously may be stifling both me and the students I encounter. . . .
>
> As a result of the Workshop, I feel altogether more free in recognizing teaching as a work of the imagination and as itself an act of scholarship rather than merely as an expression or delivery system of scholarship. One exchange revealed pedagogy as a real field for exploration, discussion, even interesting

debate, rather than as a pretentious-sounding word for simple techniques. I see more clearly now that how things are presented is nearly as important as what is presented, not simply because some method of presentation is more or less attractive to an audience, more palatable to students, but because teaching itself is a "thing," a thing that colors and shapes material, that affects how students conceive of a topic, and that reveals much about how a teacher construes his or her material. That is, teaching is not merely the packaging of the real message; it is itself part of the message, or it is its own message, and there may be untold alternative strategies to convey whatever is being conveyed. . . . .

I see more clearly now that how we go about our teaching tasks is inextricably connected to our views of the world and of our disciplines, that the ideas of our disciplines and our personal scholarship are enmeshed with how we go about structuring a course and the individual sessions in it. I even believe the Workshop has changed in some ways the entire course of my future professional life—not, again, because I did not care about teaching earlier, but because I more deeply understand the connections (implicit ones and those I will continue to create) between the subjects that I study and my presentation of them to students. (Wabash participant)

This and the preceding reflections say much about the kinds of changes to individuals' sense of themselves as teachers which the workshops brought about. More deeply, it speaks to the transformation of identity. As many affirmed, this experience consolidated the love of teaching that had brought them there in the first place, and affirmed the commitment they had each made to foreground it in their professional lives. But to return to one of the central themes of the preceding chapter, these changes did not occur in isolation. Rather, they were shaped by the entire relational dimension of the workshops. This, therefore, becomes the broader context which, in its own right, has multiple layers.

The first of these is the effect brought about by coming together with a group focused on teaching in the study of religion, an unusual experience in itself:

It was safe to assume, since teaching is not usually high among the factors that help you get tenure, that we must be there because we really wanted to be there. That was the strongest experience for me—to be with people in my field, but interacting in a very different way from what we usually do in the AAR. That was not a benefit I had necessarily expected. One

other person summed it up well: to be in this profession and know that you now have a network not based on expertise in one sense, but on a common commitment. That is one gift from the workshops I can already see coming out. (SE participant)

What was important about the pedagogical learning was that it happened with people who teach religion. I have the good fortune to be involved in all sorts of pedagogical activities here [at my school]—but they are never with people who teach the same area I do. So it was enormously helpful to rethink what I have learned about teaching with the focus on my own discipline. (SE participant)

In some cases, participants went back to their institutions and began to try to introduce what they had learned into their departments, with varying degrees of success. These efforts were undertaken not only by those already engaged in teaching full time, but by some of the graduate student participants as well:

One concrete item that came directly out of the workshop concerns the group of graduate students in religion of which I am a part [at my school]. After our session this spring—where we talked a lot about the inadequacies of most models of training graduate students to teach—one of the things the group of us decided to do was to work with one another more explicitly on teaching, rather than on dissertation writing, which is what we had been doing up until then. (SE participant)

As the AAR had originally hoped, there were also beneficial outcomes with respect to people's sense of connection within the different regions. One of the long-range expectations was that, in the various regions, nuclei of faculty would form who would engage in ongoing reflection about teaching at the regional level. This did, in fact, begin to happen, partly because the workshop teams made a point of setting aside time to discuss specific ways in which the fruits of the workshop could be carried back into the regions, and partly because individuals began to make a point of contributing more to the regional meetings in the pedagogy sessions. This suggests tremendous potential benefit to any professional organization sponsoring this kind of workshop.

I cannot emphasize too highly the value of this kind of network to junior scholars. We all have strengthened our

attachment to the region and to our working relationship together. (SW participant)

> This has been of real benefit to the regional AAR by creating a network at a level where you don't usually have one. The old codgers know each other and keep in touch, but this group now has a network at another level. Many of them may not stay in the region, but it's still an important thing for the region because it breaks us out of the mold of only knowing the people who have been here forever. (SW staff)

These practical effects within departments and schools do, indeed, corroborate some of the predictions of the original formulators of the workshops. But in addition to these effects, a second order of connection also emerged—one which people described as the fulfilling of an ideal on which many of them had given up:

> I am an idealist, and I imagined *this* when I was a graduate student—to sit around disagree respectfully, and learn from each other. Except it didn't really happen that way, a lot of the time, in grad school. (SW staff)

> This is the first positive experience I've had in the profession since I was a grad student, where people tried to be supportive of what each other was trying to do. It made me clarify certain things I had lost with grad school—the collaborative sense of being a scholar, teacher, and professional. I got that back in this workshop, because you could talk without the usual one-upsmanship. (SE participant)

> For the first time, I obtained a sense of teaching as a communal and not just an individual activity. Just as there is a community of scholars, there is also a community of teachers. As a result of the teaching workshop, I came to appreciate the way an individual teacher can draw on the resources of other teachers, both in general skills and methods, as well as in substantive content. Although the value of this may be obvious, I did not sufficiently appreciate it before. (SW participant)

> Lastly, I come to what I regard as the greatest benefit I have received from these workshops....I have never seen professors working on making community in the academy; "community" is something that we as graduate students have made over against our professors and the profession. It has been a powerful experience for me to see "real" people (i.e., professors

not just students) take seriously elements in academic culture that call us to be less than we can be, and work on changing those elements. I think this is the primary thing that I as a graduate student have received from these workshops: of all the things we have done, this is what has changed me the most. In our small group last Monday, I commented that the culture at my school has made it difficult for me to envision myself as a faculty person functioning in that environment. Participating in this workshop has been a real antidote to the estrangement of my experience of graduate school. For this I am especially grateful. (SE participant)

The future implications of such statements are far-reaching, and are perhaps more clearly understood when formulated in an older language, used by a staff member from the Southwest group:

> I've learned something about a phrase that we use all the time, "the guild." What that usually means is that you join an association, pay your dues, and get a journal, but with no sense of it *being* a guild. This workshop *did* create a sense of guild and of exactly how one should work. In the past, a guild took in apprentices at early stages in the practice of their craft and then, as they progressed in working at their craft under the supervision and advice of more advanced people, eventually they became full crafts people in their own right.
>
> I suppose getting tenure means that, but I'm seeing that we also have the increasing obligation to give back to the process, for the survival of the craft and the service the craft provides to the society. I have never had as strong a sense of doing that as I have over the past year. (SW staff)

One younger colleague commented in kind:

> One of the most important issues I'm seeing now is how to pass all of this on. I am so grateful for what's being handed on to me by my elders; I find that I now want to hand it on myself. (SW participant)

What emerges in both reflections is not only a sense of pride, but a feeling of being connected to others through a new-found sense of professional lineage.

It is important to note, in this regard, that the transformative effects reported above by the untenured faculty and graduate student were no less felt by those who played the role of staff:

I didn't expect to be as affected by it as I was. I went in thinking about my responsibilities to them, but not about my own way of relating in class and to my peers. I feel an extraordinary sense of satisfaction personally. (SW staff)

Finally, we think it is crucial that future staff members be aware of how much their participation in the workshop may ultimately modify their own subsequent teaching. In certain profound ways, the staff exists for the purpose of ultimately making itself obsolete *as staff*, that is, as authority in relation to the participants. One very real measure of the success of such planned obsolescence is the extent to which the ideas of the participants, as well as other staff members, contribute to the growth of each individual staff member as a teacher-scholar. This growth, as we experienced it, is perhaps the most unexpected personal benefit of all. (SW)

Within this broader context, what emerged as possibilities with respect to some of the potentially conflictual differences?

The unresolved issues for most of us are the same ones that are unresolved in the public discourse. The more conservative believers in the group felt no less marginalized by academia as a whole by the end of the sessions than at the beginning, but I do believe that none of us stands at enmity with any of our colleagues. Despite deep theological divisions, we insisted on civility and managed it. If in no other cases, at least among our group we can disagree and contest with one another in the intellectual arena, knowing one another well enough as people to keep us from mutual demonizing. For that reason if for no other, the workshops have served the academic community well in the Southwest and we are the better for it. (SW participant)

I'm currently struggling with the place of a convicted perspective, and with being able to come into the AAR without fear of being belittled. Here, nobody did that. The question is, what does someone like me bring to someone who identifies with a secular humanist position? Someone like that can't begin to understand *my* response to a film about the Southwest like *Tender Mercies* . . . .
An unexpected serendipity was the way the workshop increased my own sense of vocational satisfaction. As one who teaches at a conservative evangelical university, I have often felt somewhat outside of typical AAR agenda. As a generalist who emphasizes teaching, I sometimes have felt inadequate to converse with much of the specialist scholarship in the academy. Over the year, the workshops created for the participants an atmosphere that valued our differences and affirmed our genuine contributions to the larger dialogue about teaching religion. Consequently, I came away from each week more confident of the importance of my profession, more intent upon doing

serious work for every class, and more assured that I bring a particular, valuable perspective to both the academy and the larger evangelical populous. (SW participant)

Although clearly set in the midst of other issues that did not get addressed altogether adequately, these responses nevertheless suggest that deeper kinds of connection are possible, and that they hold the potential of standing alongside some of the forces that divide us.

"Knowing one another well enough as people," said the participant quoted above. That, I would contend, is at one level the most mundane effect of the workshops, and yet one of the most profound on the other.

> Something important happened here. One interesting and by now obvious consequence of the experience was that the participants grew to be genuine friends. This would be nice for its own sake, of course, but I am bothering to say it here for more pedagogical and scholarly reasons. By "genuine," I mean something like what one person observed at our final dinner when he noted that despite his wit and publicly hyperbolic and demonstrative style as a teacher-scholar, he has long felt alone in his work. He further noted that there was no one among his colleagues whom he would be likely to call up on the phone, but that this was not true of our Workshop group. People here are collaborating, staying in contact apart from the formal Workshop, sharing ideas on teaching and research, helping each other find resources, working together on a book and perhaps other essays. Among such a bright and busy group, this would not have happened unless something intellectually significant had also occurred. I sense that what happened here is likely to have value across the country. (Wabash participant)

> One of the other participants came to visit a few months ago. We did talk about teaching and about our different approaches, but it was much more than that. We found that the conversation took place in the context of friendship, so that it could also become more personal. This means you can discuss more than you would with a mere colleague. (EI participant)

> After each session, I have felt lonely when I returned to my own campus, missing the conversations and connections. Although I am not sure how we will survive as a group . . . I am absolutely convinced that relationships forged over this process will make a difference in the AAR/SBL, both at the regional and national levels. Generally, when one attempts something new within this structure, one looks to one's

friends to help start the initiative—and we now have a variety of friends ready to work on new perspectives on teaching and curricula. (SE participant)

To reiterate what others have said, the most transformative things about this has been to be together—to bridge the individual and the communal. I often think of myself in opposition to, or as different from, my students and colleagues. This has changed me, in coming up with the means, imagination, and techniques to see learning and teaching as a corporate enterprise. It has developed a model and a way of overcoming the loneliness that is very profound. The sense of community building in a classroom a department, and a university is more valuable than anything I've ever done on a particular project. (SW participant)

I address in particular to the general sense of isolation described in each of these comments—the difference between "mere colleagues" and "friends" to which each of them points, and the accompanying sense that within this newfound sense of guild, there is a sense of having created a unique sense of relationship which will, in its own right, have implications not only for people's teaching but, unexpectedly, for their other work as well. What may, in fact, grow out of this "the post-liberal paradigm for teaching" will be the unforeseen ramifications for scholarship.

What shape this will take remains to be seen. But already, those involved sense that there is more to come of it than they can currently imagine:

This changed my life, in some ways. It was a rich, stimulating experience. It's difficult to say how glad I am to have been a part of it. I hope that aspect will be true for others. If you're ever arguing for it before a skeptical audience, I can only say it was a transformative experience for me as a teacher. I will continue to learn how it affected me. (EI participant)

Tell Lilly and the AAR that the value of this workshop will be unfolding for years to come. The ways in which we will keep alive our identity as a group of Lilly Teaching Scholars in Religion in whatever way it evolves is really an important outgrowth of their initial commitment. (Wabash participant)

What they did understand was that this experience has been the closest many of them have come to experiencing the community of scholar teachers that they looked for when they first went into their professional careers—a hope often undermined by certain forms of competition and one-upsmanship that characterize the academic world at its worst.

"If only such a community of scholarship and teaching could be reduplicated at all AAR meetings!" said one person wistfully. Many of the staff members and participants realized that, for this to happen, there would have to be more workshops, some of which will have to be directed toward, as one person put it, "'the generation of people *employing* young teachers." What they know is that, as more people explore this experience, and as a network of closely knit scholars devoted to teaching emerges, "A critical mass of these scholars will eventually change our professional societies and our universities." (SW participant) This hope was perhaps the most important development of all for the future of the profession.

Appendix

Some Suggestions for Video Taping a Class Meeting[1]

- Work with the camera person ahead of time: tell them exactly what you want. Give as many concrete suggestions as possible.
- For most any in-class techniques, I recommend a hand-held camera. Even if you are lecturing, you still want to be able to scan the audience.
- Especially if you are taping small-group discussions, try to solve the sound problem: you somehow need to get the sound from one group at a time.
- In some classes, extra lighting might be needed, but avoid it if you can—students tend to freak out when the spots go on.
- Be sure to check with your students about their concerns and questions about the process and what will be done with the tape; you will also need to get their permissions in order to use it.
- Tape an entire class period: don't try to anticipate exactly which time-frames from the class will give you the "best" footage. The point of the exercise is to be "empirical," to let the eye of the camera see you and your students as you may not see yourselves. Later, if it makes sense to edit your tape to a shorter length, you can always do so.
- Use the tape as a pedigogical device for/with your students; if you learn anything from viewing the tape, most likely they will too.

---

[1] By Prof. Robert Sessions

- Relax. You won't learn much if you are uptight because of the camera—you want this to be a "normal" class period.

Guides to Viewing Others' Videotapes for Teaching Improvement[2]
Setting the Climate:

Offer the instructor something like tea or water. Ask how things are going. Don't talk about the tape or class right away. Talk with them for about ten minutes to establish a rapport and sense of mutual exploration. Make clear that this is not an evaluation. Focus on them.

Developing a Framework for Viewing:

Talk about the teacher's experience: his or her strengths, problems, uncertainties, and goals both for that particular class and in general. Ask what he or she is concerned about and would like to look for; how they happened to decide to be videotaped.

This is useful whether you are going to observe the class in person or through videotape which the faculty member has brought to you. The purpose is to get an idea of the class goals and teaching style of the instructor, and some general information about the students in the class:

1. So that you as a viewer can put yourself in the position of a student, ask about the day's assignment and other work preceding the class.

2. Invite the instructor to tell you something about what you'll be seeing on the tape—what will be happening in this class?

3. What did you hope the students would gain from this class particular class session?

4. What did you expect students to be doing in the class in order to reach the stated goals?

---

2   From a Teaching Consultation Workshop prepared and given by Dr. Mary Deane Sorcinelli, Director of the Center for Teaching at the University of Massachusetts at Amherst, on August 27 and 28, 1993 at Northeastern University, sponsored by the Massachusetts Faculty Development Consortium; from materials prepared by the Derek Bok Teaching and Learning Center, Harvard University; and from materials developed by Prof. Carol Owen, Northeastern University.

5. What can I expect you to be doing on this tape? What role did you take? What teaching methods did you use?

6. What were students asked to do to prepare for this class?

7. What was done in earlier classes to lead up to this one?

8. Was this class generally typical or representative of your teaching? If not, what was different?

9. Is there anything in particular you would like me to focus on during this viewing?

Give the instructor the video controls so that he or she can stop the film at any point during the discussion. Ask if he or she has ever seen him/herself on tape, and explain that he/she should stop the tape at points he/she would like to explore.

Let the tape run for five to six minutes to get a feel for it. Point out that the experience of viewing oneself can be disconcerting, and suggest that he or she view the next five minutes as a student.

What to Look for in the Observation of a Videotape
Knowledge of Subject Matter

Does the instructor show knowledge and mastery of content? Is material appropriate to this level of class and students?

Does the instructor show evidence of incorporating recent developments in the discipline?

Does the instructor present divergent viewpoints?

Is there too much, or not enough material included in this class session? In what ways?

Presentation Skills
Engaging student interest

Does the instructor prepare students for what is to follow by asking questions to see what students know about the topic? Perhaps through use of analogy, a question, or reference to some common experience?

Introduction

Does the instructor provide an overview of the class content? Relate today's lecture to previous classes? Use an outline either on the board or on a transparency?

Organization and Clarity

Ask what the overall structure of the class is. Does the instructor present content in a clear and logical manner that is made explicit to students? Provide transitions from topic to topic? Make distinctions between major and minor points? Periodically summarize the most important concepts or ideas? Define new concepts and terms? Use examples and illustrations to clarify difficult or abstract ideas? Use relevant, clear examples to explain major points? Provide handouts when appropriate?

Variation

Is the instructor able to vary the pattern of instruction through movement around the class, gestures, voice level, tone, and pace? Use alternative methods such as media, small groups, lecturing, questioning, or case study? Use the chalkboard effectively? Is the boardwork legible and organized? If appropriate, does the instructor use the students' own work (written assignments, homework problems, etc.)? Ask if the instructor varies the pace and activity over the course of the semester.

Closure

Does the instructor summarize and integrate major points of the lecture or discussion at the end of class? Relate current class to upcoming sessions? Announce homework or reading assignments hurriedly? Do students close notebooks or start talking before class has concluded?

After class

What happens once the class has ended? Do informal discussions take place among the students, or between the students and the instructor?

Discussion and Questioning Skills

Introduction

How is discussion initiated? Ask how the instructor decided to begin in that particular way. Are the purpose and guidelines clear to the students? Does the instructor encourage students involvement?

Kinds of Questions

Ask how the instructor finds out if the students understand. As you observe the tape, notice if the questions are rhetorical or real. Are they one at a time or multiple? Does the instructor use centering questions (to re-focus students' attention on a particular topic), probing questions (to require students to go beyond a superficial or incomplete answer), or redirecting questions (to ask for clarification or agreement from others in the class)?

Level of Questions

What level of questions does the instructor ask the students? Lower level, in which there is a "right" answer and students must recall, list or define principles or facts; or higher level, in which students are asked to genera-lize, compare, contrast, analyze, or synthesize information in meaningful patterns

What is done with student questions?

Are questions received politely/enthusiastically? Are questions answered in a direct and understandable manner?

What is done with student responses?

How long does the instructor wait for student response? Does the instructor use verbal reinforcement? Is there a non-verbal response? Does the instructor repeat the answer when necessary so the whole class can hear? Is the instructor receptive to student suggestions or viewpoints contrary to his/her own?

Presentation Style
Verbal Communication

Can the instructor's voice be easily heard? Does the instructor raise or lower voice for variety and emphasis? Is the rate of speech appropriate for note taking? are speech fillers ("you know," "in fact") distracting? Does the instructor talk to the class, or the board?

Non-verbal Communication

Does the instructor look directly at students? Scan the class when asking or responding to questions? Focus on particular students or sides of the room? Do facial and body movements contradict speeck or expressed intentions? Does the instructor use facial expression or body motions to sustain student interest?

Availability to students

Ask the instructor how available he or she is to students in addition to class time, and in what kinds of settings.

Giving Feedback

1. Ask the instructor what he/she noticed at each of the points he/she stops the tape. Comment on specific aspects of the teaching that are successful. Discuss ways to develop strengths even more.

2. Choose a few (two or three) weaknesses to focus on. Be prepared to make specific suggestions for improvement.

3. Do not give more advice than can readily be absorbed.

4. You can end with two questions: "What did you learn?" and "Did you see all the things that were good about the tape and about your teaching?"

Index